JSA VS. KOBRA

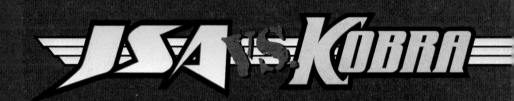

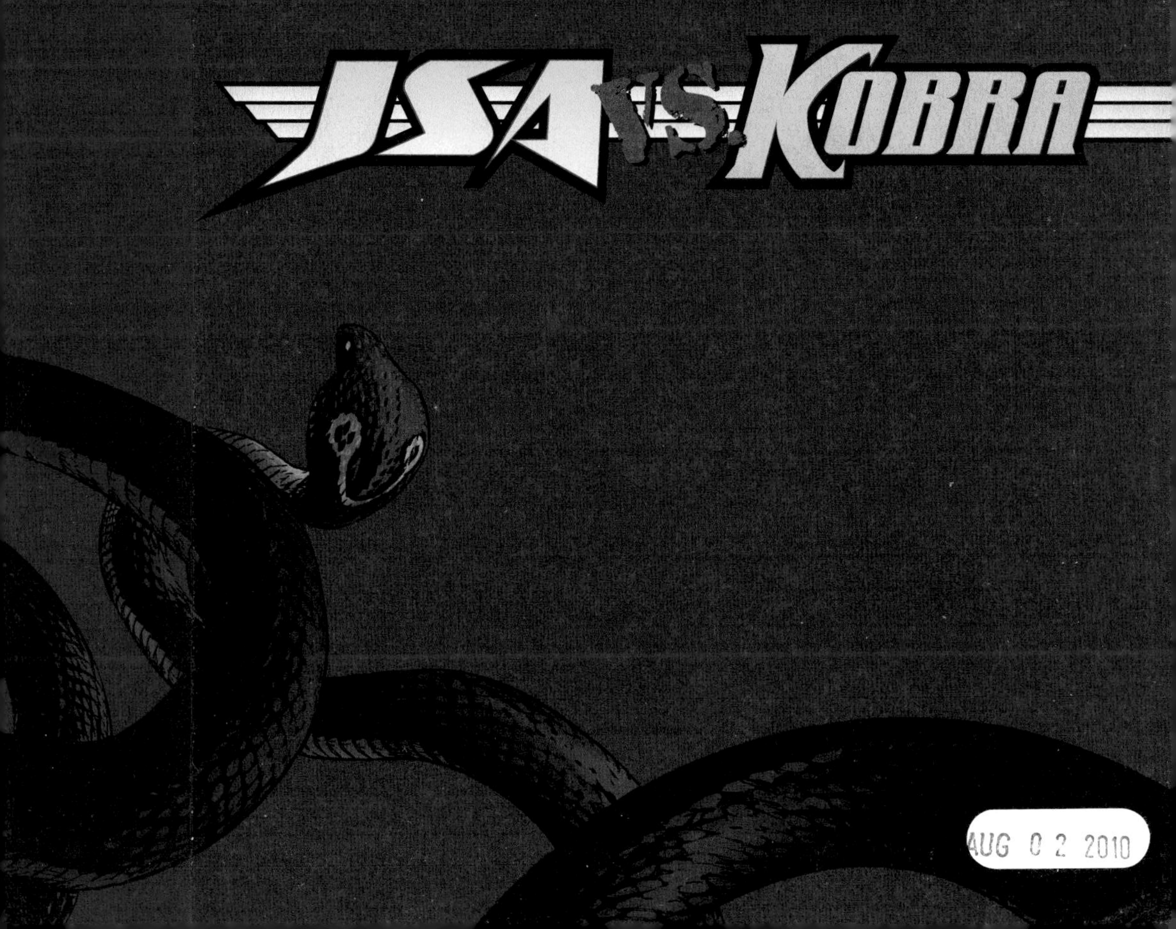

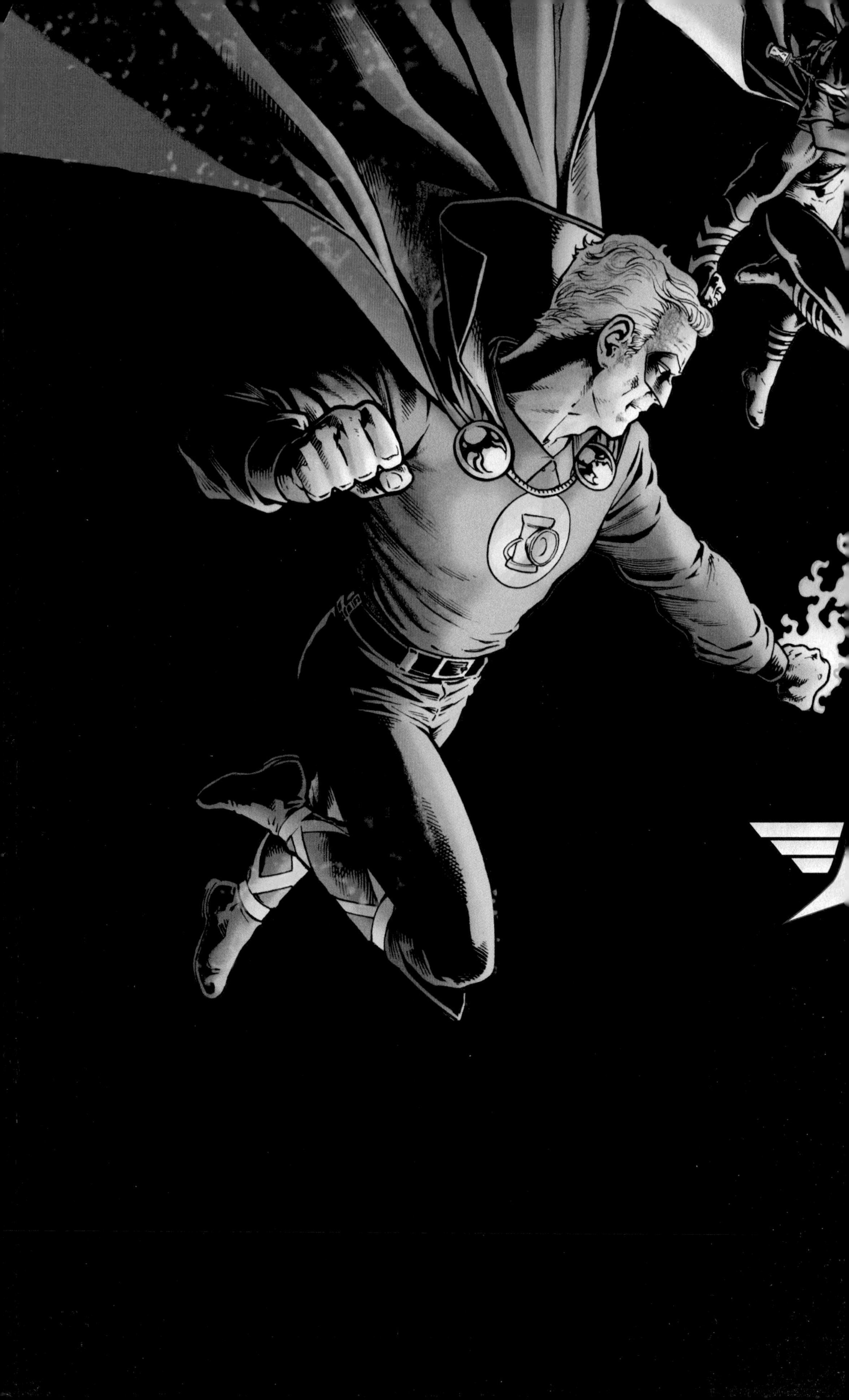

JSA vs. KOBRA

ERIC S. TRAUTMANN Writer

DON KRAMER Penciller

NEIL EDWARDS Additional Pencils — Part Five

MICHAEL BABINSKI Inker

ART LYON ALLEN PASSALAQUA Colorists

PAT BROSSEAU Letterer

GENE HA Original series covers

Rachel Gluckstern Editor-original series
Bob Harras Group Editor-Collected Editions
Anton Kawasaki Editor
Robbin Brosterman Design Director-Books

DC COMICS

Diane Nelson President
Dan DiDio and Jim Lee Co-Publishers
Geoff Johns Chief Creative Officer
Patrick Caldon EVP-Finance and Administration
John Rood EVP-Sales, Marketing
and Business Development
Amy Genkins SVP-Business and Legal Affairs
Steve Rotterdam SVP-Sales and Marketing
John Cunningham VP-Marketing
Terri Cunningham VP-Managing Editor
Alison Gill VP-Manufacturing
David Hyde VP-Publicity
Sue Pohja VP-Book Trade Sales
Alysse Soll VP-Advertising and Custom Publishing
Bob Wayne VP-Sales
Mark Chiarello Art Director

Cover by **Gene Ha**

JSA VS. KOBRA

DC Comics, 1700 Broadway, New York, NY 10019
A Warner Bros. Entertainment Company
Printed by World Color Press, Inc., Dubuque, IA,
USA. 6/30/10. First printing.
ISBN: 978-1-4012-2729-6

3 8001 00093 9722

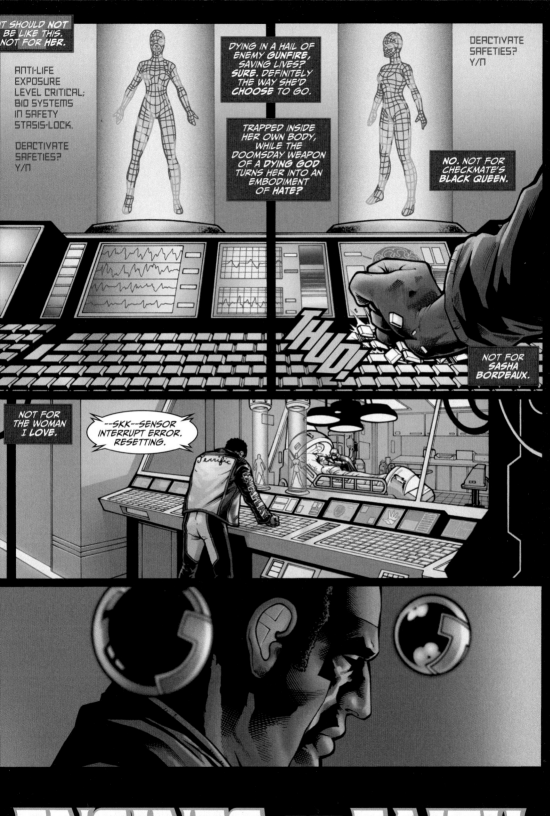

IT SHOULD NOT BE LIKE THIS. NOT FOR HER.

ANTI-LIFE EXPOSURE LEVEL CRITICAL; BIO SYSTEMS IN SAFETY STASIS-LOCK.

DEACTIVATE SAFETIES? Y/N

DYING IN A HAIL OF ENEMY GUNFIRE, SAVING LIVES? SURE. DEFINITELY THE WAY SHE'D CHOOSE TO GO.

TRAPPED INSIDE HER OWN BODY, WHILE THE DOOMSDAY WEAPON OF A DYING GOD TURNS HER INTO AN EMBODIMENT OF HATE?

DEACTIVATE SAFETIES? Y/N

NO. NOT FOR CHECKMATE'S BLACK QUEEN.

THUD!

NOT FOR SASHA BORDEAUX.

NOT FOR THE WOMAN I LOVE.

--SKK--SENSOR INTERRUPT ERROR. RESETTING.

ENGINES OF FAITH
PART ONE: BAD RELIGION

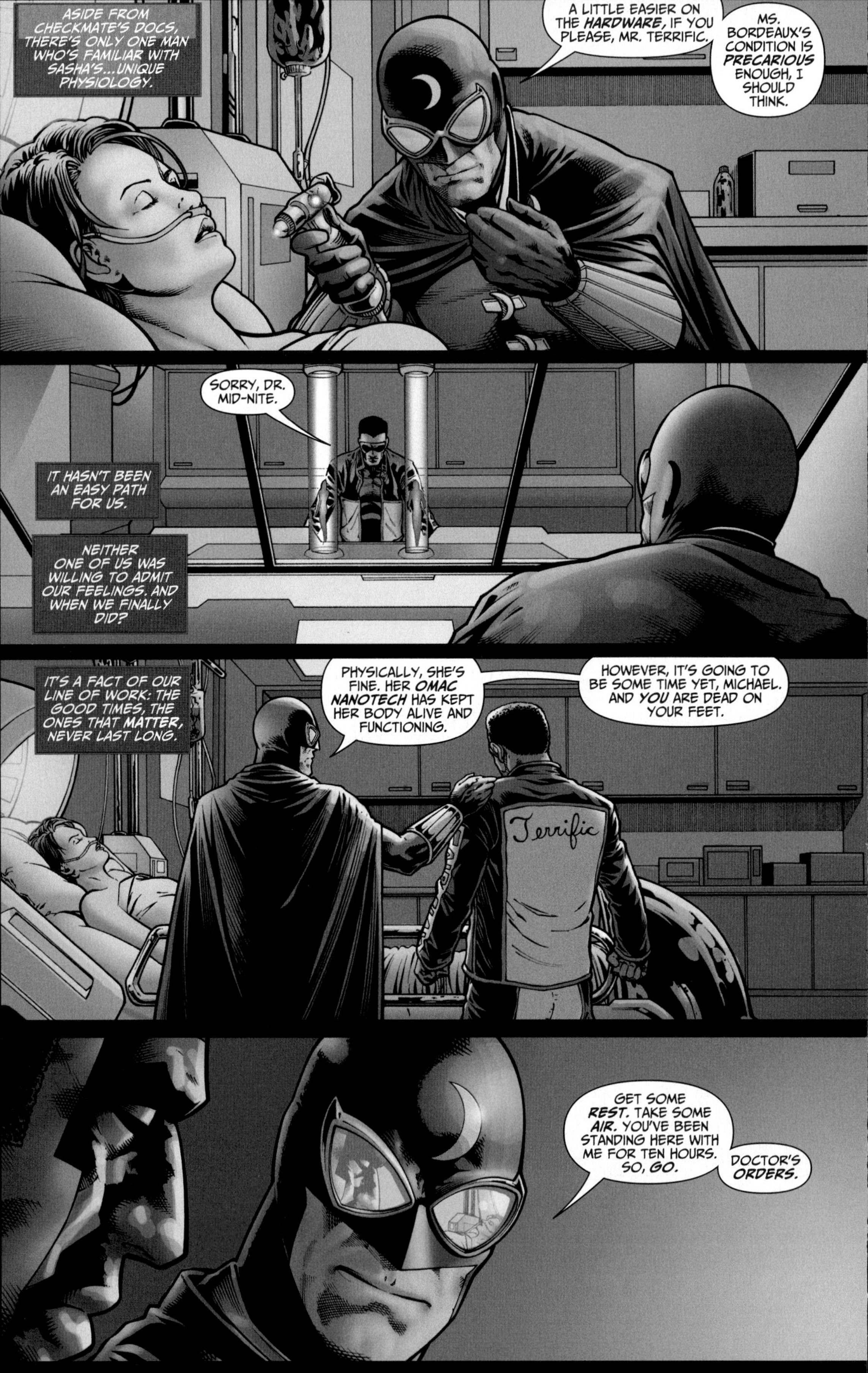
ASIDE FROM CHECKMATE'S DOCS, THERE'S ONLY ONE MAN WHO'S FAMILIAR WITH SASHA'S...UNIQUE PHYSIOLOGY.
A LITTLE EASIER ON THE HARDWARE, IF YOU PLEASE, MR. TERRIFIC.
MS. BORDEAUX'S CONDITION IS PRECARIOUS ENOUGH, I SHOULD THINK.
SORRY, DR. MID-NITE.
IT HASN'T BEEN AN EASY PATH FOR US.
NEITHER ONE OF US WAS WILLING TO ADMIT OUR FEELINGS. AND WHEN WE FINALLY DID?
IT'S A FACT OF OUR LINE OF WORK: THE GOOD TIMES, THE ONES THAT MATTER, NEVER LAST LONG.
PHYSICALLY, SHE'S FINE. HER OMAC NANOTECH HAS KEPT HER BODY ALIVE AND FUNCTIONING.
HOWEVER, IT'S GOING TO BE SOME TIME YET, MICHAEL. AND YOU ARE DEAD ON YOUR FEET.
Terrific
GET SOME REST. TAKE SOME AIR. YOU'VE BEEN STANDING HERE WITH ME FOR TEN HOURS. SO, GO.
DOCTOR'S ORDERS.

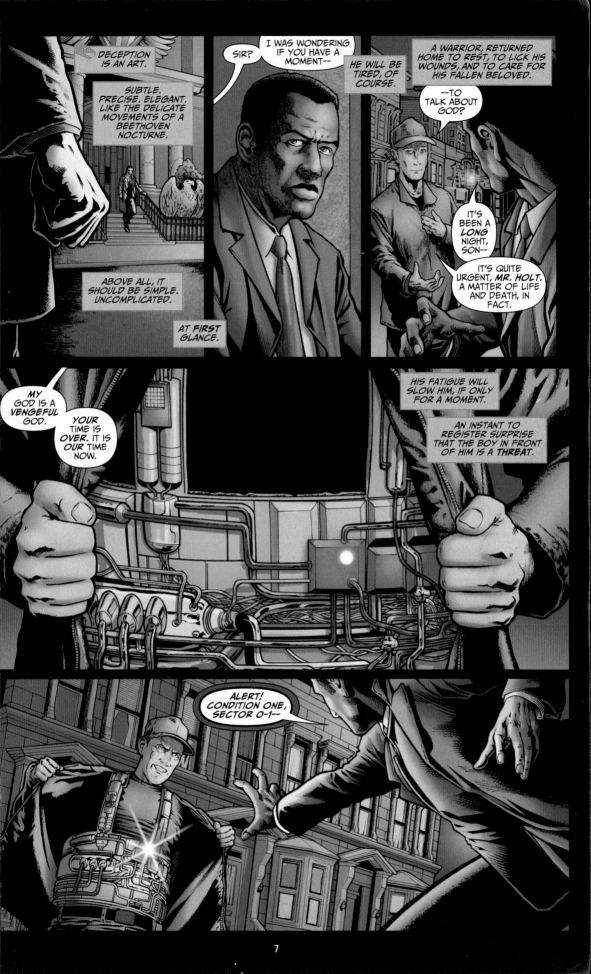

DECEPTION IS AN ART.

SUBTLE. PRECISE. ELEGANT. LIKE THE DELICATE MOVEMENTS OF A BEETHOVEN NOCTURNE.

ABOVE ALL, IT SHOULD BE SIMPLE. UNCOMPLICATED.

AT FIRST GLANCE.

SIR?

I WAS WONDERING IF YOU HAVE A MOMENT--

HE WILL BE TIRED, OF COURSE.

A WARRIOR, RETURNED HOME TO REST, TO LICK HIS WOUNDS, AND TO CARE FOR HIS FALLEN BELOVED.

--TO TALK ABOUT GOD?

IT'S BEEN A LONG NIGHT, SON--

IT'S QUITE URGENT, MR. HOLT. A MATTER OF LIFE AND DEATH, IN FACT.

MY GOD IS A VENGEFUL GOD.

YOUR TIME IS OVER. IT IS OUR TIME NOW.

HIS FATIGUE WILL SLOW HIM, IF ONLY FOR A MOMENT.

AN INSTANT TO REGISTER SURPRISE THAT THE BOY IN FRONT OF HIM IS A THREAT.

ALERT! CONDITION ONE, SECTOR O-1--

7

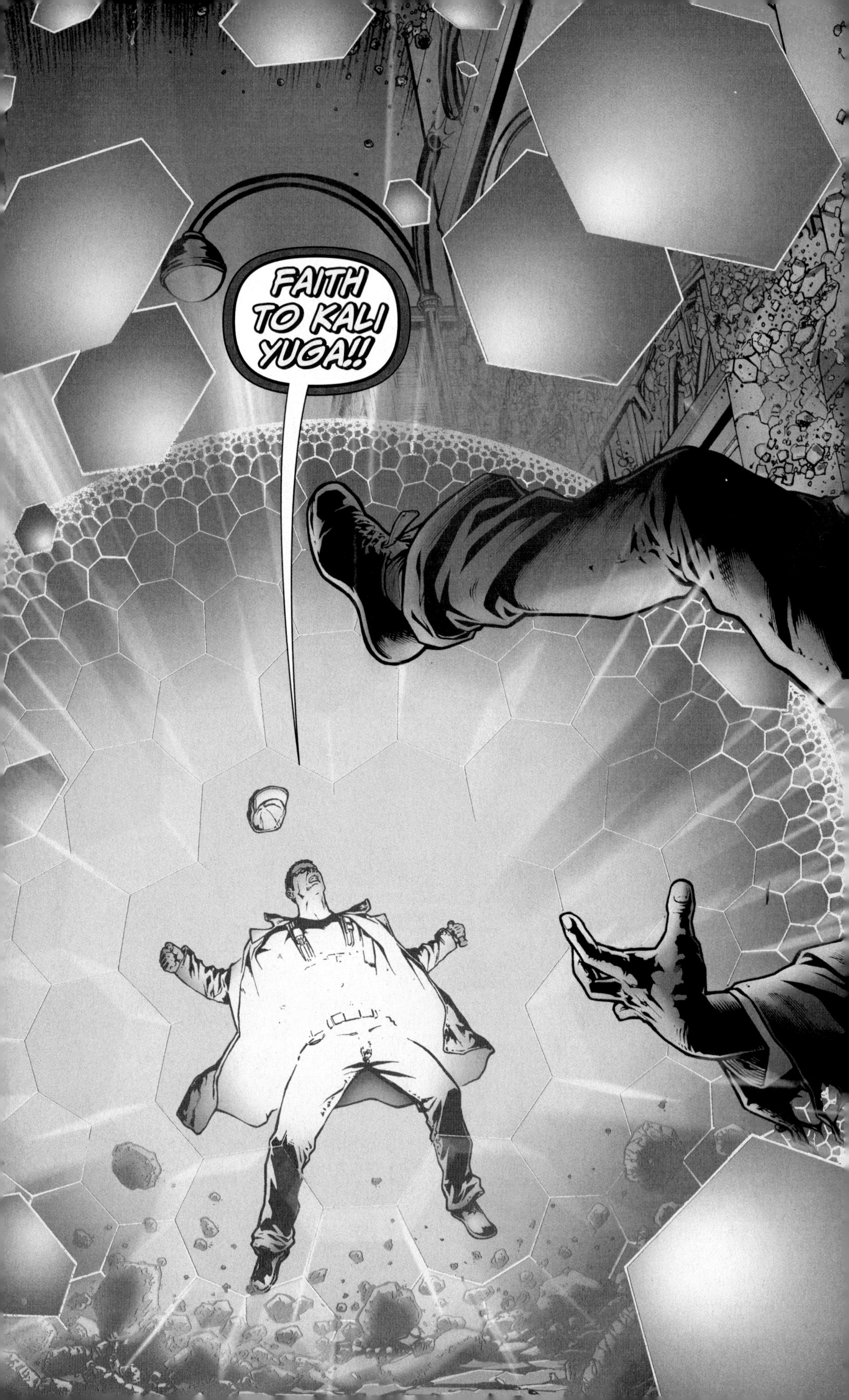
FAITH TO KALI YUGA!!

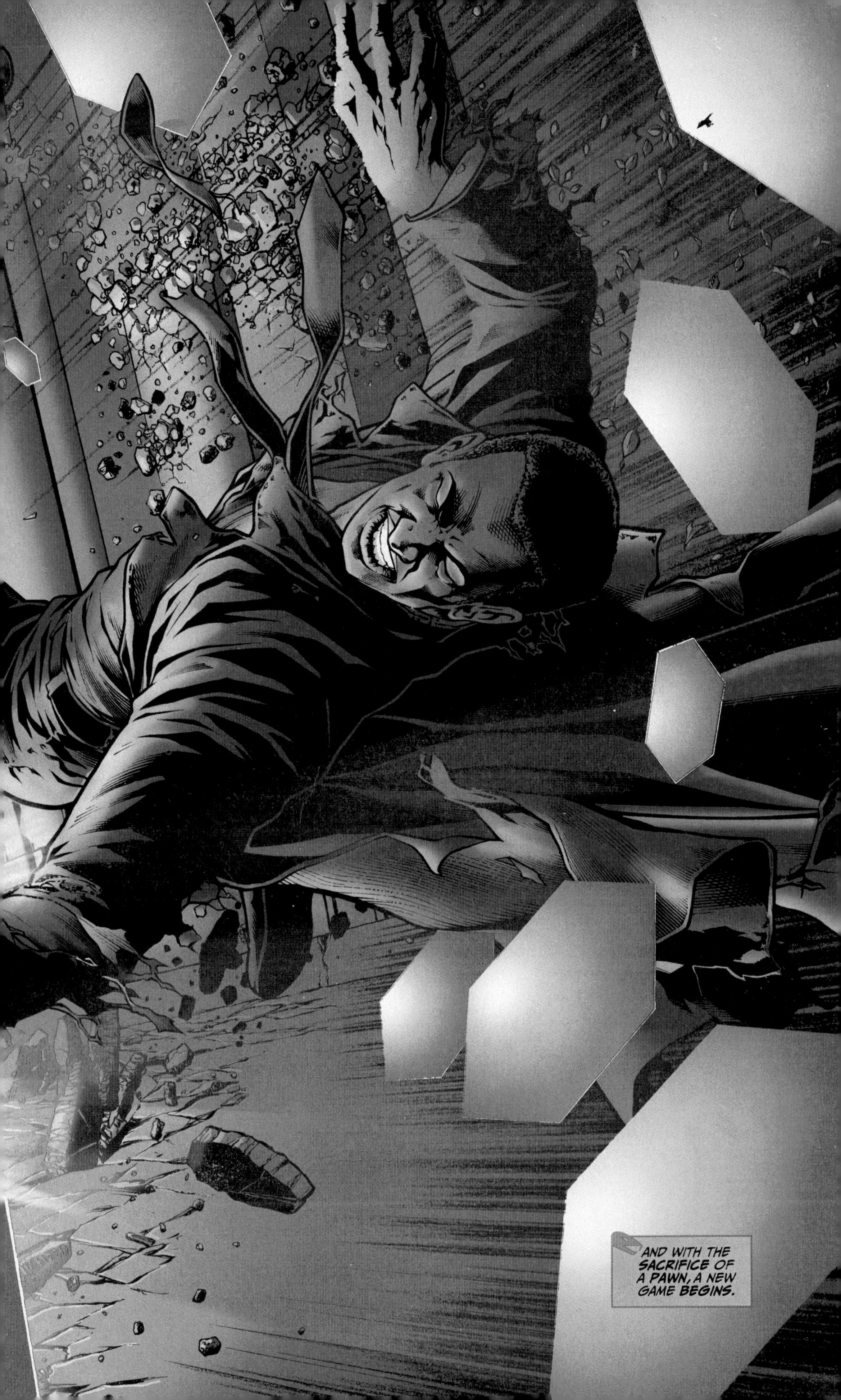
AND WITH THE SACRIFICE OF A PAWN, A NEW GAME BEGINS.

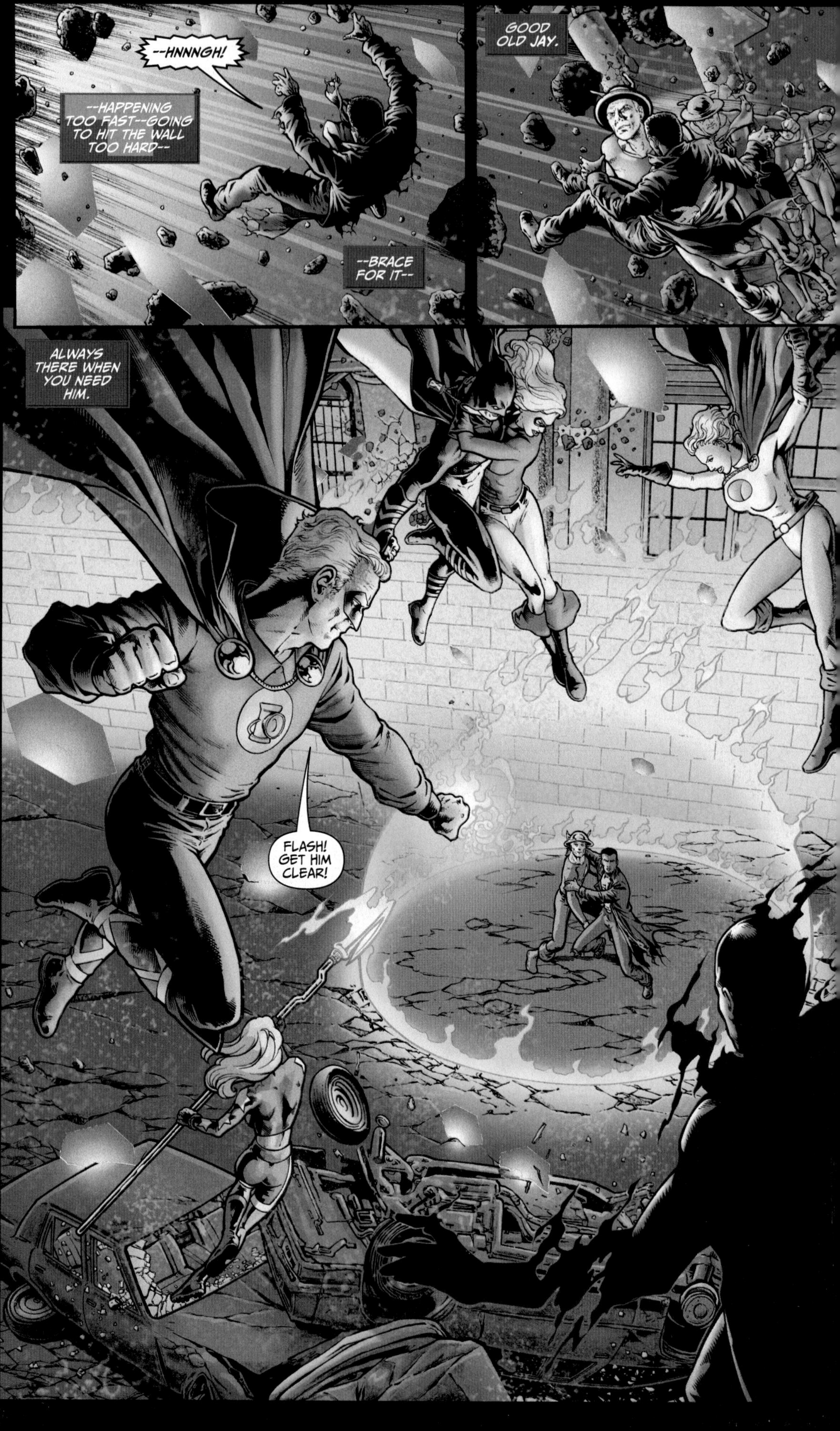
--HNNNGH!
--HAPPENING TOO FAST--GOING TO HIT THE WALL TOO HARD--
--BRACE FOR IT--
GOOD OLD JAY.
ALWAYS THERE WHEN YOU NEED HIM.
FLASH! GET HIM CLEAR!

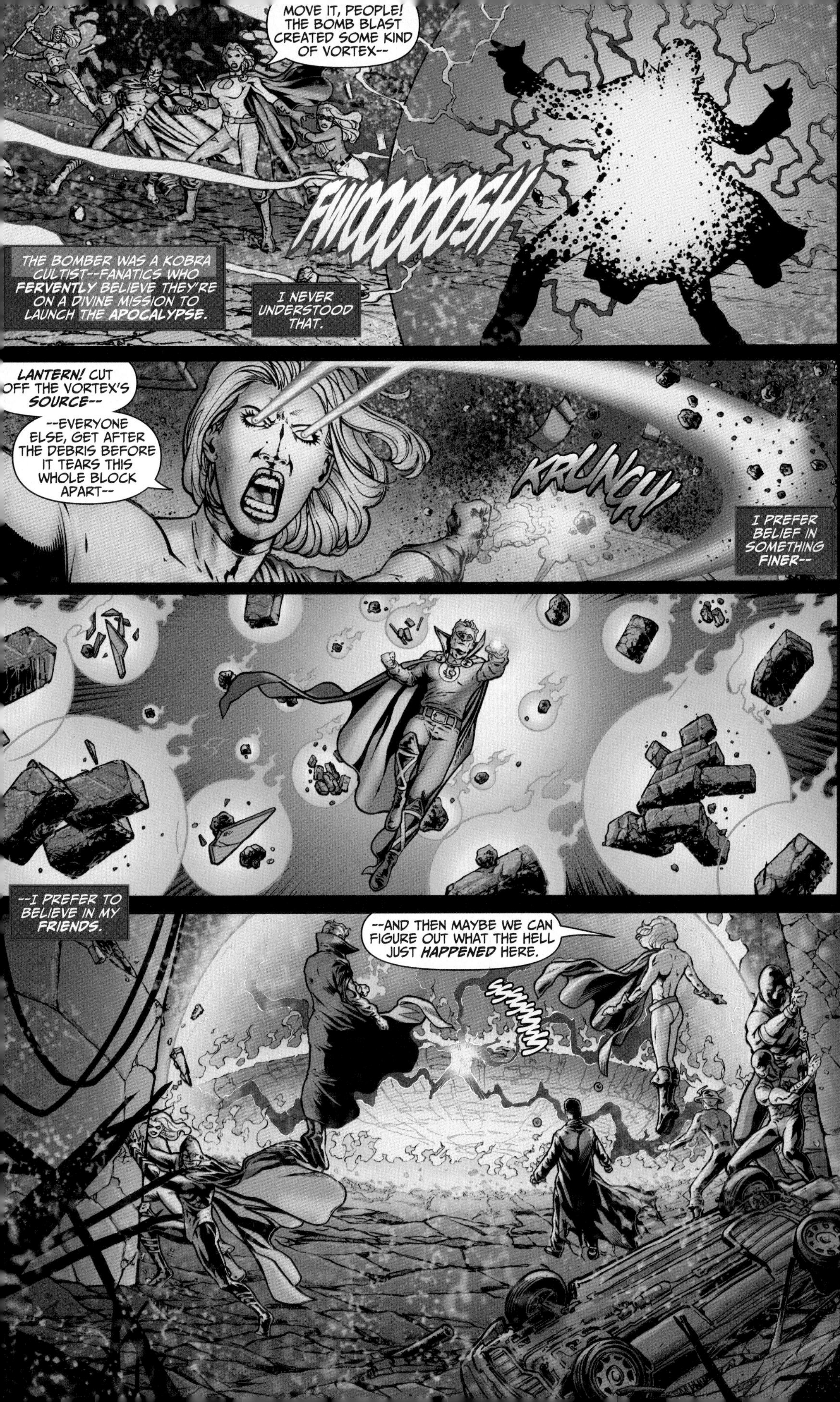
MOVE IT, PEOPLE! THE BOMB BLAST CREATED SOME KIND OF VORTEX--
FWOOOOOOSH
THE BOMBER WAS A KOBRA CULTIST--FANATICS WHO FERVENTLY BELIEVE THEY'RE ON A DIVINE MISSION TO LAUNCH THE APOCALYPSE.
I NEVER UNDERSTOOD THAT.
LANTERN! CUT OFF THE VORTEX'S SOURCE--
--EVERYONE ELSE, GET AFTER THE DEBRIS BEFORE IT TEARS THIS WHOLE BLOCK APART--
KRUNCH!
I PREFER BELIEF IN SOMETHING FINER--
--I PREFER TO BELIEVE IN MY FRIENDS.
--AND THEN MAYBE WE CAN FIGURE OUT WHAT THE HELL JUST HAPPENED HERE.

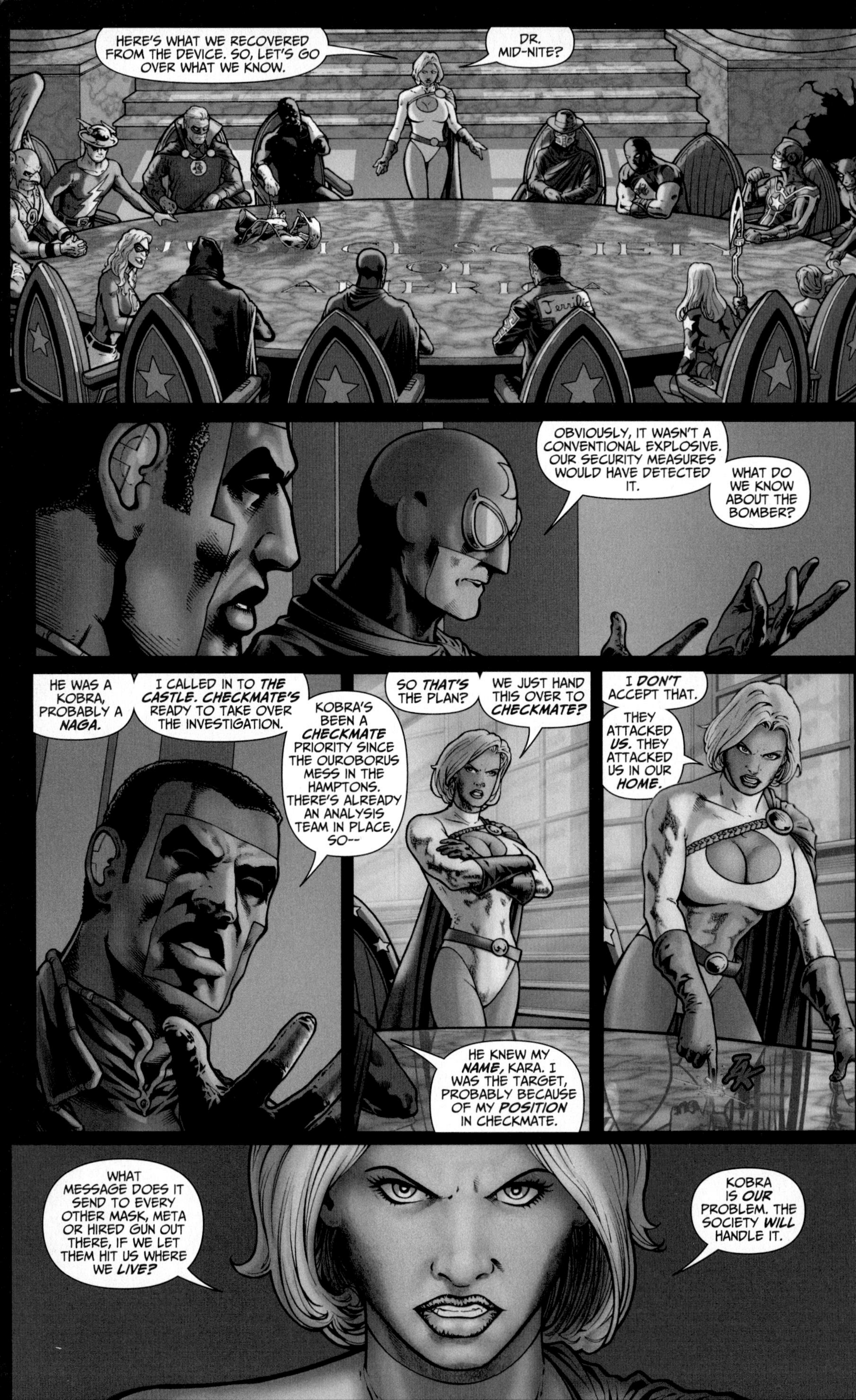
HERE'S WHAT WE RECOVERED FROM THE DEVICE. SO, LET'S GO OVER WHAT WE KNOW.
DR. MID-NITE?
OBVIOUSLY, IT WASN'T A CONVENTIONAL EXPLOSIVE. OUR SECURITY MEASURES WOULD HAVE DETECTED IT.
WHAT DO WE KNOW ABOUT THE BOMBER?
HE WAS A KOBRA, PROBABLY A NAGA.
I CALLED IN TO THE CASTLE. CHECKMATE'S READY TO TAKE OVER THE INVESTIGATION.
KOBRA'S BEEN A CHECKMATE PRIORITY SINCE THE OUROBORUS MESS IN THE HAMPTONS. THERE'S ALREADY AN ANALYSIS TEAM IN PLACE, SO--
SO THAT'S THE PLAN?
WE JUST HAND THIS OVER TO CHECKMATE?
HE KNEW MY NAME, KARA. I WAS THE TARGET, PROBABLY BECAUSE OF MY POSITION IN CHECKMATE.
I DON'T ACCEPT THAT.
THEY ATTACKED US. THEY ATTACKED US IN OUR HOME.
WHAT MESSAGE DOES IT SEND TO EVERY OTHER MASK, META OR HIRED GUN OUT THERE, IF WE LET THEM HIT US WHERE WE LIVE?
KOBRA IS OUR PROBLEM. THE SOCIETY WILL HANDLE IT.

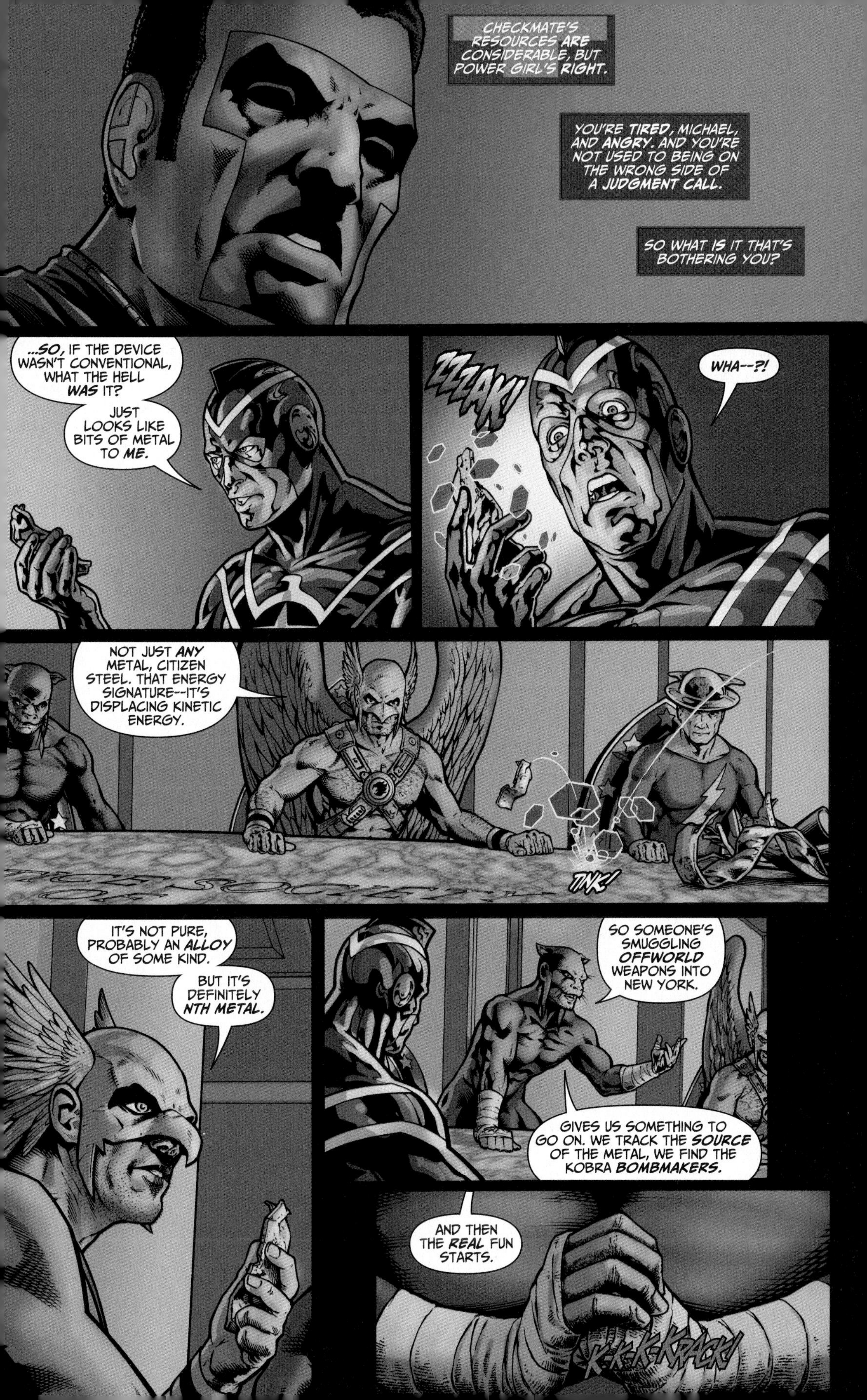
CHECKMATE'S RESOURCES ARE CONSIDERABLE, BUT POWER GIRL'S RIGHT.
YOU'RE TIRED, MICHAEL, AND ANGRY. AND YOU'RE NOT USED TO BEING ON THE WRONG SIDE OF A JUDGMENT CALL.
SO WHAT IS IT THAT'S BOTHERING YOU?
...SO, IF THE DEVICE WASN'T CONVENTIONAL, WHAT THE HELL WAS IT?
JUST LOOKS LIKE BITS OF METAL TO ME.
ZZZAK!
WHA--?!
NOT JUST ANY METAL, CITIZEN STEEL. THAT ENERGY SIGNATURE--IT'S DISPLACING KINETIC ENERGY.
TINK!
IT'S NOT PURE, PROBABLY AN ALLOY OF SOME KIND.
BUT IT'S DEFINITELY NTH METAL.
SO SOMEONE'S SMUGGLING OFFWORLD WEAPONS INTO NEW YORK.
GIVES US SOMETHING TO GO ON. WE TRACK THE SOURCE OF THE METAL, WE FIND THE KOBRA BOMBMAKERS.
AND THEN THE REAL FUN STARTS.
K-K-K-KRACK!

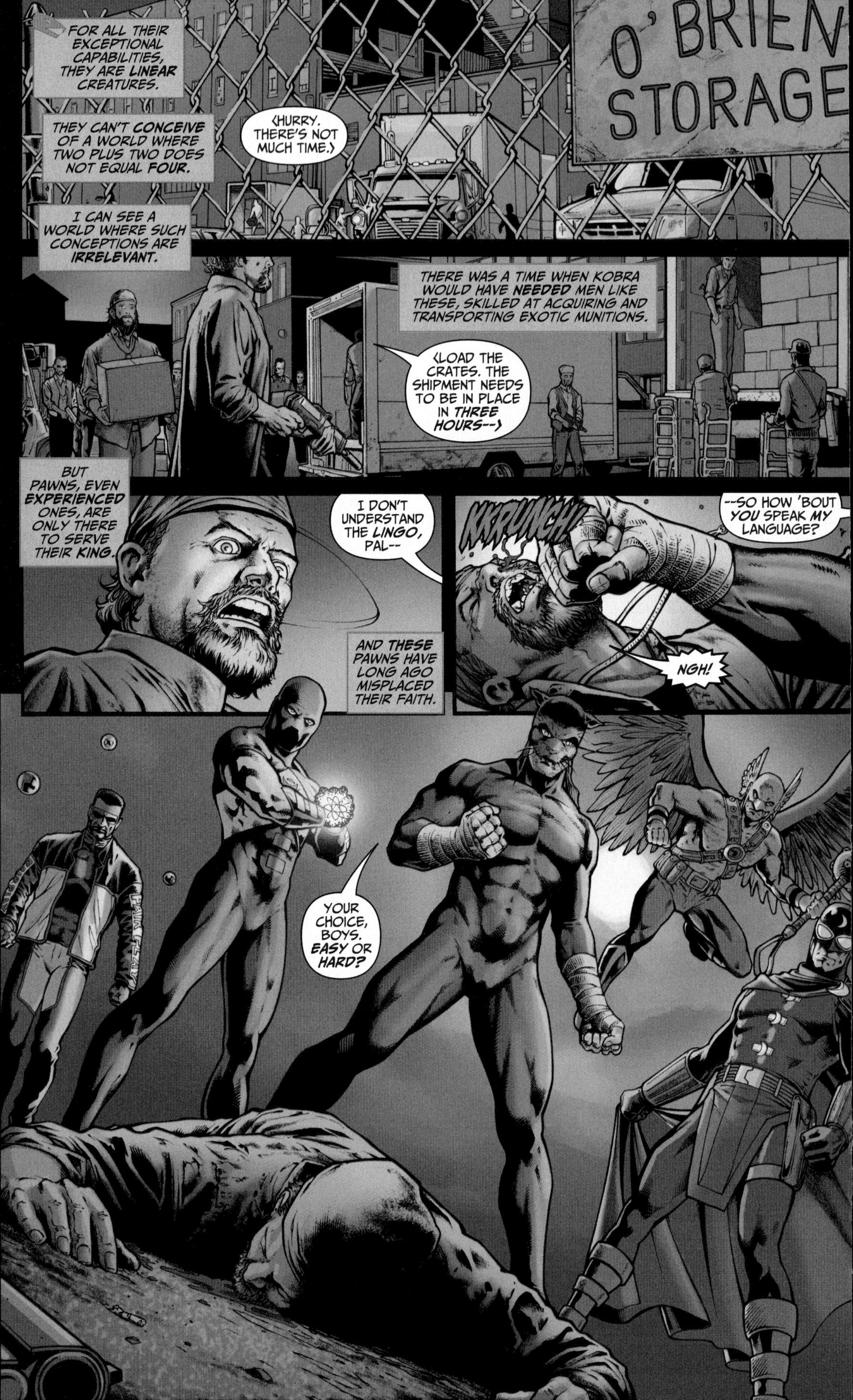
O' BRIEN
STORAGE
FOR ALL THEIR EXCEPTIONAL CAPABILITIES, THEY ARE LINEAR CREATURES.
THEY CAN'T CONCEIVE OF A WORLD WHERE TWO PLUS TWO DOES NOT EQUAL FOUR.
‹HURRY. THERE'S NOT MUCH TIME.›
I CAN SEE A WORLD WHERE SUCH CONCEPTIONS ARE IRRELEVANT.
THERE WAS A TIME WHEN KOBRA WOULD HAVE NEEDED MEN LIKE THESE, SKILLED AT ACQUIRING AND TRANSPORTING EXOTIC MUNITIONS.
‹LOAD THE CRATES. THE SHIPMENT NEEDS TO BE IN PLACE IN THREE HOURS--›
BUT PAWNS, EVEN EXPERIENCED ONES, ARE ONLY THERE TO SERVE THEIR KING.
I DON'T UNDERSTAND THE LINGO, PAL--
AND THESE PAWNS HAVE LONG AGO MISPLACED THEIR FAITH.
KKRUNCH!
--SO HOW 'BOUT YOU SPEAK MY LANGUAGE?
NGH!
YOUR CHOICE, BOYS. EASY OR HARD?

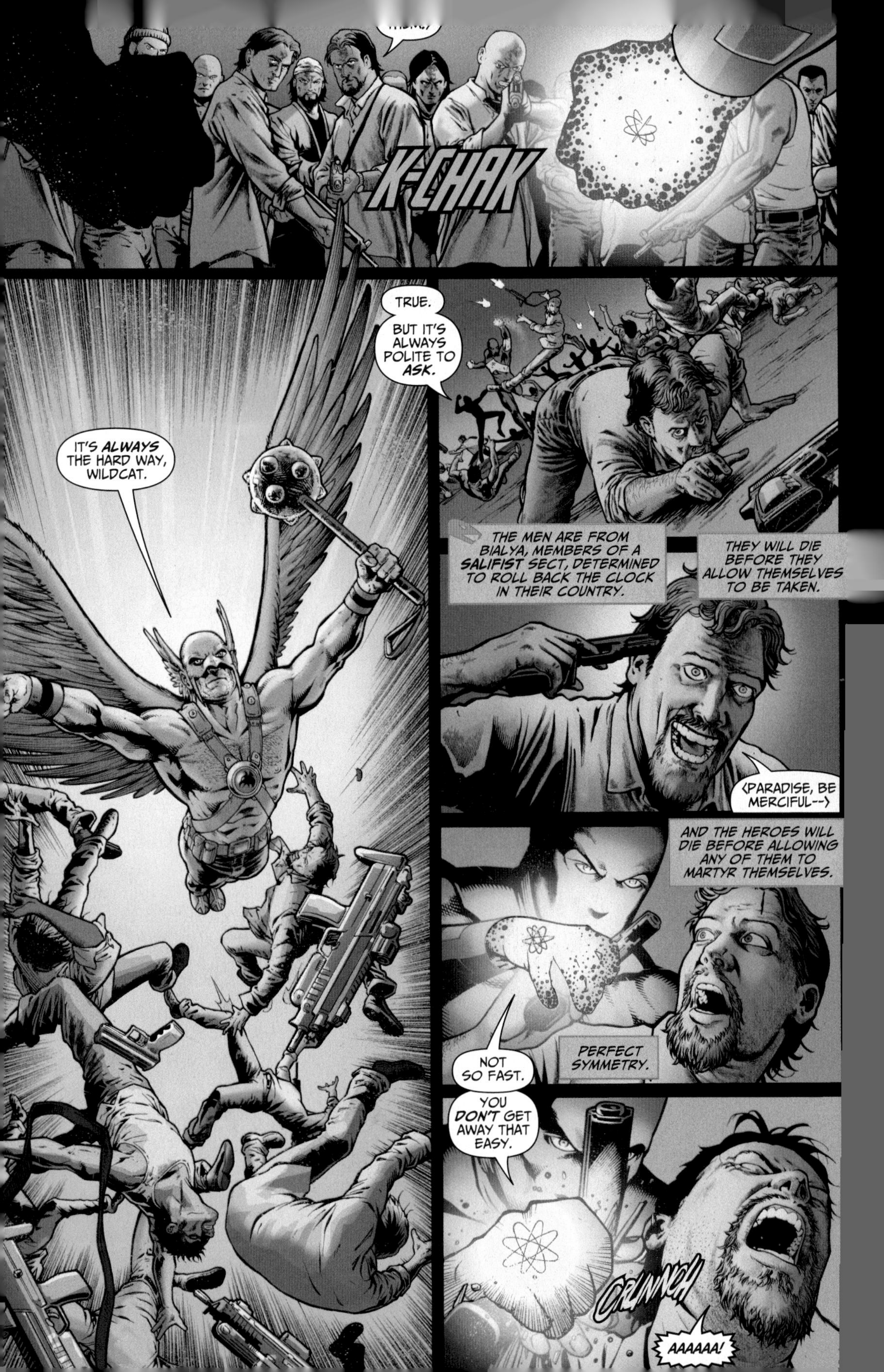
K-CHAK
TRUE.
BUT IT'S ALWAYS POLITE TO *ASK.*
IT'S *ALWAYS* THE HARD WAY, WILDCAT.
THE MEN ARE FROM BIALYA, MEMBERS OF A *SALIFIST* SECT, DETERMINED TO ROLL BACK THE CLOCK IN THEIR COUNTRY.
THEY WILL DIE BEFORE THEY ALLOW THEMSELVES TO BE TAKEN.
<PARADISE, BE MERCIFUL-->
AND THE HEROES WILL DIE BEFORE ALLOWING ANY OF THEM TO MARTYR THEMSELVES.
PERFECT SYMMETRY.
NOT SO FAST.
YOU *DON'T* GET AWAY THAT EASY.
CRUNNCH
AAAAAA!

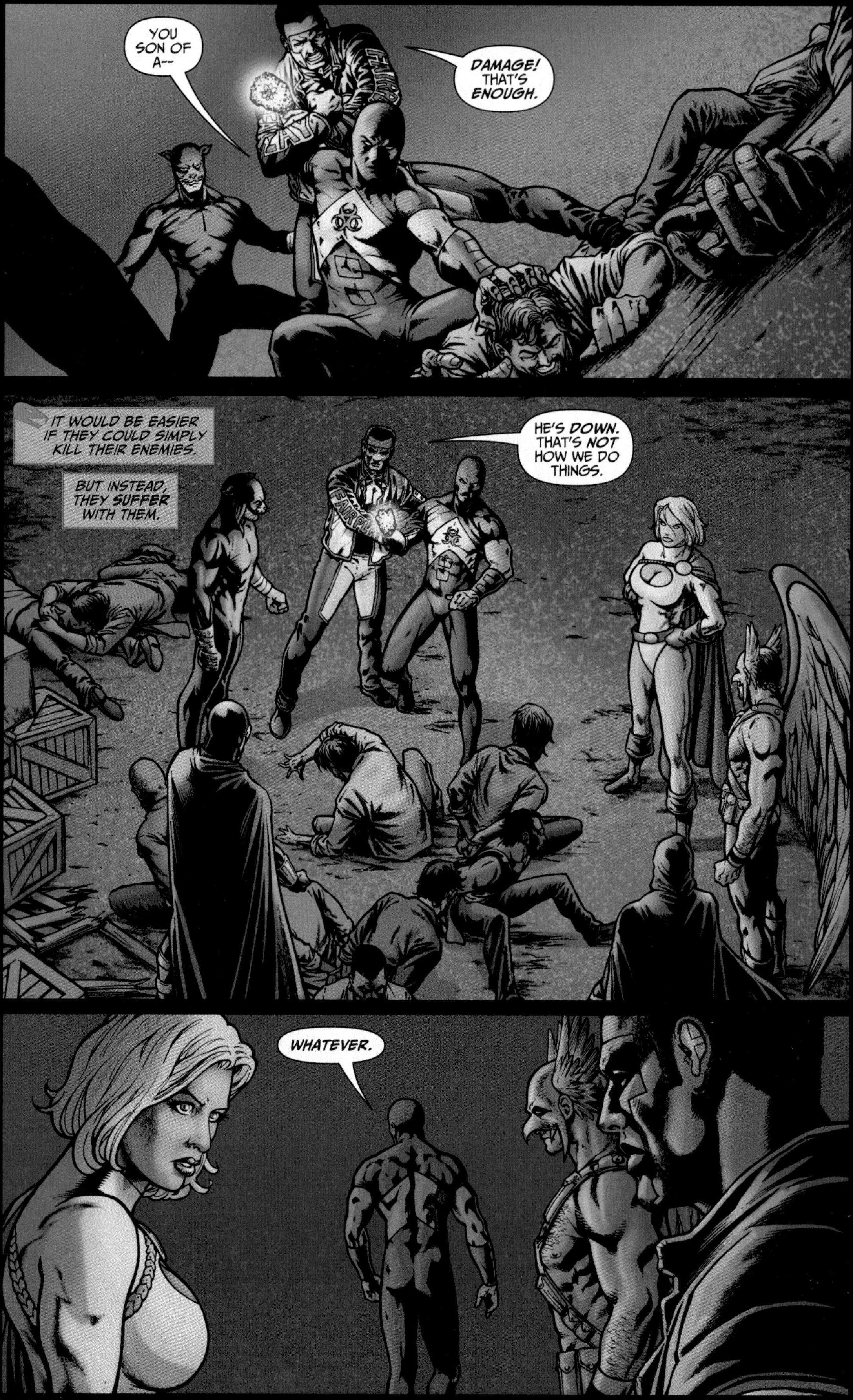
YOU SON OF A--
DAMAGE! THAT'S ENOUGH.
IT WOULD BE EASIER IF THEY COULD SIMPLY KILL THEIR ENEMIES.
BUT INSTEAD, THEY SUFFER WITH THEM.
HE'S DOWN. THAT'S NOT HOW WE DO THINGS.
WHATEVER.

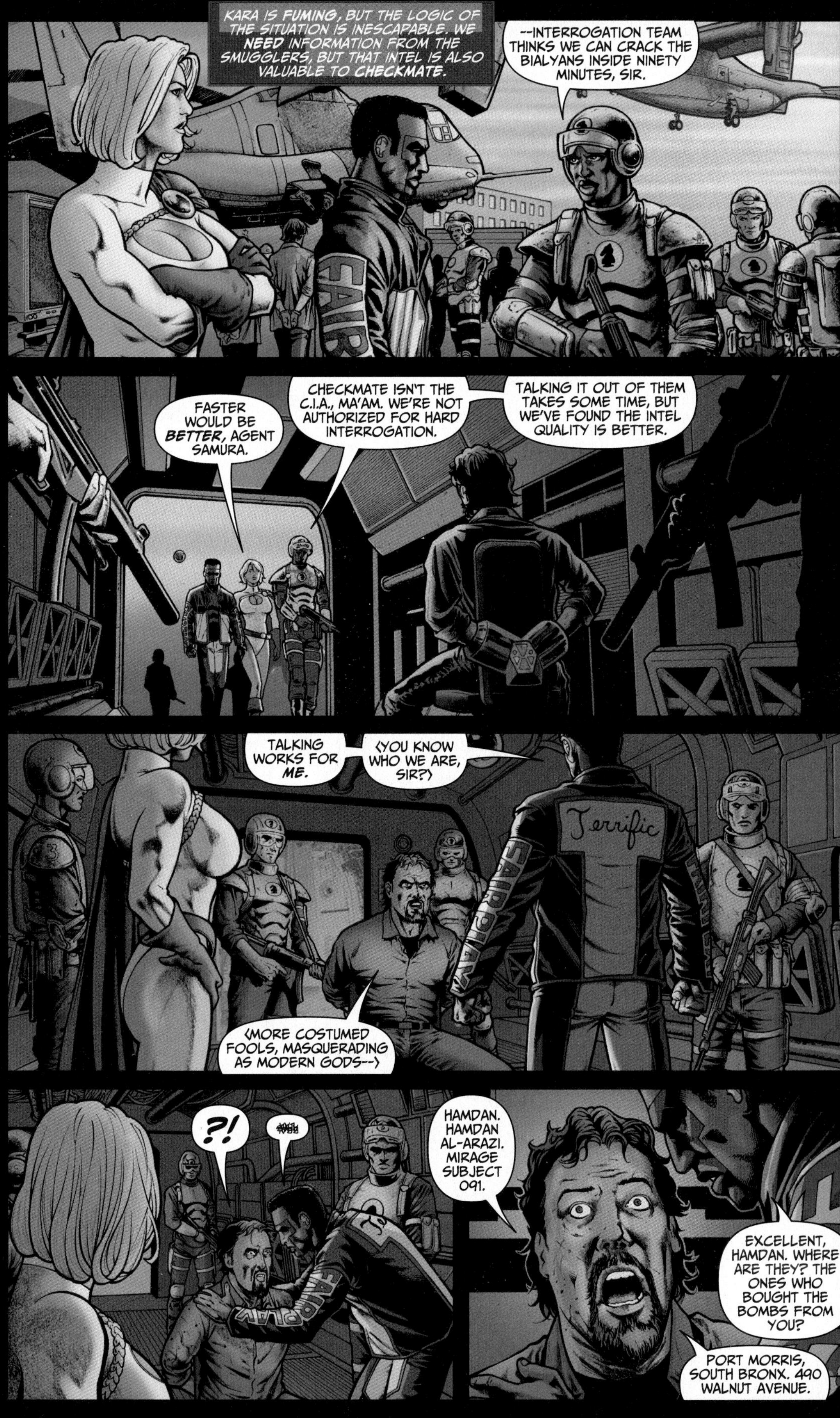
KARA IS FUMING, BUT THE LOGIC OF THE SITUATION IS INESCAPABLE. WE NEED INFORMATION FROM THE SMUGGLERS, BUT THAT INTEL IS ALSO VALUABLE TO CHECKMATE.
--INTERROGATION TEAM THINKS WE CAN CRACK THE BIALYANS INSIDE NINETY MINUTES, SIR.
FASTER WOULD BE BETTER, AGENT SAMURA.
CHECKMATE ISN'T THE C.I.A., MA'AM. WE'RE NOT AUTHORIZED FOR HARD INTERROGATION.
TALKING IT OUT OF THEM TAKES SOME TIME, BUT WE'VE FOUND THE INTEL QUALITY IS BETTER.
TALKING WORKS FOR ME.
‹YOU KNOW WHO WE ARE, SIR?›
‹MORE COSTUMED FOOLS, MASQUERADING AS MODERN GODS--›
?!
HAMDAN. HAMDAN AL-ARAZI. MIRAGE SUBJECT 091.
EXCELLENT, HAMDAN. WHERE ARE THEY? THE ONES WHO BOUGHT THE BOMBS FROM YOU?
PORT MORRIS, SOUTH BRONX. 490 WALNUT AVENUE.

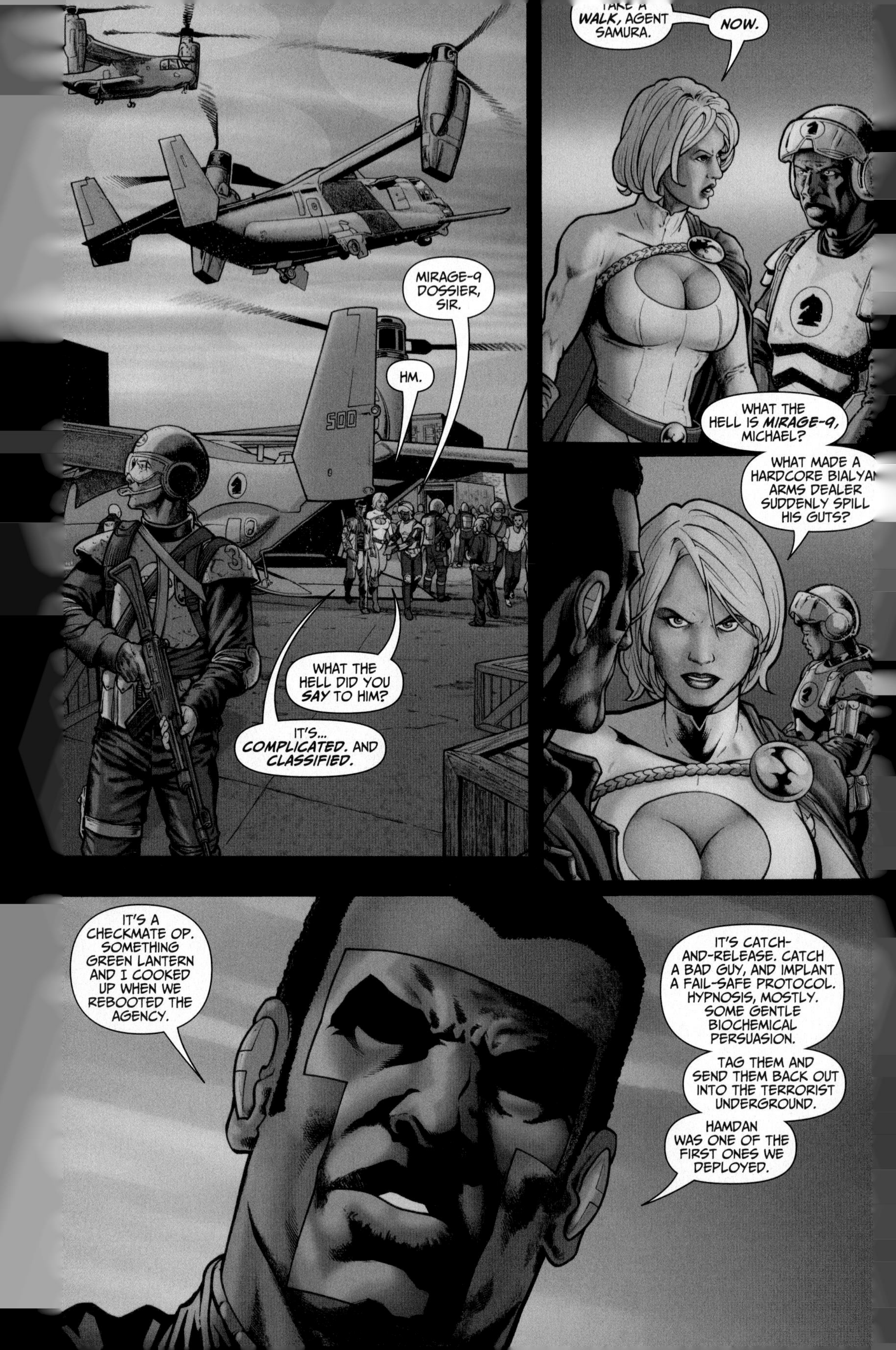
MIRAGE-9 DOSSIER, SIR.
HM.
WHAT THE HELL DID YOU *SAY* TO HIM?
IT'S... ***COMPLICATED.*** AND ***CLASSIFIED.***
WALK, AGENT SAMURA.
NOW.
WHAT THE HELL IS ***MIRAGE-9,*** MICHAEL?
WHAT MADE A HARDCORE BIALYAN ARMS DEALER SUDDENLY SPILL HIS GUTS?
IT'S A CHECKMATE OP. SOMETHING GREEN LANTERN AND I COOKED UP WHEN WE REBOOTED THE AGENCY.
IT'S CATCH-AND-RELEASE. CATCH A BAD GUY, AND IMPLANT A FAIL-SAFE PROTOCOL. HYPNOSIS, MOSTLY. SOME GENTLE BIOCHEMICAL PERSUASION.
TAG THEM AND SEND THEM BACK OUT INTO THE TERRORIST UNDERGROUND.
HAMDAN WAS ONE OF THE FIRST ONES WE DEPLOYED.

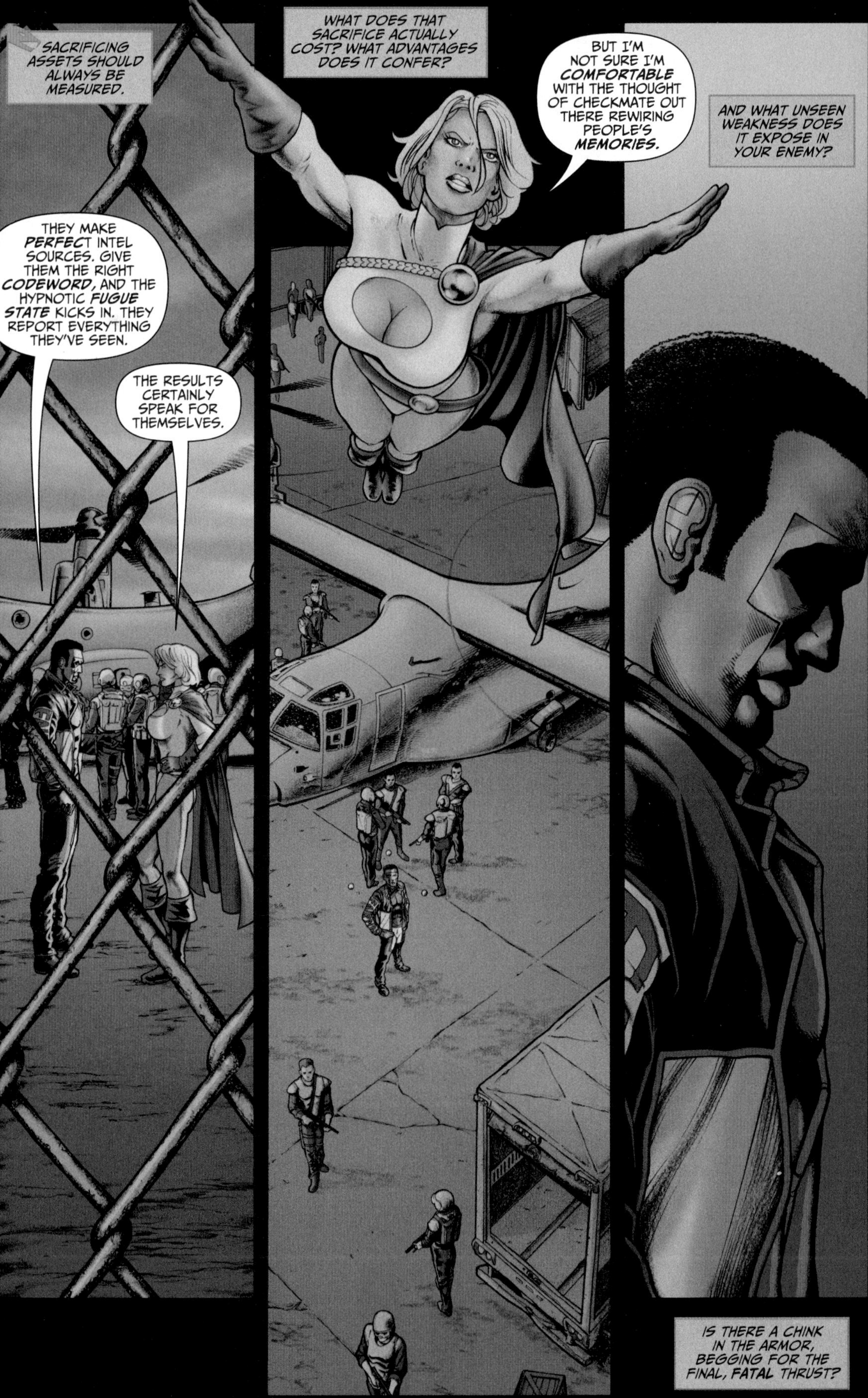
SACRIFICING ASSETS SHOULD ALWAYS BE MEASURED.
THEY MAKE PERFECT INTEL SOURCES. GIVE THEM THE RIGHT CODEWORD, AND THE HYPNOTIC FUGUE STATE KICKS IN. THEY REPORT EVERYTHING THEY'VE SEEN.
THE RESULTS CERTAINLY SPEAK FOR THEMSELVES.
WHAT DOES THAT SACRIFICE ACTUALLY COST? WHAT ADVANTAGES DOES IT CONFER?
BUT I'M NOT SURE I'M COMFORTABLE WITH THE THOUGHT OF CHECKMATE OUT THERE REWIRING PEOPLE'S MEMORIES.
AND WHAT UNSEEN WEAKNESS DOES IT EXPOSE IN YOUR ENEMY?
IS THERE A CHINK IN THE ARMOR, BEGGING FOR THE FINAL, FATAL THRUST?

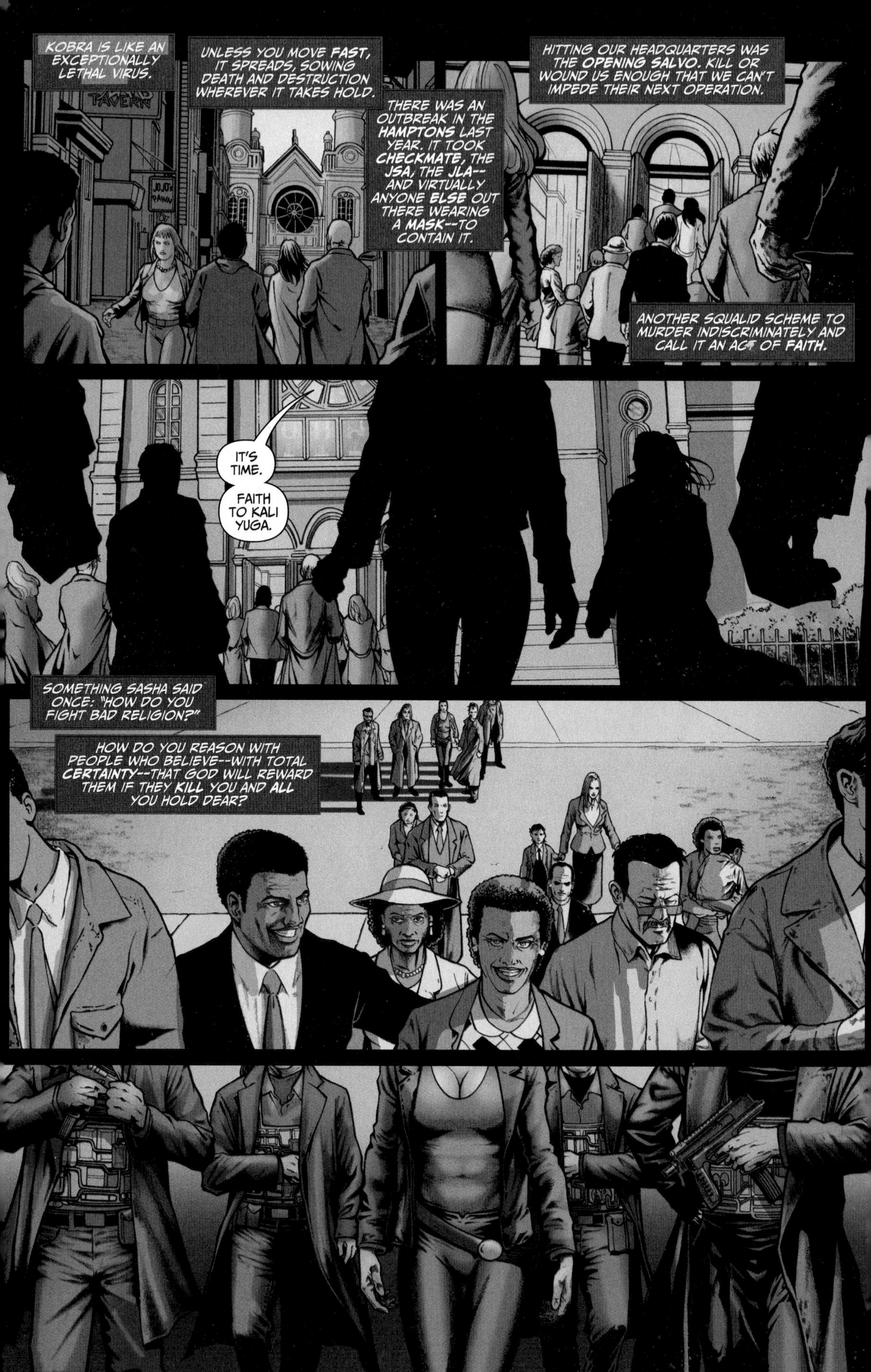

KOBRA IS LIKE AN EXCEPTIONALLY LETHAL VIRUS.
UNLESS YOU MOVE FAST, IT SPREADS, SOWING DEATH AND DESTRUCTION WHEREVER IT TAKES HOLD.
THERE WAS AN OUTBREAK IN THE HAMPTONS LAST YEAR. IT TOOK CHECKMATE, THE JSA, THE JLA--AND VIRTUALLY ANYONE ELSE OUT THERE WEARING A MASK--TO CONTAIN IT.
TAVERN
JO JO'S PAWN
HITTING OUR HEADQUARTERS WAS THE OPENING SALVO. KILL OR WOUND US ENOUGH THAT WE CAN'T IMPEDE THEIR NEXT OPERATION.
ANOTHER SQUALID SCHEME TO MURDER INDISCRIMINATELY AND CALL IT AN ACT OF FAITH.
IT'S TIME.
FAITH TO KALI YUGA.
SOMETHING SASHA SAID ONCE: "HOW DO YOU FIGHT BAD RELIGION?"
HOW DO YOU REASON WITH PEOPLE WHO BELIEVE--WITH TOTAL CERTAINTY--THAT GOD WILL REWARD THEM IF THEY KILL YOU AND ALL YOU HOLD DEAR?

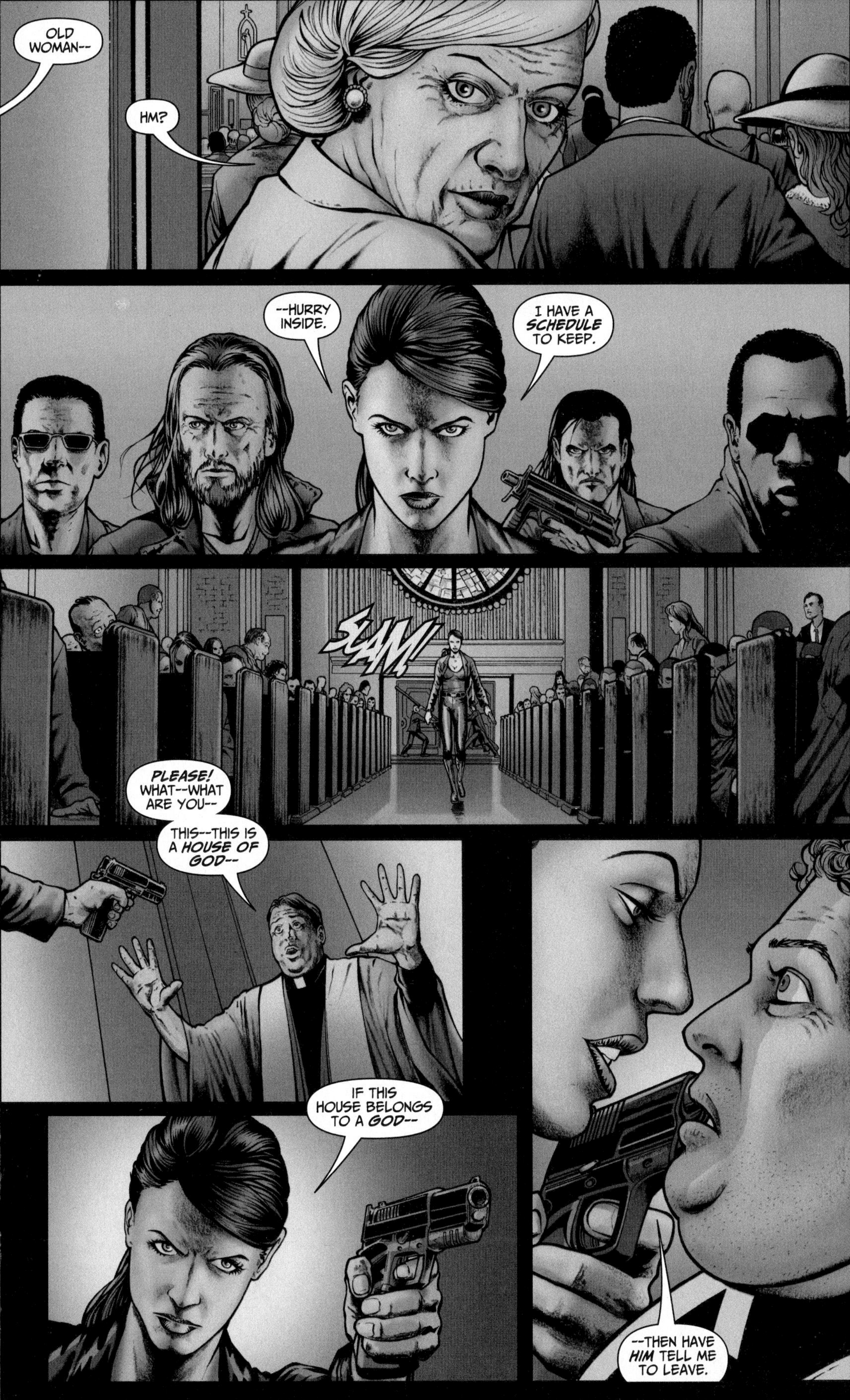
OLD WOMAN--
HM?
--HURRY INSIDE.
I HAVE A SCHEDULE TO KEEP.
SLAM!
PLEASE! WHAT--WHAT ARE YOU--
THIS--THIS IS A HOUSE OF GOD--
IF THIS HOUSE BELONGS TO A GOD--
--THEN HAVE HIM TELL ME TO LEAVE.

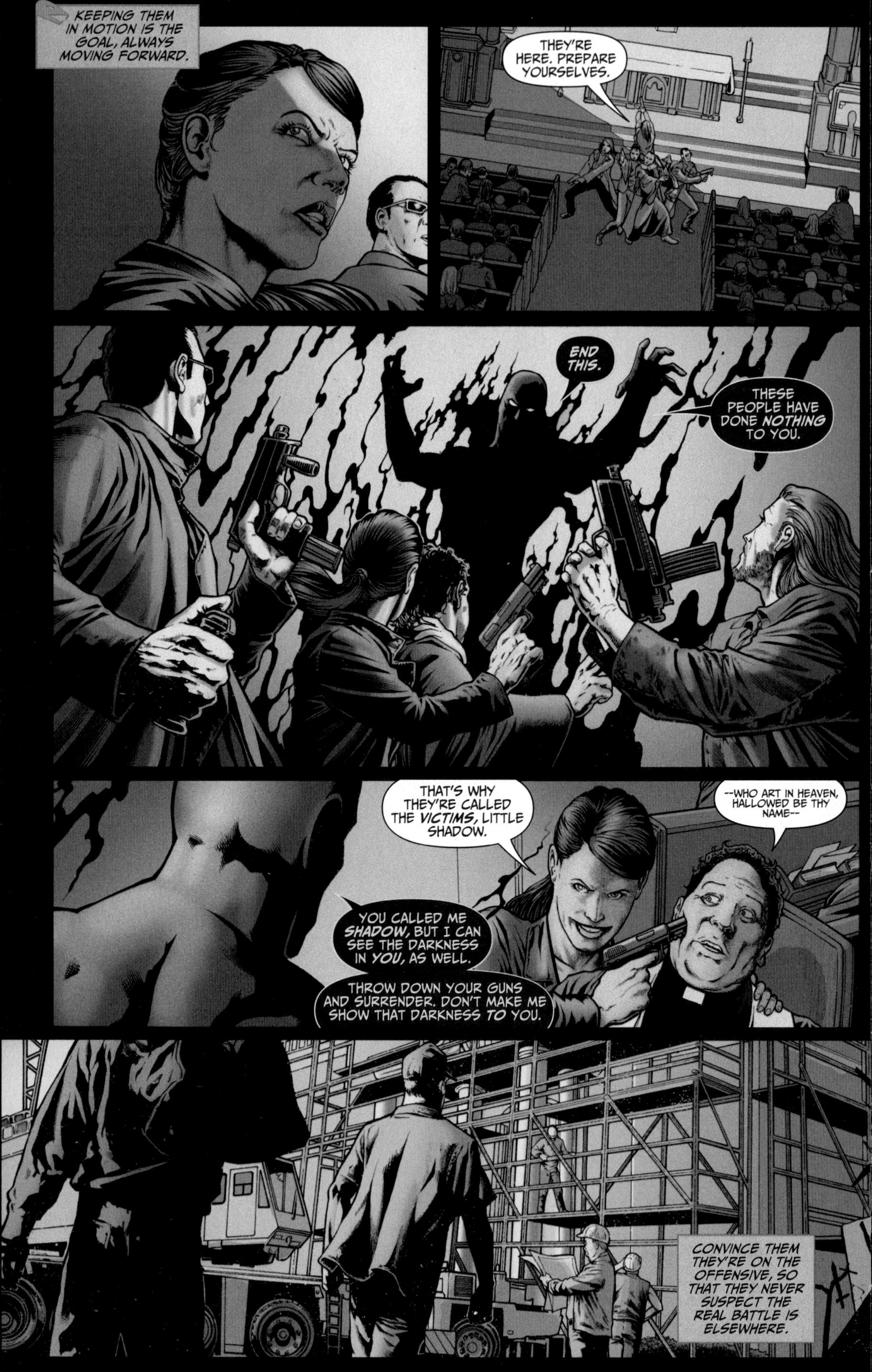
KEEPING THEM IN MOTION IS THE GOAL, ALWAYS MOVING FORWARD.
THEY'RE HERE. PREPARE YOURSELVES.
END THIS.
THESE PEOPLE HAVE DONE NOTHING TO YOU.
THAT'S WHY THEY'RE CALLED THE VICTIMS, LITTLE SHADOW.
--WHO ART IN HEAVEN, HALLOWED BE THY NAME--
YOU CALLED ME SHADOW, BUT I CAN SEE THE DARKNESS IN YOU, AS WELL.
THROW DOWN YOUR GUNS AND SURRENDER. DON'T MAKE ME SHOW THAT DARKNESS TO YOU.
CONVINCE THEM THEY'RE ON THE OFFENSIVE, SO THAT THEY NEVER SUSPECT THE REAL BATTLE IS ELSEWHERE.

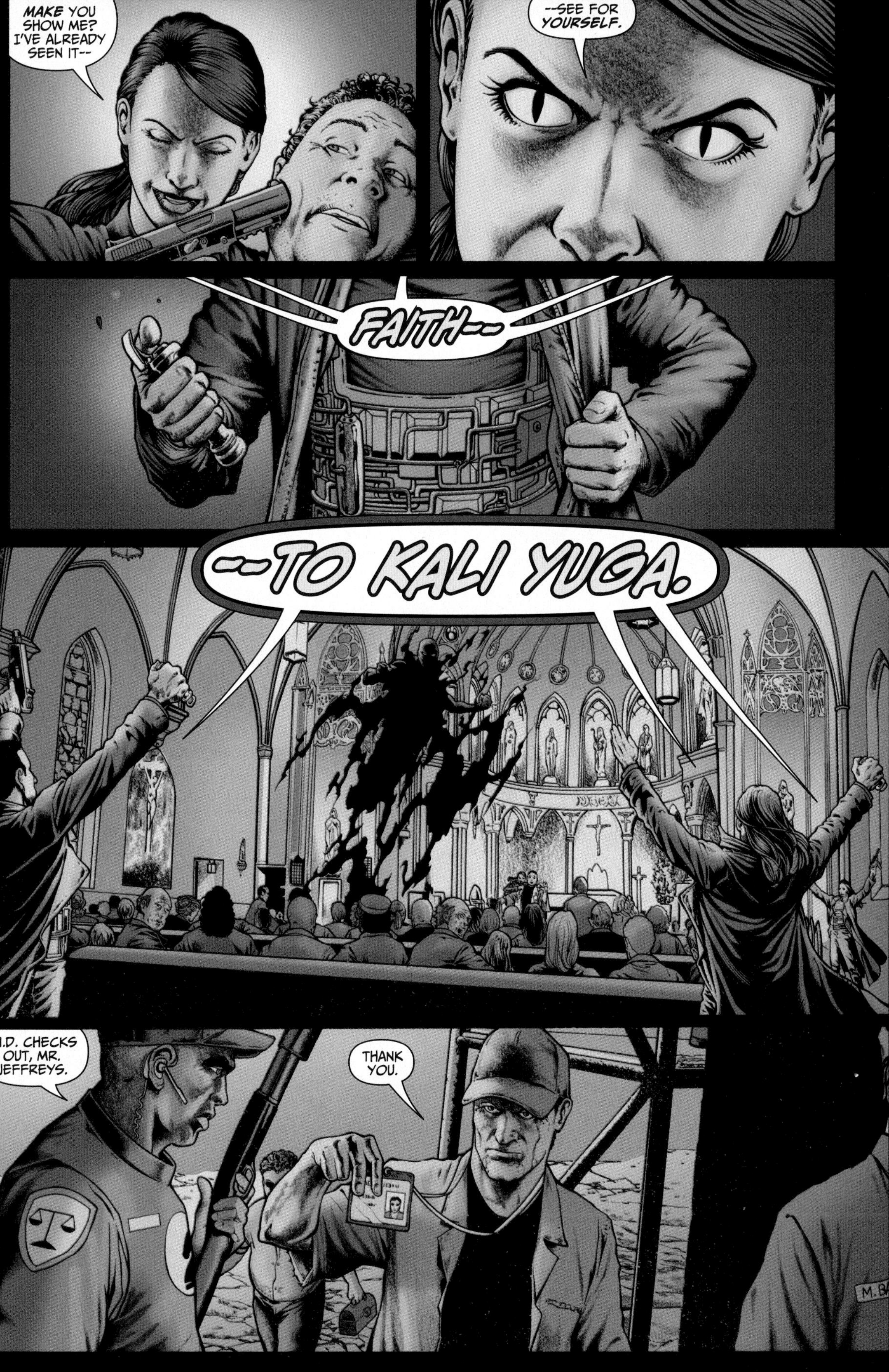
MAKE YOU SHOW ME? I'VE ALREADY SEEN IT--
--SEE FOR YOURSELF.
FAITH--
--TO KALI YUGA.
.D. CHECKS OUT, MR. JEFFREYS.
THANK YOU.
M.B

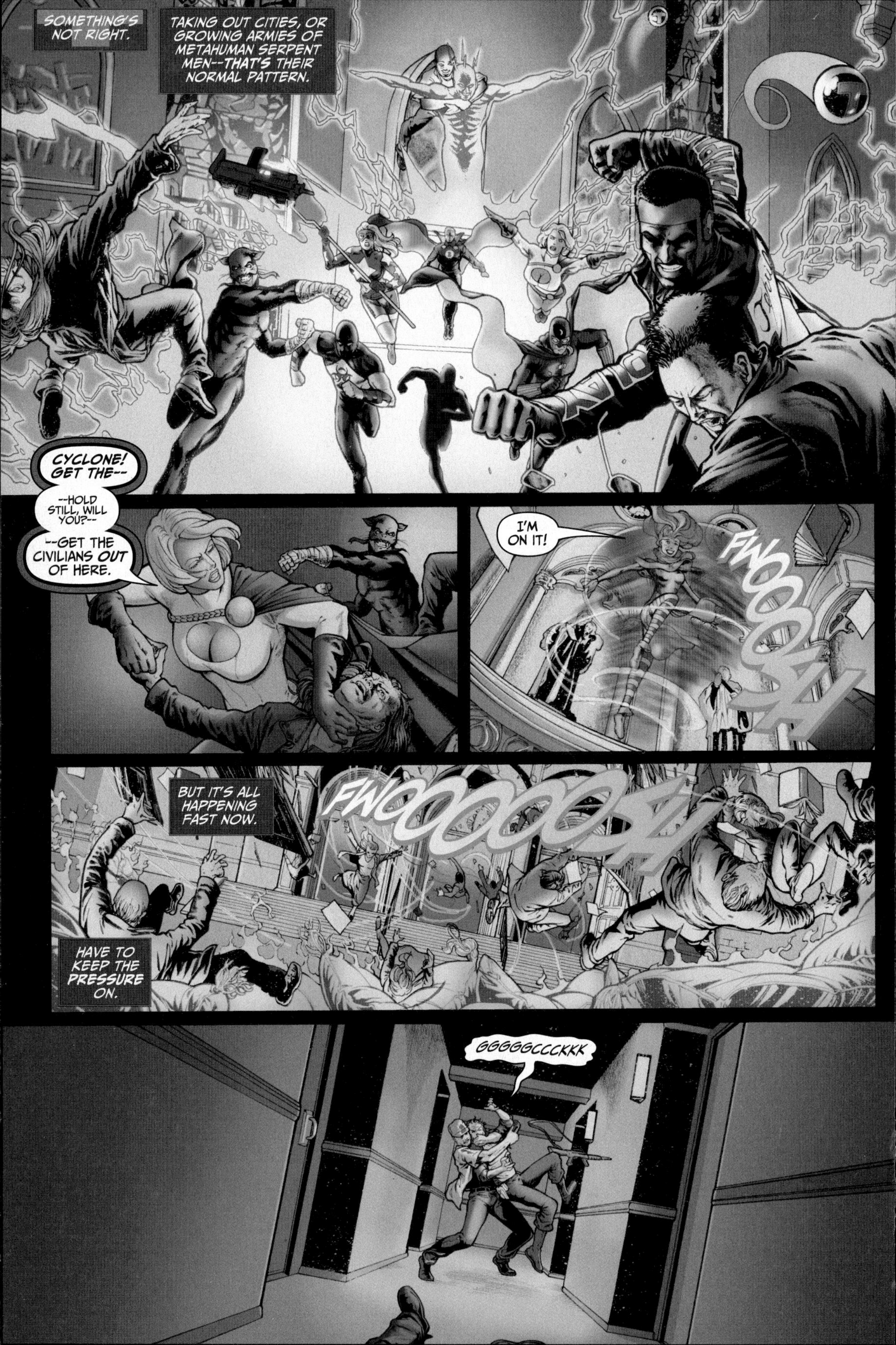
SOMETHING'S NOT RIGHT.
TAKING OUT CITIES, OR GROWING ARMIES OF METAHUMAN SERPENT MEN--THAT'S THEIR NORMAL PATTERN.
CYCLONE! GET THE--
--HOLD STILL, WILL YOU?--
--GET THE CIVILIANS OUT OF HERE.
I'M ON IT!
FWOOOOAH
BUT IT'S ALL HAPPENING FAST NOW.
FWOOOOOOAH
HAVE TO KEEP THE PRESSURE ON.
GGGGGCCCKKK

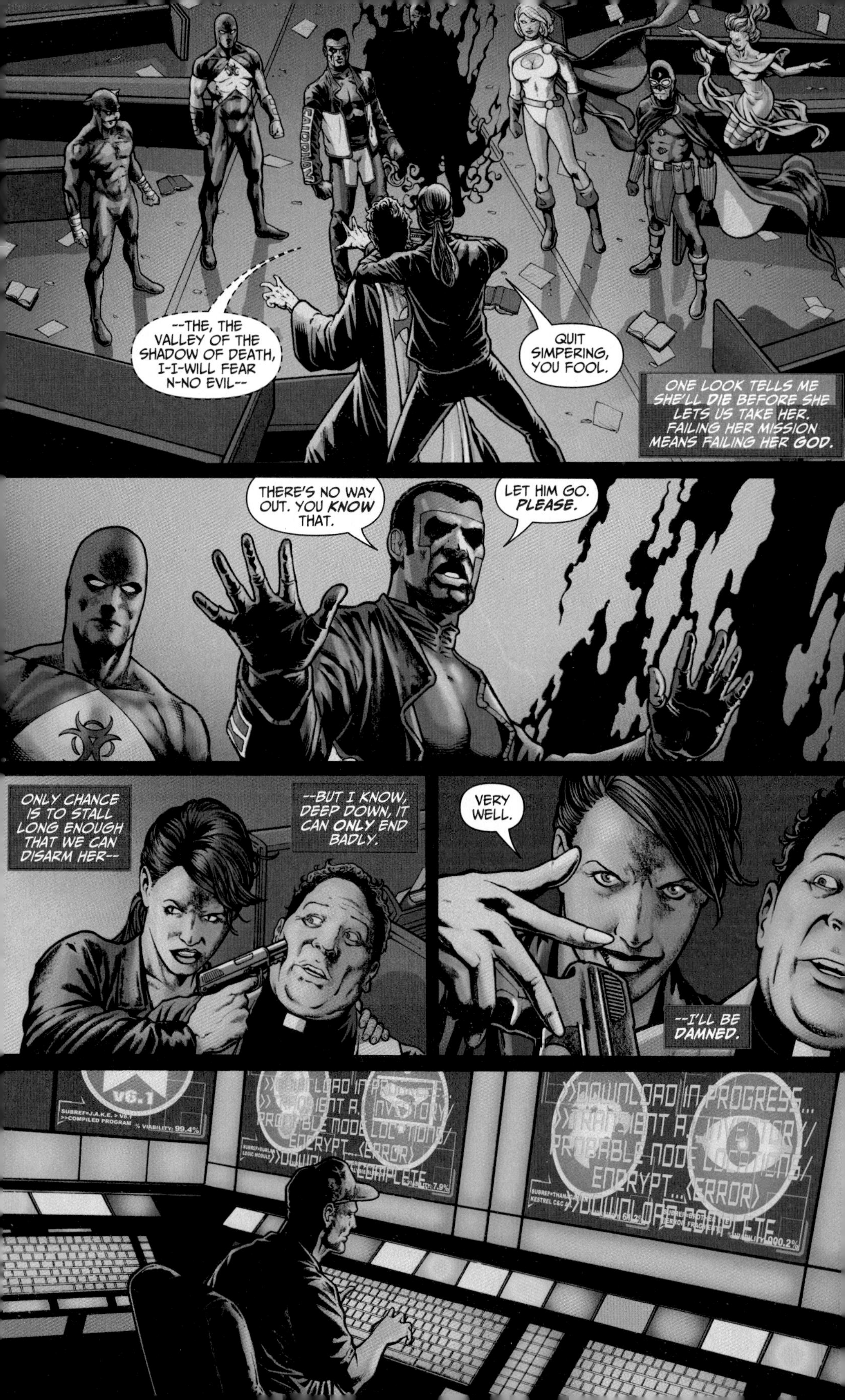
--THE, THE VALLEY OF THE SHADOW OF DEATH, I-I-WILL FEAR N-NO EVIL--
QUIT SIMPERING, YOU FOOL.
ONE LOOK TELLS ME SHE'LL DIE BEFORE SHE LETS US TAKE HER. FAILING HER MISSION MEANS FAILING HER GOD.
THERE'S NO WAY OUT. YOU KNOW THAT.
LET HIM GO. PLEASE.
ONLY CHANCE IS TO STALL LONG ENOUGH THAT WE CAN DISARM HER--
--BUT I KNOW, DEEP DOWN, IT CAN ONLY END BADLY.
VERY WELL.
--I'LL BE DAMNED.
v6.1
SUBREF=J.A.K.E. > V6.1
>>COMPILED PROGRAM
% VIABILITY: 99.4%
>>DOWNLOAD IN PROGRESS...
ENCRYPT...(ERROR)

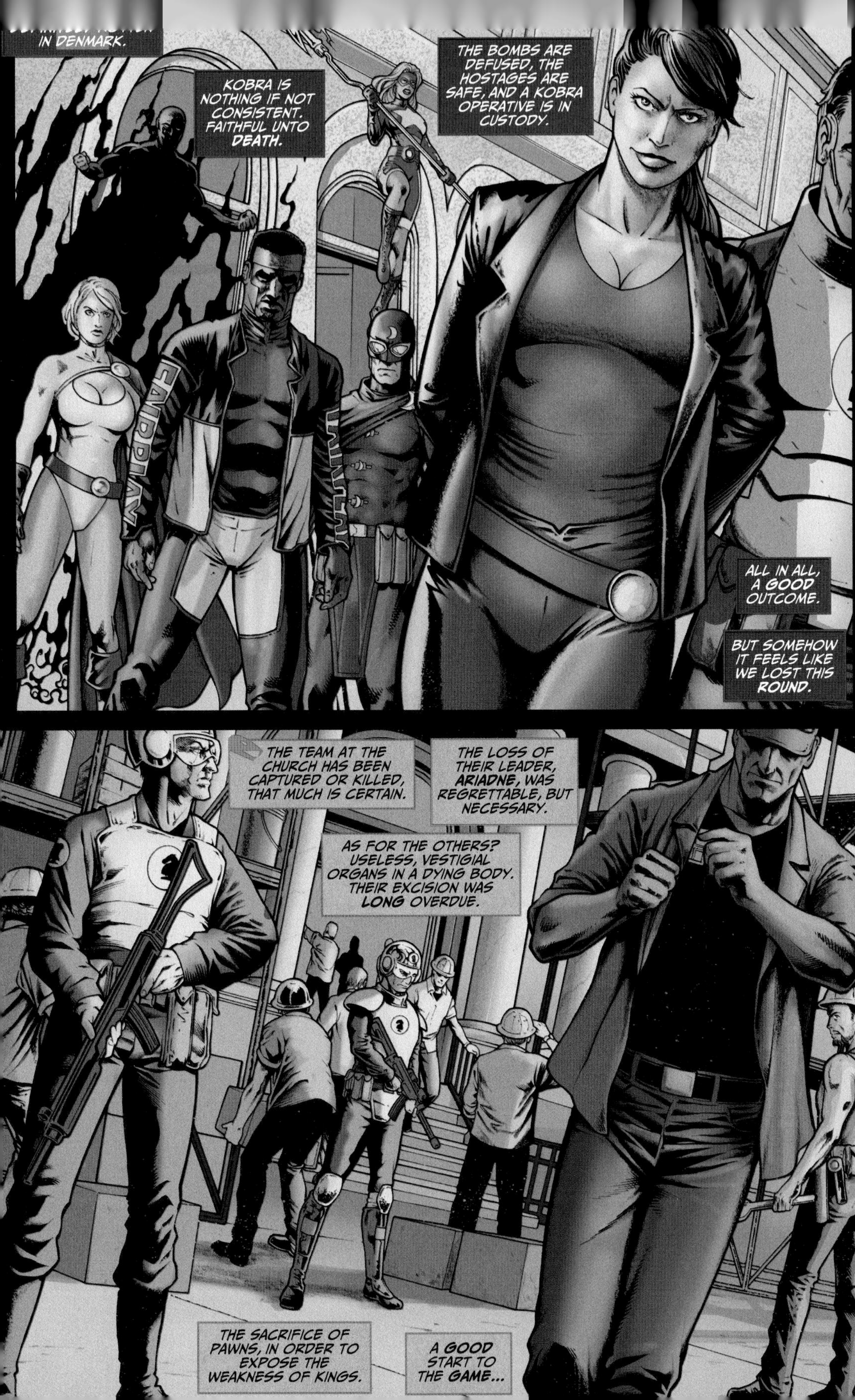
IN DENMARK.
KOBRA IS NOTHING IF NOT CONSISTENT. FAITHFUL UNTO DEATH.
THE BOMBS ARE DEFUSED, THE HOSTAGES ARE SAFE, AND A KOBRA OPERATIVE IS IN CUSTODY.
ALL IN ALL, A GOOD OUTCOME.
BUT SOMEHOW IT FEELS LIKE WE LOST THIS ROUND.
THE TEAM AT THE CHURCH HAS BEEN CAPTURED OR KILLED, THAT MUCH IS CERTAIN.
THE LOSS OF THEIR LEADER, ARIADNE, WAS REGRETTABLE, BUT NECESSARY.
AS FOR THE OTHERS? USELESS, VESTIGIAL ORGANS IN A DYING BODY. THEIR EXCISION WAS LONG OVERDUE.
THE SACRIFICE OF PAWNS, IN ORDER TO EXPOSE THE WEAKNESS OF KINGS.
A GOOD START TO THE GAME...

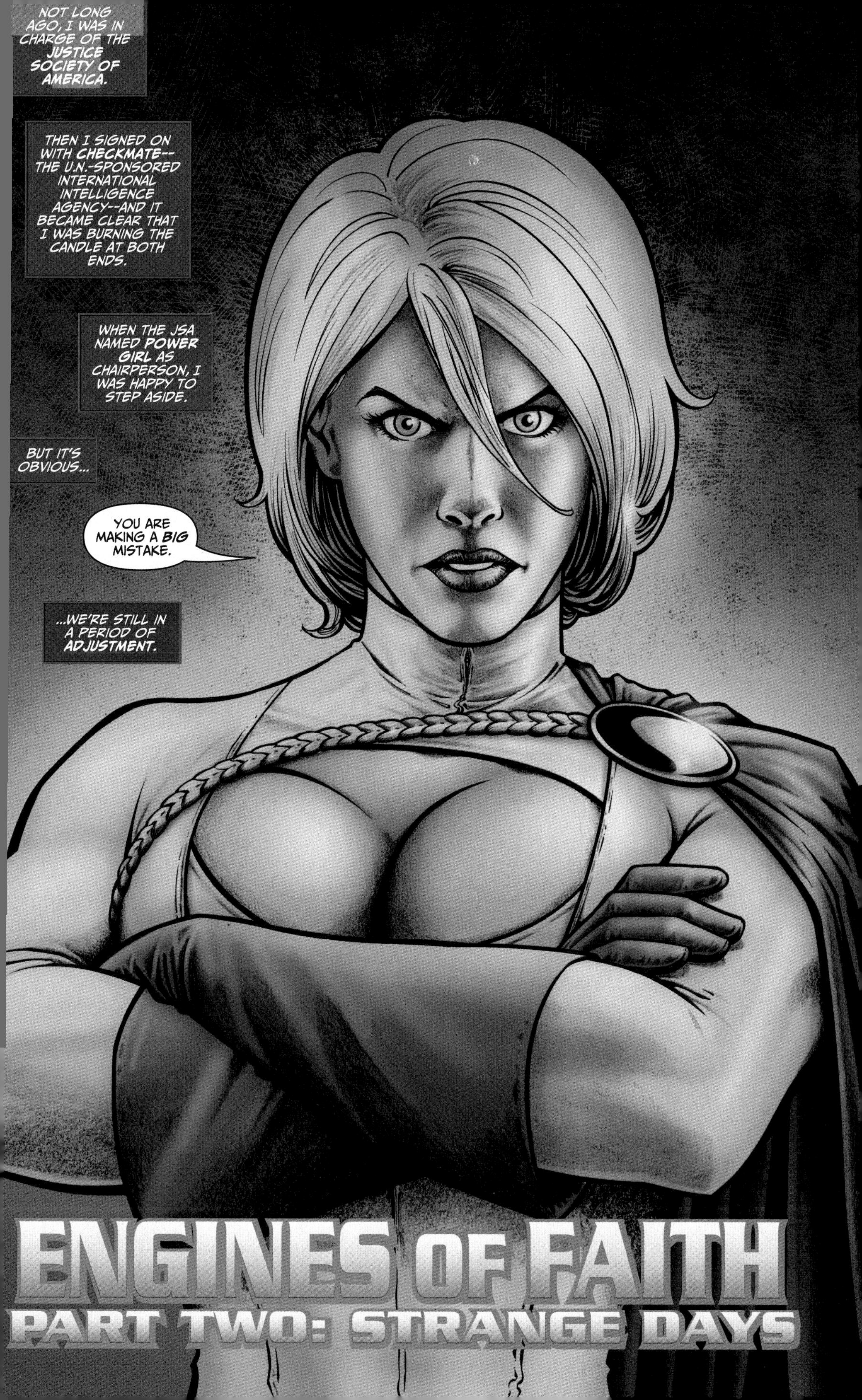

NOT LONG AGO, I WAS IN CHARGE OF THE JUSTICE SOCIETY OF AMERICA.
THEN I SIGNED ON WITH CHECKMATE-- THE U.N.-SPONSORED INTERNATIONAL INTELLIGENCE AGENCY--AND IT BECAME CLEAR THAT I WAS BURNING THE CANDLE AT BOTH ENDS.
WHEN THE JSA NAMED POWER GIRL AS CHAIRPERSON, I WAS HAPPY TO STEP ASIDE.
BUT IT'S OBVIOUS...
YOU ARE MAKING A BIG MISTAKE.
...WE'RE STILL IN A PERIOD OF ADJUSTMENT.
ENGINES OF FAITH
PART TWO: STRANGE DAYS

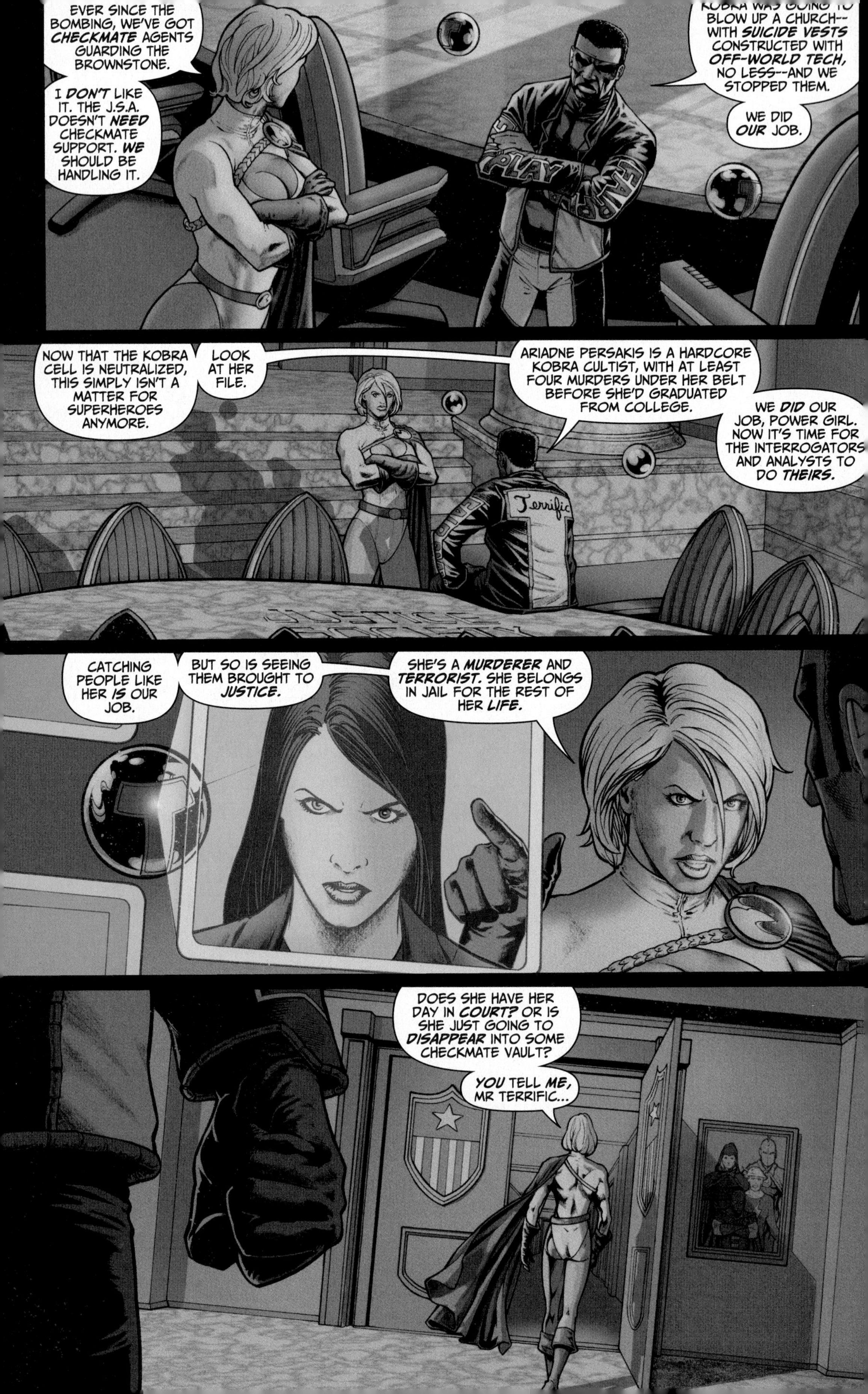

EVER SINCE THE BOMBING, WE'VE GOT **CHECKMATE** AGENTS GUARDING THE BROWNSTONE.
I **DON'T** LIKE IT. THE J.S.A. DOESN'T **NEED** CHECKMATE SUPPORT. **WE** SHOULD BE HANDLING IT.
KOBRA WAS GOING TO BLOW UP A CHURCH--WITH **SUICIDE VESTS** CONSTRUCTED WITH **OFF-WORLD TECH,** NO LESS--AND WE STOPPED THEM.
WE DID **OUR** JOB.
NOW THAT THE KOBRA CELL IS NEUTRALIZED, THIS SIMPLY ISN'T A MATTER FOR SUPERHEROES ANYMORE.
LOOK AT HER FILE.
ARIADNE PERSAKIS IS A HARDCORE KOBRA CULTIST, WITH AT LEAST FOUR MURDERS UNDER HER BELT BEFORE SHE'D GRADUATED FROM COLLEGE.
WE **DID** OUR JOB, POWER GIRL. NOW IT'S TIME FOR THE INTERROGATORS AND ANALYSTS TO DO **THEIRS.**
CATCHING PEOPLE LIKE HER **IS** OUR JOB.
BUT SO IS SEEING THEM BROUGHT TO **JUSTICE.**
SHE'S A **MURDERER** AND **TERRORIST.** SHE BELONGS IN JAIL FOR THE REST OF HER **LIFE.**
DOES SHE HAVE HER DAY IN **COURT?** OR IS SHE JUST GOING TO **DISAPPEAR** INTO SOME CHECKMATE VAULT?
YOU TELL **ME,** MR TERRIFIC...

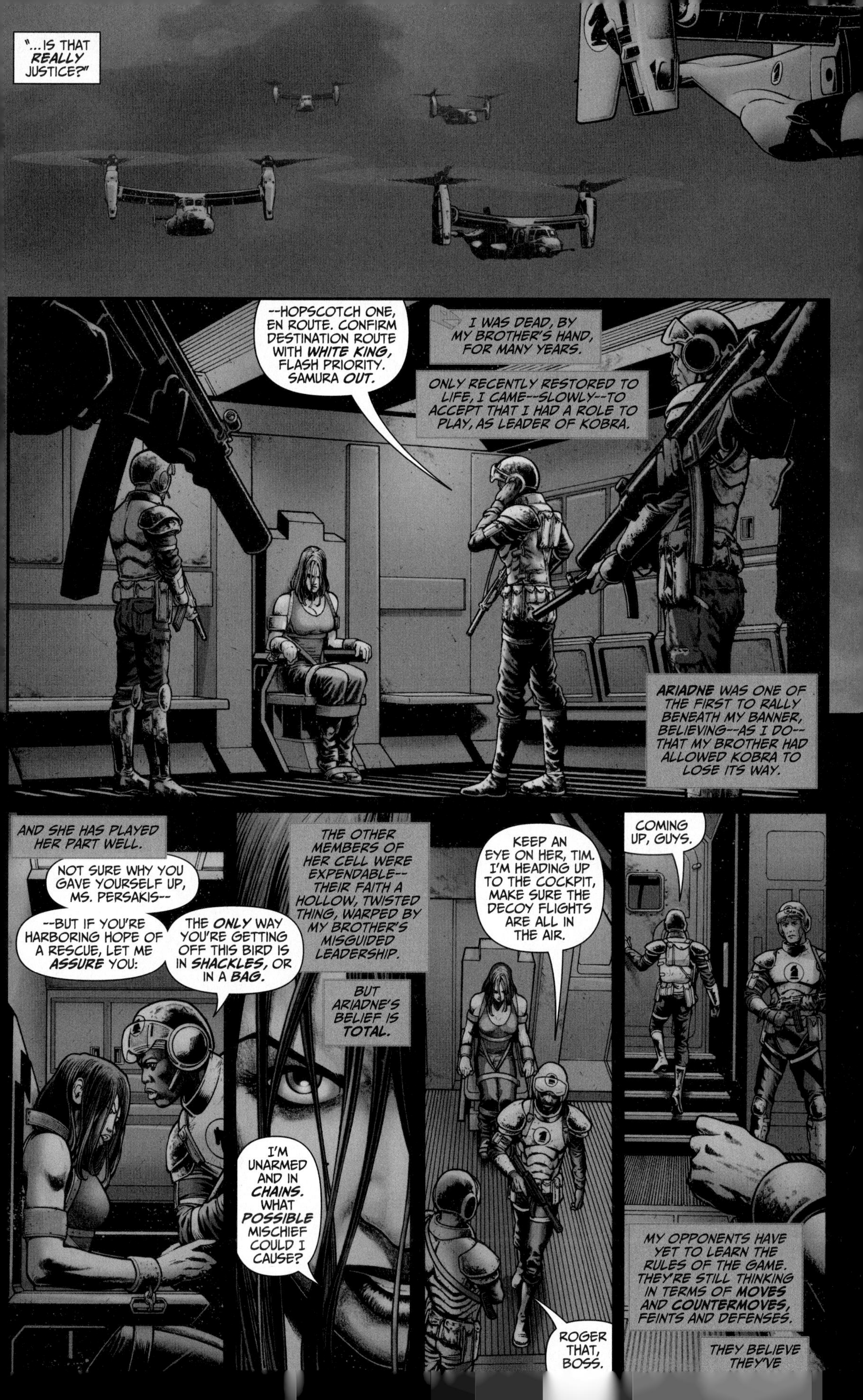
"...IS THAT REALLY JUSTICE?"
--HOPSCOTCH ONE, EN ROUTE. CONFIRM DESTINATION ROUTE WITH WHITE KING, FLASH PRIORITY. SAMURA OUT.
I WAS DEAD, BY MY BROTHER'S HAND, FOR MANY YEARS.
ONLY RECENTLY RESTORED TO LIFE, I CAME--SLOWLY--TO ACCEPT THAT I HAD A ROLE TO PLAY, AS LEADER OF KOBRA.
ARIADNE WAS ONE OF THE FIRST TO RALLY BENEATH MY BANNER, BELIEVING--AS I DO--THAT MY BROTHER HAD ALLOWED KOBRA TO LOSE ITS WAY.
AND SHE HAS PLAYED HER PART WELL.
NOT SURE WHY YOU GAVE YOURSELF UP, MS. PERSAKIS--
--BUT IF YOU'RE HARBORING HOPE OF A RESCUE, LET ME ASSURE YOU:
THE ONLY WAY YOU'RE GETTING OFF THIS BIRD IS IN SHACKLES, OR IN A BAG.
THE OTHER MEMBERS OF HER CELL WERE EXPENDABLE--THEIR FAITH A HOLLOW, TWISTED THING, WARPED BY MY BROTHER'S MISGUIDED LEADERSHIP.
BUT ARIADNE'S BELIEF IS TOTAL.
I'M UNARMED AND IN CHAINS. WHAT POSSIBLE MISCHIEF COULD I CAUSE?
KEEP AN EYE ON HER, TIM. I'M HEADING UP TO THE COCKPIT, MAKE SURE THE DECOY FLIGHTS ARE ALL IN THE AIR.
ROGER THAT, BOSS.
COMING UP, GUYS.
MY OPPONENTS HAVE YET TO LEARN THE RULES OF THE GAME. THEY'RE STILL THINKING IN TERMS OF MOVES AND COUNTERMOVES, FEINTS AND DEFENSES.
THEY BELIEVE THEY'VE

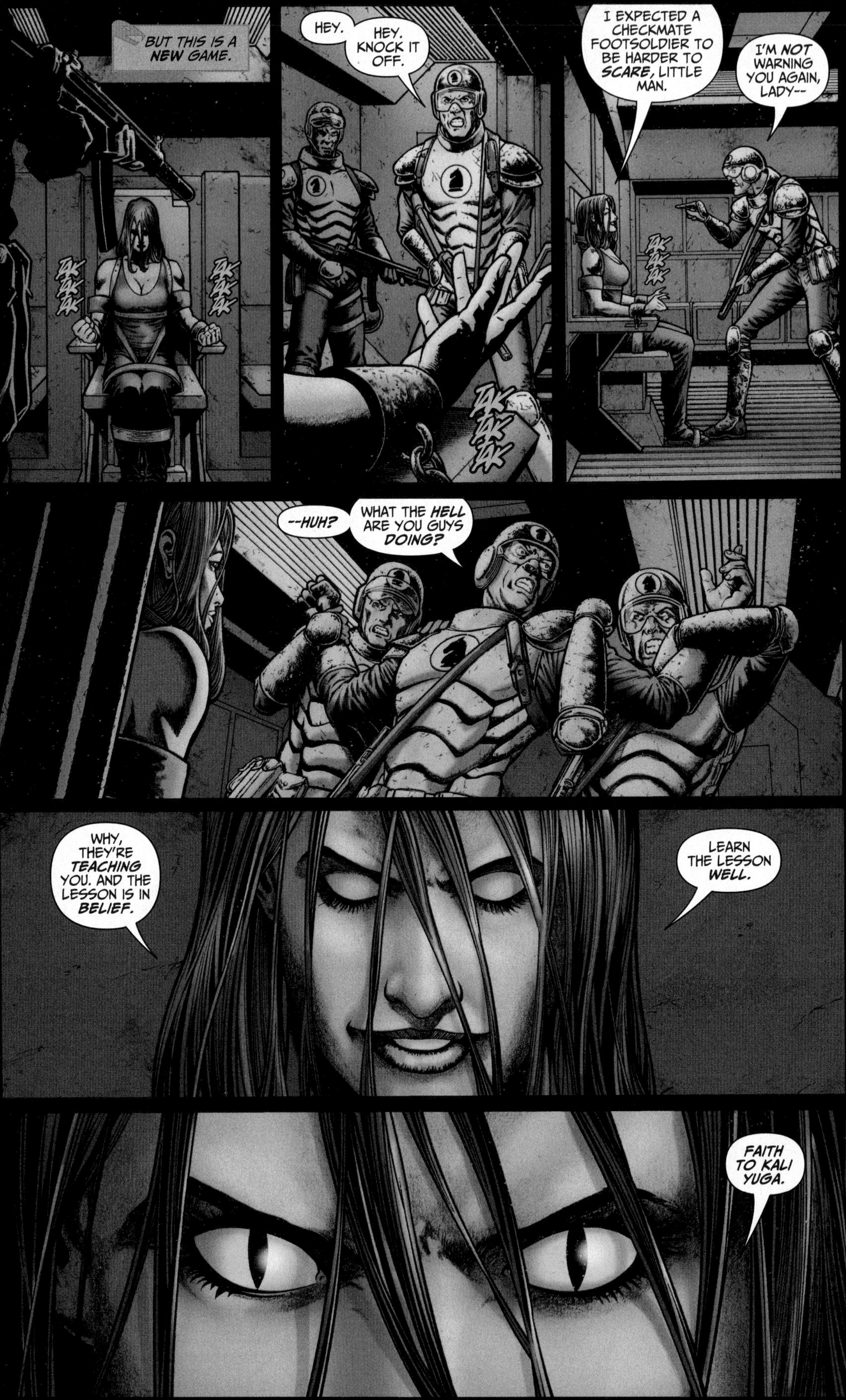
BUT THIS IS A NEW GAME.
TAK TAK TAK
TAK TAK TAK
HEY.
HEY. KNOCK IT OFF.
TAK TAK TAK
I EXPECTED A CHECKMATE FOOTSOLDIER TO BE HARDER TO SCARE, LITTLE MAN.
I'M NOT WARNING YOU AGAIN, LADY--
TAK TAK TAK
--HUH?
WHAT THE HELL ARE YOU GUYS DOING?
WHY, THEY'RE TEACHING YOU. AND THE LESSON IS IN BELIEF.
LEARN THE LESSON WELL.
FAITH TO KALI YUGA.

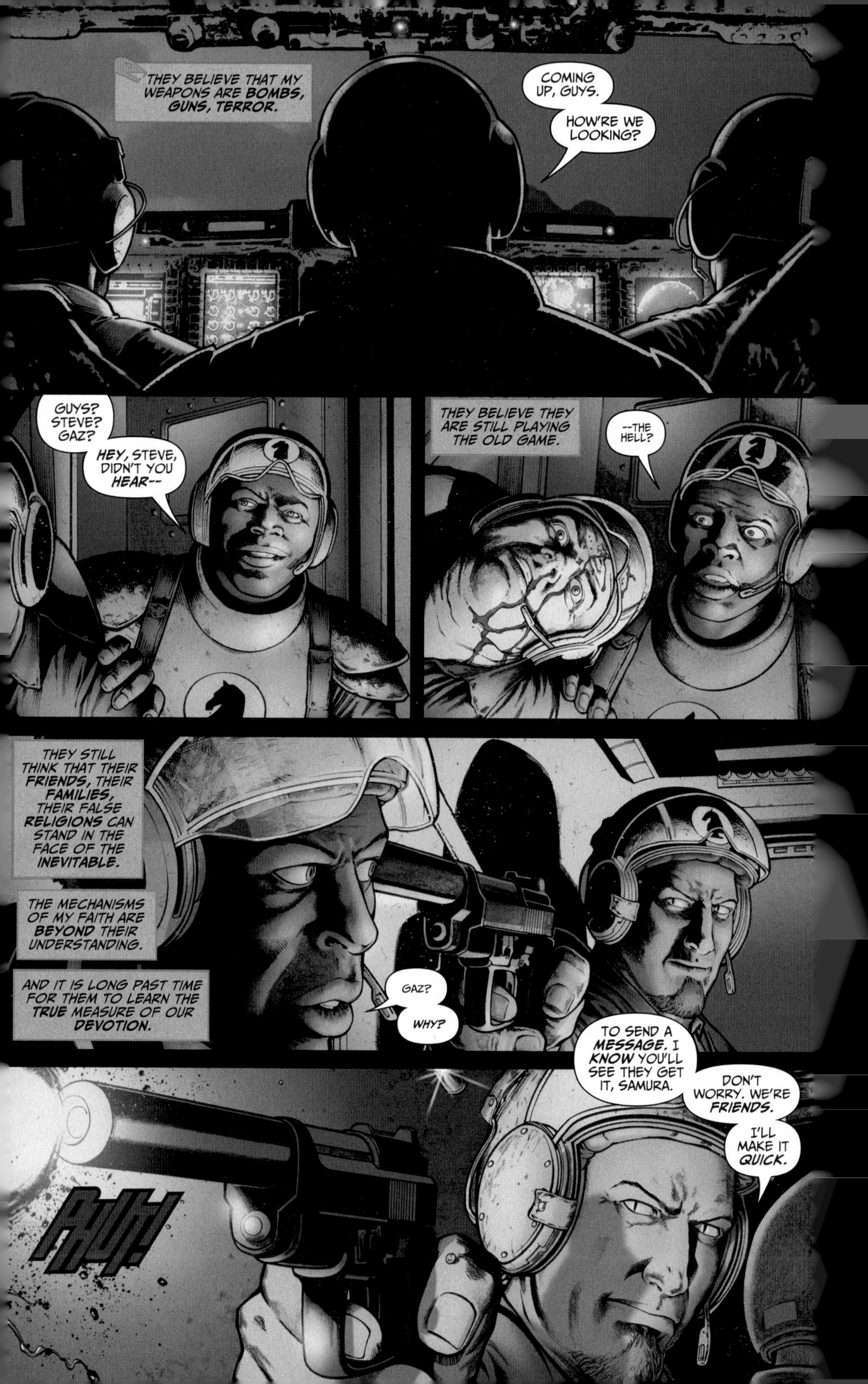
THEY BELIEVE THAT MY WEAPONS ARE BOMBS, GUNS, TERROR.
COMING UP, GUYS.
HOW'RE WE LOOKING?
GUYS? STEVE? GAZ?
HEY, STEVE, DIDN'T YOU HEAR--
THEY BELIEVE THEY ARE STILL PLAYING THE OLD GAME.
--THE HELL?
THEY STILL THINK THAT THEIR FRIENDS, THEIR FAMILIES, THEIR FALSE RELIGIONS CAN STAND IN THE FACE OF THE INEVITABLE.
THE MECHANISMS OF MY FAITH ARE BEYOND THEIR UNDERSTANDING.
AND IT IS LONG PAST TIME FOR THEM TO LEARN THE TRUE MEASURE OF OUR DEVOTION.
GAZ?
WHY?
TO SEND A MESSAGE. I KNOW YOU'LL SEE THEY GET IT, SAMURA.
DON'T WORRY. WE'RE FRIENDS.
I'LL MAKE IT QUICK.
PHUT!

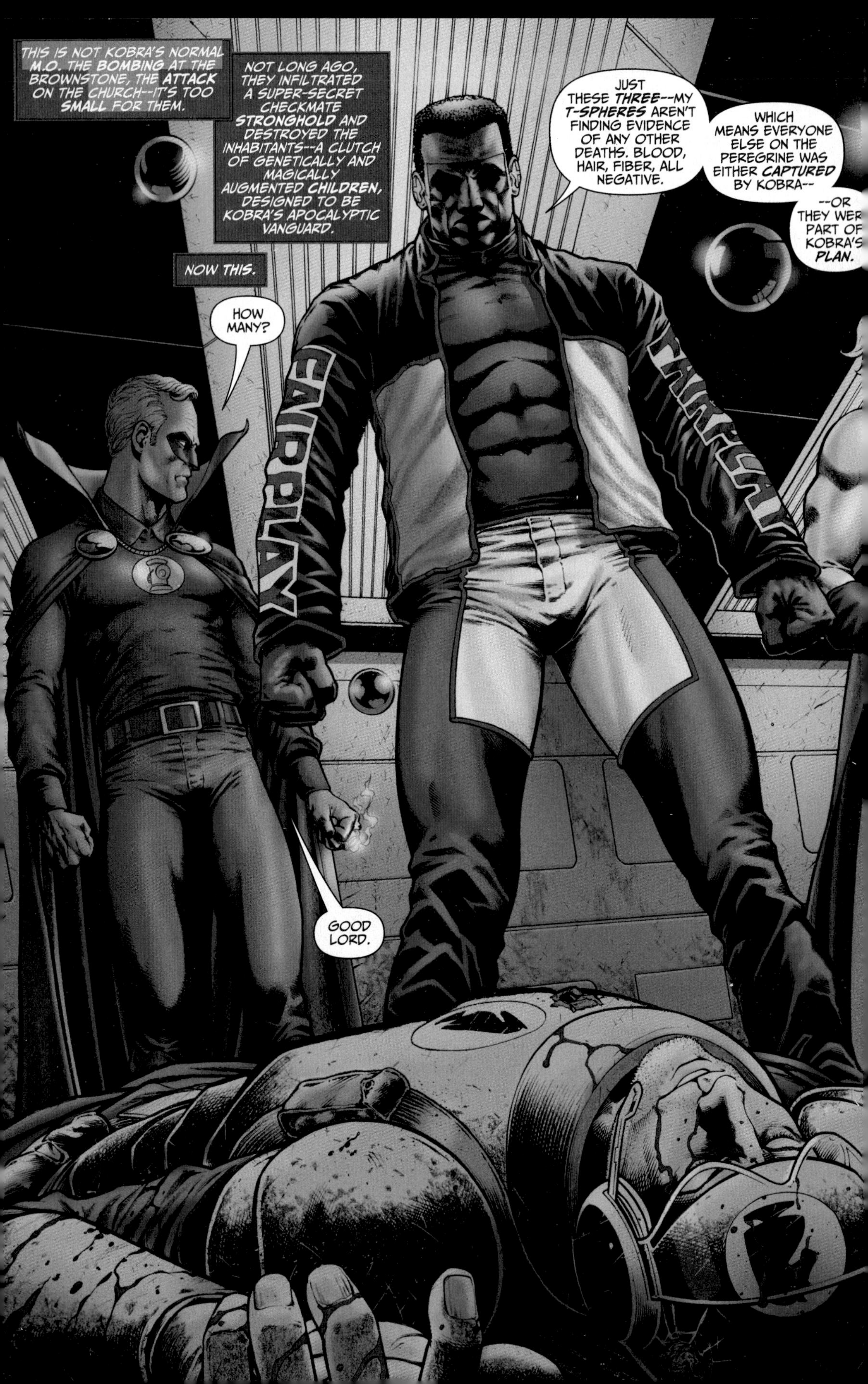

THIS IS NOT KOBRA'S NORMAL M.O. THE BOMBING AT THE BROWNSTONE, THE ATTACK ON THE CHURCH--IT'S TOO SMALL FOR THEM.
NOT LONG AGO, THEY INFILTRATED A SUPER-SECRET CHECKMATE STRONGHOLD AND DESTROYED THE INHABITANTS--A CLUTCH OF GENETICALLY AND MAGICALLY AUGMENTED CHILDREN, DESIGNED TO BE KOBRA'S APOCALYPTIC VANGUARD.
NOW THIS.
HOW MANY?
JUST THESE THREE--MY T-SPHERES AREN'T FINDING EVIDENCE OF ANY OTHER DEATHS. BLOOD, HAIR, FIBER, ALL NEGATIVE.
WHICH MEANS EVERYONE ELSE ON THE PEREGRINE WAS EITHER CAPTURED BY KOBRA--
--OR THEY WER PART OF KOBRA'S PLAN.
FAIRPLAY
FAIRPLAY
GOOD LORD.

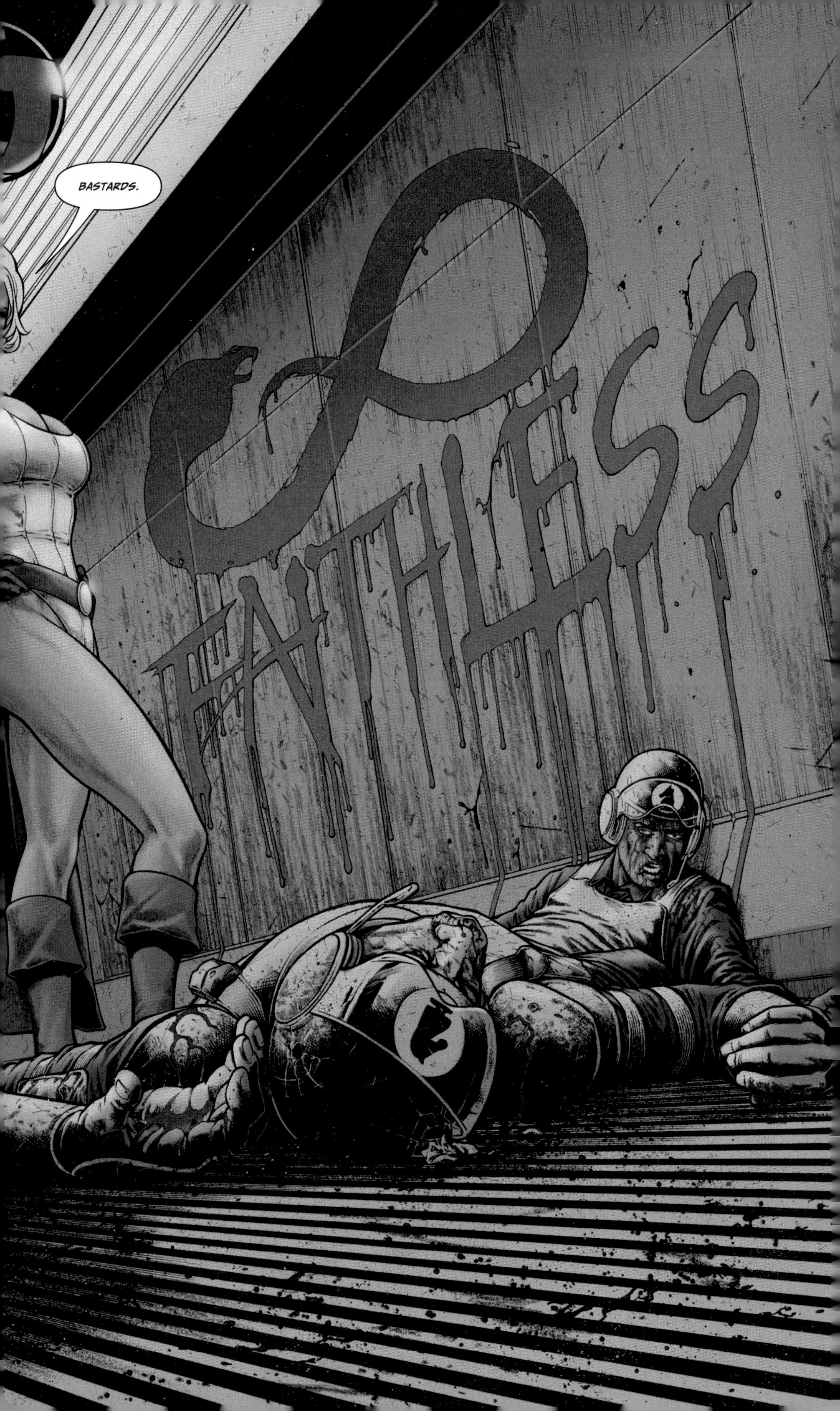
BASTARDS.
FAITHLESS

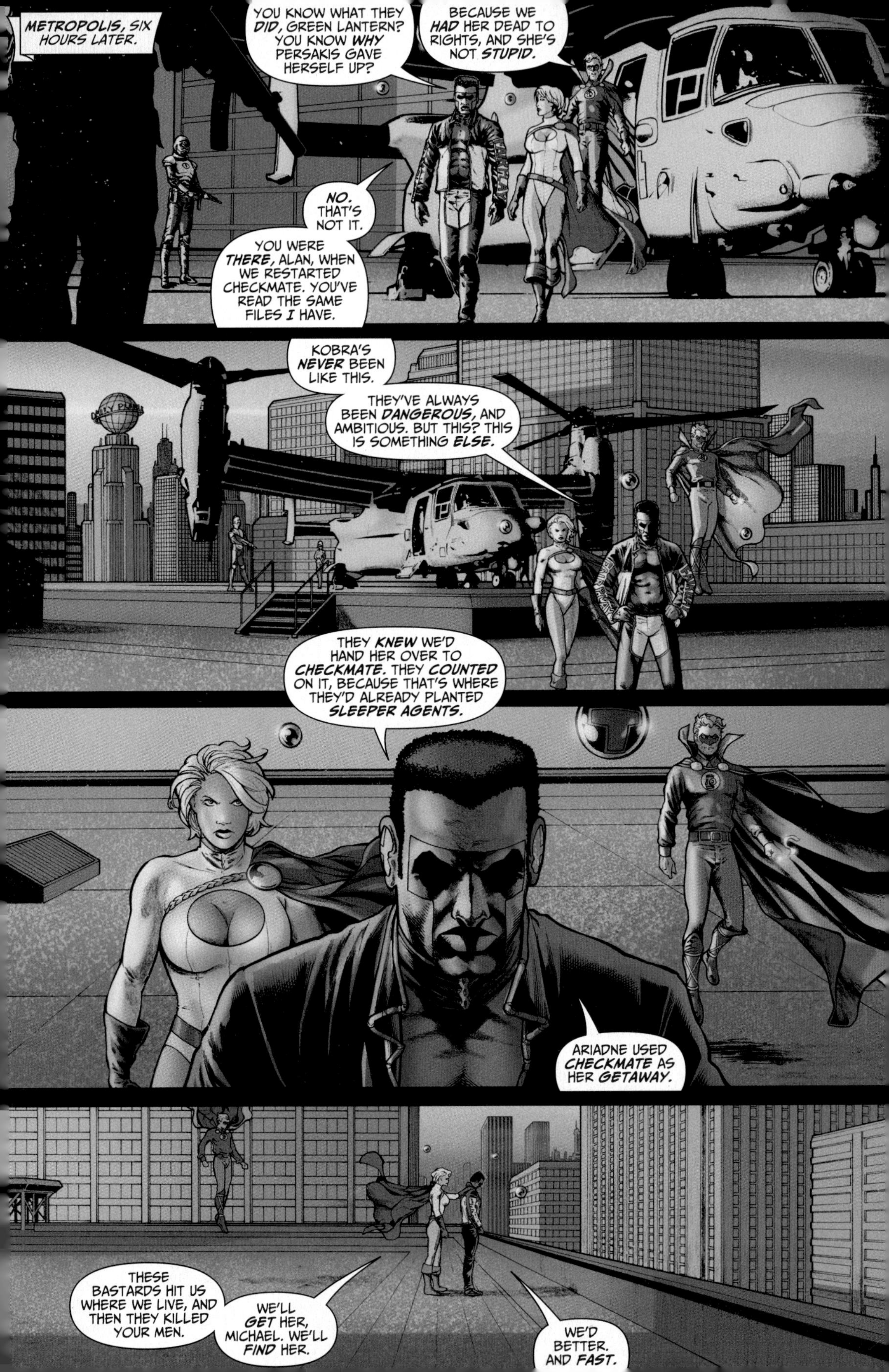
METROPOLIS, SIX HOURS LATER.
YOU KNOW WHAT THEY DID, GREEN LANTERN? YOU KNOW WHY PERSAKIS GAVE HERSELF UP?
BECAUSE WE HAD HER DEAD TO RIGHTS, AND SHE'S NOT STUPID.
NO. THAT'S NOT IT.
YOU WERE THERE, ALAN, WHEN WE RESTARTED CHECKMATE. YOU'VE READ THE SAME FILES I HAVE.
KOBRA'S NEVER BEEN LIKE THIS.
THEY'VE ALWAYS BEEN DANGEROUS, AND AMBITIOUS. BUT THIS? THIS IS SOMETHING ELSE.
THEY KNEW WE'D HAND HER OVER TO CHECKMATE. THEY COUNTED ON IT, BECAUSE THAT'S WHERE THEY'D ALREADY PLANTED SLEEPER AGENTS.
ARIADNE USED CHECKMATE AS HER GETAWAY.
THESE BASTARDS HIT US WHERE WE LIVE, AND THEN THEY KILLED YOUR MEN.
WE'LL GET HER, MICHAEL. WE'LL FIND HER.
WE'D BETTER. AND FAST.

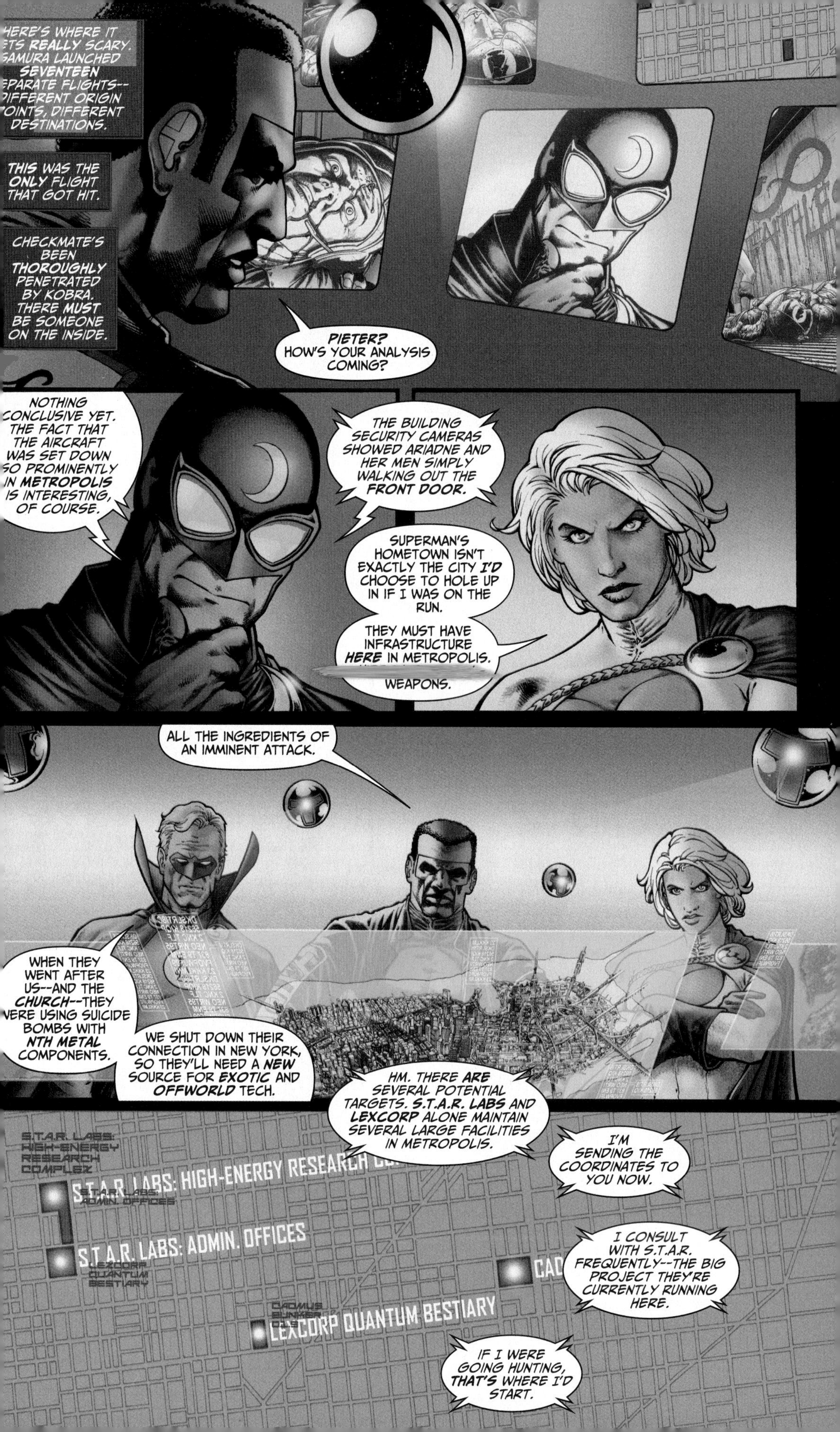
HERE'S WHERE IT ETS REALLY SCARY. SAMURA LAUNCHED SEVENTEEN EPARATE FLIGHTS-- DIFFERENT ORIGIN OINTS, DIFFERENT DESTINATIONS.
THIS WAS THE ONLY FLIGHT THAT GOT HIT.
CHECKMATE'S BEEN THOROUGHLY PENETRATED BY KOBRA. THERE MUST BE SOMEONE ON THE INSIDE.
PIETER? HOW'S YOUR ANALYSIS COMING?
NOTHING CONCLUSIVE YET. THE FACT THAT THE AIRCRAFT WAS SET DOWN SO PROMINENTLY IN METROPOLIS IS INTERESTING, OF COURSE.
THE BUILDING SECURITY CAMERAS SHOWED ARIADNE AND HER MEN SIMPLY WALKING OUT THE FRONT DOOR.
SUPERMAN'S HOMETOWN ISN'T EXACTLY THE CITY I'D CHOOSE TO HOLE UP IN IF I WAS ON THE RUN.
THEY MUST HAVE INFRASTRUCTURE HERE IN METROPOLIS.
WEAPONS.
ALL THE INGREDIENTS OF AN IMMINENT ATTACK.
WHEN THEY WENT AFTER US--AND THE CHURCH--THEY WERE USING SUICIDE BOMBS WITH NTH METAL COMPONENTS.
WE SHUT DOWN THEIR CONNECTION IN NEW YORK, SO THEY'LL NEED A NEW SOURCE FOR EXOTIC AND OFFWORLD TECH.
HM. THERE ARE SEVERAL POTENTIAL TARGETS. S.T.A.R. LABS AND LEXCORP ALONE MAINTAIN SEVERAL LARGE FACILITIES IN METROPOLIS.
I'M SENDING THE COORDINATES TO YOU NOW.
S.T.A.R. LABS: HIGH-ENERGY RESEARCH COMPLEX
S.T.A.R. LABS: HIGH-ENERGY RESEARCH CO
S.T.A.R. LABS: ADMIN. OFFICES
S.T.A.R. LABS: ADMIN. OFFICES
LEXCORP QUANTUM BESTIARY
CADMUS BUNKER
LEXCORP QUANTUM BESTIARY
CAD
I CONSULT WITH S.T.A.R. FREQUENTLY--THE BIG PROJECT THEY'RE CURRENTLY RUNNING HERE.
IF I WERE GOING HUNTING, THAT'S WHERE I'D START.

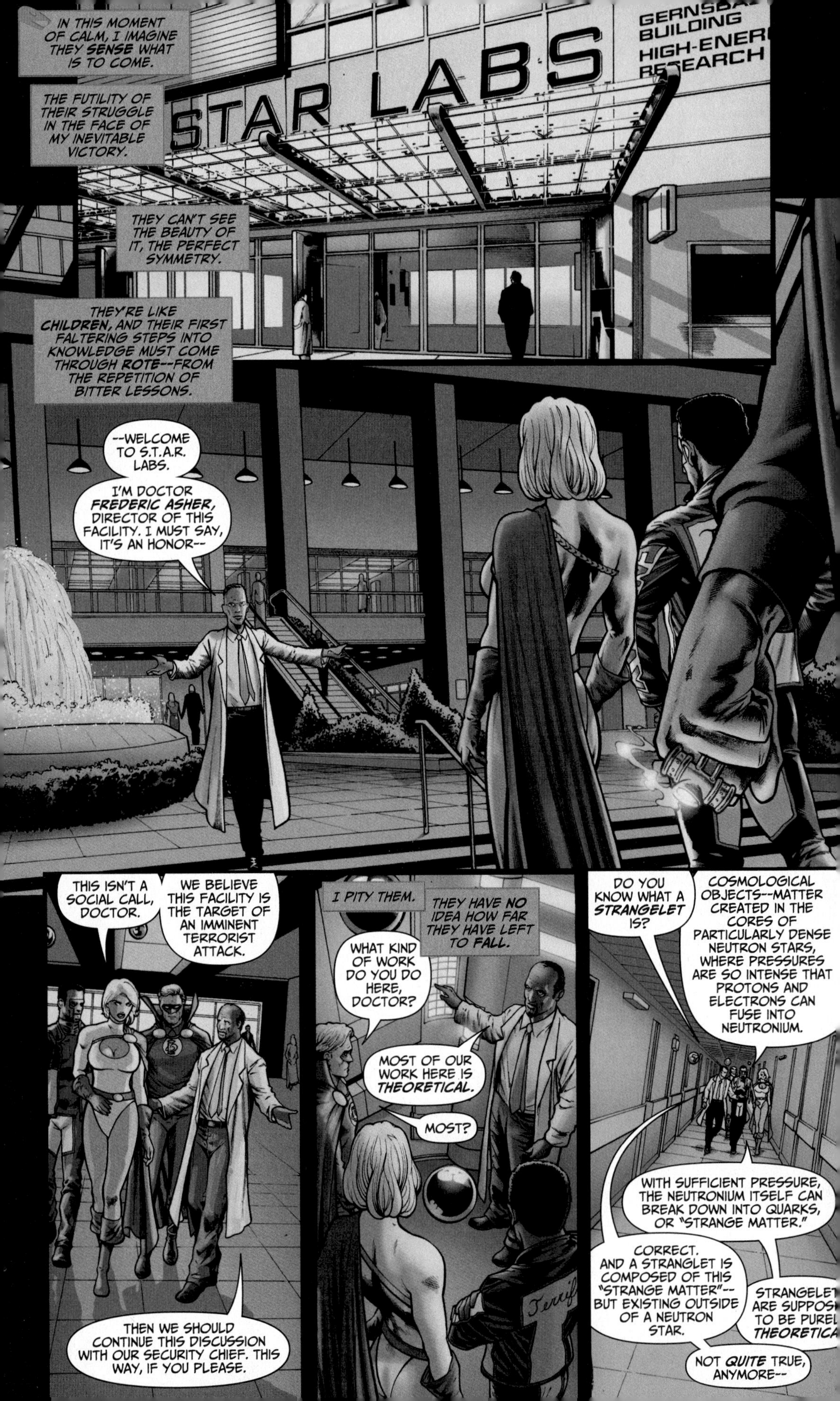

IN THIS MOMENT OF CALM, I IMAGINE THEY SENSE WHAT IS TO COME.
STAR LABS
GERNSB
BUILDING
HIGH-ENER
RESEARCH
THE FUTILITY OF THEIR STRUGGLE IN THE FACE OF MY INEVITABLE VICTORY.
THEY CAN'T SEE THE BEAUTY OF IT, THE PERFECT SYMMETRY.
THEY'RE LIKE CHILDREN, AND THEIR FIRST FALTERING STEPS INTO KNOWLEDGE MUST COME THROUGH ROTE--FROM THE REPETITION OF BITTER LESSONS.
--WELCOME TO S.T.A.R. LABS.
I'M DOCTOR FREDERIC ASHER, DIRECTOR OF THIS FACILITY. I MUST SAY, IT'S AN HONOR--
THIS ISN'T A SOCIAL CALL, DOCTOR.
WE BELIEVE THIS FACILITY IS THE TARGET OF AN IMMINENT TERRORIST ATTACK.
THEN WE SHOULD CONTINUE THIS DISCUSSION WITH OUR SECURITY CHIEF. THIS WAY, IF YOU PLEASE.
I PITY THEM.
THEY HAVE NO IDEA HOW FAR THEY HAVE LEFT TO FALL.
WHAT KIND OF WORK DO YOU DO HERE, DOCTOR?
MOST OF OUR WORK HERE IS THEORETICAL.
MOST?
DO YOU KNOW WHAT A STRANGELET IS?
COSMOLOGICAL OBJECTS--MATTER CREATED IN THE CORES OF PARTICULARLY DENSE NEUTRON STARS, WHERE PRESSURES ARE SO INTENSE THAT PROTONS AND ELECTRONS CAN FUSE INTO NEUTRONIUM.
WITH SUFFICIENT PRESSURE, THE NEUTRONIUM ITSELF CAN BREAK DOWN INTO QUARKS, OR "STRANGE MATTER."
CORRECT. AND A STRANGLET IS COMPOSED OF THIS "STRANGE MATTER"--BUT EXISTING OUTSIDE OF A NEUTRON STAR.
STRANGELE ARE SUPPOS TO BE PUREL THEORETICA
NOT QUITE TRUE, ANYMORE--

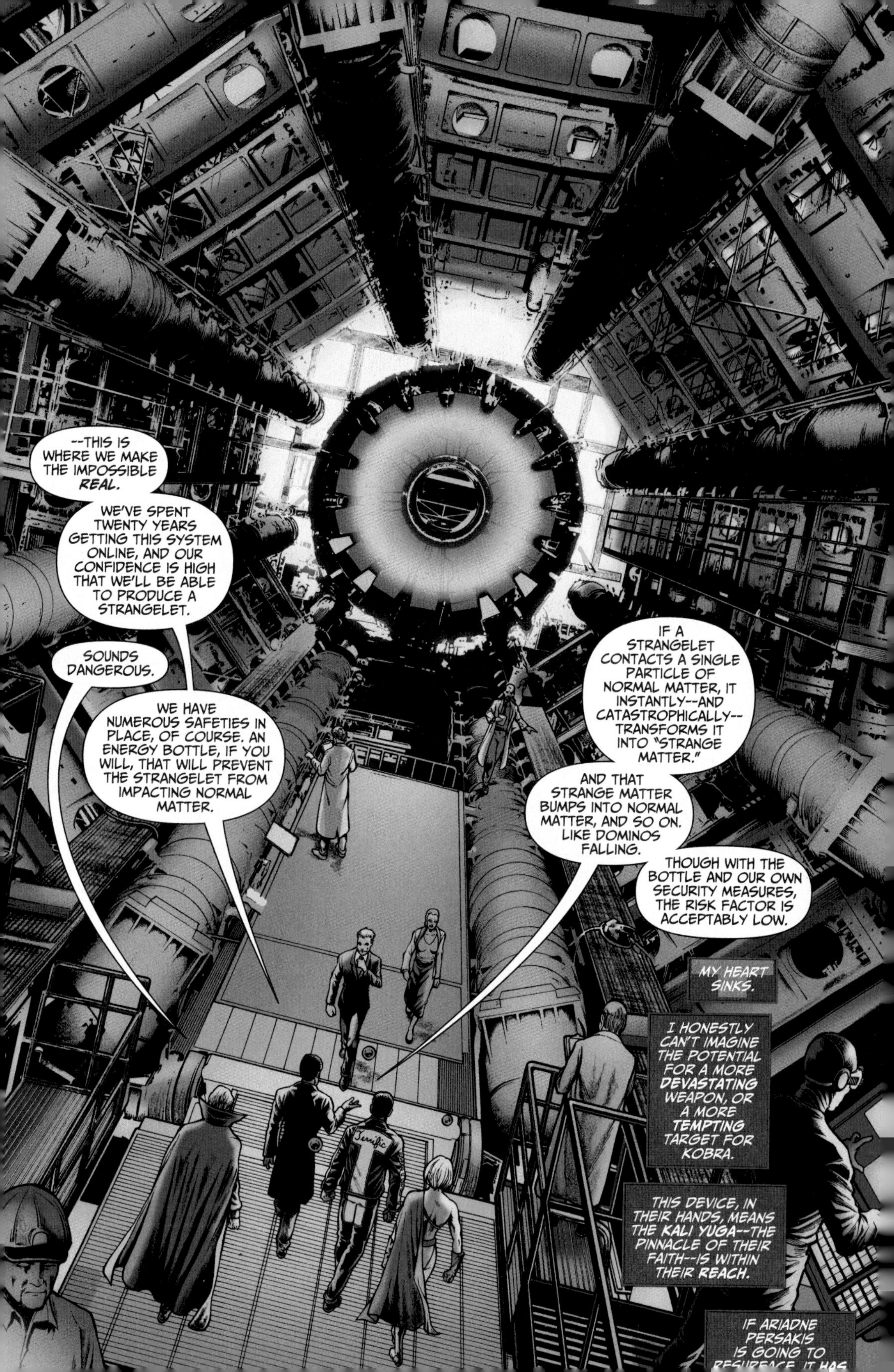
--THIS IS WHERE WE MAKE THE IMPOSSIBLE *REAL.*
WE'VE SPENT TWENTY YEARS GETTING THIS SYSTEM ONLINE, AND OUR CONFIDENCE IS HIGH THAT WE'LL BE ABLE TO PRODUCE A STRANGELET.
SOUNDS DANGEROUS.
WE HAVE NUMEROUS SAFETIES IN PLACE, OF COURSE. AN ENERGY BOTTLE, IF YOU WILL, THAT WILL PREVENT THE STRANGELET FROM IMPACTING NORMAL MATTER.
IF A STRANGELET CONTACTS A SINGLE PARTICLE OF NORMAL MATTER, IT INSTANTLY--AND CATASTROPHICALLY--TRANSFORMS IT INTO "STRANGE MATTER."
AND THAT STRANGE MATTER BUMPS INTO NORMAL MATTER, AND SO ON. LIKE DOMINOS FALLING.
THOUGH WITH THE BOTTLE AND OUR OWN SECURITY MEASURES, THE RISK FACTOR IS ACCEPTABLY LOW.
MY HEART SINKS.
I HONESTLY CAN'T IMAGINE THE POTENTIAL FOR A MORE **DEVASTATING** WEAPON, OR A MORE **TEMPTING** TARGET FOR KOBRA.
THIS DEVICE, IN THEIR HANDS, MEANS THE **KALI YUGA**--THE PINNACLE OF THEIR FAITH--IS WITHIN THEIR **REACH.**
IF ARIADNE PERSAKIS IS GOING TO

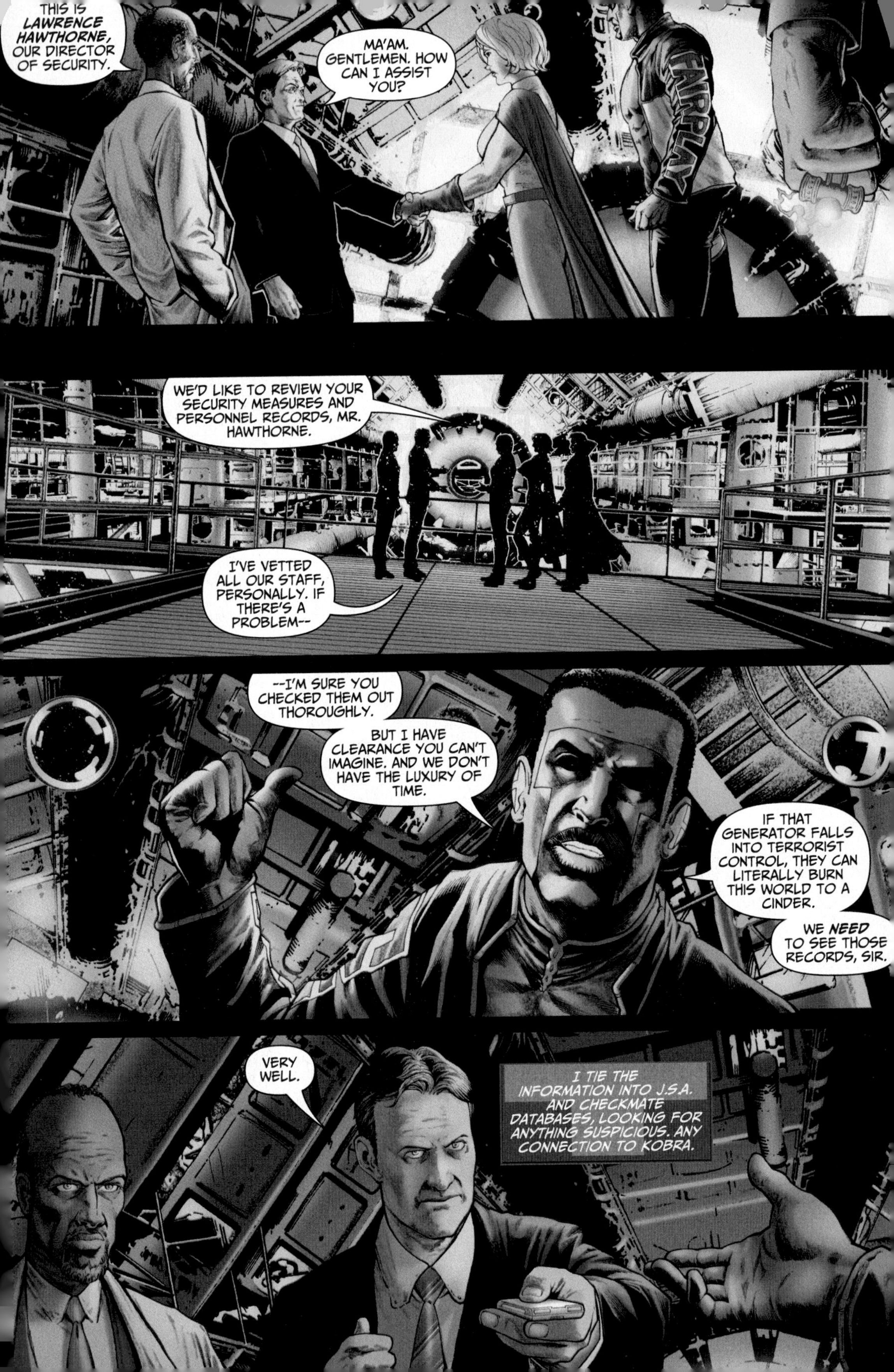
THIS IS LAWRENCE HAWTHORNE, OUR DIRECTOR OF SECURITY.
MA'AM. GENTLEMEN. HOW CAN I ASSIST YOU?
FAIRPLAY
WE'D LIKE TO REVIEW YOUR SECURITY MEASURES AND PERSONNEL RECORDS, MR. HAWTHORNE.
I'VE VETTED ALL OUR STAFF, PERSONALLY. IF THERE'S A PROBLEM--
--I'M SURE YOU CHECKED THEM OUT THOROUGHLY.
BUT I HAVE CLEARANCE YOU CAN'T IMAGINE. AND WE DON'T HAVE THE LUXURY OF TIME.
IF THAT GENERATOR FALLS INTO TERRORIST CONTROL, THEY CAN LITERALLY BURN THIS WORLD TO A CINDER.
WE NEED TO SEE THOSE RECORDS, SIR.
VERY WELL.
I TIE THE INFORMATION INTO J.S.A. AND CHECKMATE DATABASES, LOOKING FOR ANYTHING SUSPICIOUS. ANY CONNECTION TO KOBRA.

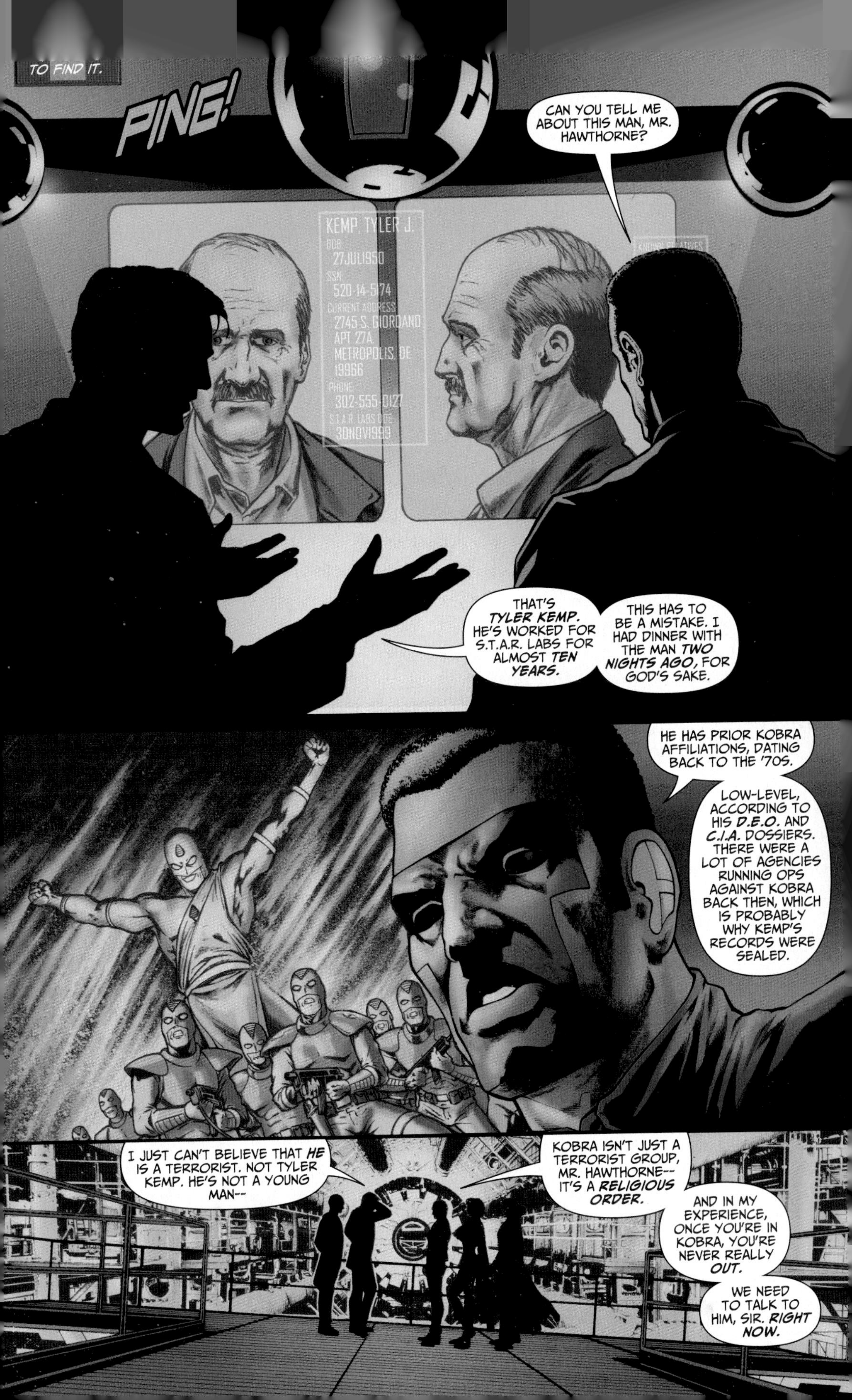
TO FIND IT.
PING!
CAN YOU TELL ME ABOUT THIS MAN, MR. HAWTHORNE?
KEMP, TYLER J.
DOB: 27JUL1950
SSN: 520-14-5174
CURRENT ADDRESS: 2745 S. GIORDANO APT 27A. METROPOLIS, DE 19966
PHONE: 302-555-0127
S.T.A.R. LABS DOE: 30NOV1999
THAT'S TYLER KEMP. HE'S WORKED FOR S.T.A.R. LABS FOR ALMOST TEN YEARS.
THIS HAS TO BE A MISTAKE. I HAD DINNER WITH THE MAN TWO NIGHTS AGO, FOR GOD'S SAKE.
HE HAS PRIOR KOBRA AFFILIATIONS, DATING BACK TO THE '70S.
LOW-LEVEL, ACCORDING TO HIS D.E.O. AND C.I.A. DOSSIERS. THERE WERE A LOT OF AGENCIES RUNNING OPS AGAINST KOBRA BACK THEN, WHICH IS PROBABLY WHY KEMP'S RECORDS WERE SEALED.
I JUST CAN'T BELIEVE THAT HE IS A TERRORIST. NOT TYLER KEMP. HE'S NOT A YOUNG MAN--
KOBRA ISN'T JUST A TERRORIST GROUP, MR. HAWTHORNE-- IT'S A RELIGIOUS ORDER.
AND IN MY EXPERIENCE, ONCE YOU'RE IN KOBRA, YOU'RE NEVER REALLY OUT.
WE NEED TO TALK TO HIM, SIR. RIGHT NOW.

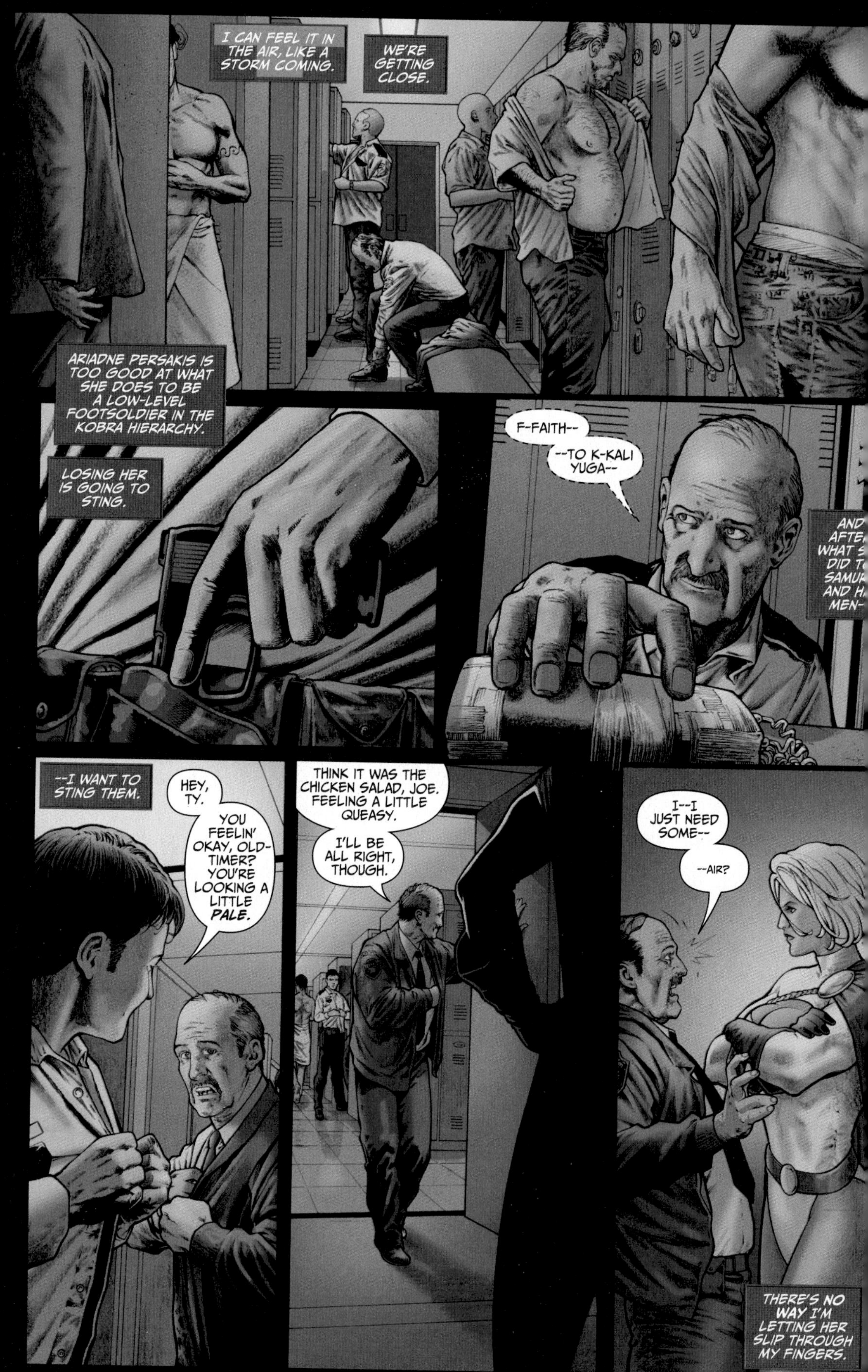

I CAN FEEL IT IN THE AIR, LIKE A STORM COMING.
WE'RE GETTING CLOSE.
ARIADNE PERSAKIS IS TOO GOOD AT WHAT SHE DOES TO BE A LOW-LEVEL FOOTSOLDIER IN THE KOBRA HIERARCHY.
LOSING HER IS GOING TO STING.
F-FAITH--
--TO K-KALI YUGA--
--I WANT TO STING THEM.
HEY, TY.
YOU FEELIN' OKAY, OLD-TIMER? YOU'RE LOOKING A LITTLE PALE.
THINK IT WAS THE CHICKEN SALAD, JOE. FEELING A LITTLE QUEASY.
I'LL BE ALL RIGHT, THOUGH.
I--I JUST NEED SOME--
--AIR?
THERE'S NO WAY I'M LETTING HER SLIP THROUGH MY FINGERS.

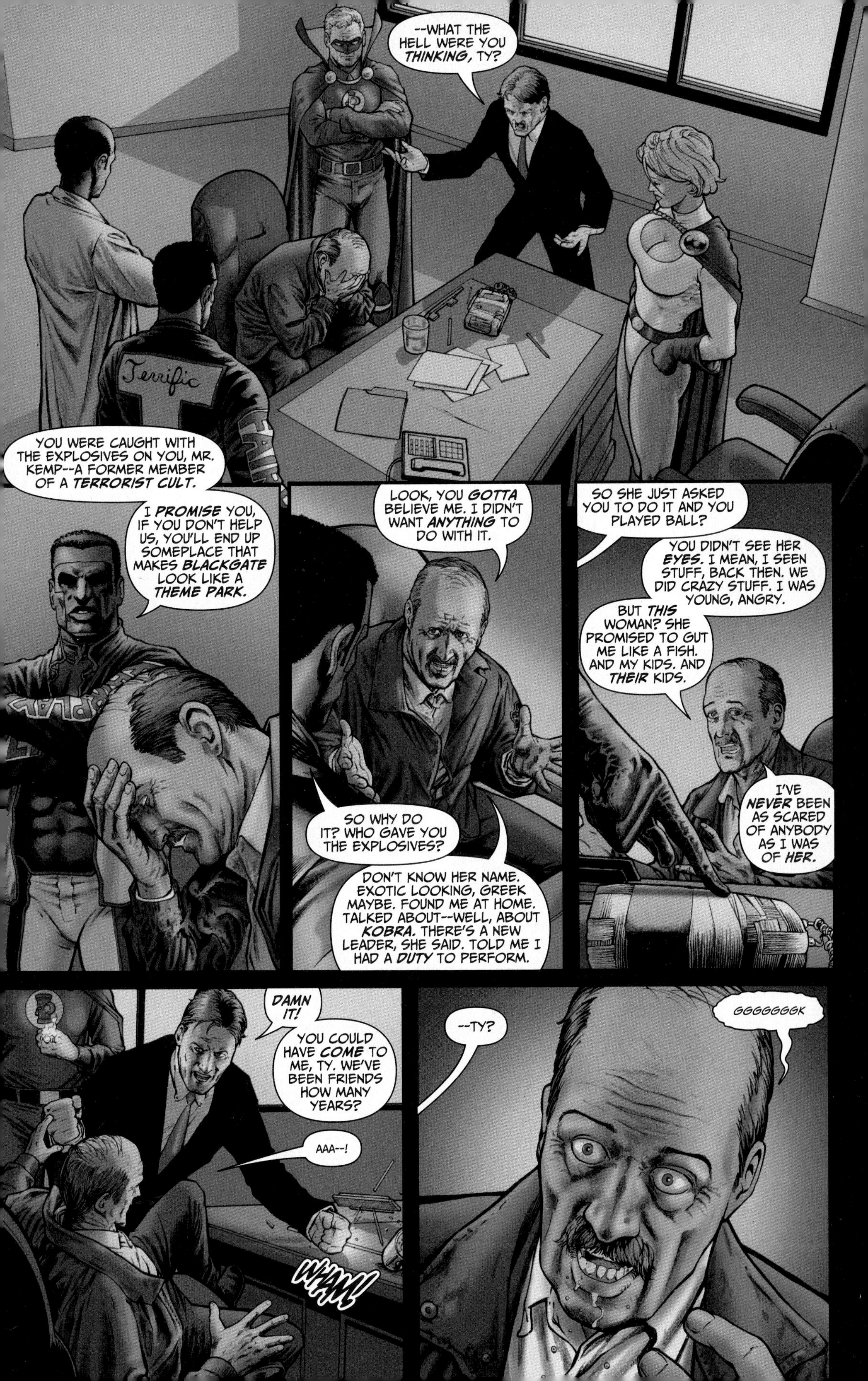

--WHAT THE HELL WERE YOU *THINKING*, TY?
Terrific
YOU WERE CAUGHT WITH THE EXPLOSIVES ON YOU, MR. KEMP--A FORMER MEMBER OF A *TERRORIST CULT.*
I *PROMISE* YOU, IF YOU DON'T HELP US, YOU'LL END UP SOMEPLACE THAT MAKES *BLACKGATE* LOOK LIKE A *THEME PARK.*
LOOK, YOU *GOTTA* BELIEVE ME. I DIDN'T WANT *ANYTHING* TO DO WITH IT.
SO WHY DO IT? WHO GAVE YOU THE EXPLOSIVES?
DON'T KNOW HER NAME. EXOTIC LOOKING, GREEK MAYBE. FOUND ME AT HOME. TALKED ABOUT--WELL, ABOUT *KOBRA.* THERE'S A NEW LEADER, SHE SAID. TOLD ME I HAD A *DUTY* TO PERFORM.
SO SHE JUST ASKED YOU TO DO IT AND YOU PLAYED BALL?
YOU DIDN'T SEE HER *EYES.* I MEAN, I SEEN STUFF, BACK THEN. WE DID CRAZY STUFF. I WAS YOUNG, ANGRY.
BUT *THIS* WOMAN? SHE PROMISED TO GUT ME LIKE A FISH. AND MY KIDS. AND *THEIR* KIDS.
I'VE *NEVER* BEEN AS SCARED OF ANYBODY AS I WAS OF *HER.*
DAMN IT!
YOU COULD HAVE *COME* TO ME, TY. WE'VE BEEN FRIENDS HOW MANY YEARS?
AAA--!
WHAM!
--TY?
GGGGGGGK

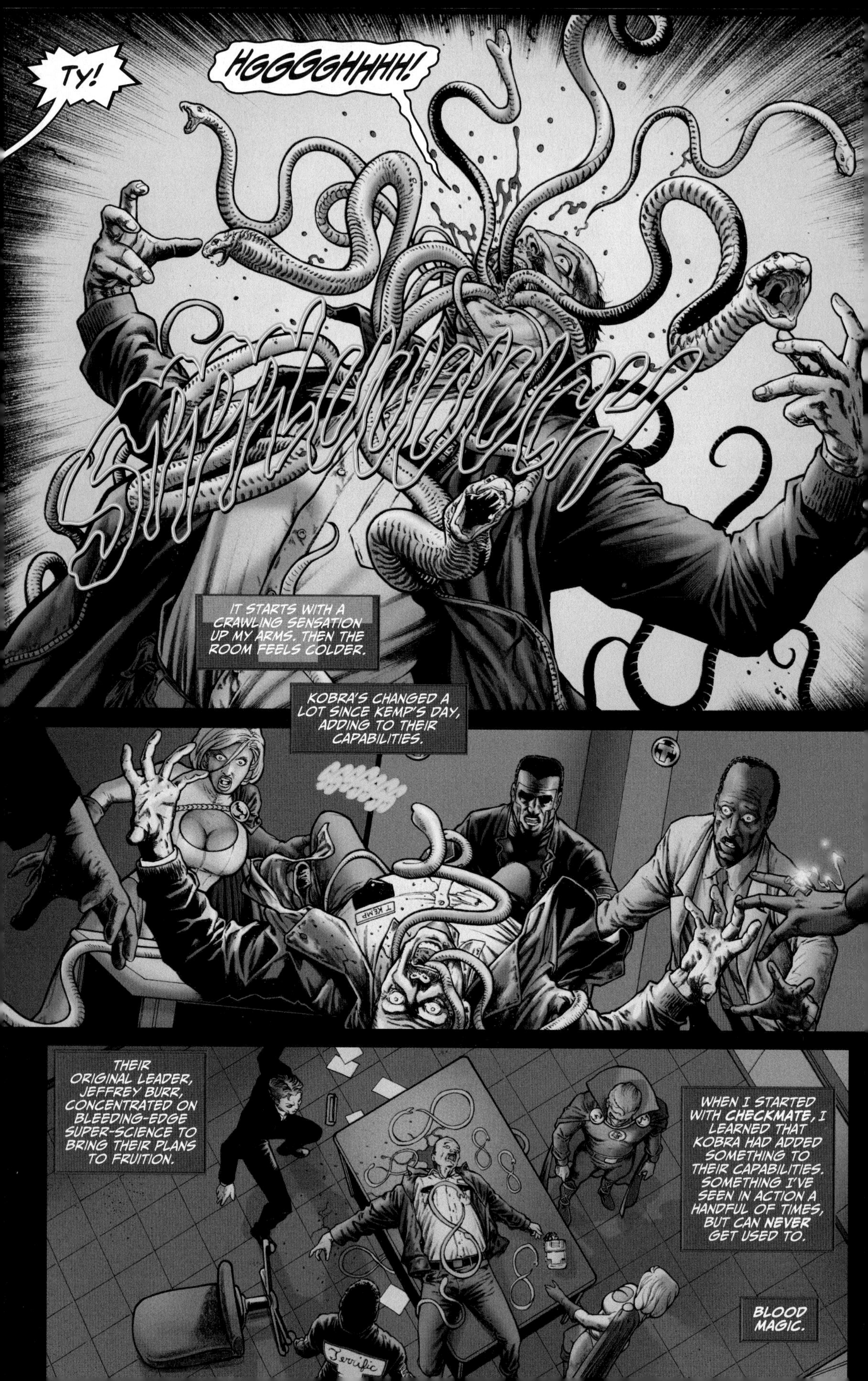
TY!
HGGGGHHHH!
IT STARTS WITH A CRAWLING SENSATION UP MY ARMS. THEN THE ROOM FEELS COLDER.
KOBRA'S CHANGED A LOT SINCE KEMP'S DAY, ADDING TO THEIR CAPABILITIES.
T KEMP
THEIR ORIGINAL LEADER, JEFFREY BURR, CONCENTRATED ON BLEEDING-EDGE SUPER-SCIENCE TO BRING THEIR PLANS TO FRUITION.
WHEN I STARTED WITH CHECKMATE, I LEARNED THAT KOBRA HAD ADDED SOMETHING TO THEIR CAPABILITIES. SOMETHING I'VE SEEN IN ACTION A HANDFUL OF TIMES, BUT CAN NEVER GET USED TO.
BLOOD MAGIC.
Terrific

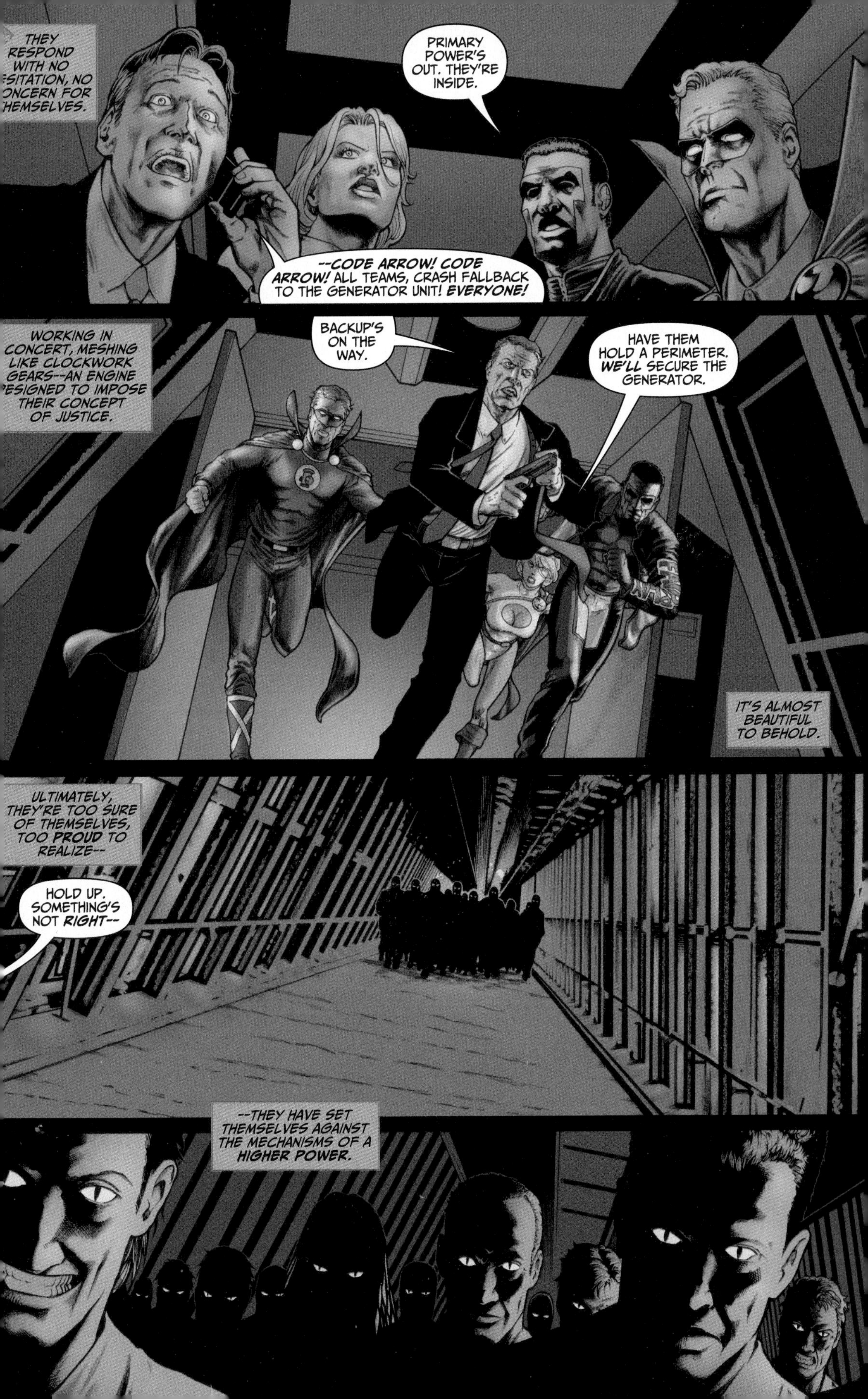

THEY RESPOND WITH NO HESITATION, NO CONCERN FOR THEMSELVES.
PRIMARY POWER'S OUT. THEY'RE INSIDE.
--CODE ARROW! CODE ARROW! ALL TEAMS, CRASH FALLBACK TO THE GENERATOR UNIT! EVERYONE!
WORKING IN CONCERT, MESHING LIKE CLOCKWORK GEARS--AN ENGINE DESIGNED TO IMPOSE THEIR CONCEPT OF JUSTICE.
BACKUP'S ON THE WAY.
HAVE THEM HOLD A PERIMETER. WE'LL SECURE THE GENERATOR.
IT'S ALMOST BEAUTIFUL TO BEHOLD.
ULTIMATELY, THEY'RE TOO SURE OF THEMSELVES, TOO PROUD TO REALIZE--
HOLD UP. SOMETHING'S NOT RIGHT--
--THEY HAVE SET THEMSELVES AGAINST THE MECHANISMS OF A HIGHER POWER.

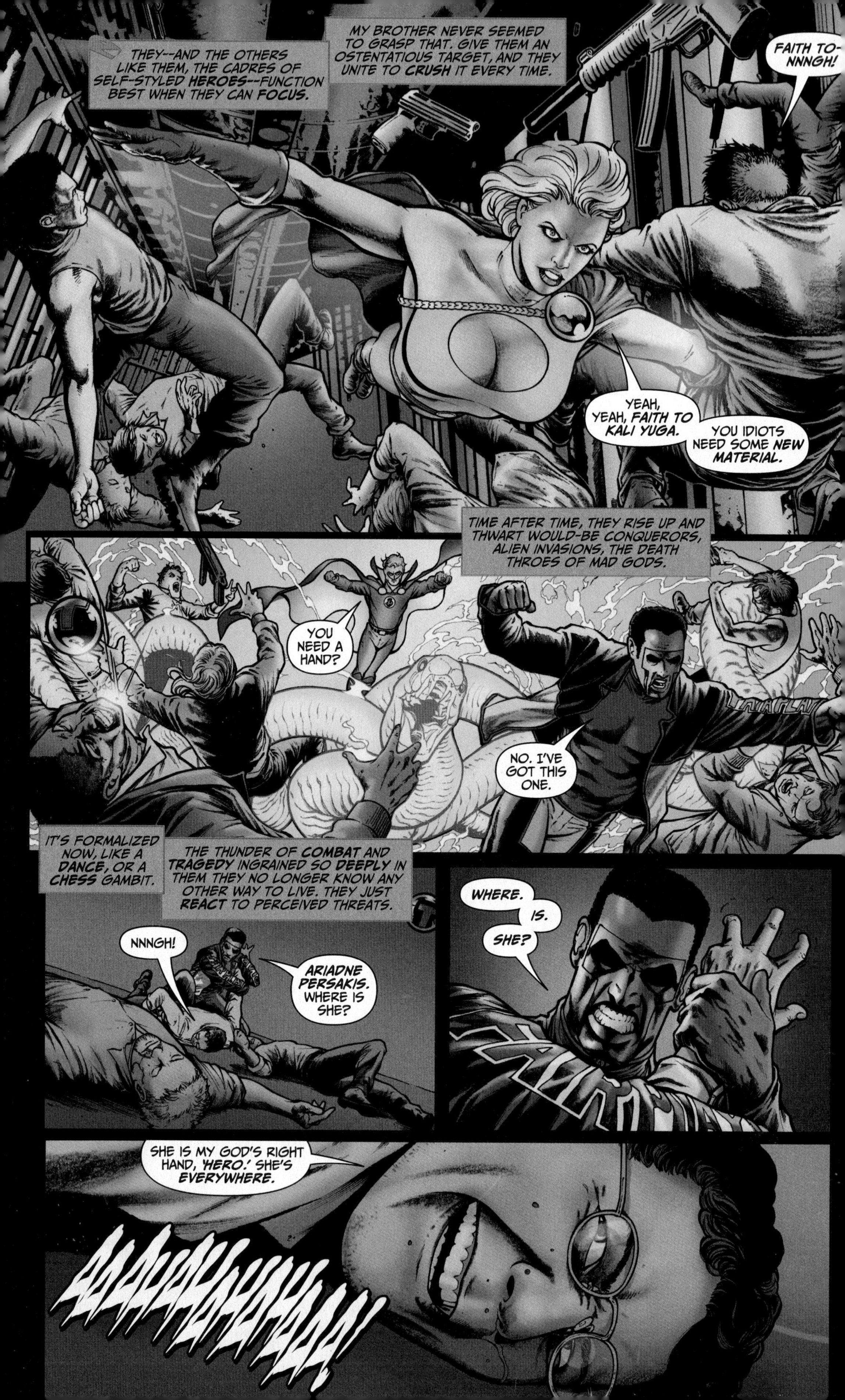
THEY--AND THE OTHERS LIKE THEM, THE CADRES OF SELF-STYLED HEROES--FUNCTION BEST WHEN THEY CAN FOCUS.
MY BROTHER NEVER SEEMED TO GRASP THAT. GIVE THEM AN OSTENTATIOUS TARGET, AND THEY UNITE TO CRUSH IT EVERY TIME.
FAITH TO-NNNGH!
YEAH, YEAH, FAITH TO KALI YUGA.
YOU IDIOTS NEED SOME NEW MATERIAL.
TIME AFTER TIME, THEY RISE UP AND THWART WOULD-BE CONQUERORS, ALIEN INVASIONS, THE DEATH THROES OF MAD GODS.
YOU NEED A HAND?
NO. I'VE GOT THIS ONE.
IT'S FORMALIZED NOW, LIKE A DANCE, OR A CHESS GAMBIT.
THE THUNDER OF COMBAT AND TRAGEDY INGRAINED SO DEEPLY IN THEM THEY NO LONGER KNOW ANY OTHER WAY TO LIVE. THEY JUST REACT TO PERCEIVED THREATS.
NNNGH!
ARIADNE PERSAKIS. WHERE IS SHE?
WHERE.
IS.
SHE?
SHE IS MY GOD'S RIGHT HAND, 'HERO.' SHE'S EVERYWHERE.
AAAHAHHAHAA!

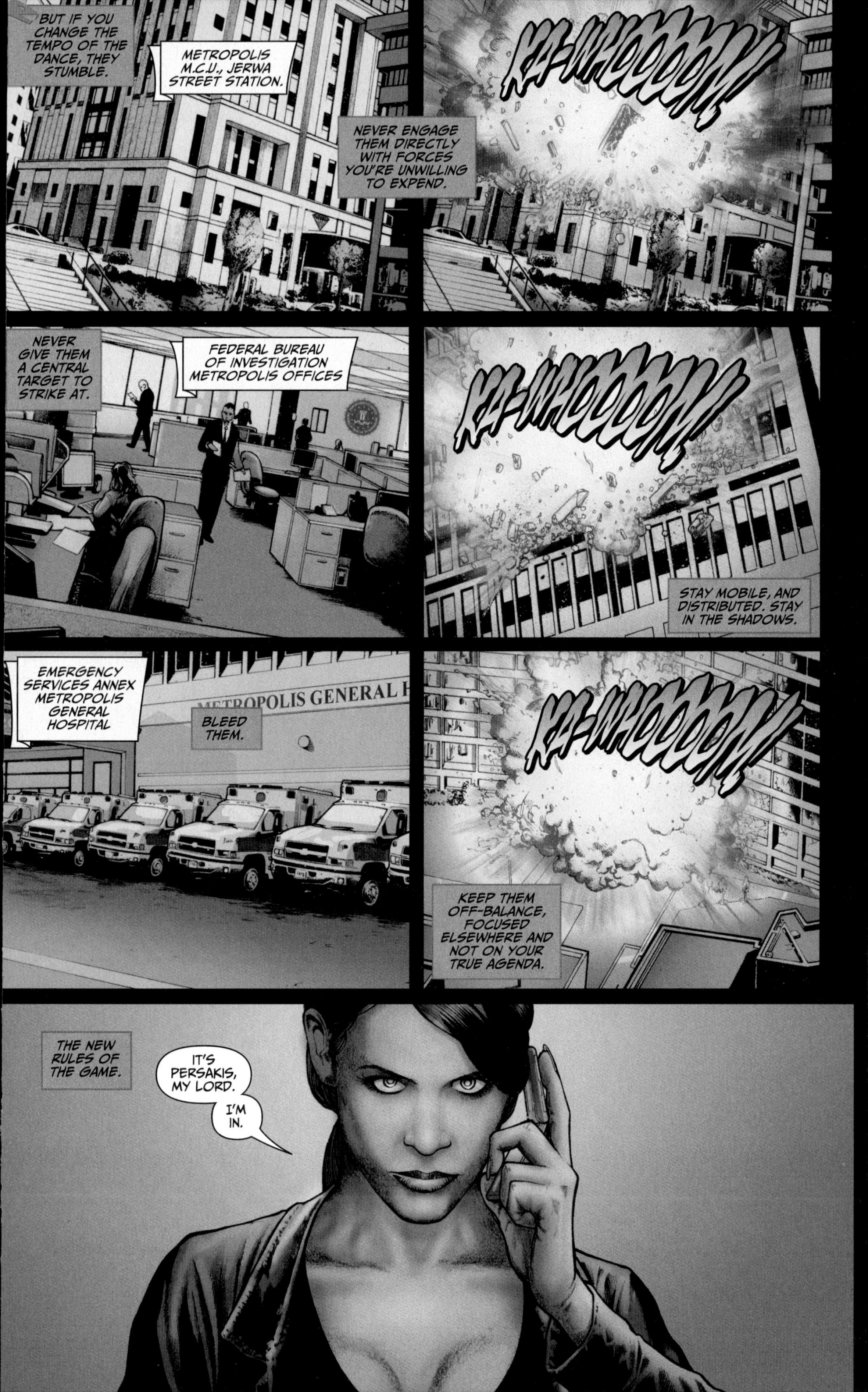
BUT IF YOU CHANGE THE TEMPO OF THE DANCE, THEY STUMBLE.
METROPOLIS M.C.U., JERWA STREET STATION.
NEVER ENGAGE THEM DIRECTLY WITH FORCES YOU'RE UNWILLING TO EXPEND.
KA-WHOOOOM!
NEVER GIVE THEM A CENTRAL TARGET TO STRIKE AT.
FEDERAL BUREAU OF INVESTIGATION METROPOLIS OFFICES
KA-WHOOOOM!
STAY MOBILE, AND DISTRIBUTED. STAY IN THE SHADOWS.
EMERGENCY SERVICES ANNEX METROPOLIS GENERAL HOSPITAL
METROPOLIS GENERAL H
BLEED THEM.
KA-WHOOOOM!
KEEP THEM OFF-BALANCE, FOCUSED ELSEWHERE AND NOT ON YOUR TRUE AGENDA.
THE NEW RULES OF THE GAME.
IT'S PERSAKIS, MY LORD.
I'M IN.

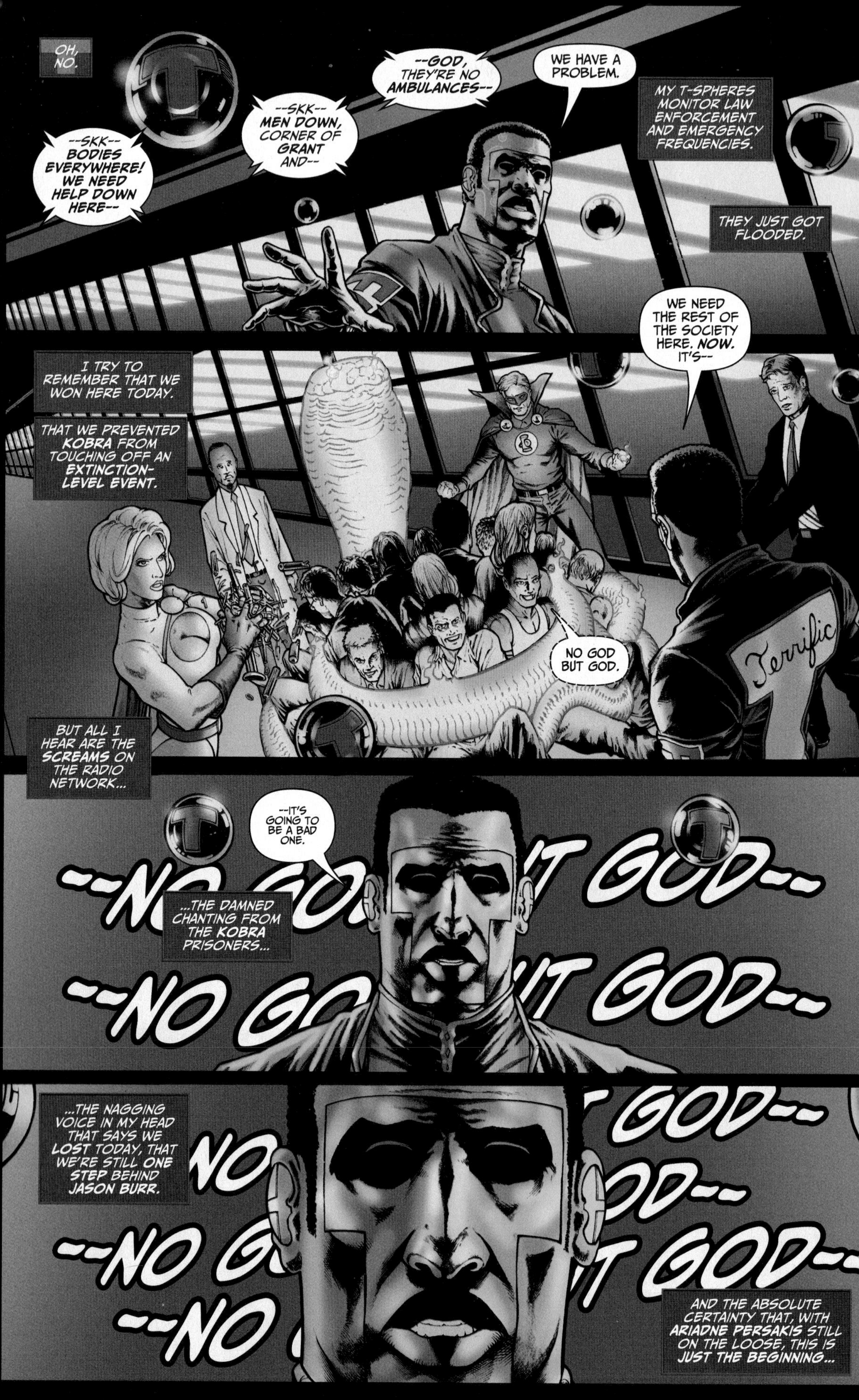
OH, NO.
--SKK-- BODIES EVERYWHERE! WE NEED HELP DOWN HERE--
--SKK-- MEN DOWN, CORNER OF GRANT AND--
--GOD, THEY'RE NO AMBULANCES--
WE HAVE A PROBLEM.
MY T-SPHERES MONITOR LAW ENFORCEMENT AND EMERGENCY FREQUENCIES.
THEY JUST GOT FLOODED.
I TRY TO REMEMBER THAT WE WON HERE TODAY.
THAT WE PREVENTED KOBRA FROM TOUCHING OFF AN EXTINCTION-LEVEL EVENT.
WE NEED THE REST OF THE SOCIETY HERE. NOW. IT'S--
Terrific
NO GOD BUT GOD.
BUT ALL I HEAR ARE THE SCREAMS ON THE RADIO NETWORK...
--IT'S GOING TO BE A BAD ONE.
--NO GO T GOD--
...THE DAMNED CHANTING FROM THE KOBRA PRISONERS...
--NO GO T GOD--
...THE NAGGING VOICE IN MY HEAD THAT SAYS WE LOST TODAY, THAT WE'RE STILL ONE STEP BEHIND JASON BURR.
NO T GOD--
OD--
--NO G T GOD--
--NO
AND THE ABSOLUTE CERTAINTY THAT, WITH ARIADNE PERSAKIS STILL ON THE LOOSE, THIS IS JUST THE BEGINNING...

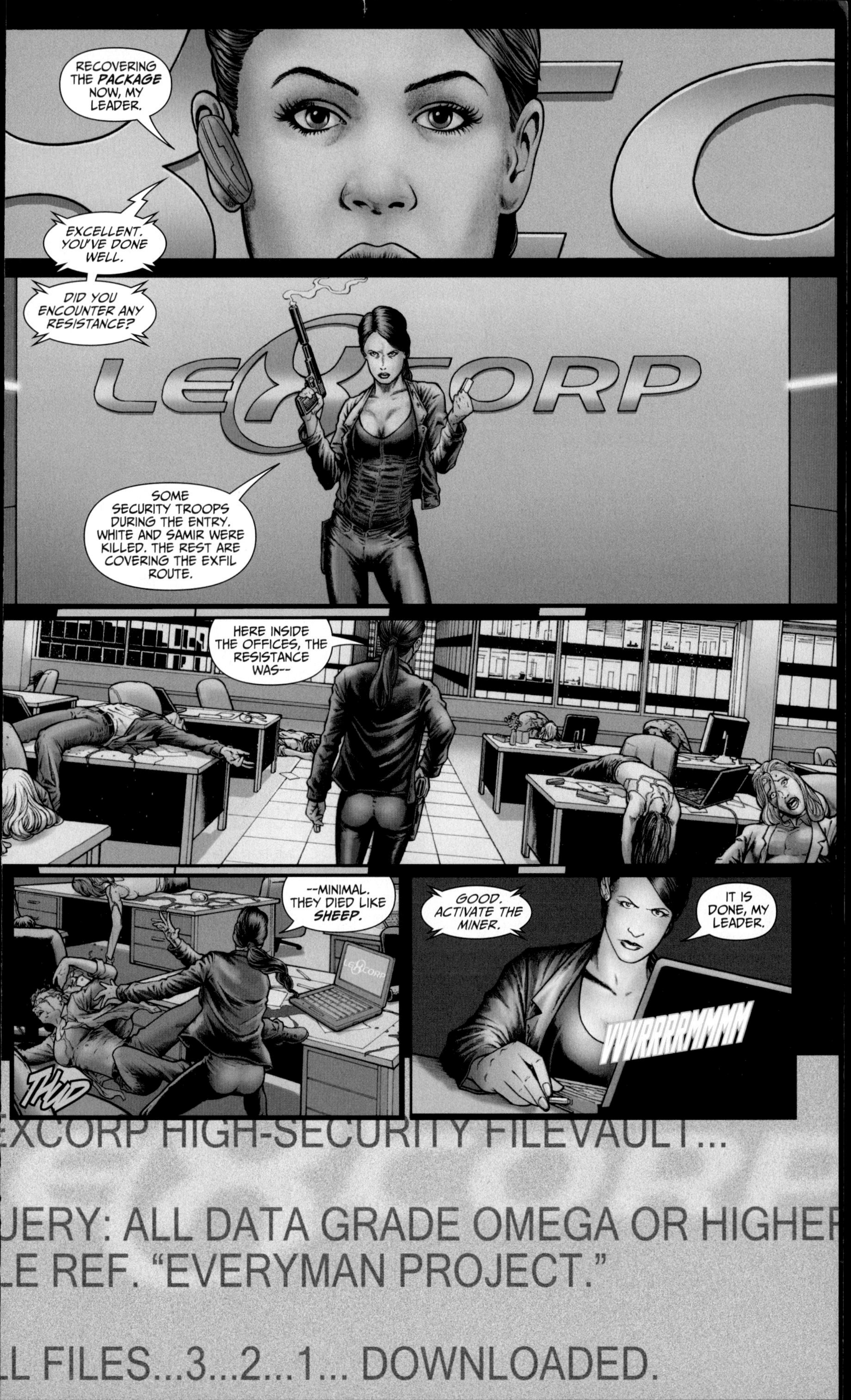
RECOVERING THE PACKAGE NOW, MY LEADER.
EXCELLENT. YOU'VE DONE WELL.
DID YOU ENCOUNTER ANY RESISTANCE?
LEXCORP
SOME SECURITY TROOPS DURING THE ENTRY. WHITE AND SAMIR WERE KILLED. THE REST ARE COVERING THE EXFIL ROUTE.
HERE INSIDE THE OFFICES, THE RESISTANCE WAS--
--MINIMAL. THEY DIED LIKE SHEEP.
THUD
GOOD. ACTIVATE THE MINER.
IT IS DONE, MY LEADER.
VVVRRRRMMMM
EXCORP HIGH-SECURITY FILEVAULT...
UERY: ALL DATA GRADE OMEGA OR HIGHE
LE REF. "EVERYMAN PROJECT."
L FILES...3...2...1... DOWNLOADED.

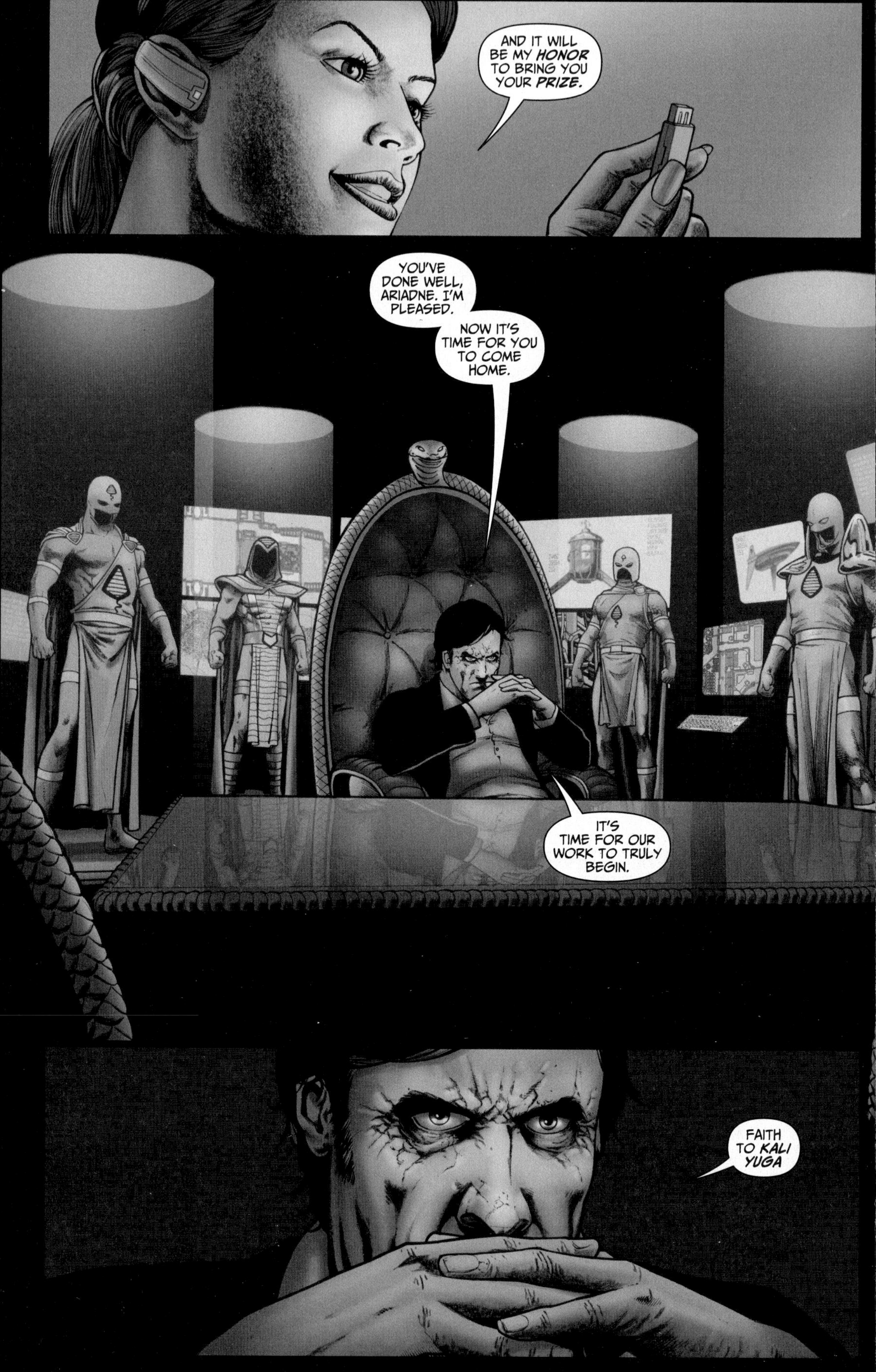
AND IT WILL BE MY ***HONOR*** TO BRING YOU YOUR ***PRIZE.***
YOU'VE DONE WELL, ARIADNE. I'M PLEASED.
NOW IT'S TIME FOR YOU TO COME HOME.
IT'S TIME FOR OUR WORK TO TRULY BEGIN.
FAITH TO ***KALI YUGA***

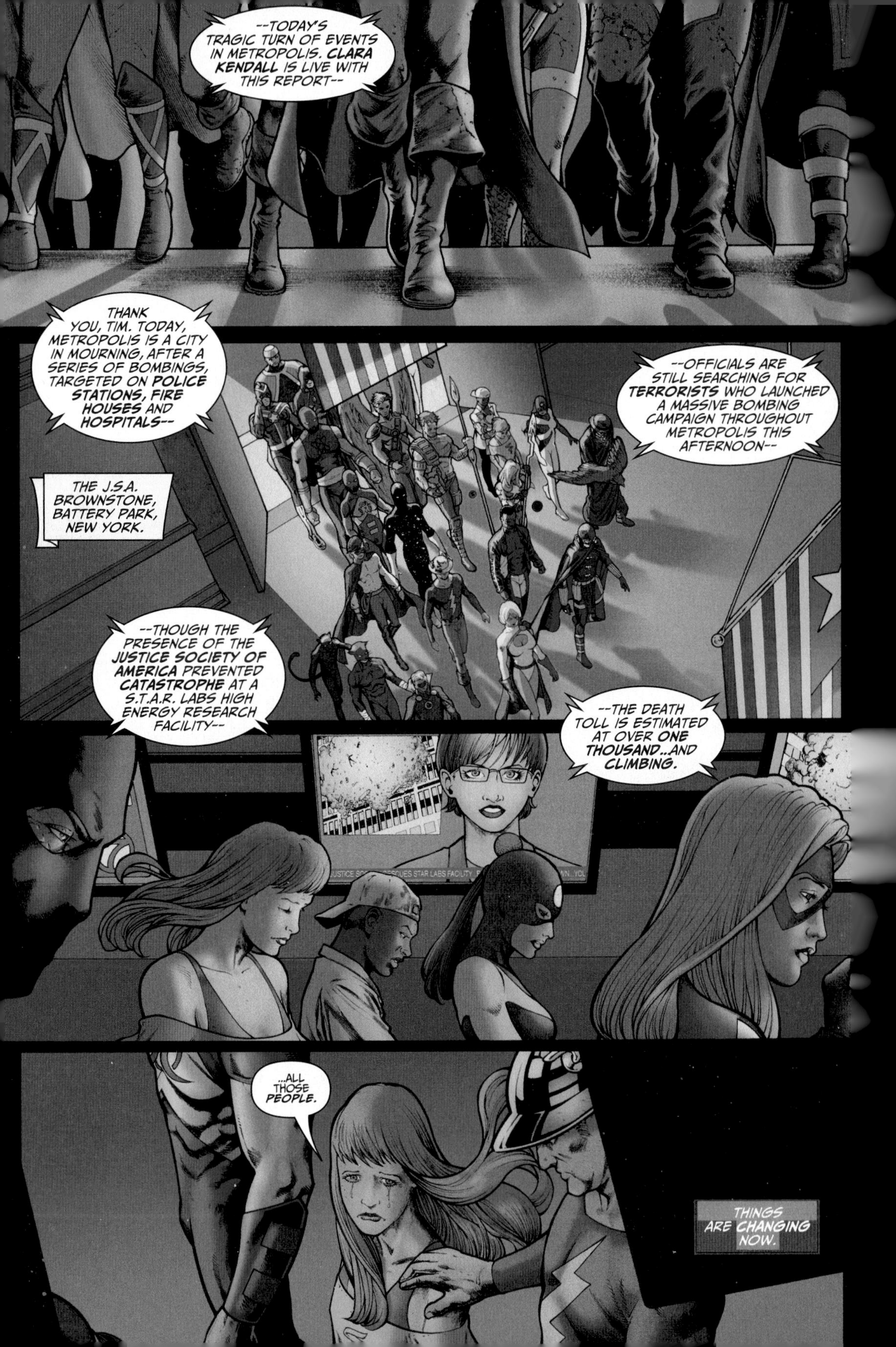
--TODAY'S TRAGIC TURN OF EVENTS IN METROPOLIS. CLARA KENDALL IS LIVE WITH THIS REPORT--
THANK YOU, TIM. TODAY, METROPOLIS IS A CITY IN MOURNING, AFTER A SERIES OF BOMBINGS, TARGETED ON POLICE STATIONS, FIRE HOUSES AND HOSPITALS--
--OFFICIALS ARE STILL SEARCHING FOR TERRORISTS WHO LAUNCHED A MASSIVE BOMBING CAMPAIGN THROUGHOUT METROPOLIS THIS AFTERNOON--
THE J.S.A. BROWNSTONE, BATTERY PARK, NEW YORK.
--THOUGH THE PRESENCE OF THE JUSTICE SOCIETY OF AMERICA PREVENTED CATASTROPHE AT A S.T.A.R. LABS HIGH ENERGY RESEARCH FACILITY--
--THE DEATH TOLL IS ESTIMATED AT OVER ONE THOUSAND...AND CLIMBING.
...ALL THOSE PEOPLE.
THINGS ARE CHANGING NOW.

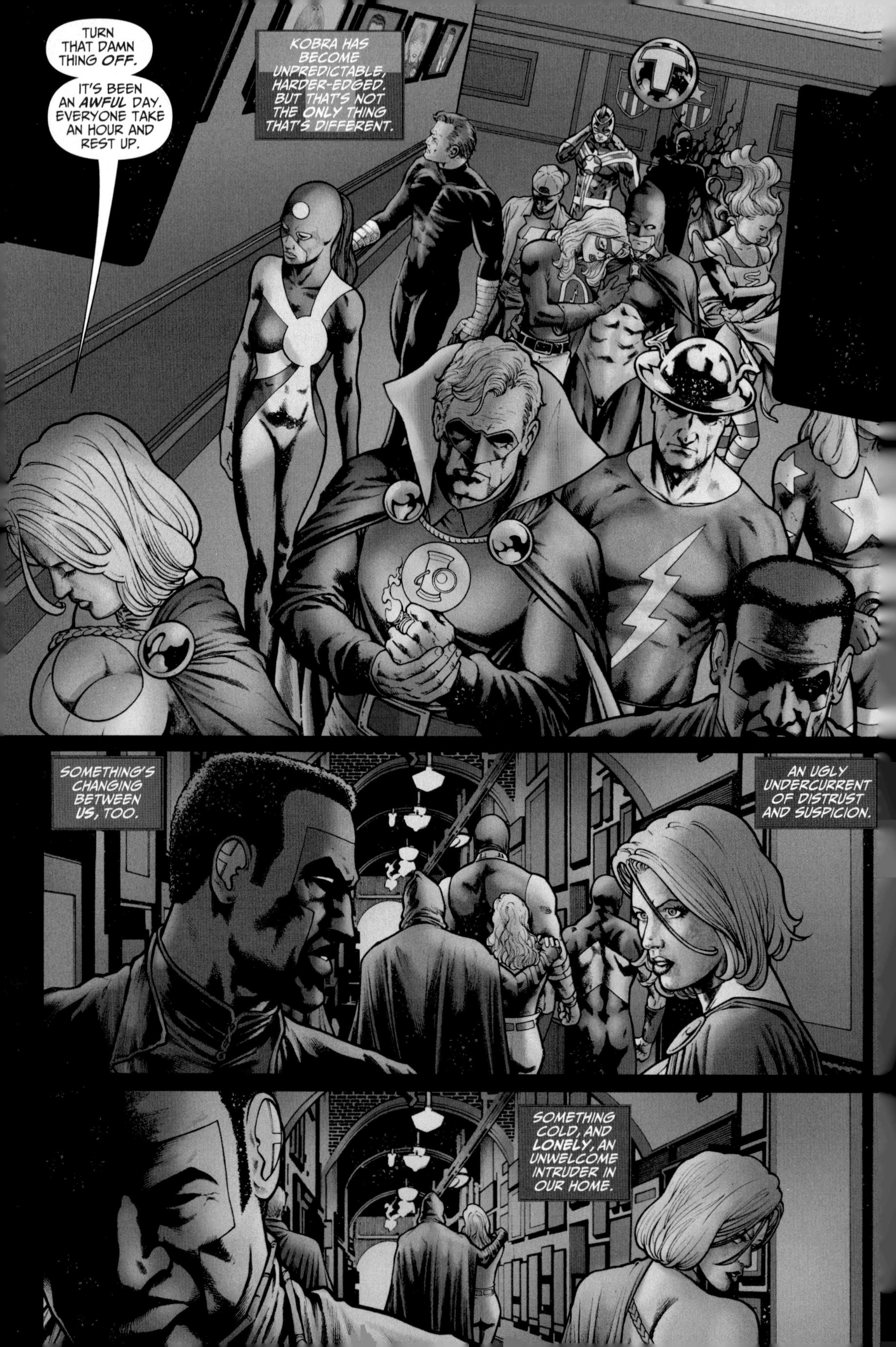
TURN THAT DAMN THING OFF.
IT'S BEEN AN AWFUL DAY. EVERYONE TAKE AN HOUR AND REST UP.
KOBRA HAS BECOME UNPREDICTABLE, HARDER-EDGED. BUT THAT'S NOT THE ONLY THING THAT'S DIFFERENT.
SOMETHING'S CHANGING BETWEEN US, TOO.
AN UGLY UNDERCURRENT OF DISTRUST AND SUSPICION.
SOMETHING COLD, AND LONELY, AN UNWELCOME INTRUDER IN OUR HOME.

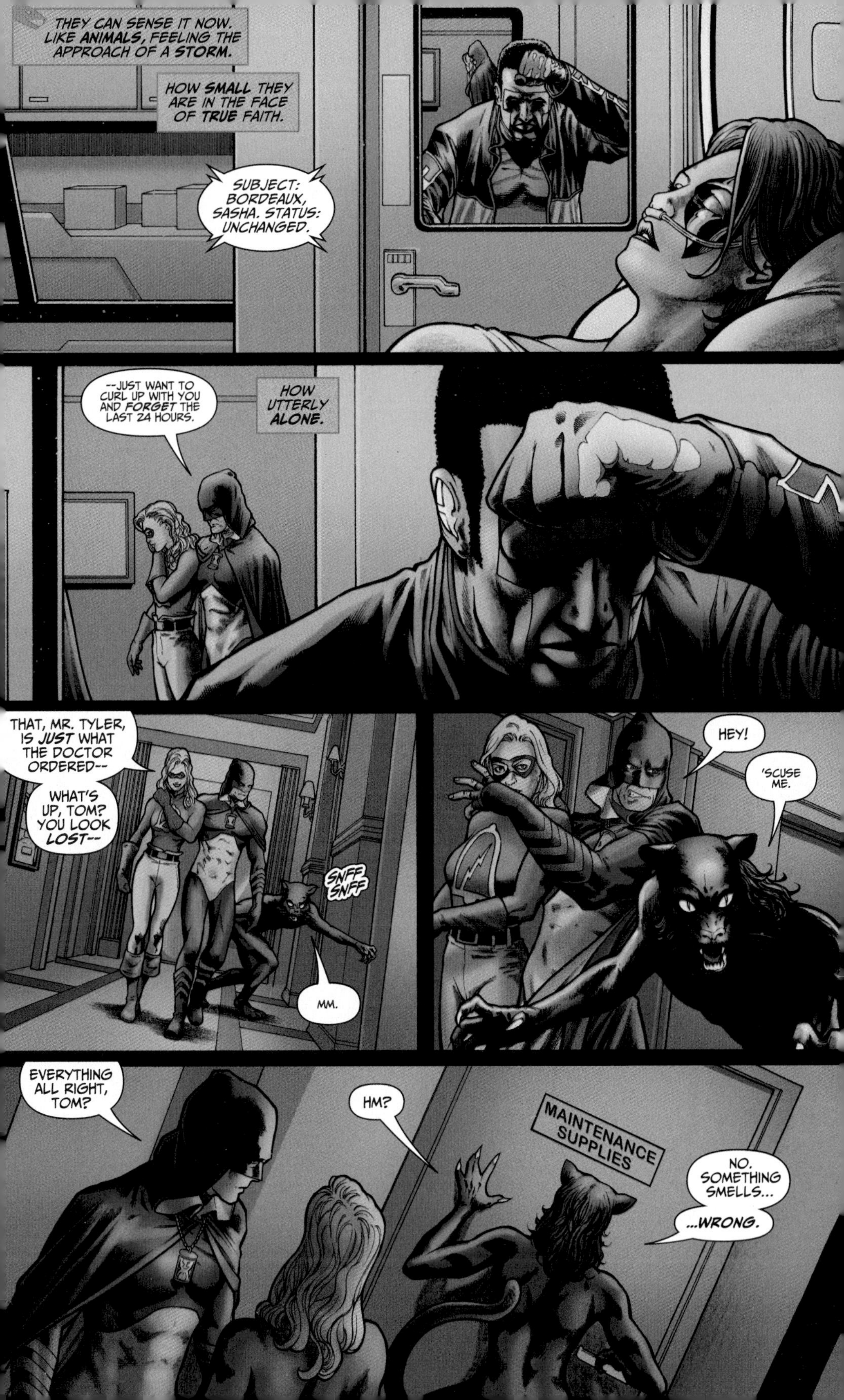
THEY CAN SENSE IT NOW. LIKE ANIMALS, FEELING THE APPROACH OF A STORM.
HOW SMALL THEY ARE IN THE FACE OF TRUE FAITH.
SUBJECT: BORDEAUX, SASHA. STATUS: UNCHANGED.
--JUST WANT TO CURL UP WITH YOU AND FORGET THE LAST 24 HOURS.
HOW UTTERLY ALONE.
THAT, MR. TYLER, IS JUST WHAT THE DOCTOR ORDERED--
WHAT'S UP, TOM? YOU LOOK LOST--
SNFF SNFF
MM.
HEY!
'SCUSE ME.
EVERYTHING ALL RIGHT, TOM?
HM?
MAINTENANCE SUPPLIES
NO. SOMETHING SMELLS...
...WRONG.

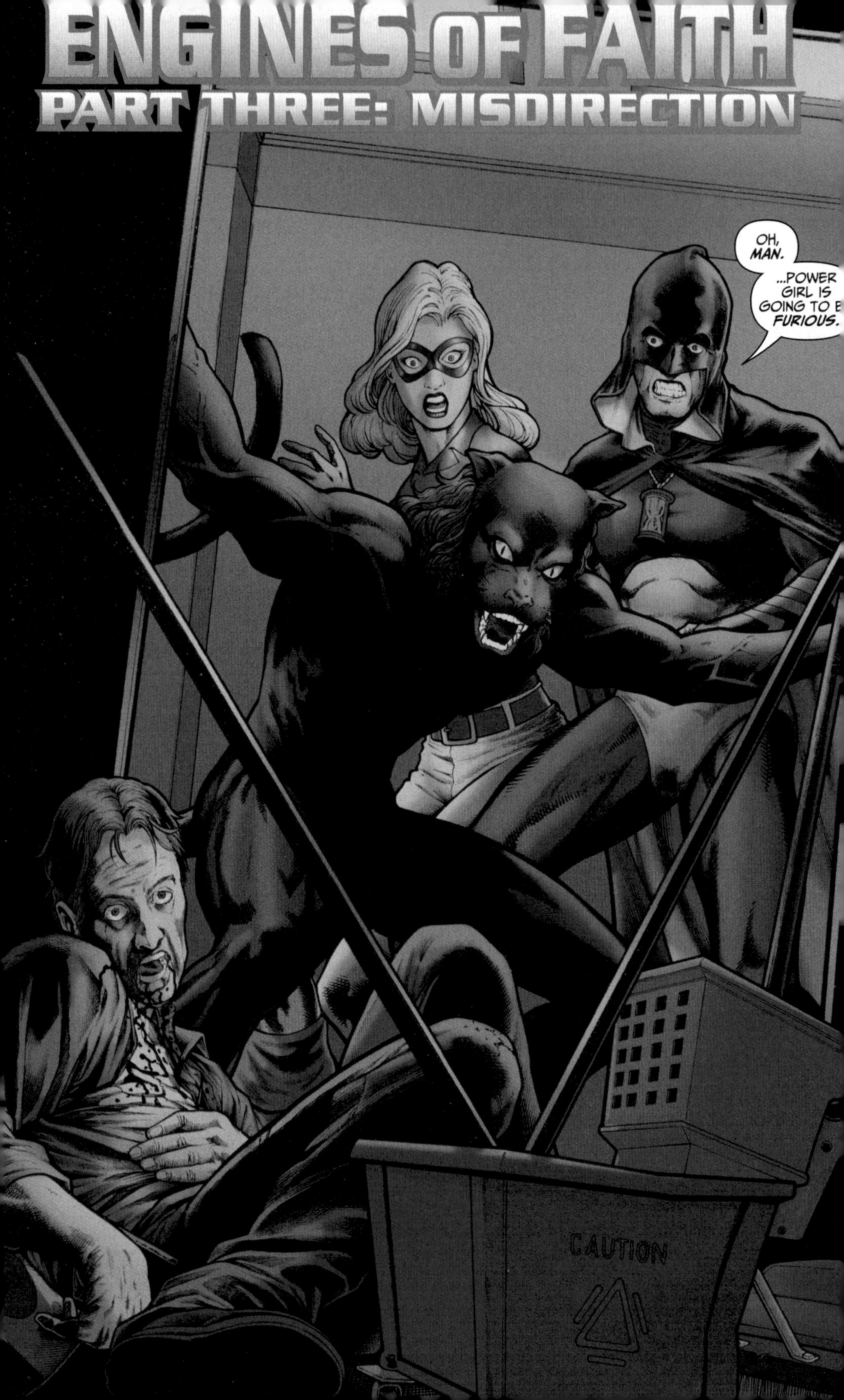
ENGINES OF FAITH
PART THREE: MISDIRECTION
OH, MAN.
...POWER GIRL IS GOING TO B FURIOUS.
CAUTION

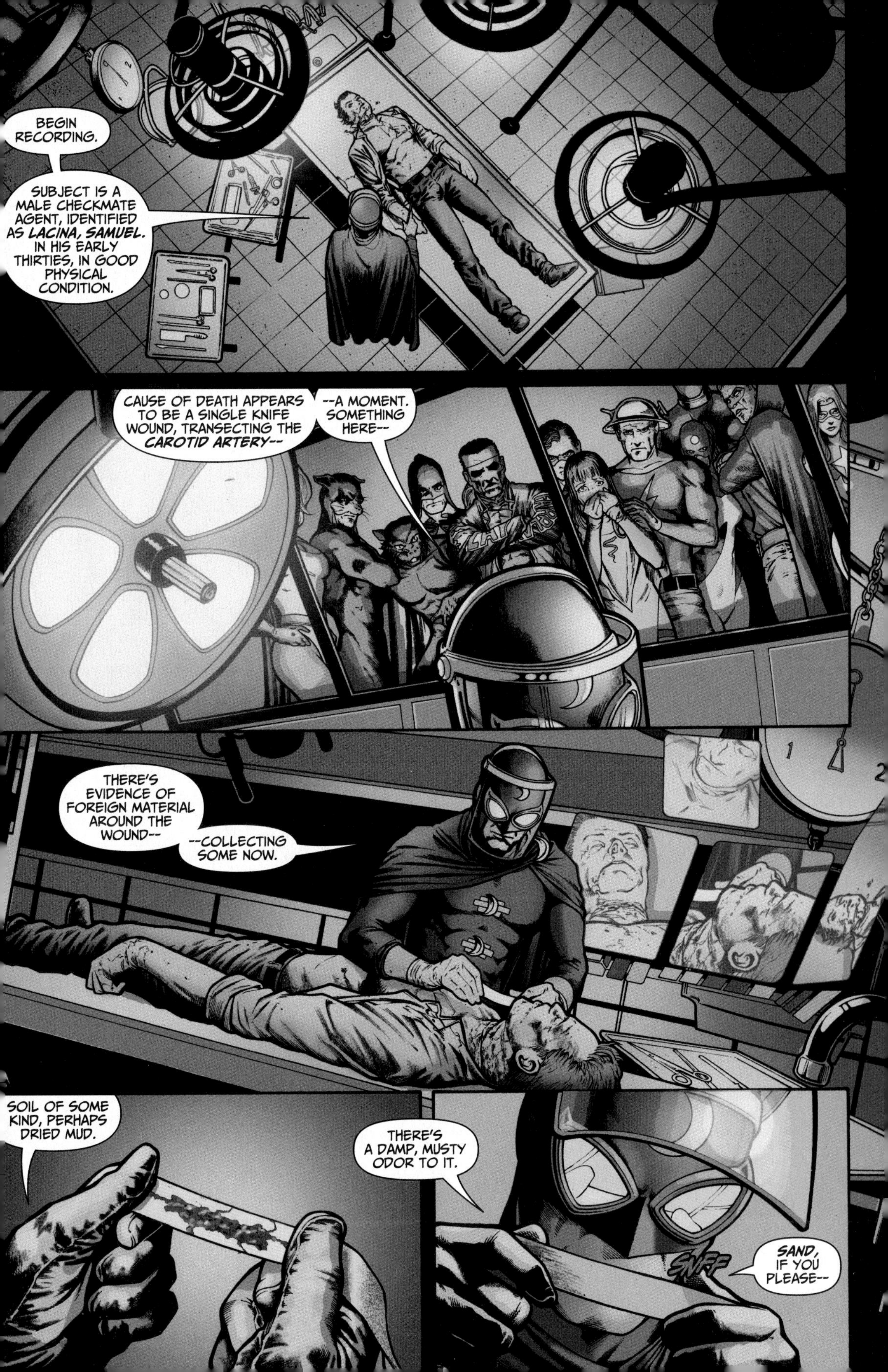

BEGIN RECORDING.
SUBJECT IS A MALE CHECKMATE AGENT, IDENTIFIED AS LACINA, SAMUEL. IN HIS EARLY THIRTIES, IN GOOD PHYSICAL CONDITION.
CAUSE OF DEATH APPEARS TO BE A SINGLE KNIFE WOUND, TRANSECTING THE CAROTID ARTERY--
--A MOMENT. SOMETHING HERE--
THERE'S EVIDENCE OF FOREIGN MATERIAL AROUND THE WOUND--
--COLLECTING SOME NOW.
SOIL OF SOME KIND, PERHAPS DRIED MUD.
THERE'S A DAMP, MUSTY ODOR TO IT.
SNFF
SAND, IF YOU PLEASE--

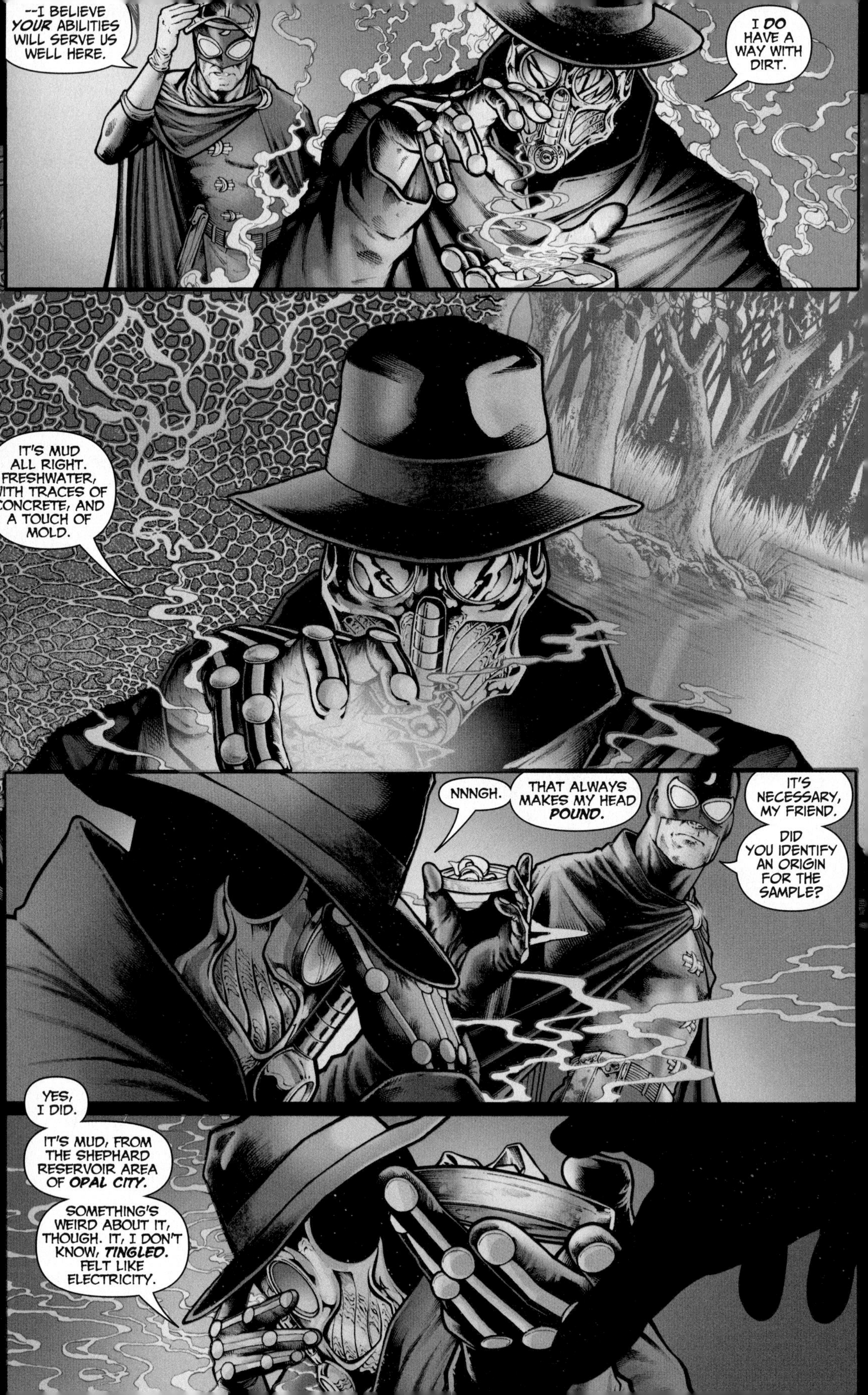
--I BELIEVE *YOUR* ABILITIES WILL SERVE US WELL HERE.
I *DO* HAVE A WAY WITH DIRT.
IT'S MUD ALL RIGHT. FRESHWATER, WITH TRACES OF CONCRETE, AND A TOUCH OF MOLD.
NNNGH.
THAT ALWAYS MAKES MY HEAD ***POUND.***
IT'S NECESSARY, MY FRIEND.
DID YOU IDENTIFY AN ORIGIN FOR THE SAMPLE?
YES, I DID.
IT'S MUD, FROM THE SHEPHARD RESERVOIR AREA OF ***OPAL CITY.***
SOMETHING'S WEIRD ABOUT IT, THOUGH. IT, I DON'T KNOW, ***TINGLED.*** FELT LIKE ELECTRICITY.

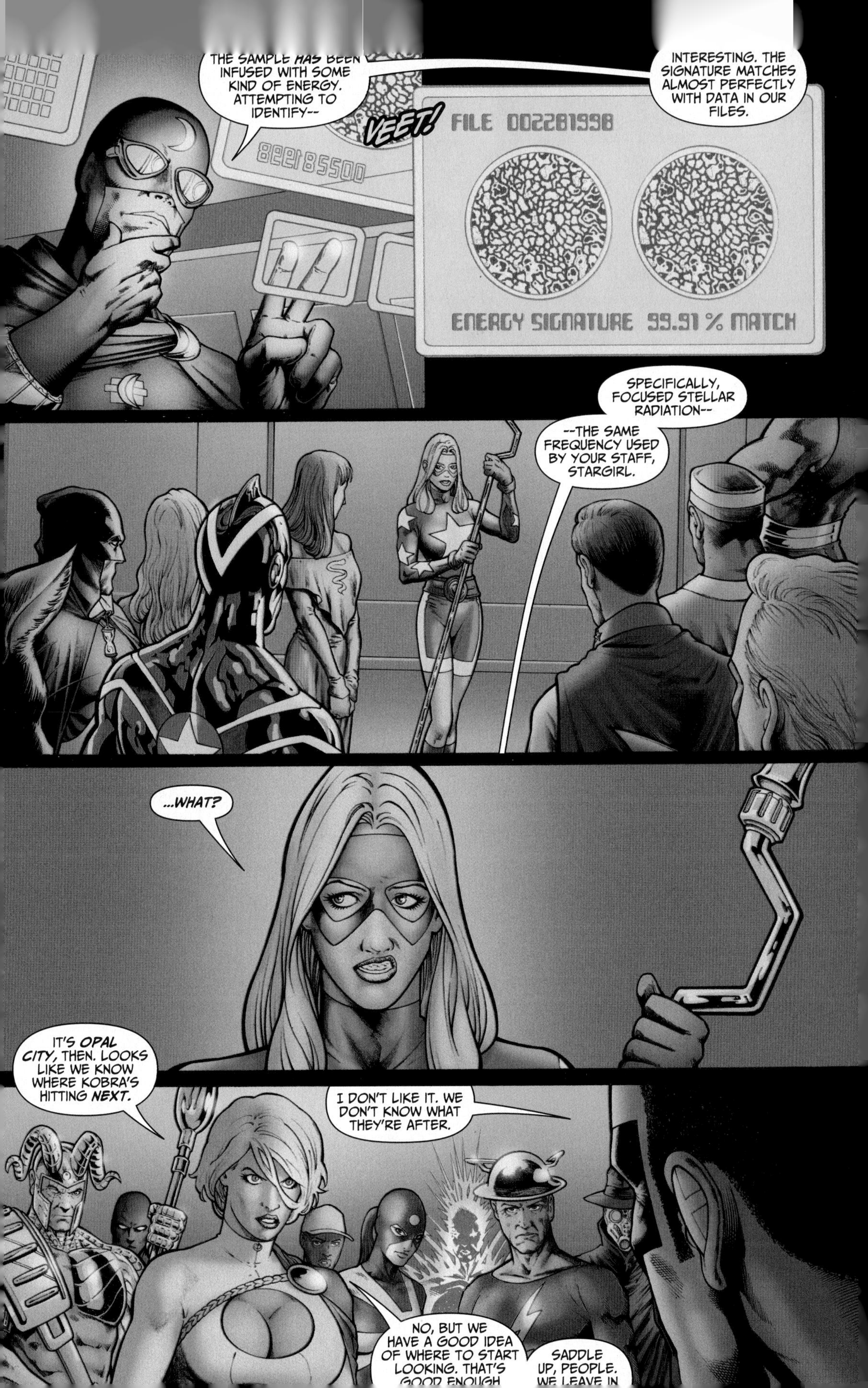

THE SAMPLE HAS BEEN INFUSED WITH SOME KIND OF ENERGY. ATTEMPTING TO IDENTIFY--
VEET!
INTERESTING. THE SIGNATURE MATCHES ALMOST PERFECTLY WITH DATA IN OUR FILES.
FILE 00228199B
ENERGY SIGNATURE 99.91 % MATCH
SPECIFICALLY, FOCUSED STELLAR RADIATION--
--THE SAME FREQUENCY USED BY YOUR STAFF, STARGIRL.
...WHAT?
IT'S OPAL CITY, THEN. LOOKS LIKE WE KNOW WHERE KOBRA'S HITTING NEXT.
I DON'T LIKE IT. WE DON'T KNOW WHAT THEY'RE AFTER.
NO, BUT WE HAVE A GOOD IDEA OF WHERE TO START LOOKING. THAT'S
SADDLE UP, PEOPLE.

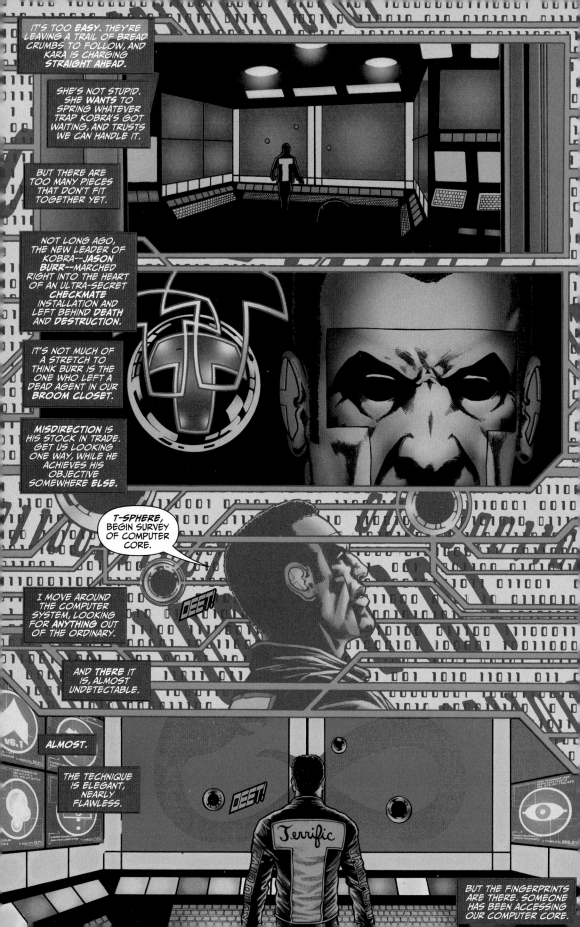

IT'S TOO *EASY.* THEY'RE LEAVING A TRAIL OF BREAD CRUMBS TO FOLLOW, AND KARA IS CHARGING STRAIGHT AHEAD.

SHE'S NOT STUPID. SHE *WANTS* TO SPRING WHATEVER TRAP KOBRA'S GOT WAITING, AND TRUSTS WE CAN HANDLE IT.

BUT THERE ARE TOO MANY PIECES THAT DON'T FIT TOGETHER YET.

NOT LONG AGO, THE NEW LEADER OF KOBRA--*JASON BURR*--MARCHED RIGHT INTO THE HEART OF AN ULTRA-SECRET *CHECKMATE* INSTALLATION AND LEFT BEHIND DEATH AND *DESTRUCTION.*

IT'S NOT MUCH OF A STRETCH TO THINK BURR IS THE ONE WHO LEFT A DEAD AGENT IN OUR *BROOM CLOSET.*

MISDIRECTION IS HIS STOCK IN TRADE. GET US LOOKING ONE WAY, WHILE HE ACHIEVES HIS *OBJECTIVE* SOMEWHERE ELSE.

T-SPHERE, BEGIN SURVEY OF COMPUTER CORE.

I MOVE AROUND THE COMPUTER SYSTEM, LOOKING FOR *ANYTHING* OUT OF THE ORDINARY.

AND *THERE* IT IS, ALMOST UNDETECTABLE.

ALMOST.

THE TECHNIQUE IS ELEGANT, NEARLY *FLAWLESS.*

BUT THE FINGERPRINTS ARE THERE. SOMEONE HAS BEEN ACCESSING OUR COMPUTER CORE.

DEET!

DEET!

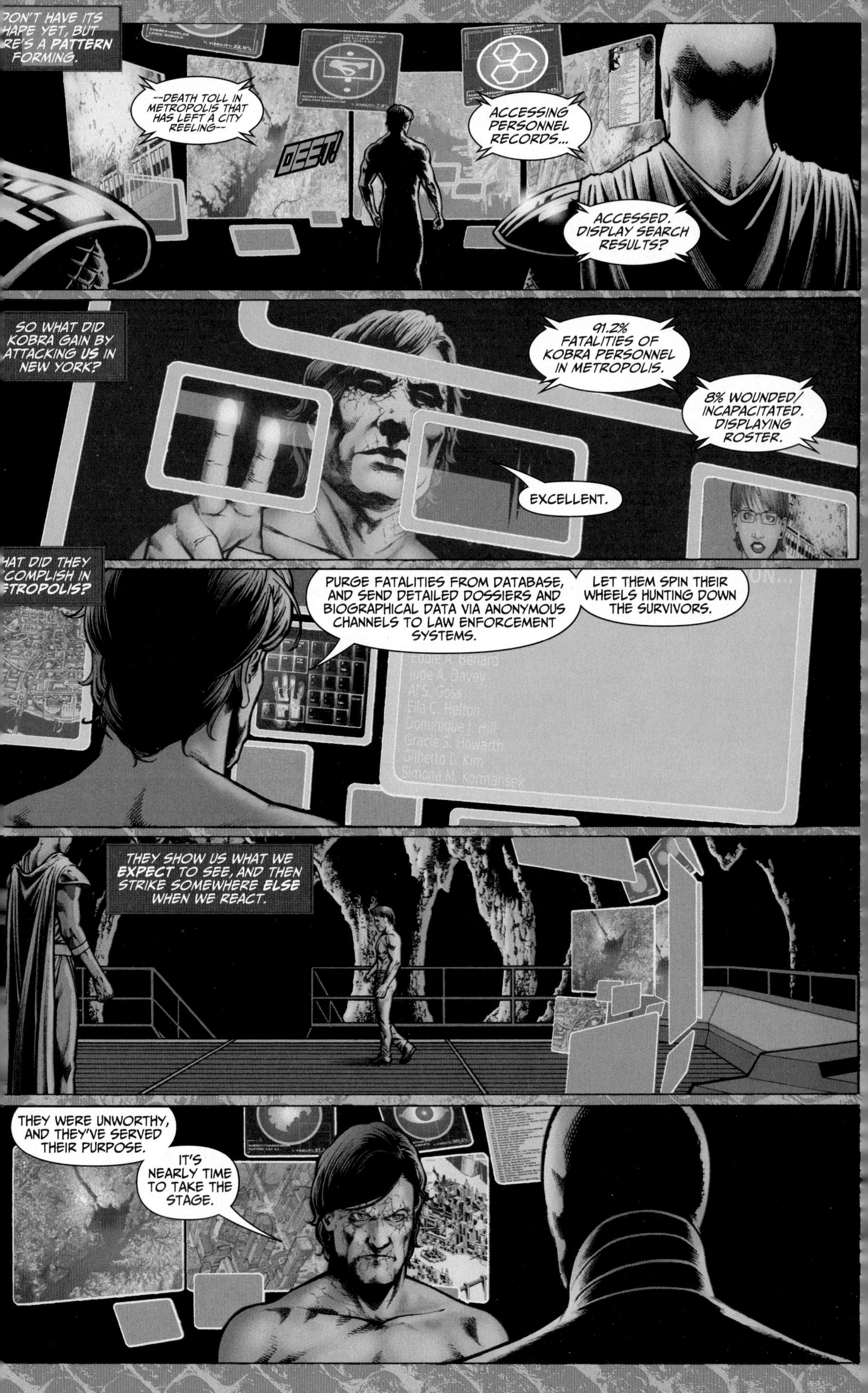

ON'T HAVE ITS HAPE YET, BUT RE'S A PATTERN FORMING.
--DEATH TOLL IN METROPOLIS THAT HAS LEFT A CITY REELING--
DEET!
ACCESSING PERSONNEL RECORDS...
ACCESSED. DISPLAY SEARCH RESULTS?
SO WHAT DID KOBRA GAIN BY ATTACKING US IN NEW YORK?
91.2% FATALITIES OF KOBRA PERSONNEL IN METROPOLIS.
8% WOUNDED/ INCAPACITATED. DISPLAYING ROSTER.
EXCELLENT.
HAT DID THEY COMPLISH IN ETROPOLIS?
PURGE FATALITIES FROM DATABASE, AND SEND DETAILED DOSSIERS AND BIOGRAPHICAL DATA VIA ANONYMOUS CHANNELS TO LAW ENFORCEMENT SYSTEMS.
LET THEM SPIN THEIR WHEELS HUNTING DOWN THE SURVIVORS.
Eddie A. Benard
Jude A. Davey
Al S. Goss
Ella C. Helton
Dominique J. Hill
Gracie S. Howarth
Gilberto L. Kim
Simona M. Kormansek
THEY SHOW US WHAT WE EXPECT TO SEE, AND THEN STRIKE SOMEWHERE ELSE WHEN WE REACT.
THEY WERE UNWORTHY, AND THEY'VE SERVED THEIR PURPOSE.
IT'S NEARLY TIME TO TAKE THE STAGE.

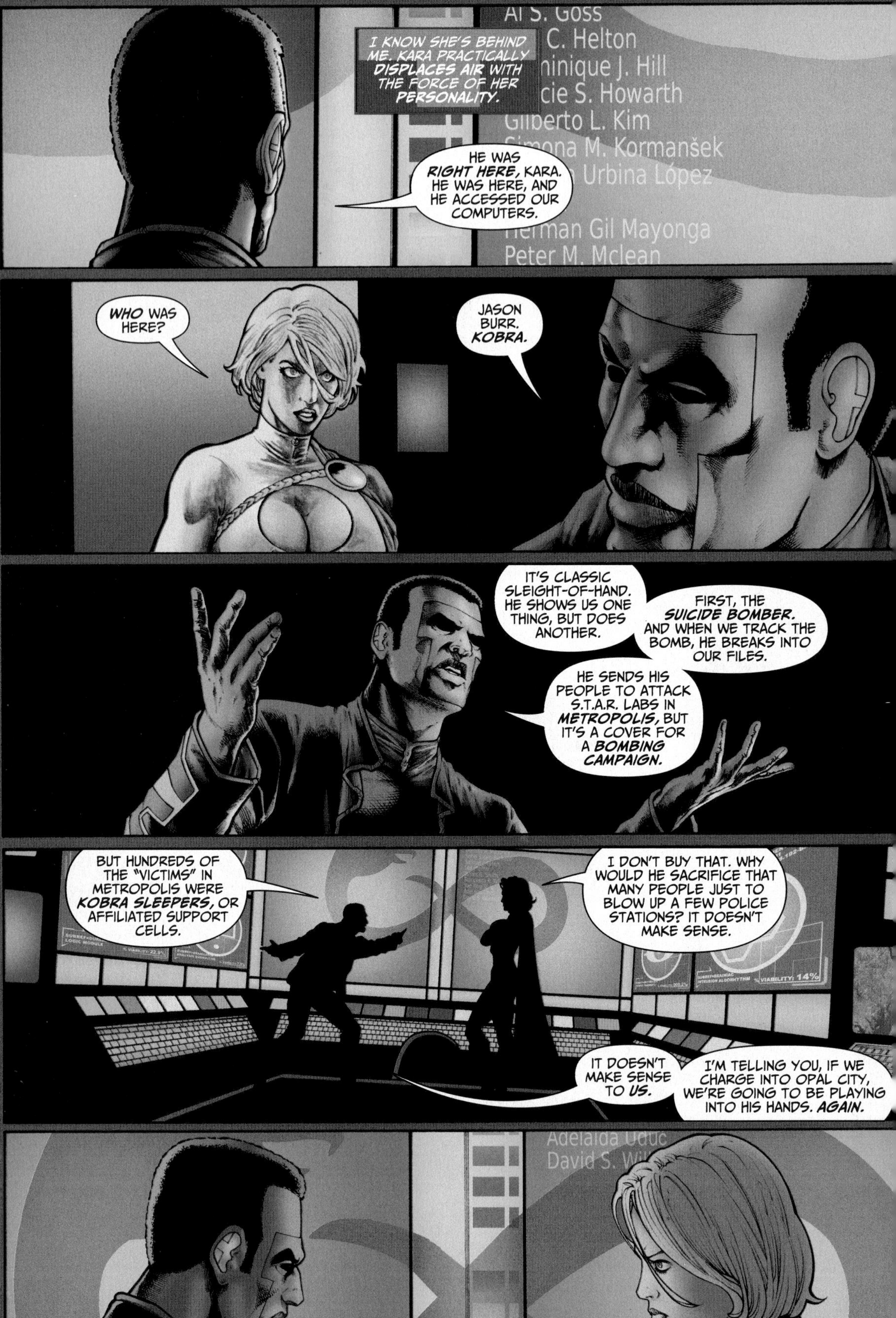
I KNOW SHE'S BEHIND ME. KARA PRACTICALLY DISPLACES AIR WITH THE FORCE OF HER PERSONALITY.
HE WAS RIGHT HERE, KARA. HE WAS HERE, AND HE ACCESSED OUR COMPUTERS.
Gilberto L. Kim
Herman Gil Mayonga
Peter M. Mclean
WHO WAS HERE?
JASON BURR. KOBRA.
IT'S CLASSIC SLEIGHT-OF-HAND. HE SHOWS US ONE THING, BUT DOES ANOTHER.
FIRST, THE SUICIDE BOMBER. AND WHEN WE TRACK THE BOMB, HE BREAKS INTO OUR FILES.
HE SENDS HIS PEOPLE TO ATTACK S.T.A.R. LABS IN METROPOLIS, BUT IT'S A COVER FOR A BOMBING CAMPAIGN.
BUT HUNDREDS OF THE "VICTIMS" IN METROPOLIS WERE KOBRA SLEEPERS, OR AFFILIATED SUPPORT CELLS.
I DON'T BUY THAT. WHY WOULD HE SACRIFICE THAT MANY PEOPLE JUST TO BLOW UP A FEW POLICE STATIONS? IT DOESN'T MAKE SENSE.
IT DOESN'T MAKE SENSE TO US.
I'M TELLING YOU, IF WE CHARGE INTO OPAL CITY, WE'RE GOING TO BE PLAYING INTO HIS HANDS. AGAIN.

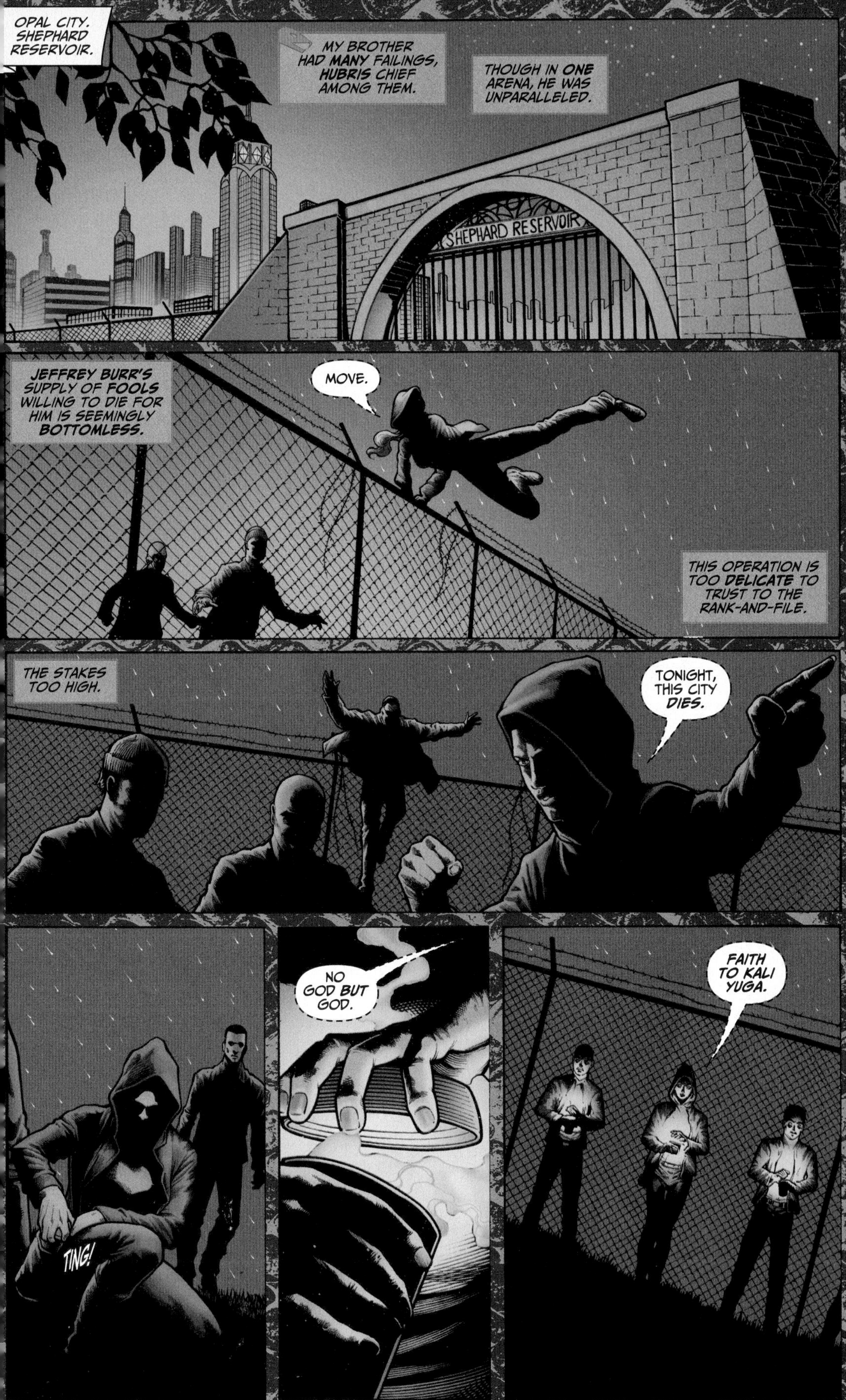
OPAL CITY. SHEPHARD RESERVOIR.
MY BROTHER HAD MANY FAILINGS, HUBRIS CHIEF AMONG THEM.
THOUGH IN ONE ARENA, HE WAS UNPARALLELED.
SHEPHARD RESERVOIR
JEFFREY BURR'S SUPPLY OF FOOLS WILLING TO DIE FOR HIM IS SEEMINGLY BOTTOMLESS.
MOVE.
THIS OPERATION IS TOO DELICATE TO TRUST TO THE RANK-AND-FILE.
THE STAKES TOO HIGH.
TONIGHT, THIS CITY DIES.
TING!
NO GOD BUT GOD.
FAITH TO KALI YUGA.

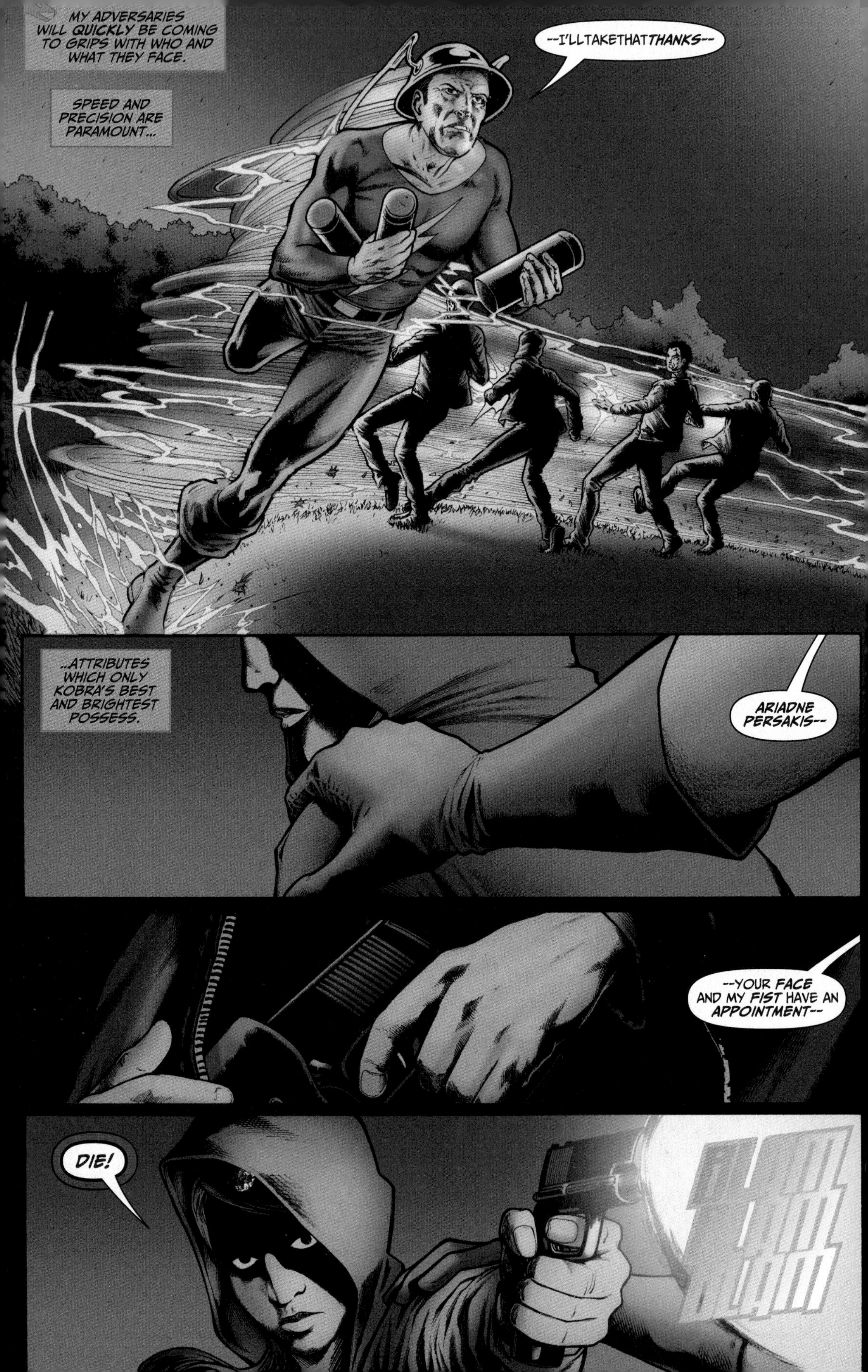

MY ADVERSARIES WILL QUICKLY BE COMING TO GRIPS WITH WHO AND WHAT THEY FACE.
--I'LLTAKETHATTHANKS--
SPEED AND PRECISION ARE PARAMOUNT...
...ATTRIBUTES WHICH ONLY KOBRA'S BEST AND BRIGHTEST POSSESS.
ARIADNE PERSAKIS--
--YOUR FACE AND MY FIST HAVE AN APPOINTMENT--
DIE!
BLAM BLAM BLAM

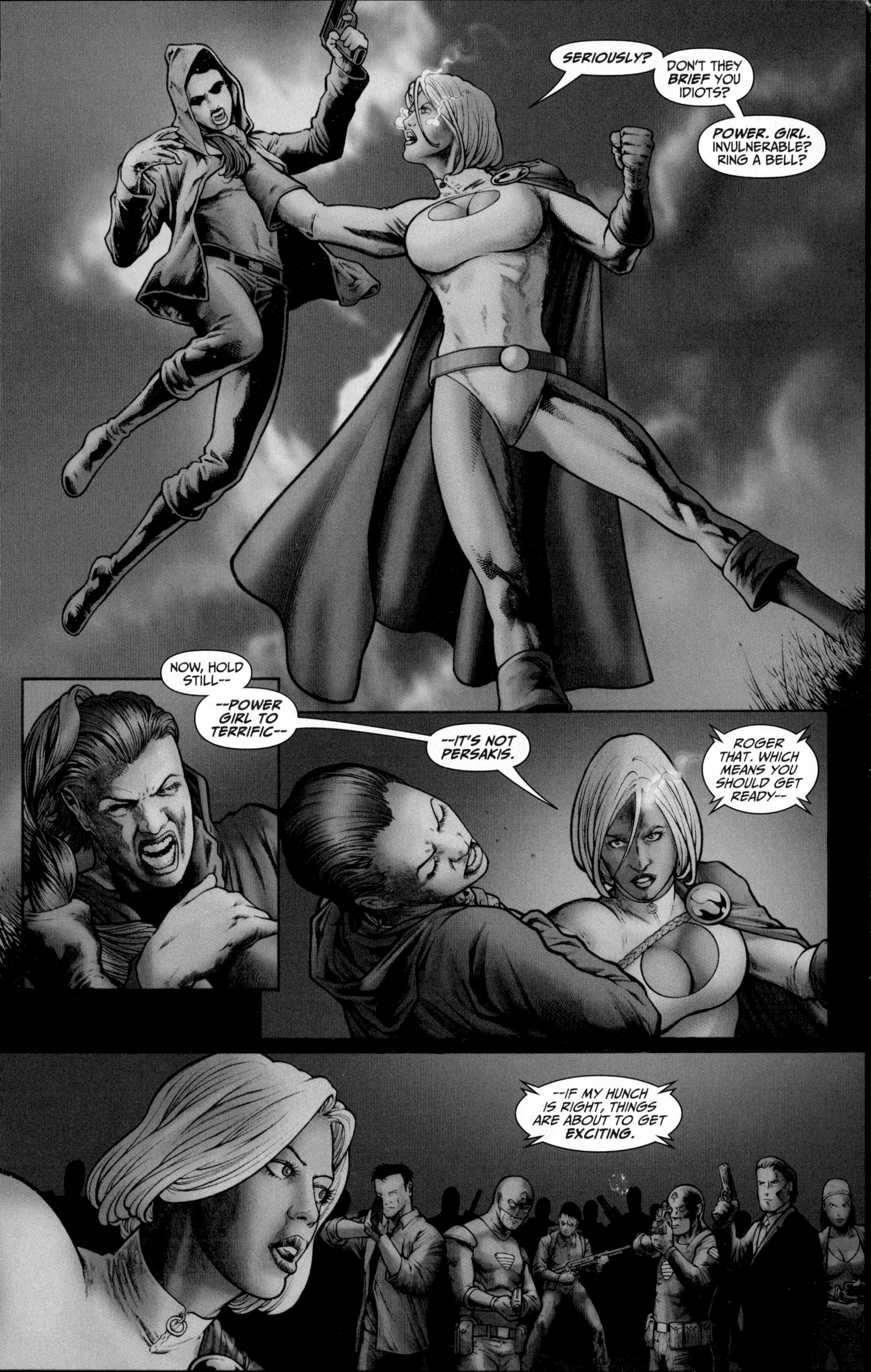
SERIOUSLY?
DON'T THEY BRIEF YOU IDIOTS?
POWER. GIRL. INVULNERABLE? RING A BELL?
NOW, HOLD STILL--
--POWER GIRL TO TERRIFIC--
--IT'S NOT PERSAKIS.
ROGER THAT. WHICH MEANS YOU SHOULD GET READY--
--IF MY HUNCH IS RIGHT, THINGS ARE ABOUT TO GET EXCITING.

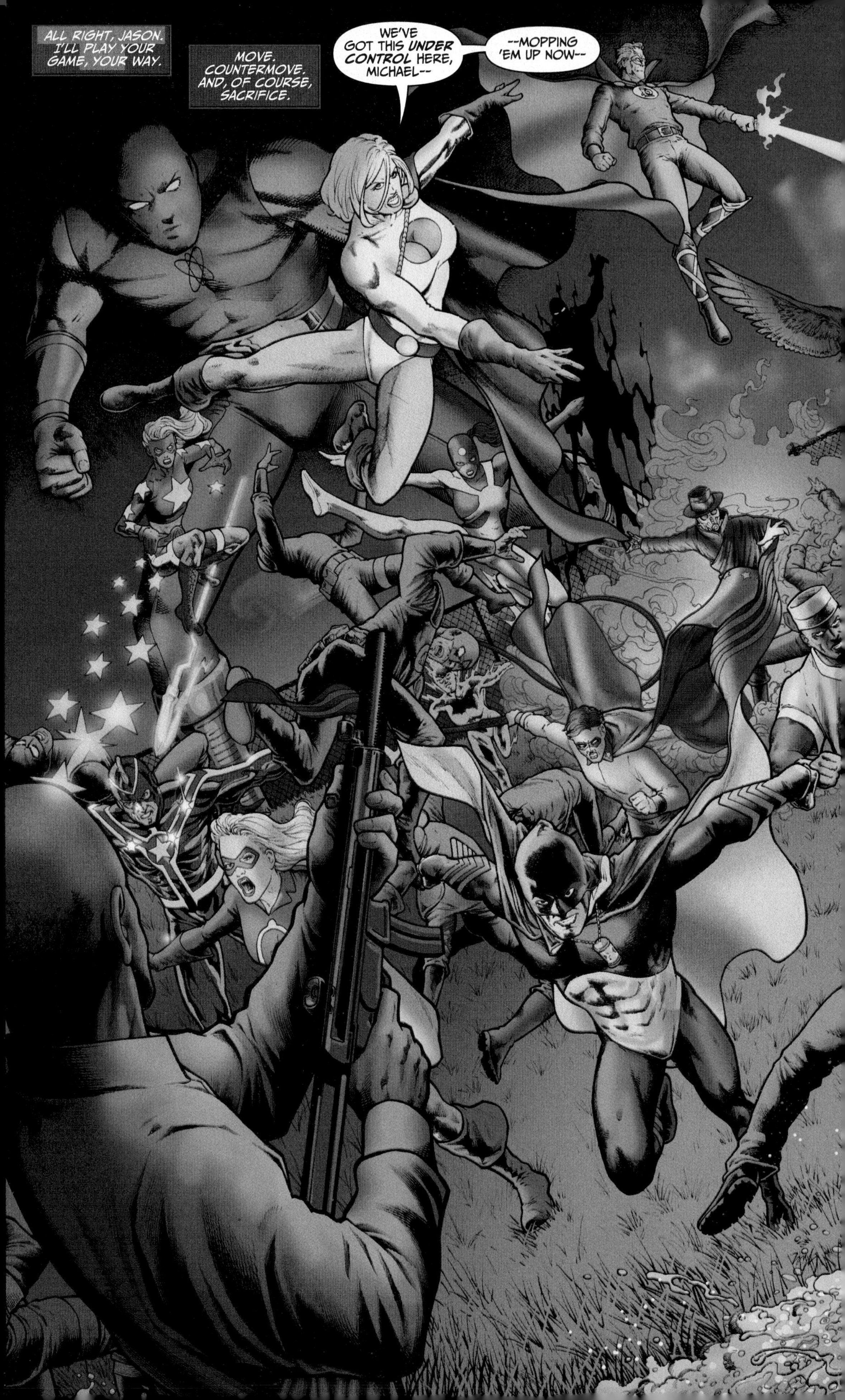
ALL RIGHT, JASON. I'LL PLAY YOUR GAME, YOUR WAY.
MOVE. COUNTERMOVE. AND, OF COURSE, SACRIFICE.
WE'VE GOT THIS UNDER CONTROL HERE, MICHAEL--
--MOPPING 'EM UP NOW--

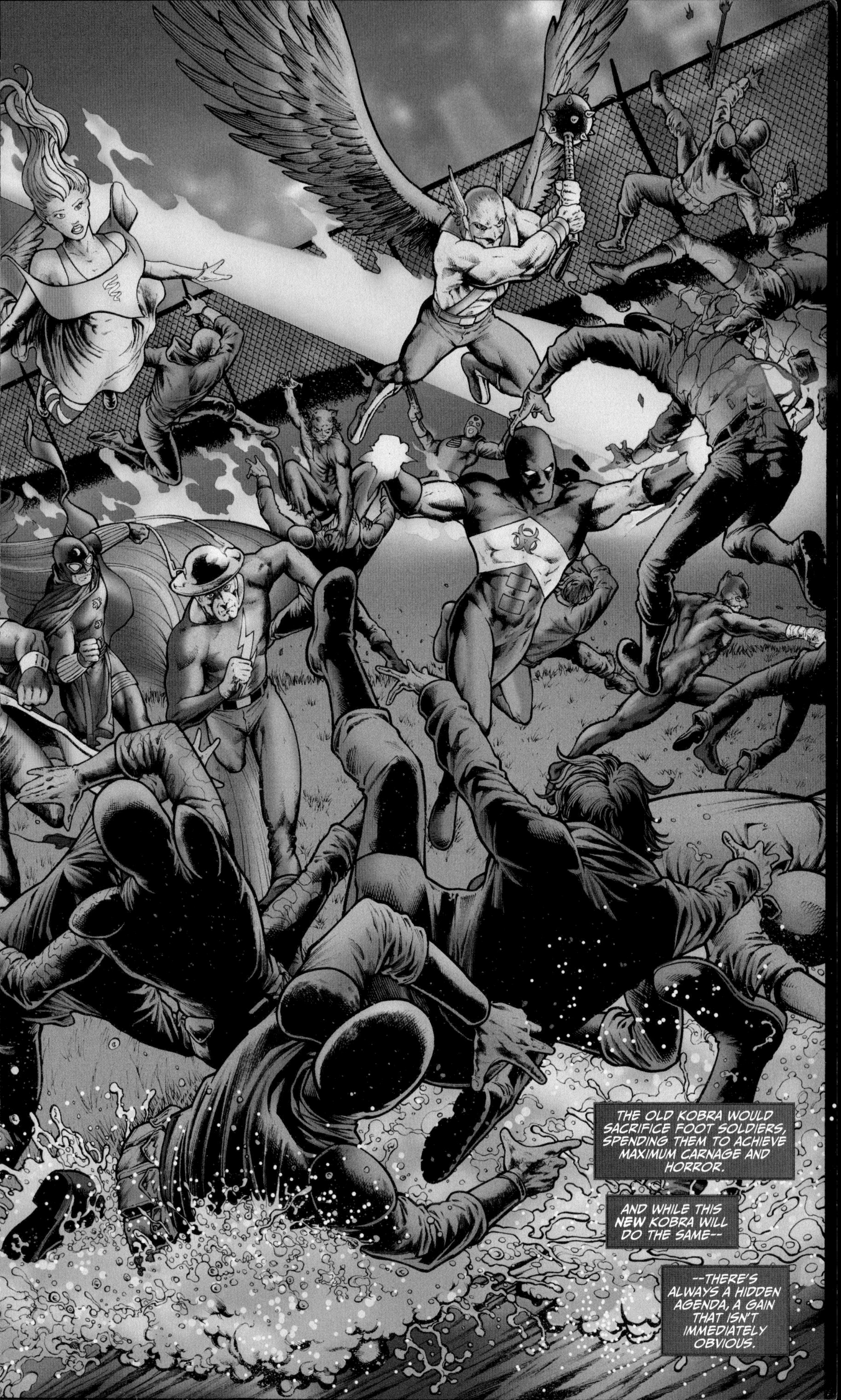
THE OLD KOBRA WOULD SACRIFICE FOOT SOLDIERS, SPENDING THEM TO ACHIEVE MAXIMUM CARNAGE AND HORROR.
AND WHILE THIS NEW KOBRA WILL DO THE SAME--
--THERE'S ALWAYS A HIDDEN AGENDA, A GAIN THAT ISN'T IMMEDIATELY OBVIOUS.

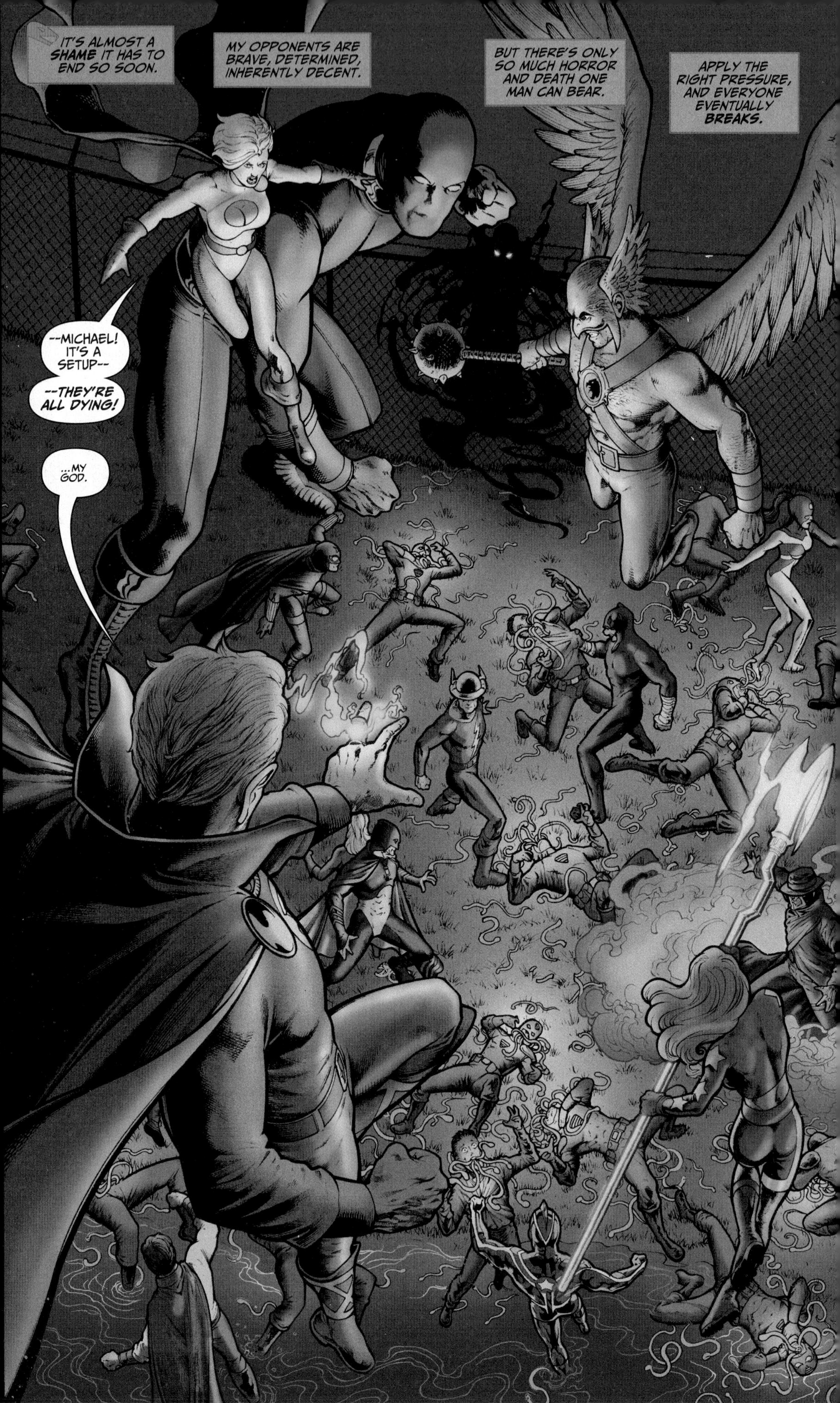

IT'S ALMOST A SHAME IT HAS TO END SO SOON.
MY OPPONENTS ARE BRAVE, DETERMINED, INHERENTLY DECENT.
BUT THERE'S ONLY SO MUCH HORROR AND DEATH ONE MAN CAN BEAR.
APPLY THE RIGHT PRESSURE, AND EVERYONE EVENTUALLY BREAKS.
--MICHAEL! IT'S A SETUP--
--THEY'RE ALL DYING!
...MY GOD.

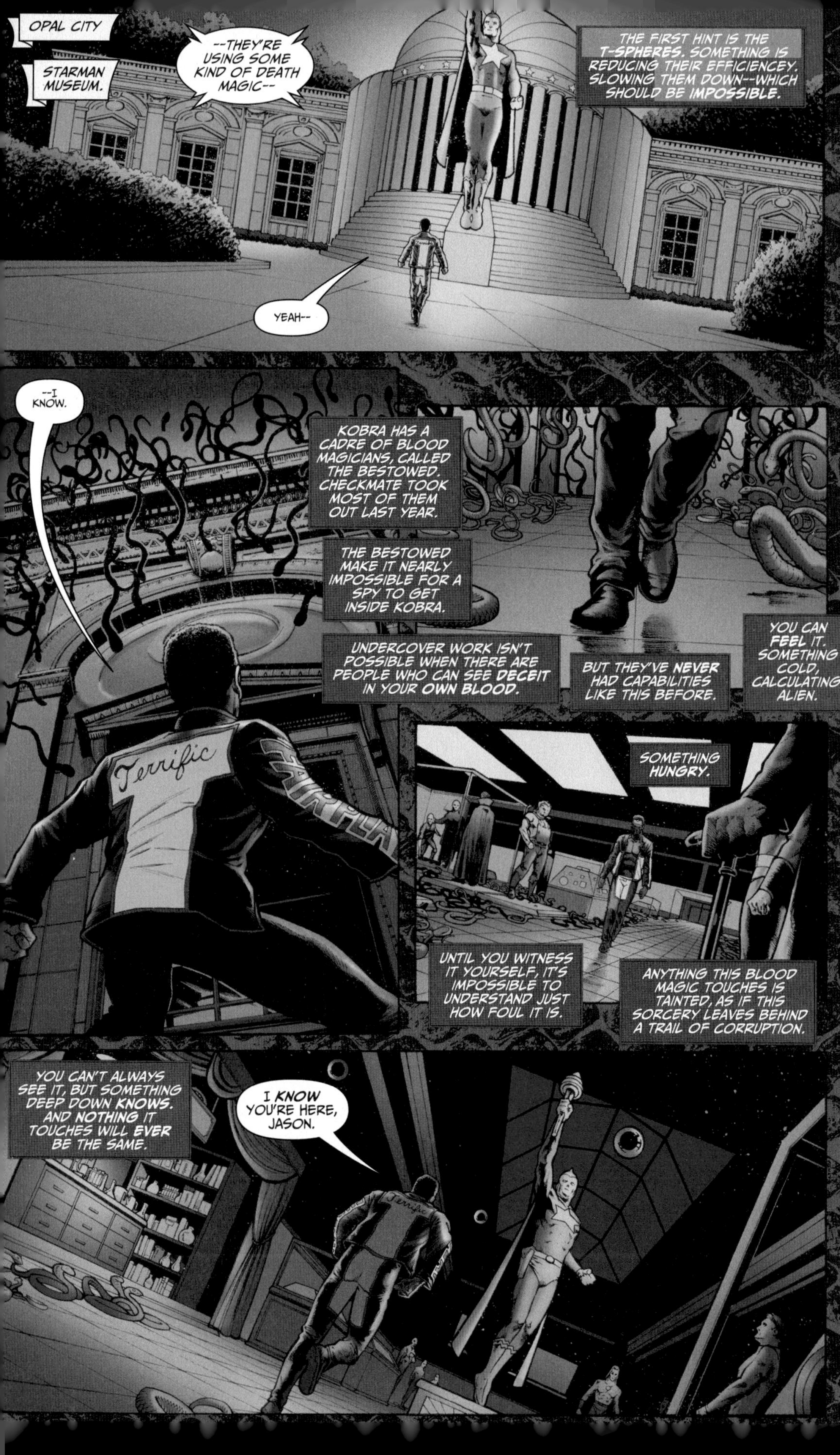

OPAL CITY
STARMAN MUSEUM.
--THEY'RE USING SOME KIND OF DEATH MAGIC--
THE FIRST HINT IS THE T-SPHERES. SOMETHING IS REDUCING THEIR EFFICIENCEY. SLOWING THEM DOWN--WHICH SHOULD BE IMPOSSIBLE.
YEAH--
--I KNOW.
KOBRA HAS A CADRE OF BLOOD MAGICIANS, CALLED THE BESTOWED. CHECKMATE TOOK MOST OF THEM OUT LAST YEAR.
THE BESTOWED MAKE IT NEARLY IMPOSSIBLE FOR A SPY TO GET INSIDE KOBRA.
UNDERCOVER WORK ISN'T POSSIBLE WHEN THERE ARE PEOPLE WHO CAN SEE DECEIT IN YOUR OWN BLOOD.
BUT THEY'VE NEVER HAD CAPABILITIES LIKE THIS BEFORE.
YOU CAN FEEL IT. SOMETHING COLD, CALCULATING, ALIEN.
SOMETHING HUNGRY.
UNTIL YOU WITNESS IT YOURSELF, IT'S IMPOSSIBLE TO UNDERSTAND JUST HOW FOUL IT IS.
ANYTHING THIS BLOOD MAGIC TOUCHES IS TAINTED, AS IF THIS SORCERY LEAVES BEHIND A TRAIL OF CORRUPTION.
YOU CAN'T ALWAYS SEE IT, BUT SOMETHING DEEP DOWN KNOWS. AND NOTHING IT TOUCHES WILL EVER BE THE SAME.
I KNOW YOU'RE HERE, JASON.

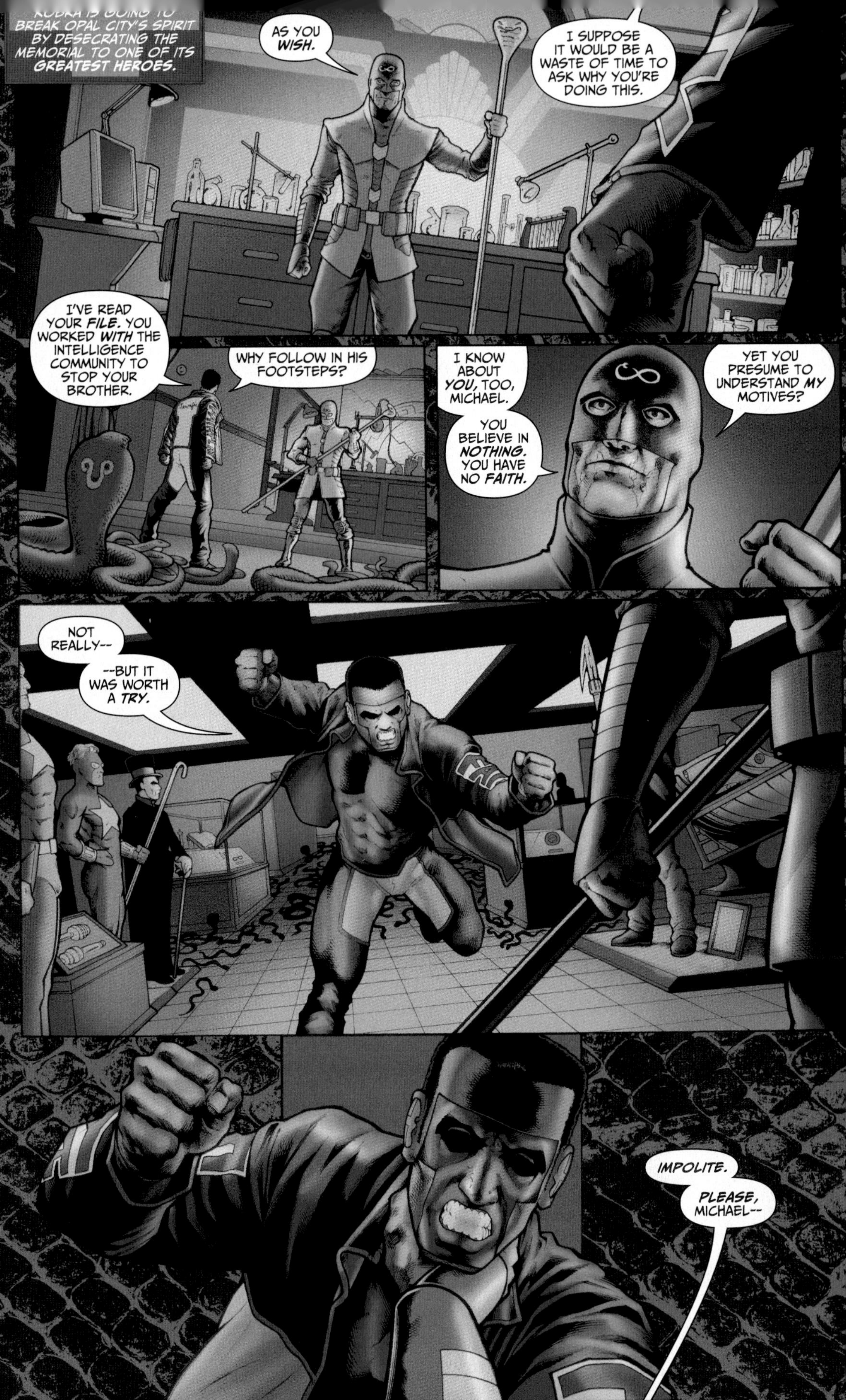
BREAK OPAL CITY'S SPIRIT BY DESECRATING THE MEMORIAL TO ONE OF ITS GREATEST HEROES.
AS YOU WISH.
I SUPPOSE IT WOULD BE A WASTE OF TIME TO ASK WHY YOU'RE DOING THIS.
I'VE READ YOUR FILE. YOU WORKED WITH THE INTELLIGENCE COMMUNITY TO STOP YOUR BROTHER.
WHY FOLLOW IN HIS FOOTSTEPS?
I KNOW ABOUT YOU, TOO, MICHAEL.
YOU BELIEVE IN NOTHING. YOU HAVE NO FAITH.
YET YOU PRESUME TO UNDERSTAND MY MOTIVES?
NOT REALLY--
--BUT IT WAS WORTH A TRY.
IMPOLITE.
PLEASE, MICHAEL--

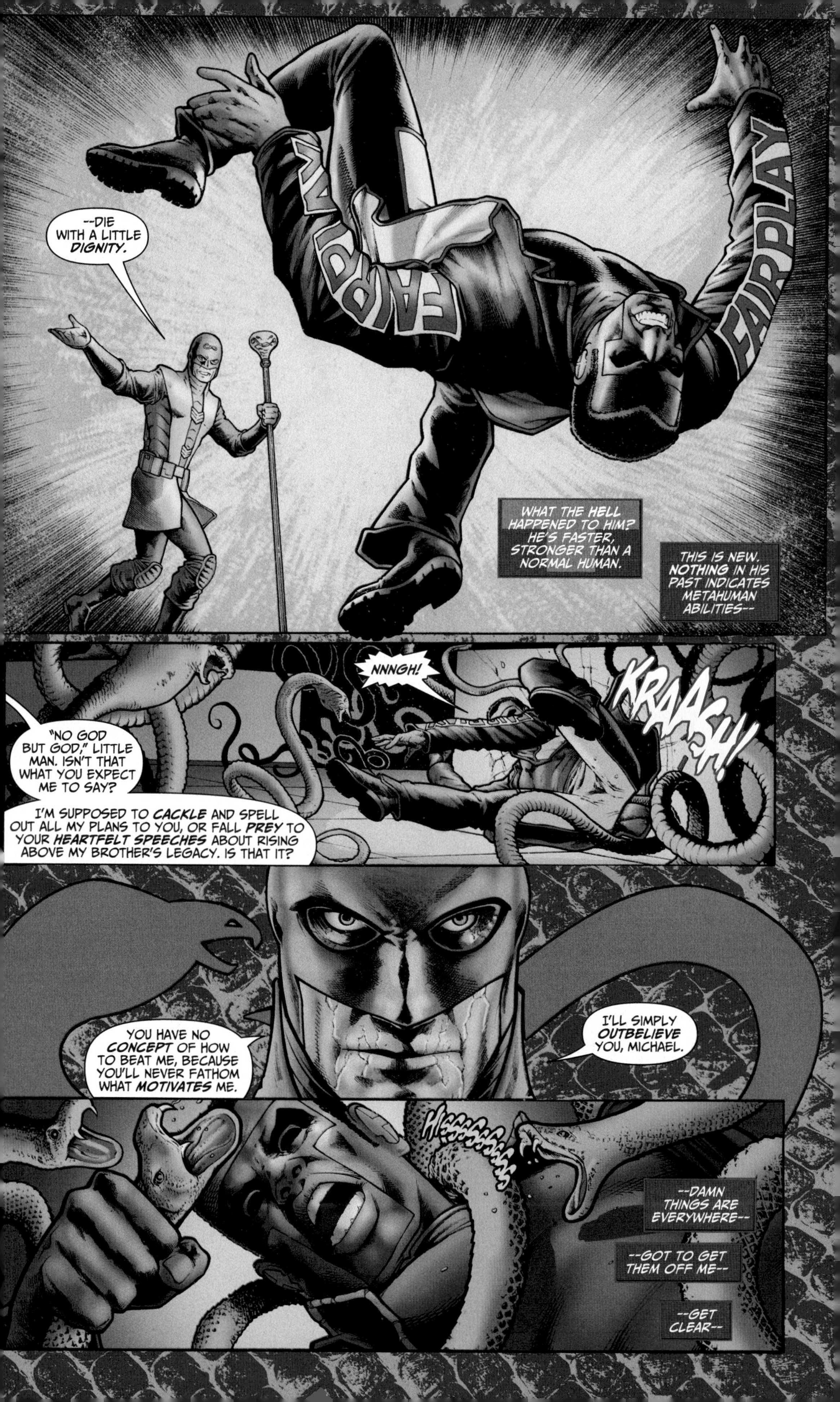

--DIE WITH A LITTLE DIGNITY.
FAIRPLAY
FAIRPLAY
WHAT THE HELL HAPPENED TO HIM? HE'S FASTER, STRONGER THAN A NORMAL HUMAN.
THIS IS NEW. NOTHING IN HIS PAST INDICATES METAHUMAN ABILITIES--
NNNGH!
KRAASH!
"NO GOD BUT GOD," LITTLE MAN. ISN'T THAT WHAT YOU EXPECT ME TO SAY?
I'M SUPPOSED TO CACKLE AND SPELL OUT ALL MY PLANS TO YOU, OR FALL PREY TO YOUR HEARTFELT SPEECHES ABOUT RISING ABOVE MY BROTHER'S LEGACY. IS THAT IT?
YOU HAVE NO CONCEPT OF HOW TO BEAT ME, BECAUSE YOU'LL NEVER FATHOM WHAT MOTIVATES ME.
I'LL SIMPLY OUTBELIEVE YOU, MICHAEL.
HISSSSSSSSS
--DAMN THINGS ARE EVERYWHERE--
--GOT TO GET THEM OFF ME--
--GET CLEAR--

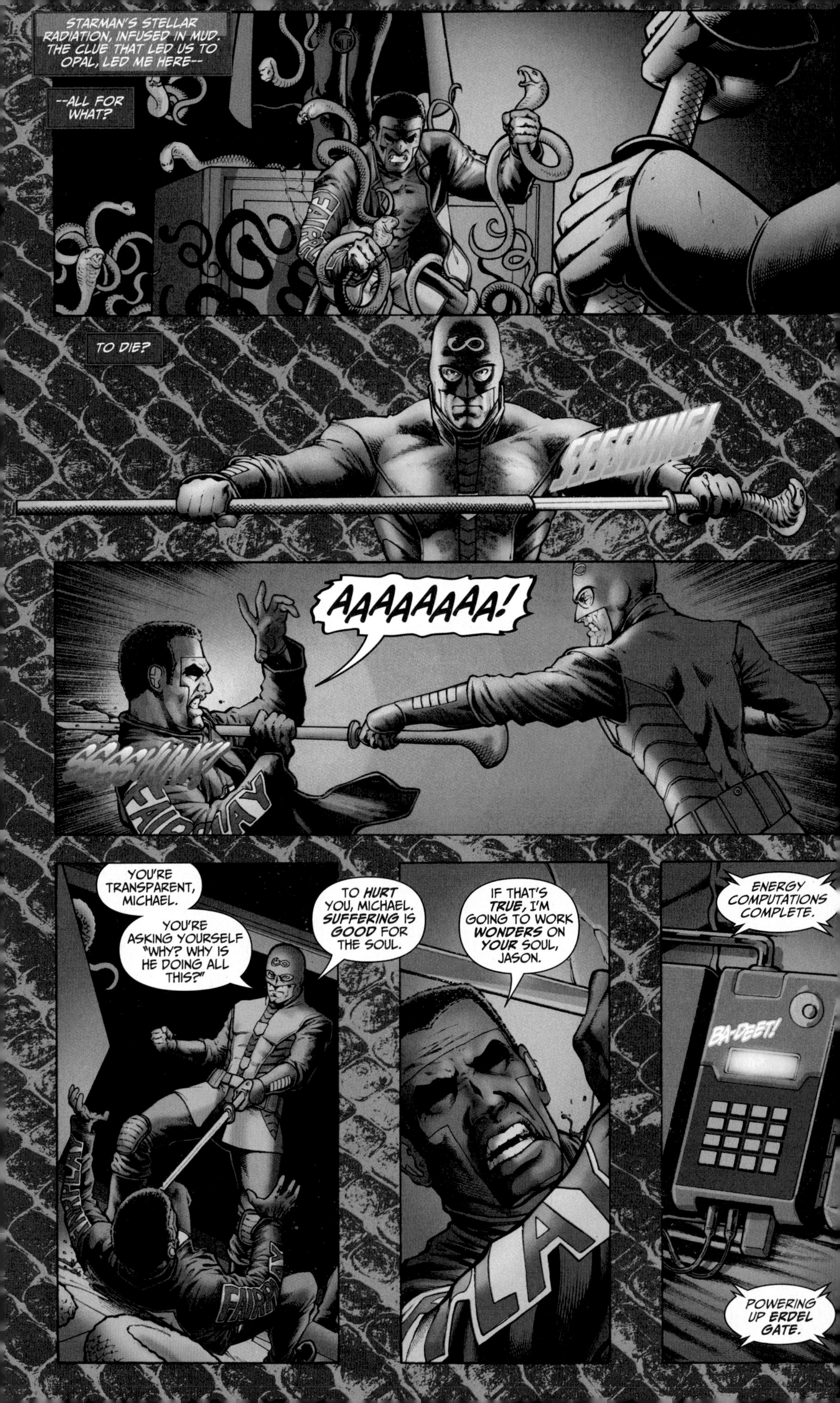
STARMAN'S STELLAR RADIATION, INFUSED IN MUD. THE CLUE THAT LED US TO OPAL, LED ME HERE--
--ALL FOR WHAT?
TO DIE?
SSSSHUNG!
AAAAAAAA!
SSSHUNK!
YOU'RE TRANSPARENT, MICHAEL.
YOU'RE ASKING YOURSELF "WHY? WHY IS HE DOING ALL THIS?"
TO HURT YOU, MICHAEL. SUFFERING IS GOOD FOR THE SOUL.
IF THAT'S TRUE, I'M GOING TO WORK WONDERS ON YOUR SOUL, JASON.
ENERGY COMPUTATIONS COMPLETE.
BA-DEET!
POWERING UP ERDEL GATE.

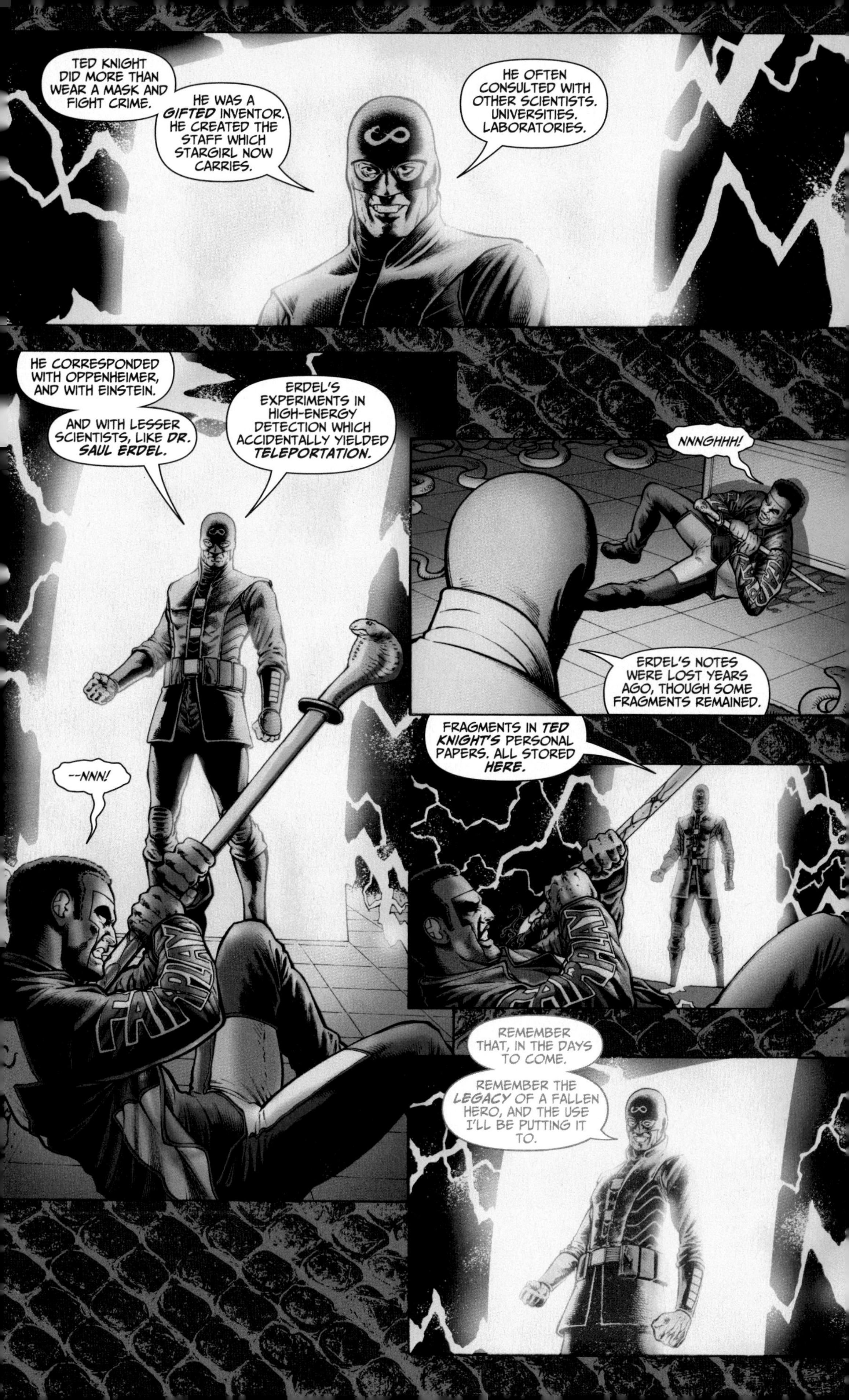

TED KNIGHT DID MORE THAN WEAR A MASK AND FIGHT CRIME.
HE WAS A GIFTED INVENTOR. HE CREATED THE STAFF WHICH STARGIRL NOW CARRIES.
HE OFTEN CONSULTED WITH OTHER SCIENTISTS. UNIVERSITIES. LABORATORIES.
HE CORRESPONDED WITH OPPENHEIMER, AND WITH EINSTEIN.
AND WITH LESSER SCIENTISTS, LIKE DR. SAUL ERDEL.
ERDEL'S EXPERIMENTS IN HIGH-ENERGY DETECTION WHICH ACCIDENTALLY YIELDED TELEPORTATION.
--NNN!
NNNGHHH!
ERDEL'S NOTES WERE LOST YEARS AGO, THOUGH SOME FRAGMENTS REMAINED.
FRAGMENTS IN TED KNIGHT'S PERSONAL PAPERS. ALL STORED HERE.
REMEMBER THAT, IN THE DAYS TO COME.
REMEMBER THE LEGACY OF A FALLEN HERO, AND THE USE I'LL BE PUTTING IT TO.

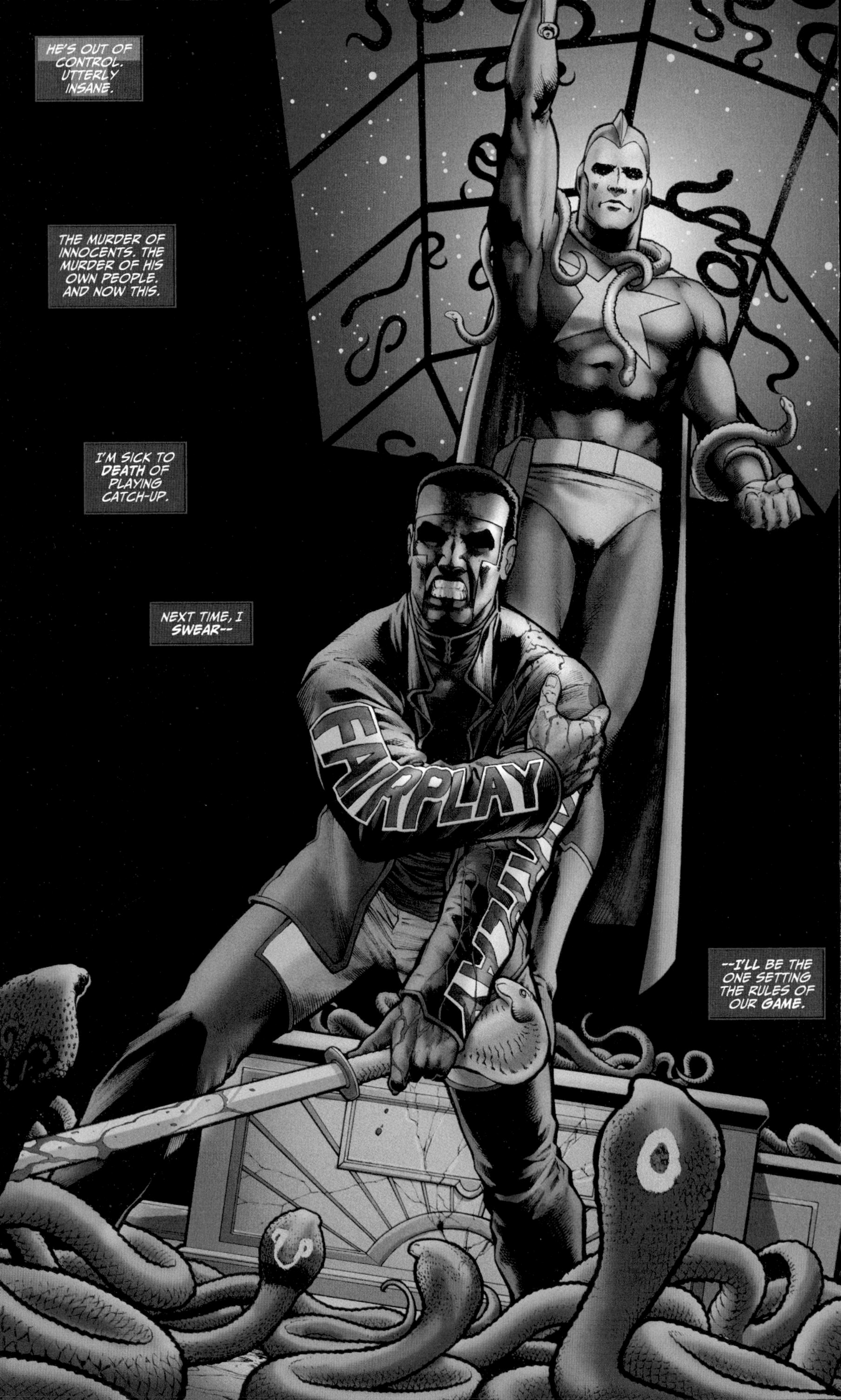
HE'S OUT OF CONTROL. UTTERLY INSANE.
THE MURDER OF INNOCENTS. THE MURDER OF HIS OWN PEOPLE. AND NOW THIS.
I'M SICK TO DEATH OF PLAYING CATCH-UP.
NEXT TIME, I SWEAR--
FAIRPLAY
--I'LL BE THE ONE SETTING THE RULES OF OUR GAME.

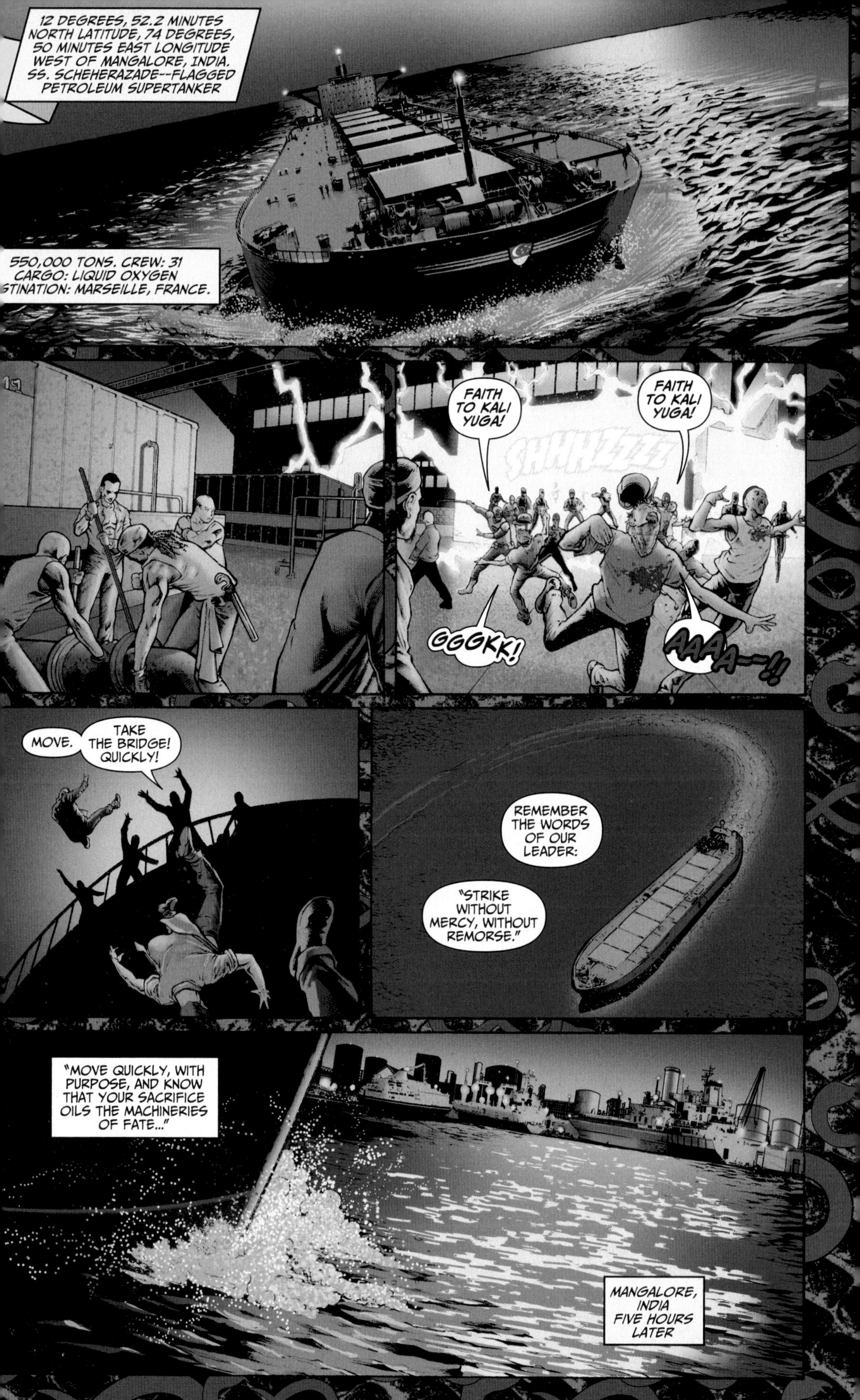
12 DEGREES, 52.2 MINUTES NORTH LATITUDE, 74 DEGREES, 50 MINUTES EAST LONGITUDE WEST OF MANGALORE, INDIA. SS. SCHEHERAZADE--FLAGGED PETROLEUM SUPERTANKER
550,000 TONS. CREW: 31 CARGO: LIQUID OXYGEN STINATION: MARSEILLE, FRANCE.
FAITH TO KALI YUGA!
FAITH TO KALI YUGA!
SHHHZZZZ
GGGKK!
AAAA--!!
MOVE.
TAKE THE BRIDGE! QUICKLY!
REMEMBER THE WORDS OF OUR LEADER:
"STRIKE WITHOUT MERCY, WITHOUT REMORSE."
"MOVE QUICKLY, WITH PURPOSE, AND KNOW THAT YOUR SACRIFICE OILS THE MACHINERIES OF FATE..."
MANGALORE, INDIA FIVE HOURS LATER

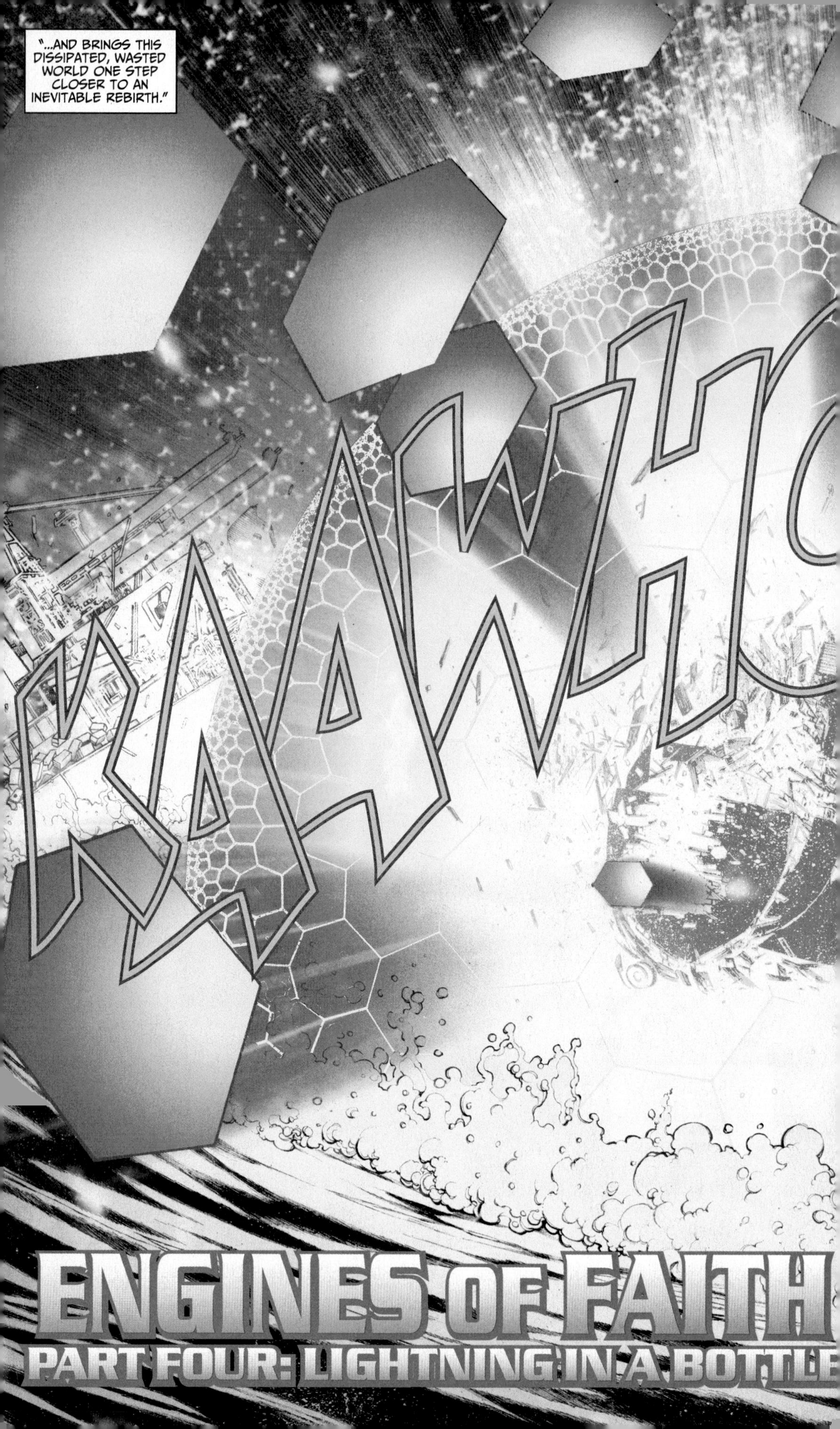
"...AND BRINGS THIS DISSIPATED, WASTED WORLD ONE STEP CLOSER TO AN INEVITABLE REBIRTH."
KAWHO
ENGINES OF FAITH
PART FOUR: LIGHTNING IN A BOTTLE

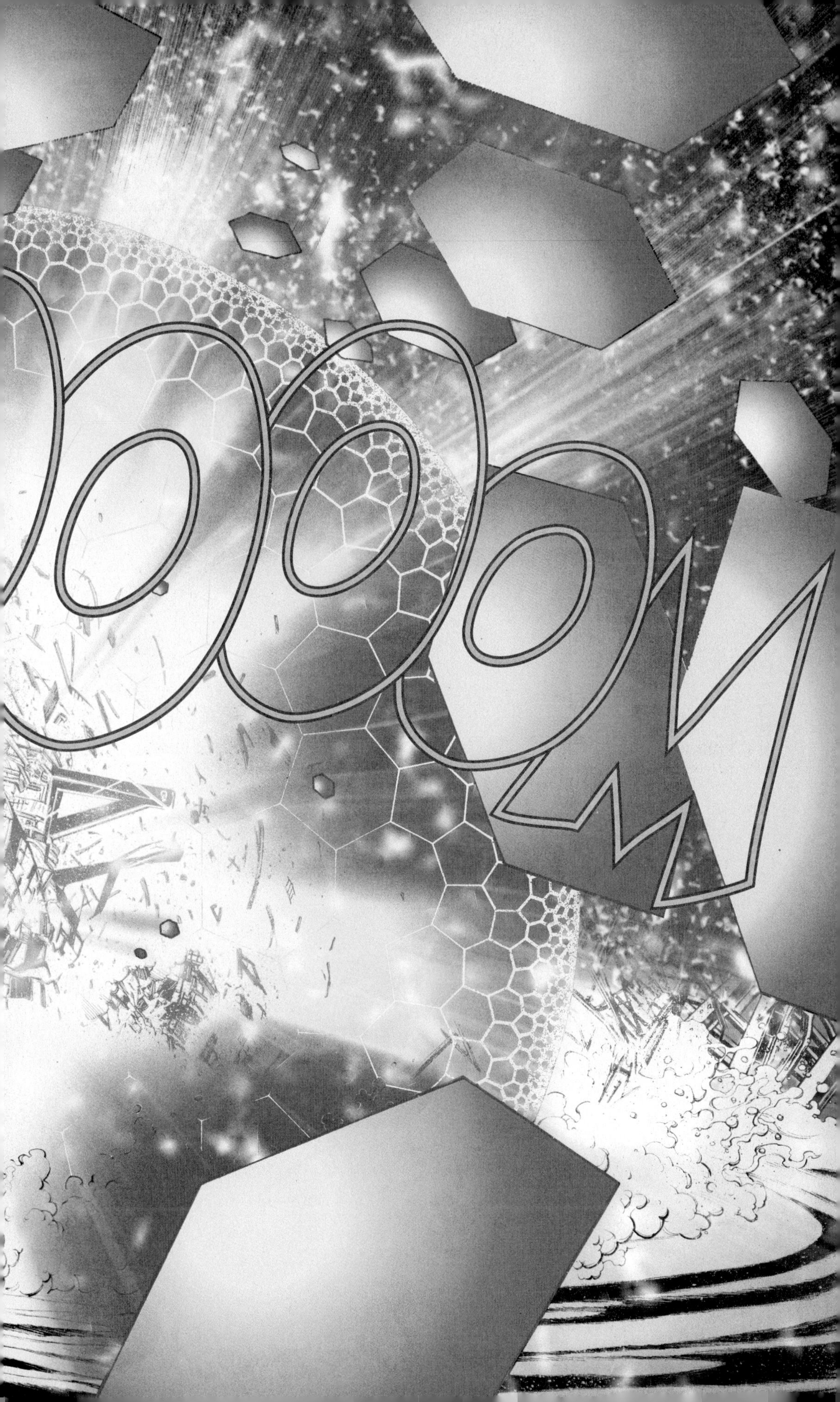
OOOOM

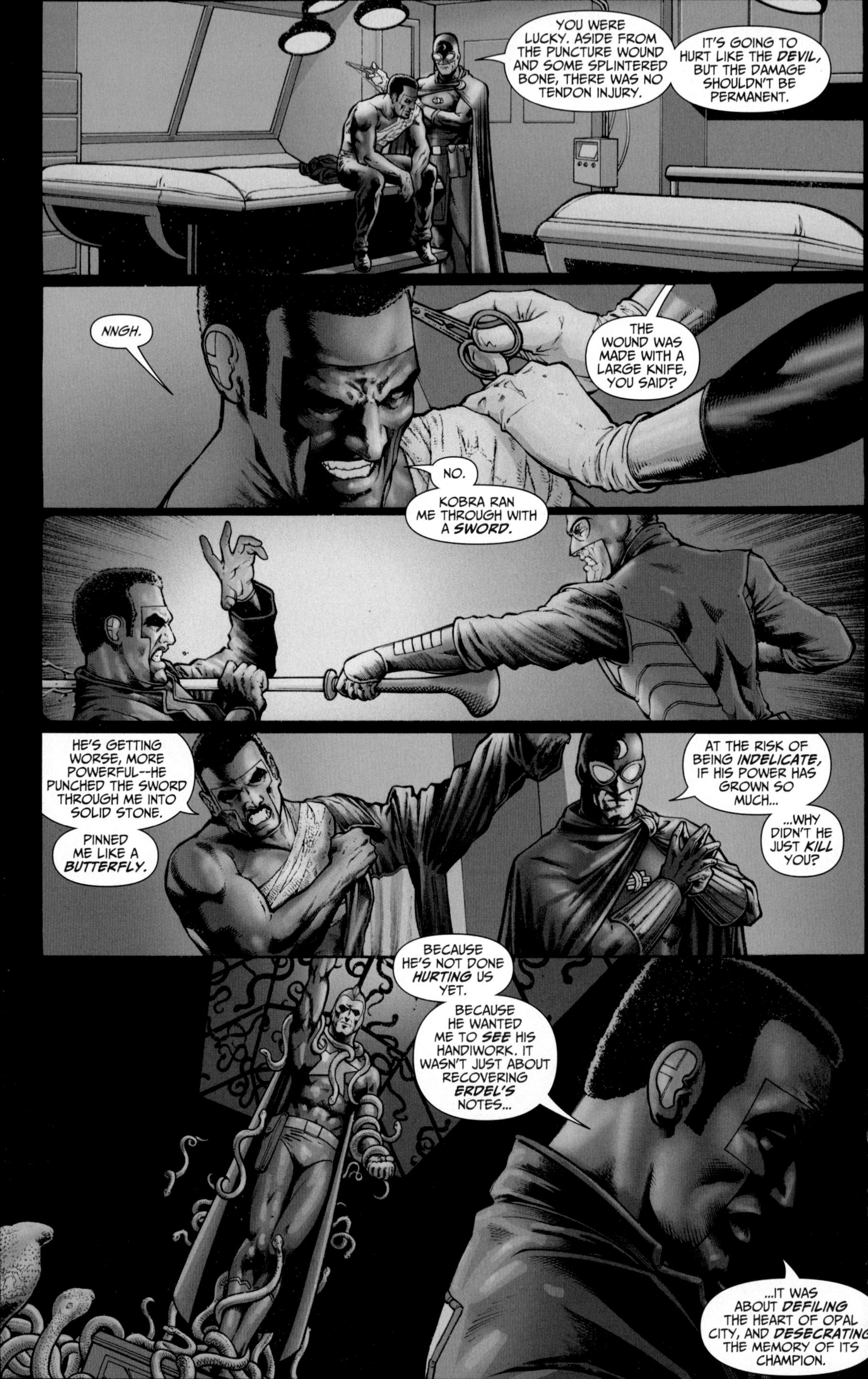
YOU WERE LUCKY. ASIDE FROM THE PUNCTURE WOUND AND SOME SPLINTERED BONE, THERE WAS NO TENDON INJURY.
IT'S GOING TO HURT LIKE THE DEVIL, BUT THE DAMAGE SHOULDN'T BE PERMANENT.
NNGH.
THE WOUND WAS MADE WITH A LARGE KNIFE, YOU SAID?
NO.
KOBRA RAN ME THROUGH WITH A SWORD.
HE'S GETTING WORSE, MORE POWERFUL--HE PUNCHED THE SWORD THROUGH ME INTO SOLID STONE.
PINNED ME LIKE A BUTTERFLY.
AT THE RISK OF BEING INDELICATE, IF HIS POWER HAS GROWN SO MUCH...
...WHY DIDN'T HE JUST KILL YOU?
BECAUSE HE'S NOT DONE HURTING US YET.
BECAUSE HE WANTED ME TO SEE HIS HANDIWORK. IT WASN'T JUST ABOUT RECOVERING ERDEL'S NOTES...
...IT WAS ABOUT DEFILING THE HEART OF OPAL CITY, AND DESECRATING THE MEMORY OF ITS CHAMPION.

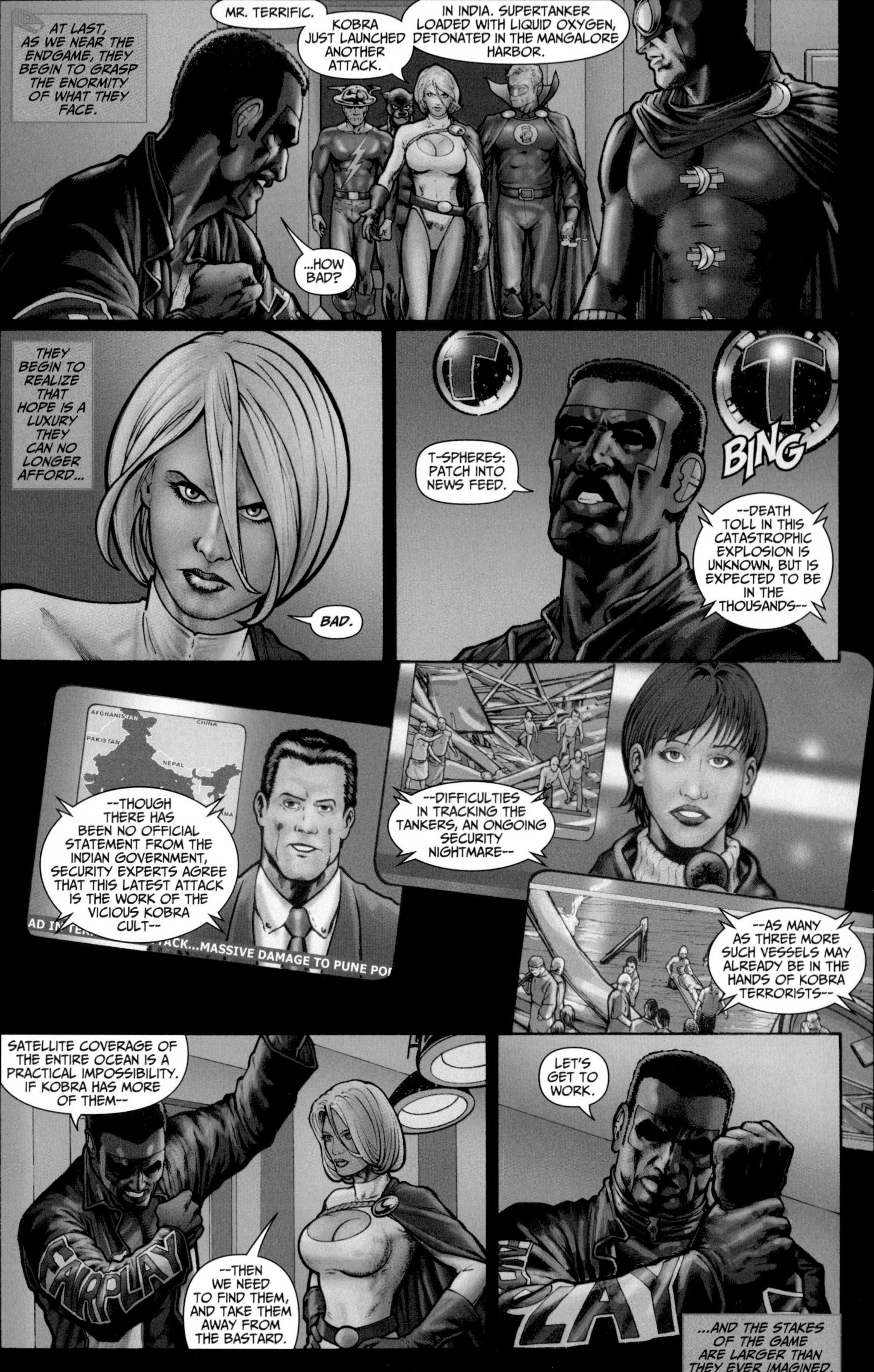

AT LAST, AS WE NEAR THE ENDGAME, THEY BEGIN TO GRASP THE ENORMITY OF WHAT THEY FACE.
MR. TERRIFIC.
KOBRA JUST LAUNCHED ANOTHER ATTACK.
IN INDIA. SUPERTANKER LOADED WITH LIQUID OXYGEN, DETONATED IN THE MANGALORE HARBOR.
...HOW BAD?
THEY BEGIN TO REALIZE THAT HOPE IS A LUXURY THEY CAN NO LONGER AFFORD...
BAD.
T-SPHERES: PATCH INTO NEWS FEED.
BING
--DEATH TOLL IN THIS CATASTROPHIC EXPLOSION IS UNKNOWN, BUT IS EXPECTED TO BE IN THE THOUSANDS--
AFGHANISTAN
CHINA
PAKISTAN
NEPAL
--THOUGH THERE HAS BEEN NO OFFICIAL STATEMENT FROM THE INDIAN GOVERNMENT, SECURITY EXPERTS AGREE THAT THIS LATEST ATTACK IS THE WORK OF THE VICIOUS KOBRA CULT--
...MASSIVE DAMAGE TO PUNE PO
--DIFFICULTIES IN TRACKING THE TANKERS, AN ONGOING SECURITY NIGHTMARE--
--AS MANY AS THREE MORE SUCH VESSELS MAY ALREADY BE IN THE HANDS OF KOBRA TERRORISTS--
SATELLITE COVERAGE OF THE ENTIRE OCEAN IS A PRACTICAL IMPOSSIBILITY. IF KOBRA HAS MORE OF THEM--
FAIRPLAY
--THEN WE NEED TO FIND THEM, AND TAKE THEM AWAY FROM THE BASTARD.
LET'S GET TO WORK.
...AND THE STAKES OF THE GAME ARE LARGER THAN THEY EVER IMAGINED.

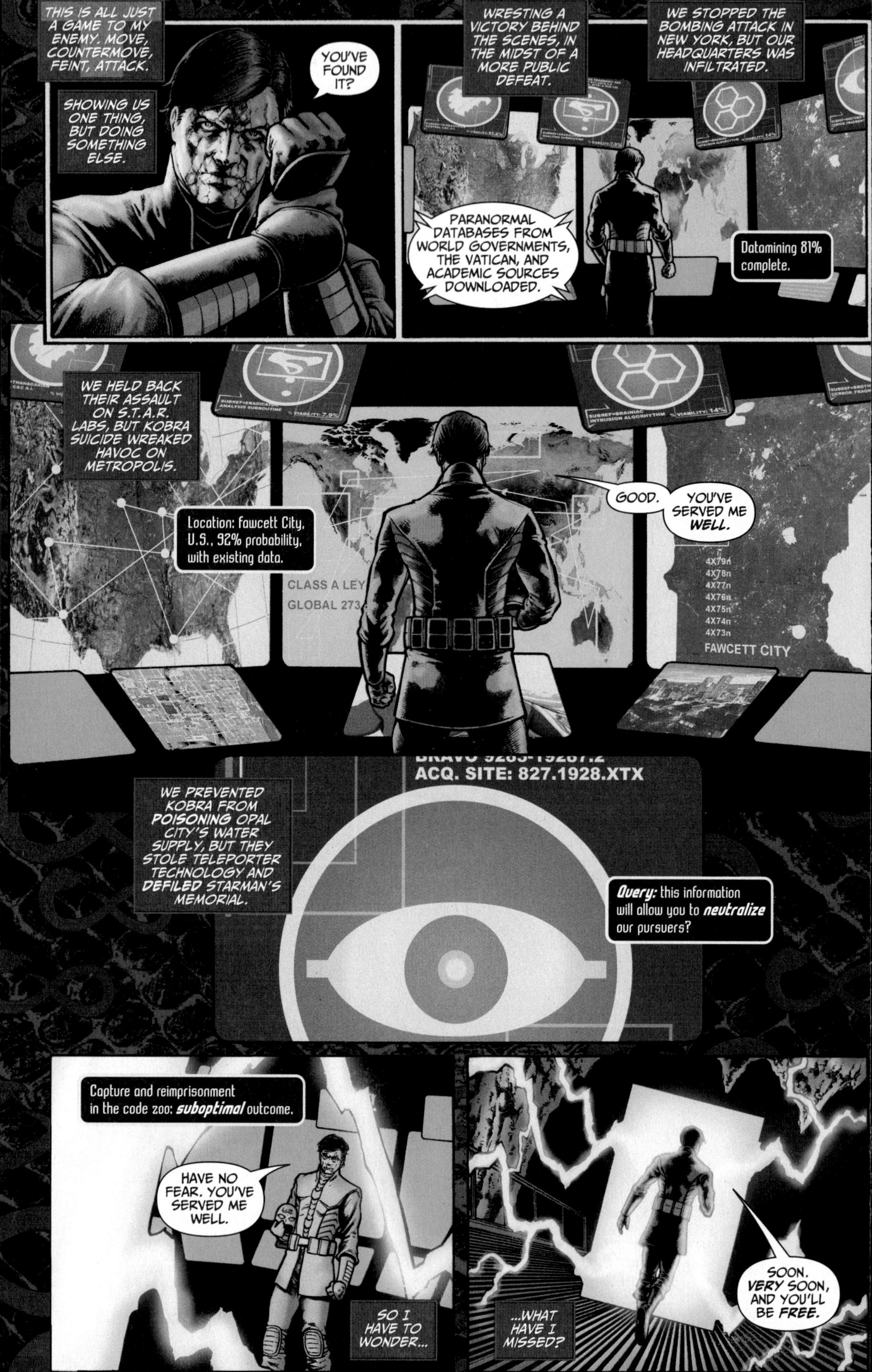
THIS IS ALL JUST A GAME TO MY ENEMY. MOVE, COUNTERMOVE, FEINT, ATTACK.
SHOWING US ONE THING, BUT DOING SOMETHING ELSE.
YOU'VE FOUND IT?
WRESTING A VICTORY BEHIND THE SCENES, IN THE MIDST OF A MORE PUBLIC DEFEAT.
WE STOPPED THE BOMBING ATTACK IN NEW YORK, BUT OUR HEADQUARTERS WAS INFILTRATED.
PARANORMAL DATABASES FROM WORLD GOVERNMENTS, THE VATICAN, AND ACADEMIC SOURCES DOWNLOADED.
Datamining 81% complete.
WE HELD BACK THEIR ASSAULT ON S.T.A.R. LABS, BUT KOBRA SUICIDE WREAKED HAVOC ON METROPOLIS.
Location: fawcett City, U.S., 92% probability, with existing data.
CLASS A LEY
GLOBAL 273
GOOD.
YOU'VE SERVED ME WELL.
4X79n
4X78n
4X77n
4X76n
4X75n
4X74n
4X73n
FAWCETT CITY
ACQ. SITE: 827.1928.XTX
WE PREVENTED KOBRA FROM POISONING OPAL CITY'S WATER SUPPLY, BUT THEY STOLE TELEPORTER TECHNOLOGY AND DEFILED STARMAN'S MEMORIAL.
Query: this information will allow you to neutralize our pursuers?
Capture and reimprisonment in the code zoo: suboptimal outcome.
HAVE NO FEAR. YOU'VE SERVED ME WELL.
SO I HAVE TO WONDER...
...WHAT HAVE I MISSED?
SOON. VERY SOON, AND YOU'LL BE FREE.

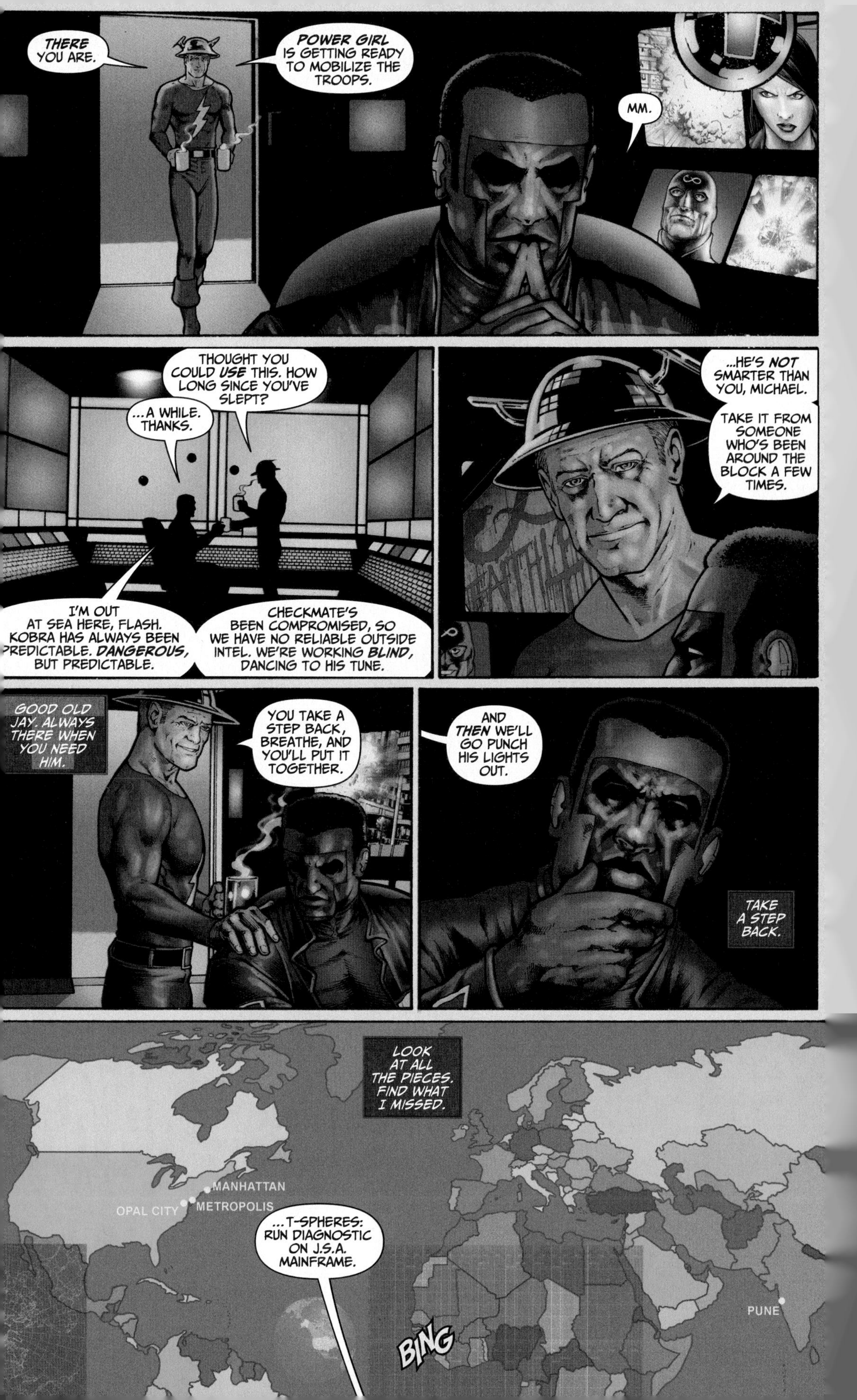
THERE YOU ARE.
POWER GIRL IS GETTING READY TO MOBILIZE THE TROOPS.
MM.
THOUGHT YOU COULD USE THIS. HOW LONG SINCE YOU'VE SLEPT?
...A WHILE. THANKS.
I'M OUT AT SEA HERE, FLASH. KOBRA HAS ALWAYS BEEN PREDICTABLE. DANGEROUS, BUT PREDICTABLE.
CHECKMATE'S BEEN COMPROMISED, SO WE HAVE NO RELIABLE OUTSIDE INTEL. WE'RE WORKING BLIND, DANCING TO HIS TUNE.
...HE'S NOT SMARTER THAN YOU, MICHAEL.
TAKE IT FROM SOMEONE WHO'S BEEN AROUND THE BLOCK A FEW TIMES.
GOOD OLD JAY. ALWAYS THERE WHEN YOU NEED HIM.
YOU TAKE A STEP BACK, BREATHE, AND YOU'LL PUT IT TOGETHER.
AND THEN WE'LL GO PUNCH HIS LIGHTS OUT.
TAKE A STEP BACK.
LOOK AT ALL THE PIECES. FIND WHAT I MISSED.
MANHATTAN
OPAL CITY
METROPOLIS
...T-SPHERES: RUN DIAGNOSTIC ON J.S.A. MAINFRAME.
PUNE
BING

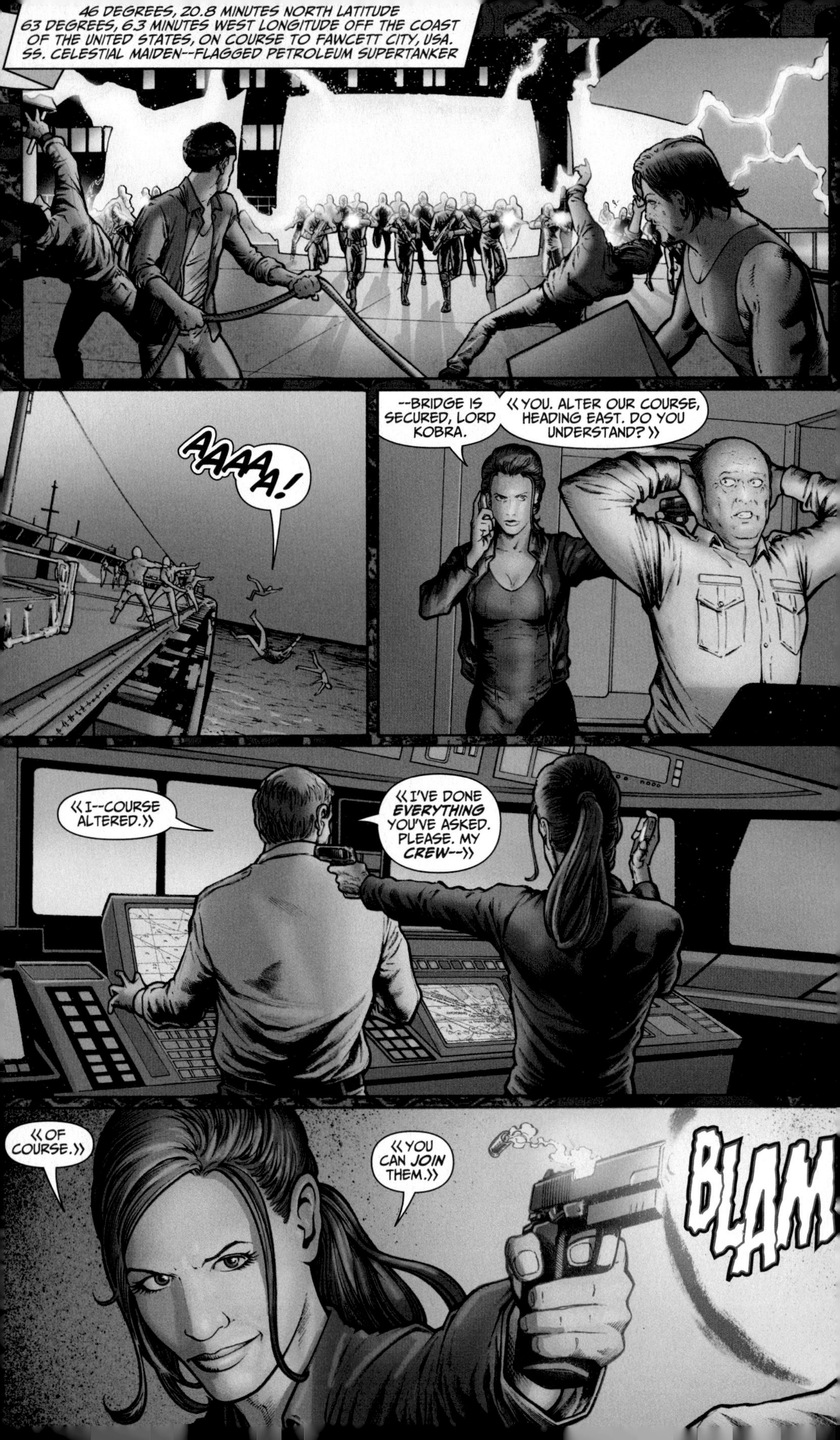
46 DEGREES, 20.8 MINUTES NORTH LATITUDE 63 DEGREES, 6.3 MINUTES WEST LONGITUDE OFF THE COAST OF THE UNITED STATES, ON COURSE TO FAWCETT CITY, USA. SS. CELESTIAL MAIDEN--FLAGGED PETROLEUM SUPERTANKER
AAAAA!
--BRIDGE IS SECURED, LORD KOBRA.
«YOU. ALTER OUR COURSE, HEADING EAST. DO YOU UNDERSTAND?»
«I--COURSE ALTERED.»
«I'VE DONE EVERYTHING YOU'VE ASKED. PLEASE. MY CREW--»
«OF COURSE.»
«YOU CAN JOIN THEM.»
BLAM

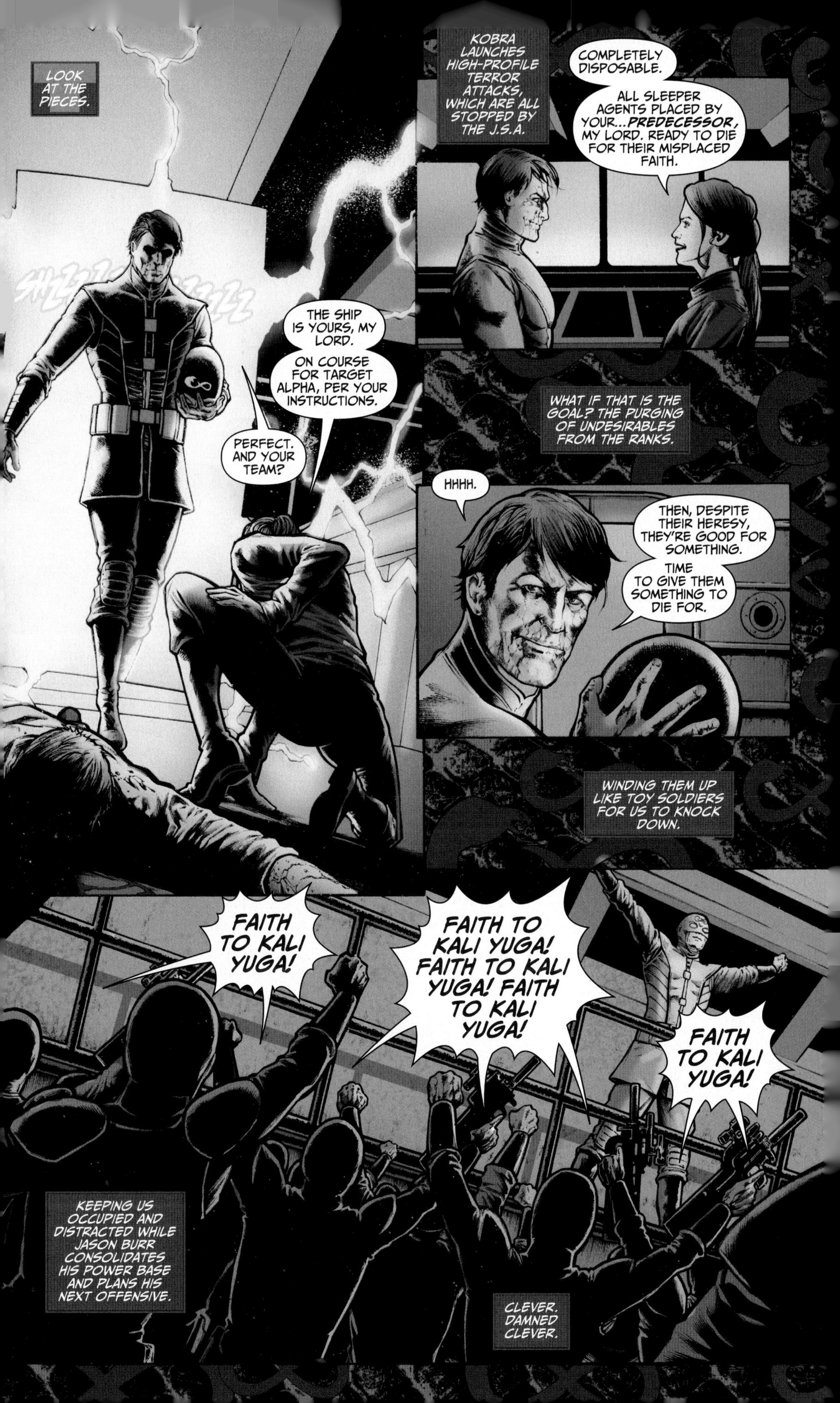

LOOK AT THE PIECES.
THE SHIP IS YOURS, MY LORD.
ON COURSE FOR TARGET ALPHA, PER YOUR INSTRUCTIONS.
PERFECT. AND YOUR TEAM?
KOBRA LAUNCHES HIGH-PROFILE TERROR ATTACKS, WHICH ARE ALL STOPPED BY THE J.S.A.
COMPLETELY DISPOSABLE.
ALL SLEEPER AGENTS PLACED BY YOUR...PREDECESSOR, MY LORD. READY TO DIE FOR THEIR MISPLACED FAITH.
WHAT IF THAT IS THE GOAL? THE PURGING OF UNDESIRABLES FROM THE RANKS.
HHHH.
THEN, DESPITE THEIR HERESY, THEY'RE GOOD FOR SOMETHING.
TIME TO GIVE THEM SOMETHING TO DIE FOR.
WINDING THEM UP LIKE TOY SOLDIERS FOR US TO KNOCK DOWN.
FAITH TO KALI YUGA!
FAITH TO KALI YUGA! FAITH TO KALI YUGA! FAITH TO KALI YUGA!
FAITH TO KALI YUGA!
KEEPING US OCCUPIED AND DISTRACTED WHILE JASON BURR CONSOLIDATES HIS POWER BASE AND PLANS HIS NEXT OFFENSIVE.
CLEVER. DAMNED CLEVER.

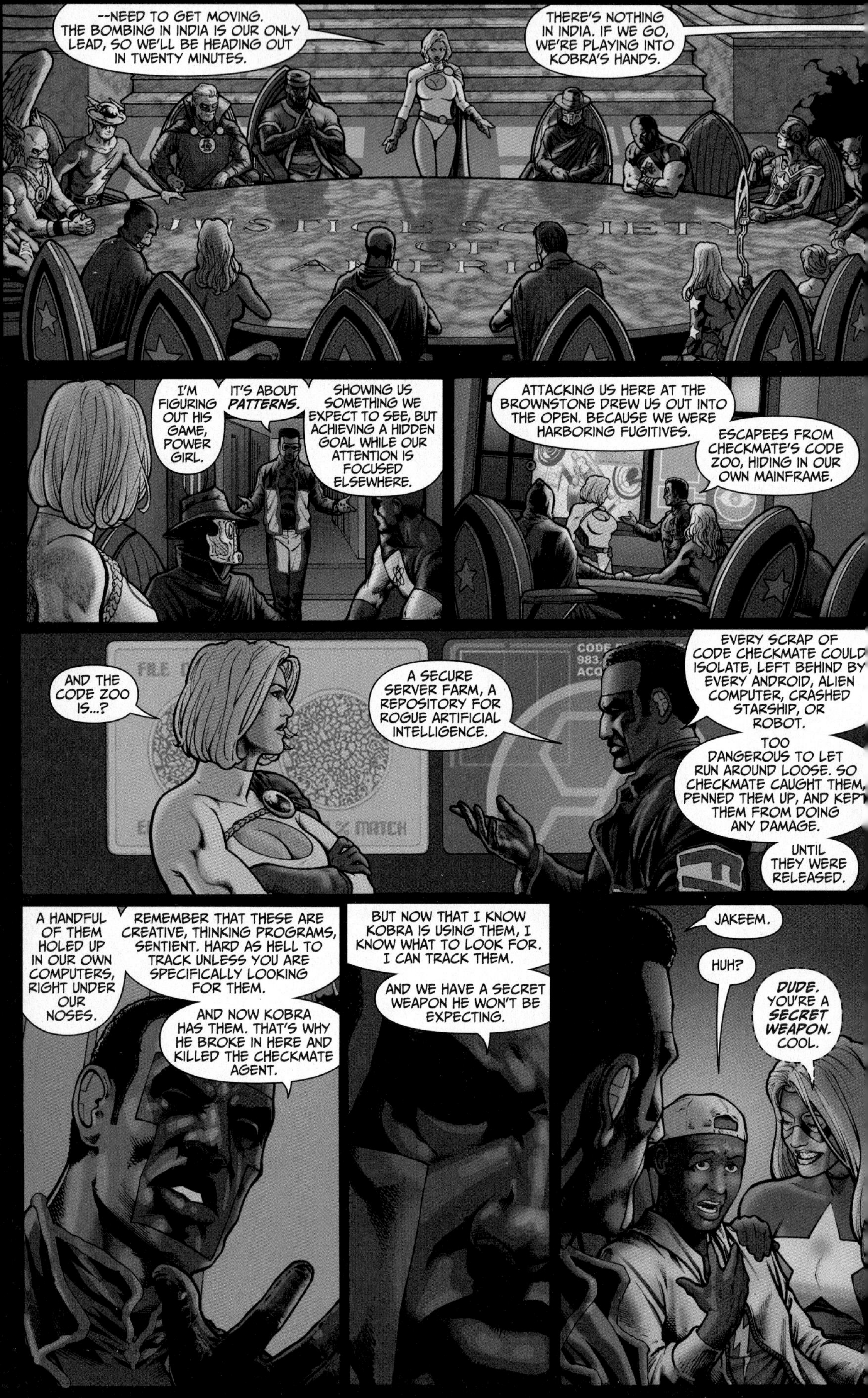

--NEED TO GET MOVING. THE BOMBING IN INDIA IS OUR ONLY LEAD, SO WE'LL BE HEADING OUT IN TWENTY MINUTES.
THERE'S NOTHING IN INDIA. IF WE GO, WE'RE PLAYING INTO KOBRA'S HANDS.
JUSTICE SOCIETY OF AMERICA
I'M FIGURING OUT HIS GAME, POWER GIRL.
IT'S ABOUT *PATTERNS.*
SHOWING US SOMETHING WE EXPECT TO SEE, BUT ACHIEVING A HIDDEN GOAL WHILE OUR ATTENTION IS FOCUSED ELSEWHERE.
ATTACKING US HERE AT THE BROWNSTONE DREW US OUT INTO THE OPEN. BECAUSE WE WERE HARBORING FUGITIVES.
ESCAPEES FROM CHECKMATE'S CODE ZOO, HIDING IN OUR OWN MAINFRAME.
AND THE CODE ZOO IS...?
A SECURE SERVER FARM, A REPOSITORY FOR ROGUE ARTIFICIAL INTELLIGENCE.
EVERY SCRAP OF CODE CHECKMATE COULD ISOLATE, LEFT BEHIND BY EVERY ANDROID, ALIEN COMPUTER, CRASHED STARSHIP, OR ROBOT.
TOO DANGEROUS TO LET RUN AROUND LOOSE. SO CHECKMATE CAUGHT THEM, PENNED THEM UP, AND KEPT THEM FROM DOING ANY DAMAGE.
UNTIL THEY WERE RELEASED.
A HANDFUL OF THEM HOLED UP IN OUR OWN COMPUTERS, RIGHT UNDER OUR NOSES.
REMEMBER THAT THESE ARE CREATIVE, THINKING PROGRAMS, SENTIENT. HARD AS HELL TO TRACK UNLESS YOU ARE SPECIFICALLY LOOKING FOR THEM.
AND NOW KOBRA HAS THEM. THAT'S WHY HE BROKE IN HERE AND KILLED THE CHECKMATE AGENT.
BUT NOW THAT I KNOW KOBRA IS USING THEM, I KNOW WHAT TO LOOK FOR. I CAN TRACK THEM.
AND WE HAVE A SECRET WEAPON HE WON'T BE EXPECTING.
JAKEEM.
HUH?
DUDE. YOU'RE A *SECRET WEAPON.* COOL.

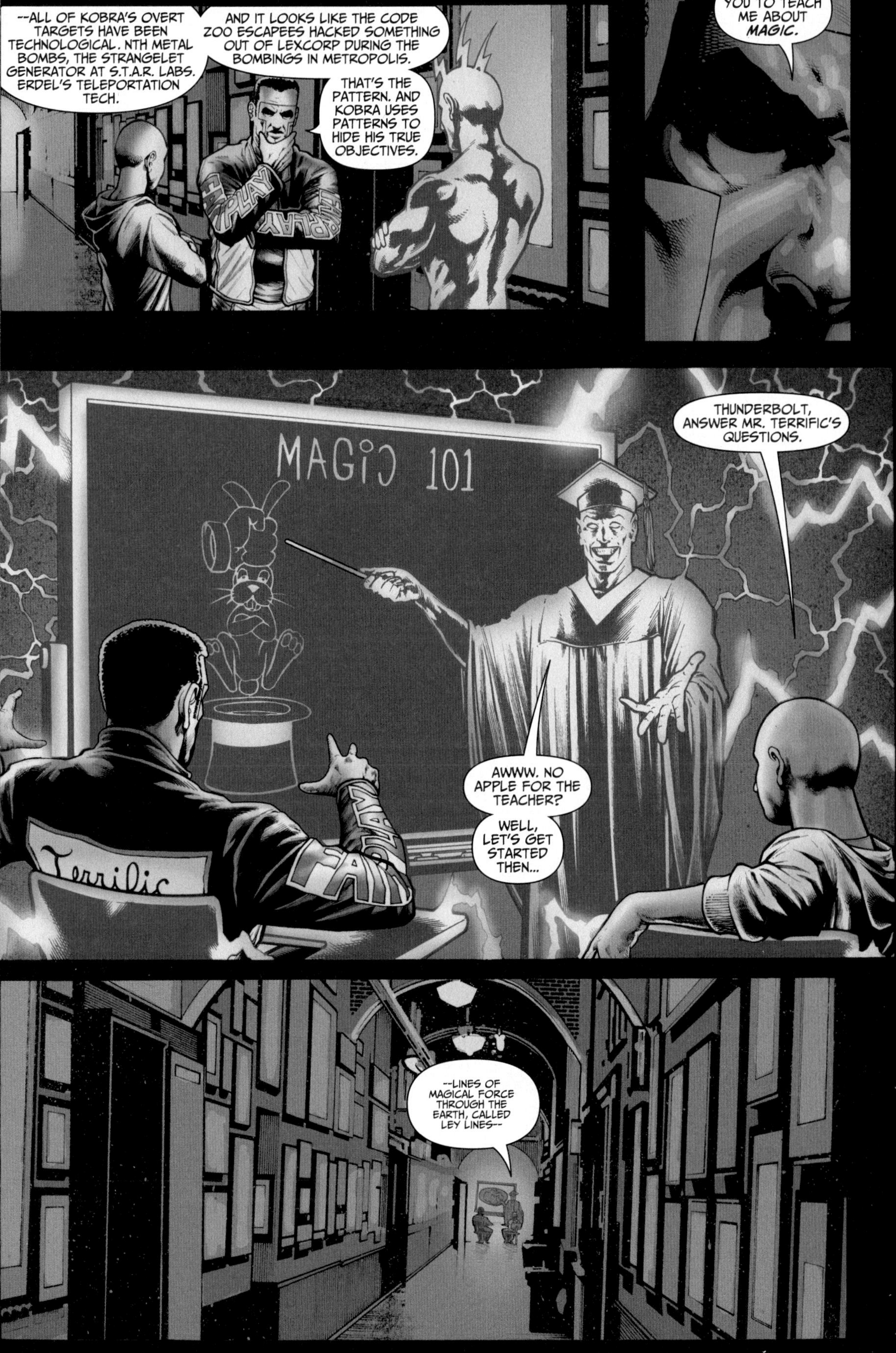
--ALL OF KOBRA'S OVERT TARGETS HAVE BEEN TECHNOLOGICAL. NTH METAL BOMBS, THE STRANGELET GENERATOR AT S.T.A.R. LABS. ERDEL'S TELEPORTATION TECH.
AND IT LOOKS LIKE THE CODE ZOO ESCAPEES HACKED SOMETHING OUT OF LEXCORP DURING THE BOMBINGS IN METROPOLIS.
THAT'S THE PATTERN. AND KOBRA USES PATTERNS TO HIDE HIS TRUE OBJECTIVES.
SO I WANT YOU TO TEACH ME ABOUT *MAGIC.*
MAGIC 101
THUNDERBOLT, ANSWER MR. TERRIFIC'S QUESTIONS.
AWWW. NO APPLE FOR THE TEACHER?
WELL, LET'S GET STARTED THEN...
--LINES OF MAGICAL FORCE THROUGH THE EARTH, CALLED LEY LINES--

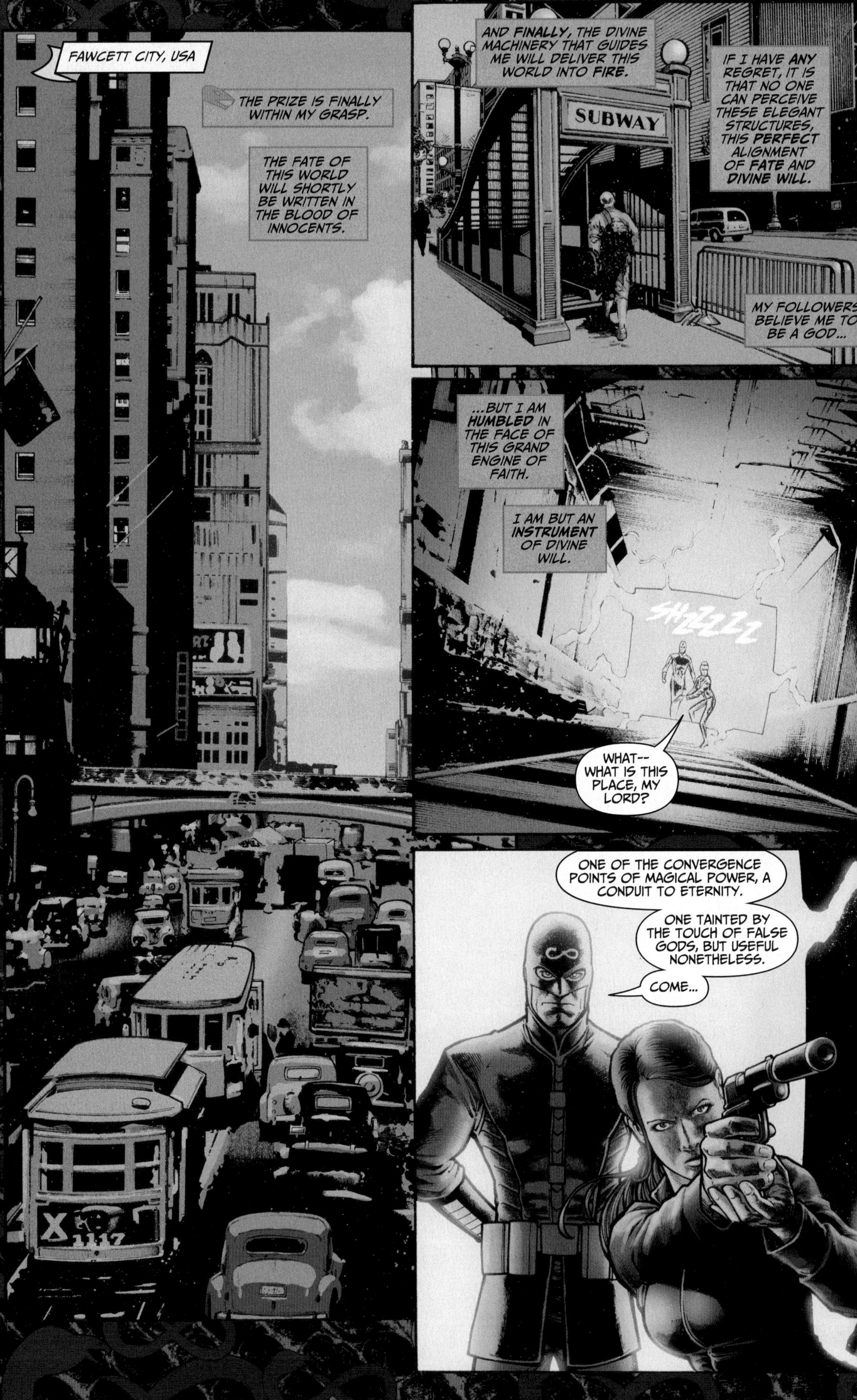
FAWCETT CITY, USA
THE PRIZE IS FINALLY WITHIN MY GRASP.
THE FATE OF THIS WORLD WILL SHORTLY BE WRITTEN IN THE BLOOD OF INNOCENTS.
AND FINALLY, THE DIVINE MACHINERY THAT GUIDES ME WILL DELIVER THIS WORLD INTO FIRE.
SUBWAY
IF I HAVE ANY REGRET, IT IS THAT NO ONE CAN PERCEIVE THESE ELEGANT STRUCTURES, THIS PERFECT ALIGNMENT OF FATE AND DIVINE WILL.
MY FOLLOWERS BELIEVE ME TO BE A GOD...
...BUT I AM HUMBLED IN THE FACE OF THIS GRAND ENGINE OF FAITH.
I AM BUT AN INSTRUMENT OF DIVINE WILL.
SHZZZZZ
WHAT-- WHAT IS THIS PLACE, MY LORD?
ONE OF THE CONVERGENCE POINTS OF MAGICAL POWER, A CONDUIT TO ETERNITY.
ONE TAINTED BY THE TOUCH OF FALSE GODS, BUT USEFUL NONETHELESS.
COME...
X 1117

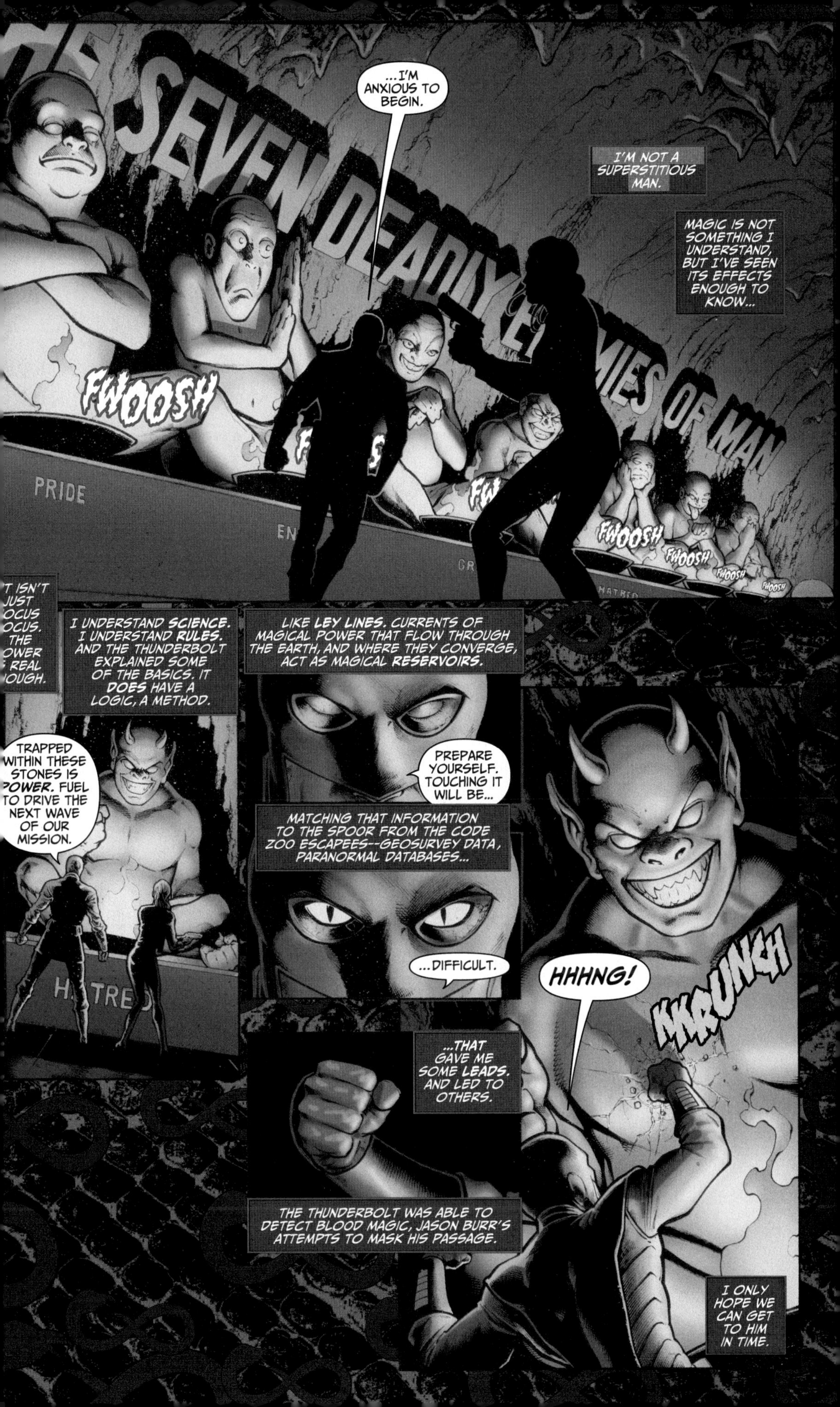

HE SEVEN DEADLY
MIES OF MAN
...I'M ANXIOUS TO BEGIN.
I'M NOT A SUPERSTITIOUS MAN.
MAGIC IS NOT SOMETHING I UNDERSTAND, BUT I'VE SEEN ITS EFFECTS ENOUGH TO KNOW...
FWOOSH
PRIDE
FWOOSH
FWOOSH
FWOOSH
FWOOSH
T ISN'T JUST OCUS OCUS. THE OWER REAL OUGH.
I UNDERSTAND SCIENCE. I UNDERSTAND RULES. AND THE THUNDERBOLT EXPLAINED SOME OF THE BASICS. IT DOES HAVE A LOGIC, A METHOD.
TRAPPED WITHIN THESE STONES IS POWER. FUEL TO DRIVE THE NEXT WAVE OF OUR MISSION.
LIKE LEY LINES. CURRENTS OF MAGICAL POWER THAT FLOW THROUGH THE EARTH, AND WHERE THEY CONVERGE, ACT AS MAGICAL RESERVOIRS.
PREPARE YOURSELF. TOUCHING IT WILL BE...
MATCHING THAT INFORMATION TO THE SPOOR FROM THE CODE ZOO ESCAPEES--GEOSURVEY DATA, PARANORMAL DATABASES...
...DIFFICULT.
HHHNG!
KKRUNCH
...THAT GAVE ME SOME LEADS. AND LED TO OTHERS.
THE THUNDERBOLT WAS ABLE TO DETECT BLOOD MAGIC, JASON BURR'S ATTEMPTS TO MASK HIS PASSAGE.
I ONLY HOPE WE CAN GET TO HIM IN TIME.

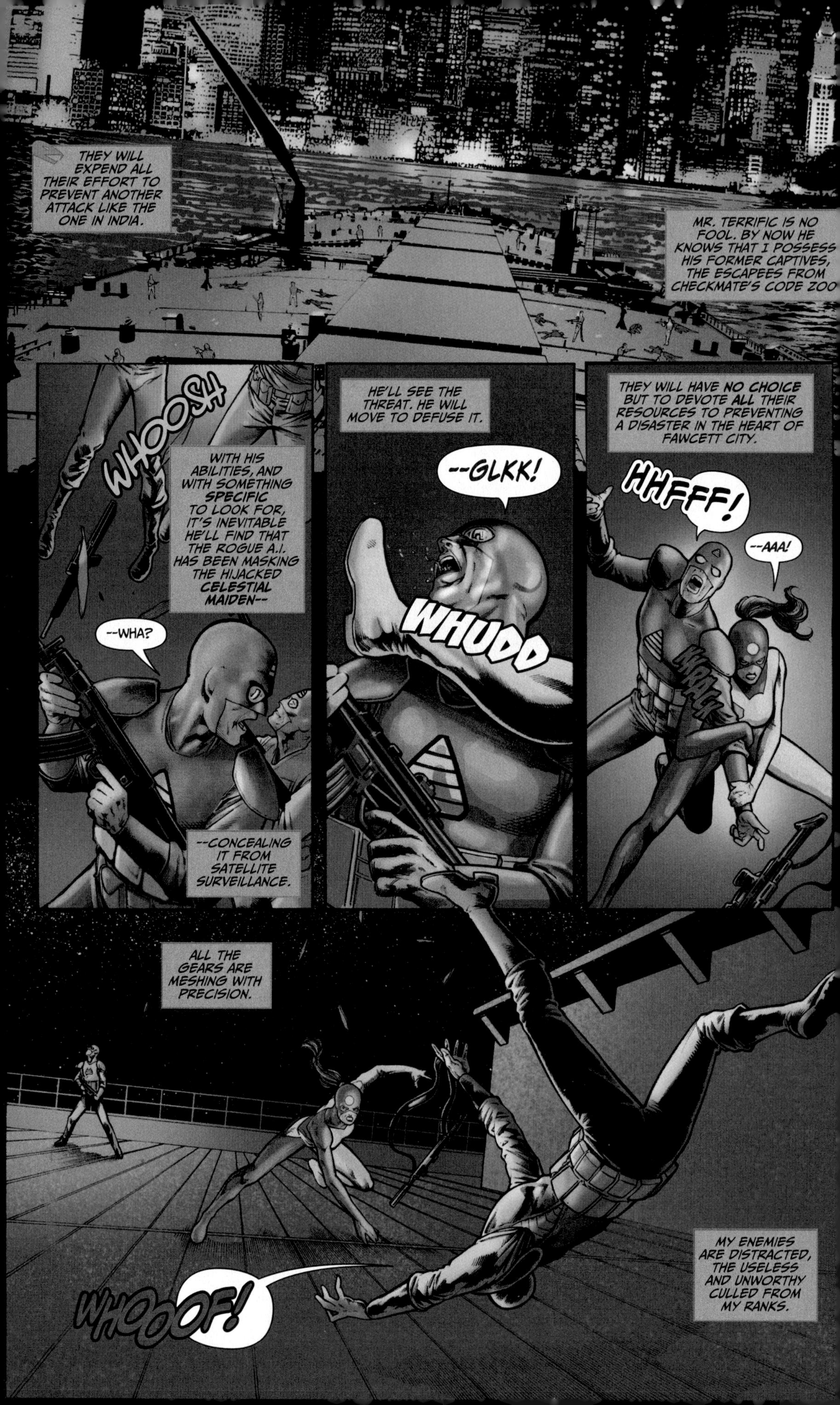
THEY WILL EXPEND ALL THEIR EFFORT TO PREVENT ANOTHER ATTACK LIKE THE ONE IN INDIA.
MR. TERRIFIC IS NO FOOL. BY NOW HE KNOWS THAT I POSSESS HIS FORMER CAPTIVES, THE ESCAPEES FROM CHECKMATE'S CODE ZOO
WHOOSH
WITH HIS ABILITIES, AND WITH SOMETHING SPECIFIC TO LOOK FOR, IT'S INEVITABLE HE'LL FIND THAT THE ROGUE A.I. HAS BEEN MASKING THE HIJACKED CELESTIAL MAIDEN--
--WHA?
--CONCEALING IT FROM SATELLITE SURVEILLANCE.
HE'LL SEE THE THREAT. HE WILL MOVE TO DEFUSE IT.
--GLKK!
WHUDD
THEY WILL HAVE NO CHOICE BUT TO DEVOTE ALL THEIR RESOURCES TO PREVENTING A DISASTER IN THE HEART OF FAWCETT CITY.
HHFFFF!
--AAA!
WKRACK
ALL THE GEARS ARE MESHING WITH PRECISION.
MY ENEMIES ARE DISTRACTED, THE USELESS AND UNWORTHY CULLED FROM MY RANKS.
WHOOOF!

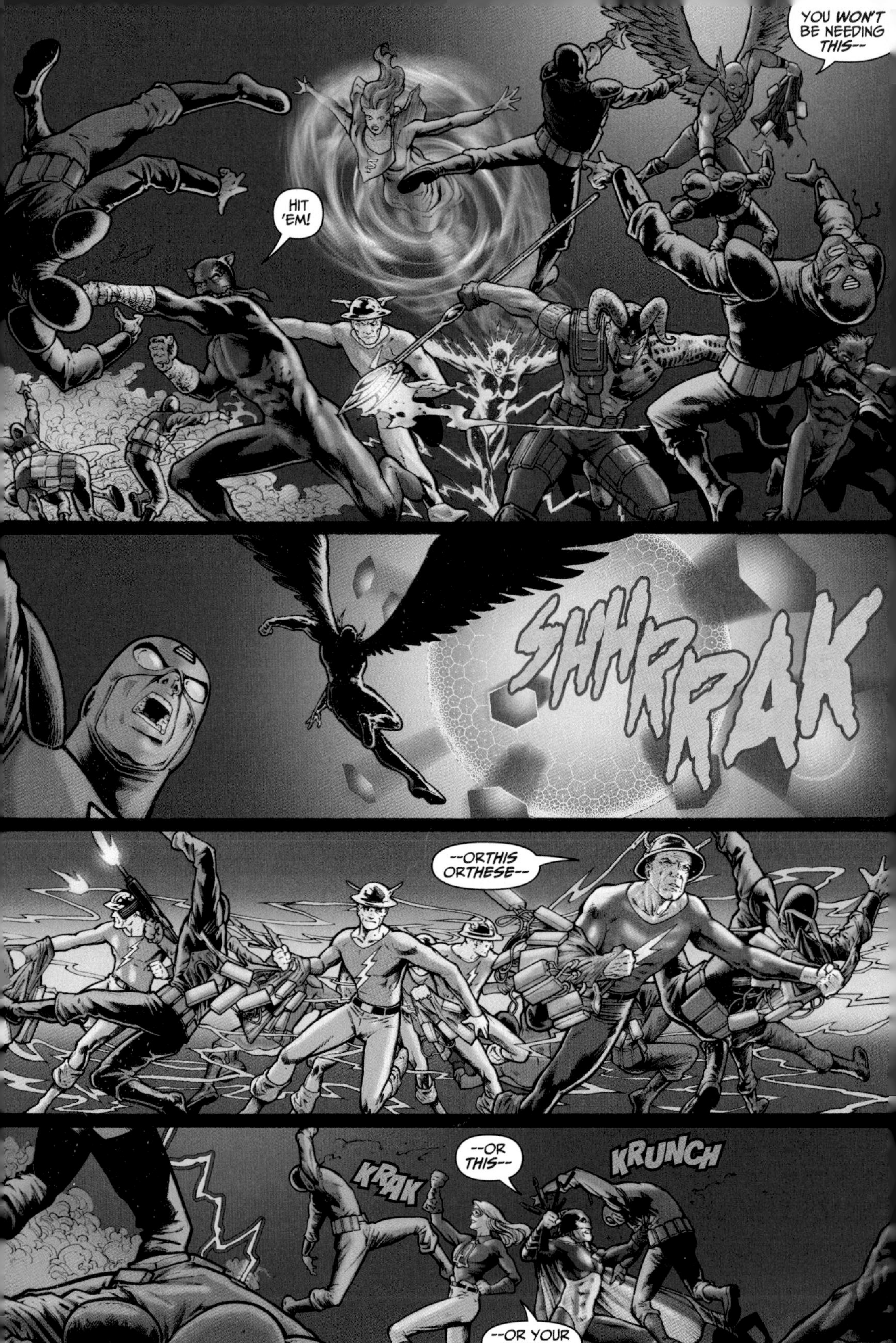
YOU WON'T BE NEEDING THIS--
HIT 'EM!
SHHRRAK
--OR THIS OR THESE--
KRAK
--OR THIS--
KRUNCH
--OR YOUR TEETH--

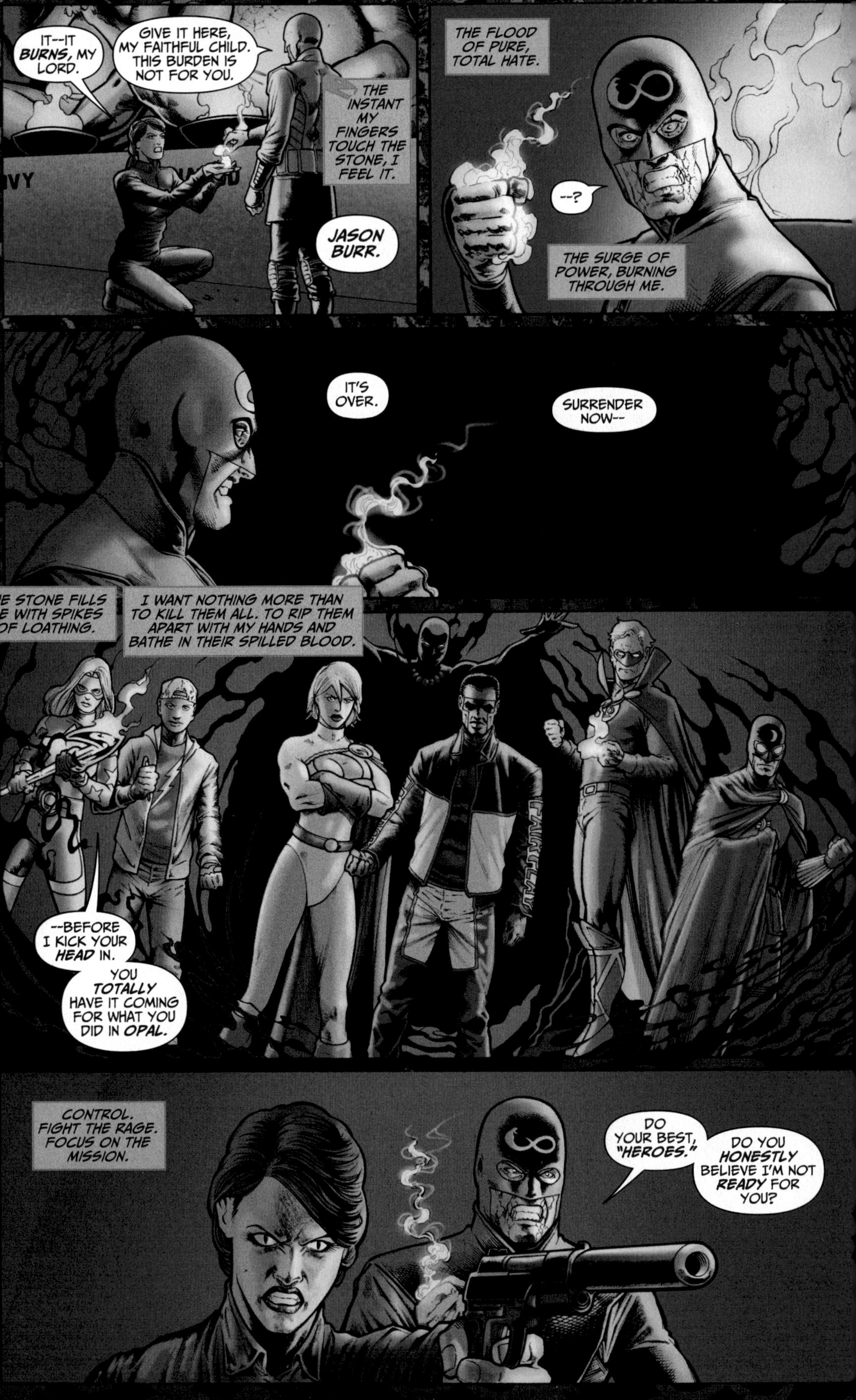
IT--IT BURNS, MY LORD.
GIVE IT HERE, MY FAITHFUL CHILD. THIS BURDEN IS NOT FOR YOU.
THE INSTANT MY FINGERS TOUCH THE STONE, I FEEL IT.
JASON BURR.
THE FLOOD OF PURE, TOTAL HATE.
--?
THE SURGE OF POWER, BURNING THROUGH ME.
IT'S OVER.
SURRENDER NOW--
THE STONE FILLS ME WITH SPIKES OF LOATHING.
I WANT NOTHING MORE THAN TO KILL THEM ALL. TO RIP THEM APART WITH MY HANDS AND BATHE IN THEIR SPILLED BLOOD.
--BEFORE I KICK YOUR HEAD IN.
YOU TOTALLY HAVE IT COMING FOR WHAT YOU DID IN OPAL.
CONTROL. FIGHT THE RAGE. FOCUS ON THE MISSION.
DO YOUR BEST, "HEROES."
DO YOU HONESTLY BELIEVE I'M NOT READY FOR YOU?

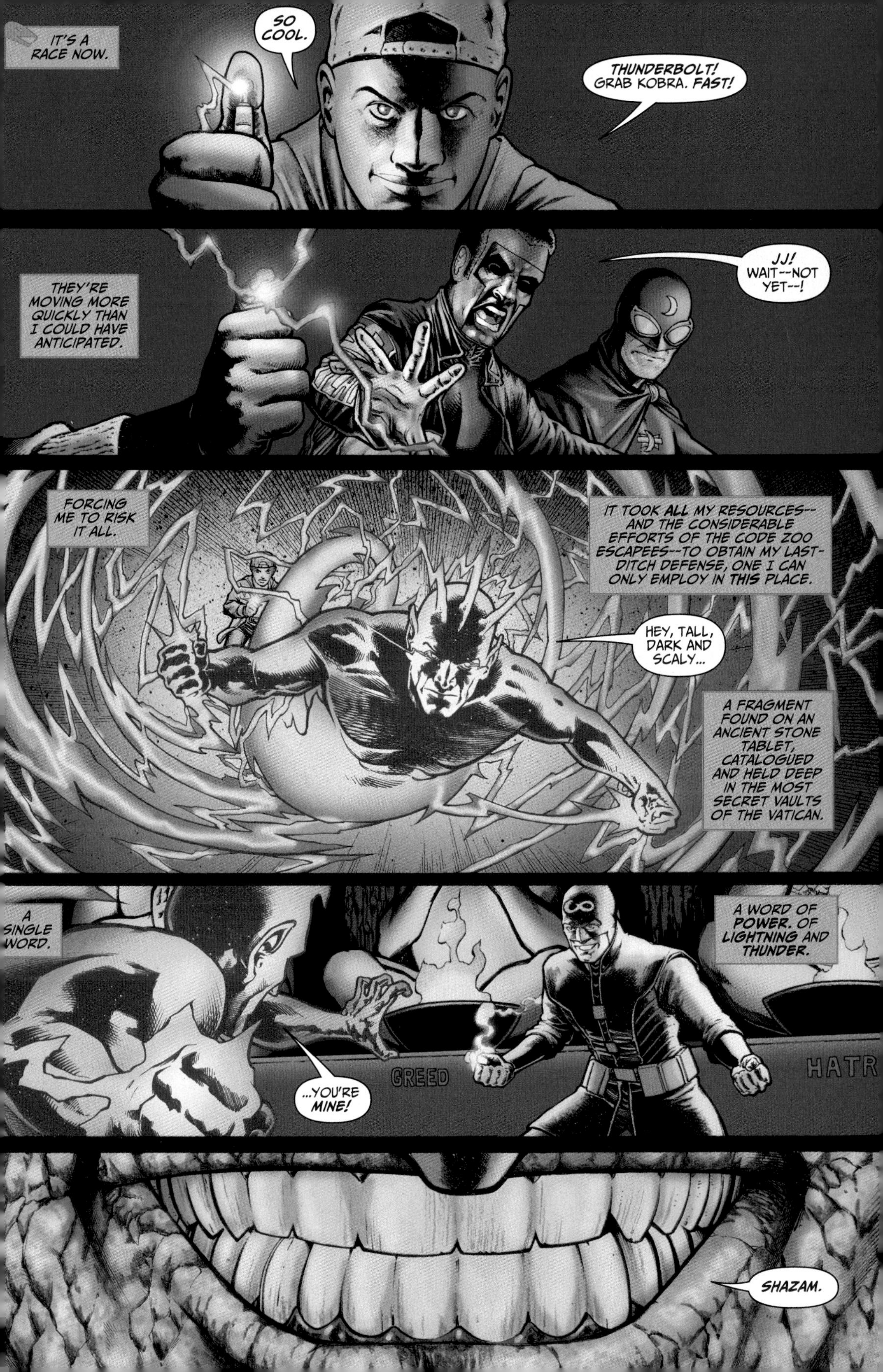
IT'S A RACE NOW.
SO COOL.
THUNDERBOLT! GRAB KOBRA. FAST!
THEY'RE MOVING MORE QUICKLY THAN I COULD HAVE ANTICIPATED.
JJ! WAIT--NOT YET--!
FORCING ME TO RISK IT ALL.
IT TOOK ALL MY RESOURCES--AND THE CONSIDERABLE EFFORTS OF THE CODE ZOO ESCAPEES--TO OBTAIN MY LAST-DITCH DEFENSE, ONE I CAN ONLY EMPLOY IN THIS PLACE.
HEY, TALL, DARK AND SCALY...
A FRAGMENT FOUND ON AN ANCIENT STONE TABLET, CATALOGUED AND HELD DEEP IN THE MOST SECRET VAULTS OF THE VATICAN.
A SINGLE WORD.
A WORD OF POWER. OF LIGHTNING AND THUNDER.
GREED
HATR
...YOU'RE MINE!
SHAZAM.

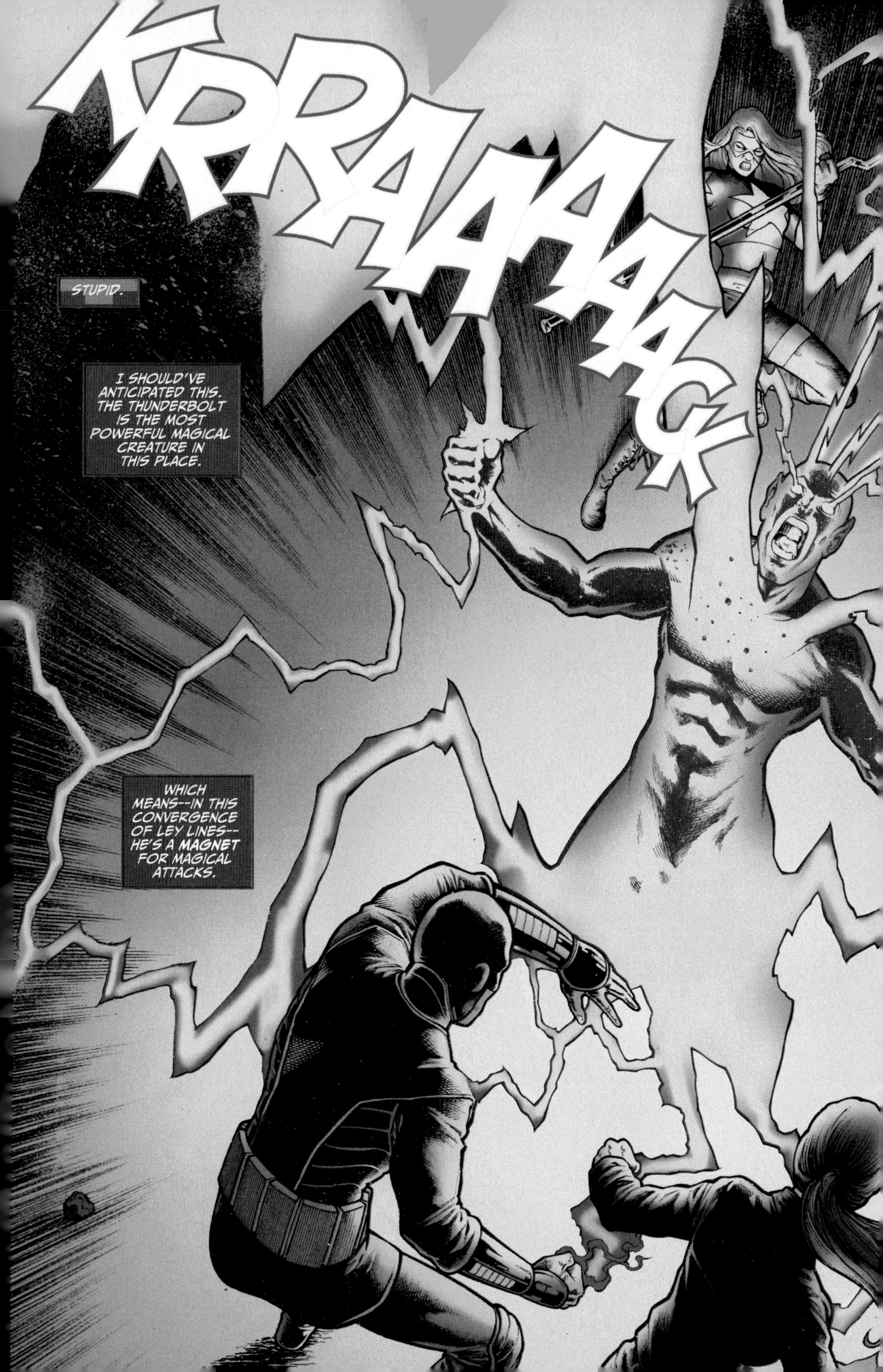
KRRAAAAACK
STUPID.
I SHOULD'VE ANTICIPATED THIS. THE THUNDERBOLT IS THE MOST POWERFUL MAGICAL CREATURE IN THIS PLACE.
WHICH MEANS--IN THIS CONVERGENCE OF LEY LINES--HE'S A MAGNET FOR MAGICAL ATTACKS.

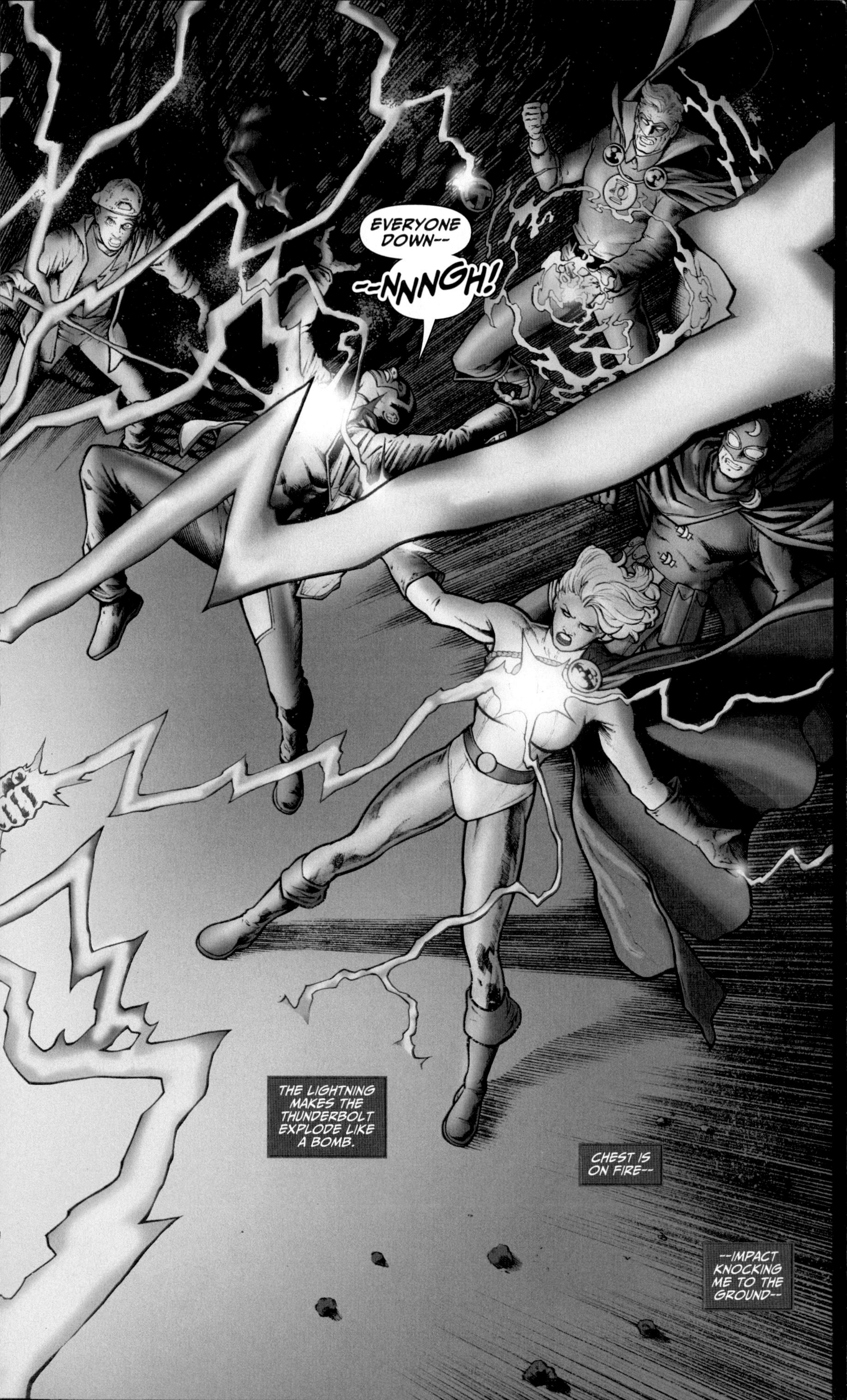
EVERYONE DOWN--
--NNNGH!
THE LIGHTNING MAKES THE THUNDERBOLT EXPLODE LIKE A BOMB.
CHEST IS ON FIRE--
--IMPACT KNOCKING ME TO THE GROUND--

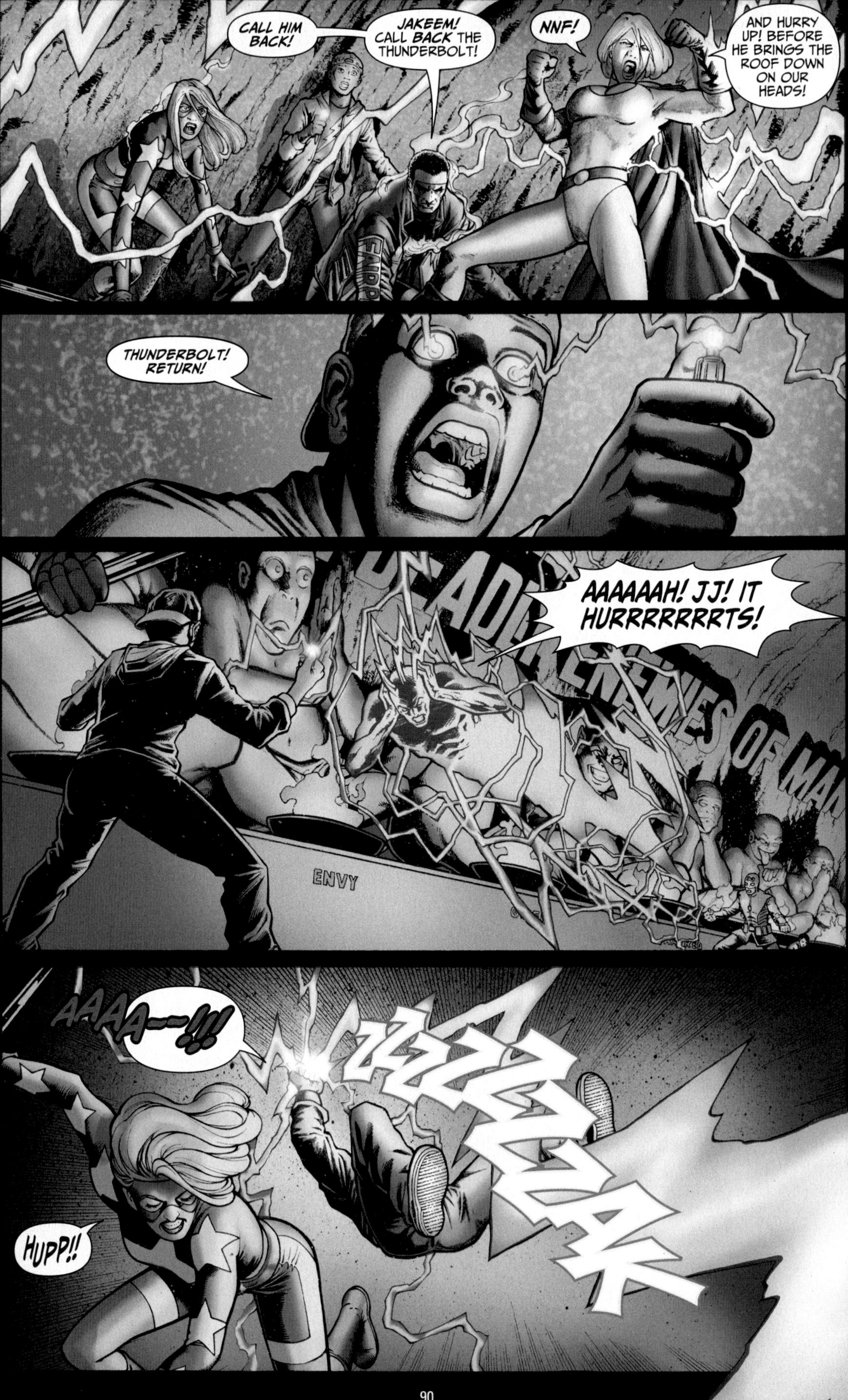

CALL HIM BACK!
JAKEEM! CALL BACK THE THUNDERBOLT!
NNF!
AND HURRY UP! BEFORE HE BRINGS THE ROOF DOWN ON OUR HEADS!
THUNDERBOLT! RETURN!
AAAAAAH! JJ! IT HURRRRRRRTS!
ENVY
AAAA--!!!
ZZZZZZAK
HUPP!!

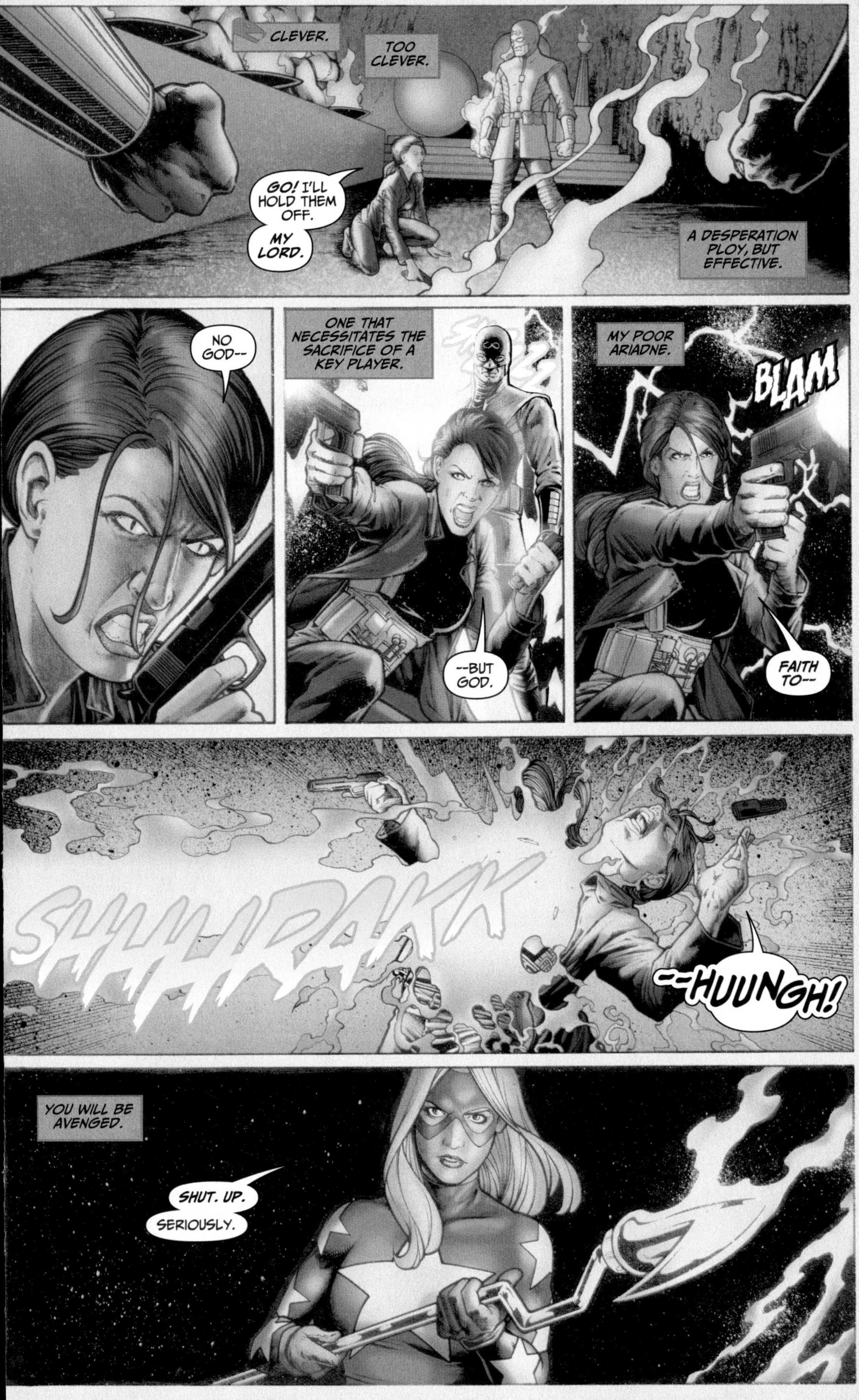
CLEVER.
TOO CLEVER.
GO! I'LL HOLD THEM OFF.
MY LORD.
A DESPERATION PLOY, BUT EFFECTIVE.
NO GOD--
ONE THAT NECESSITATES THE SACRIFICE OF A KEY PLAYER.
--BUT GOD.
MY POOR ARIADNE.
BLAM
FAITH TO--
SHHRAKK
--HUUNGH!
YOU WILL BE AVENGED.
SHUT. UP.
SERIOUSLY.

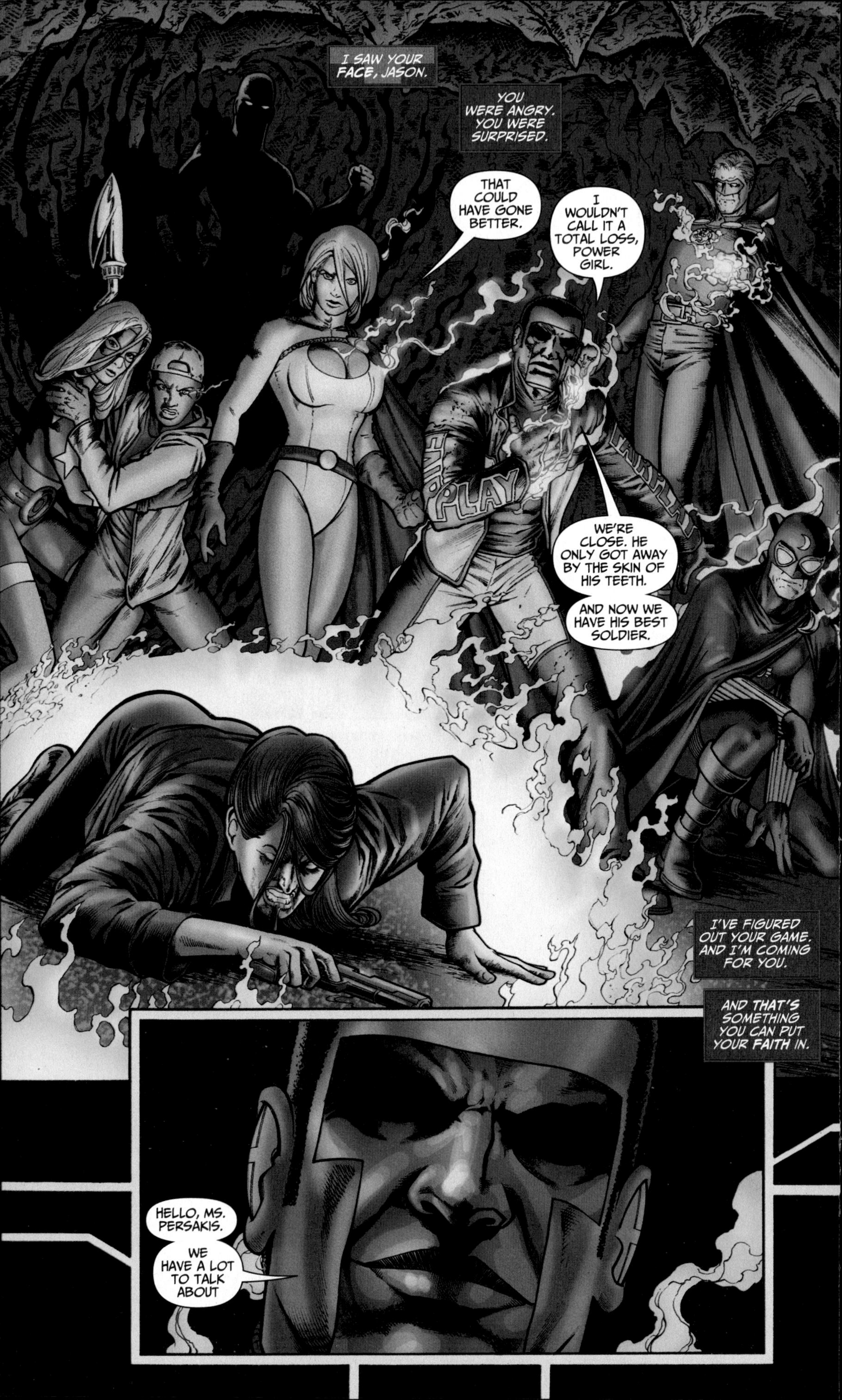
I SAW YOUR FACE, JASON.
YOU WERE ANGRY. YOU WERE SURPRISED.
THAT COULD HAVE GONE BETTER.
I WOULDN'T CALL IT A TOTAL LOSS, POWER GIRL.
WE'RE CLOSE. HE ONLY GOT AWAY BY THE SKIN OF HIS TEETH.
AND NOW WE HAVE HIS BEST SOLDIER.
I'VE FIGURED OUT YOUR GAME. AND I'M COMING FOR YOU.
AND THAT'S SOMETHING YOU CAN PUT YOUR FAITH IN.
HELLO, MS. PERSAKIS.
WE HAVE A LOT TO TALK ABOUT

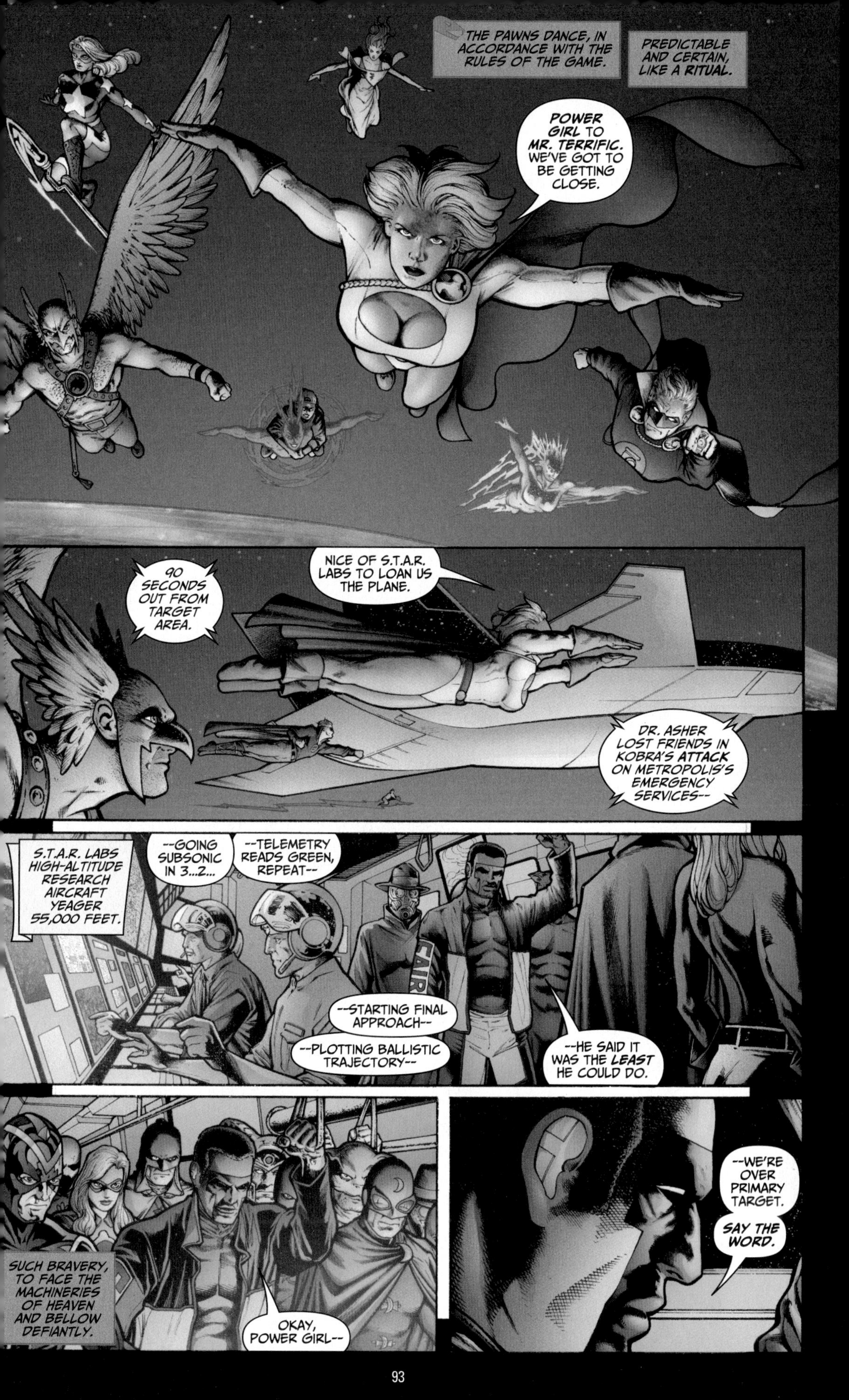

THE PAWNS DANCE, IN ACCORDANCE WITH THE RULES OF THE GAME.
PREDICTABLE AND CERTAIN, LIKE A RITUAL.
POWER GIRL TO MR. TERRIFIC. WE'VE GOT TO BE GETTING CLOSE.
90 SECONDS OUT FROM TARGET AREA.
NICE OF S.T.A.R. LABS TO LOAN US THE PLANE.
DR. ASHER LOST FRIENDS IN KOBRA'S ATTACK ON METROPOLIS'S EMERGENCY SERVICES--
S.T.A.R. LABS HIGH-ALTITUDE RESEARCH AIRCRAFT YEAGER 55,000 FEET.
--GOING SUBSONIC IN 3...2...
--TELEMETRY READS GREEN, REPEAT--
--STARTING FINAL APPROACH--
--PLOTTING BALLISTIC TRAJECTORY--
--HE SAID IT WAS THE LEAST HE COULD DO.
SUCH BRAVERY, TO FACE THE MACHINERIES OF HEAVEN AND BELLOW DEFIANTLY.
OKAY, POWER GIRL--
--WE'RE OVER PRIMARY TARGET.
SAY THE WORD.

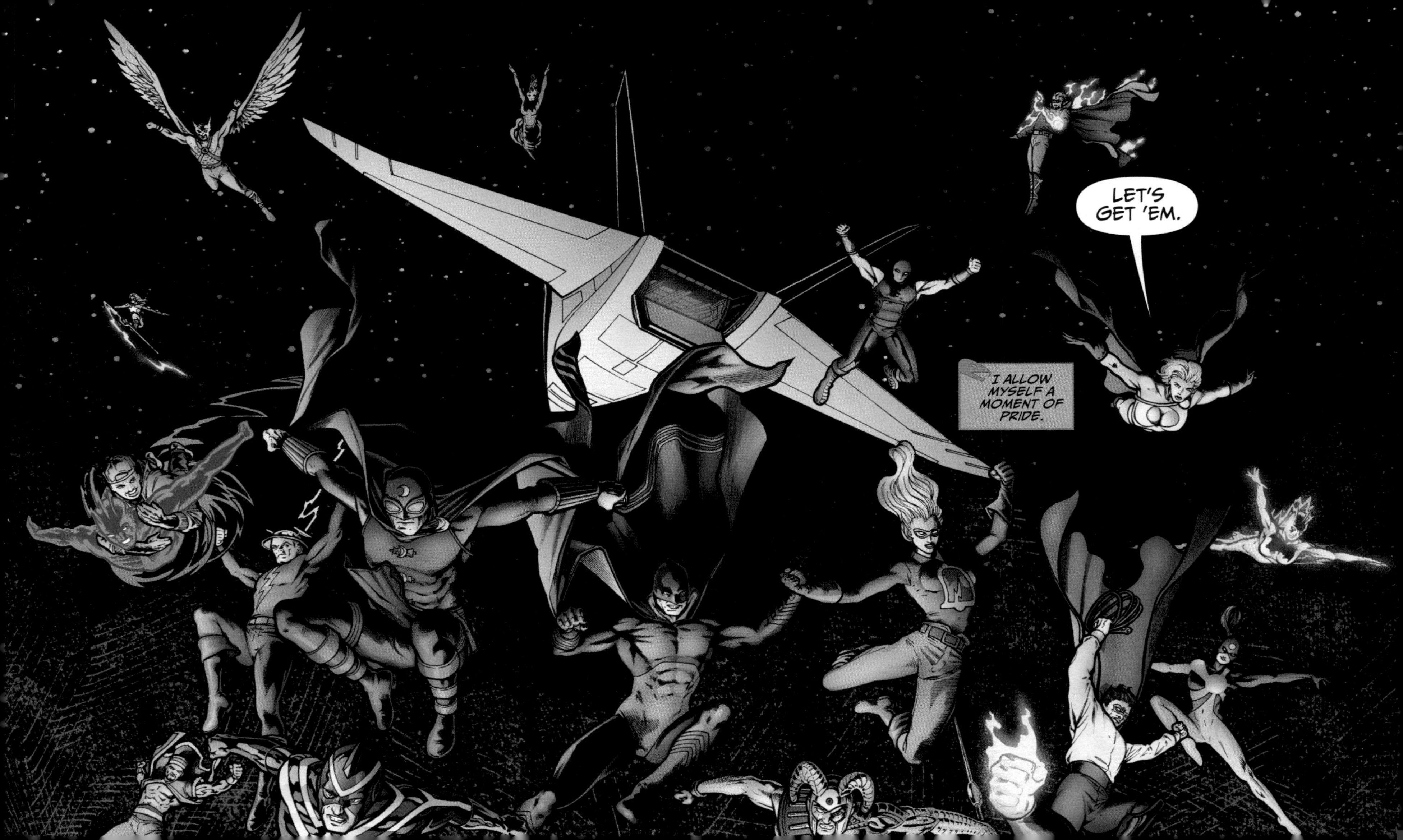
I ALLOW MYSELF A MOMENT OF PRIDE.
LET'S GET 'EM.

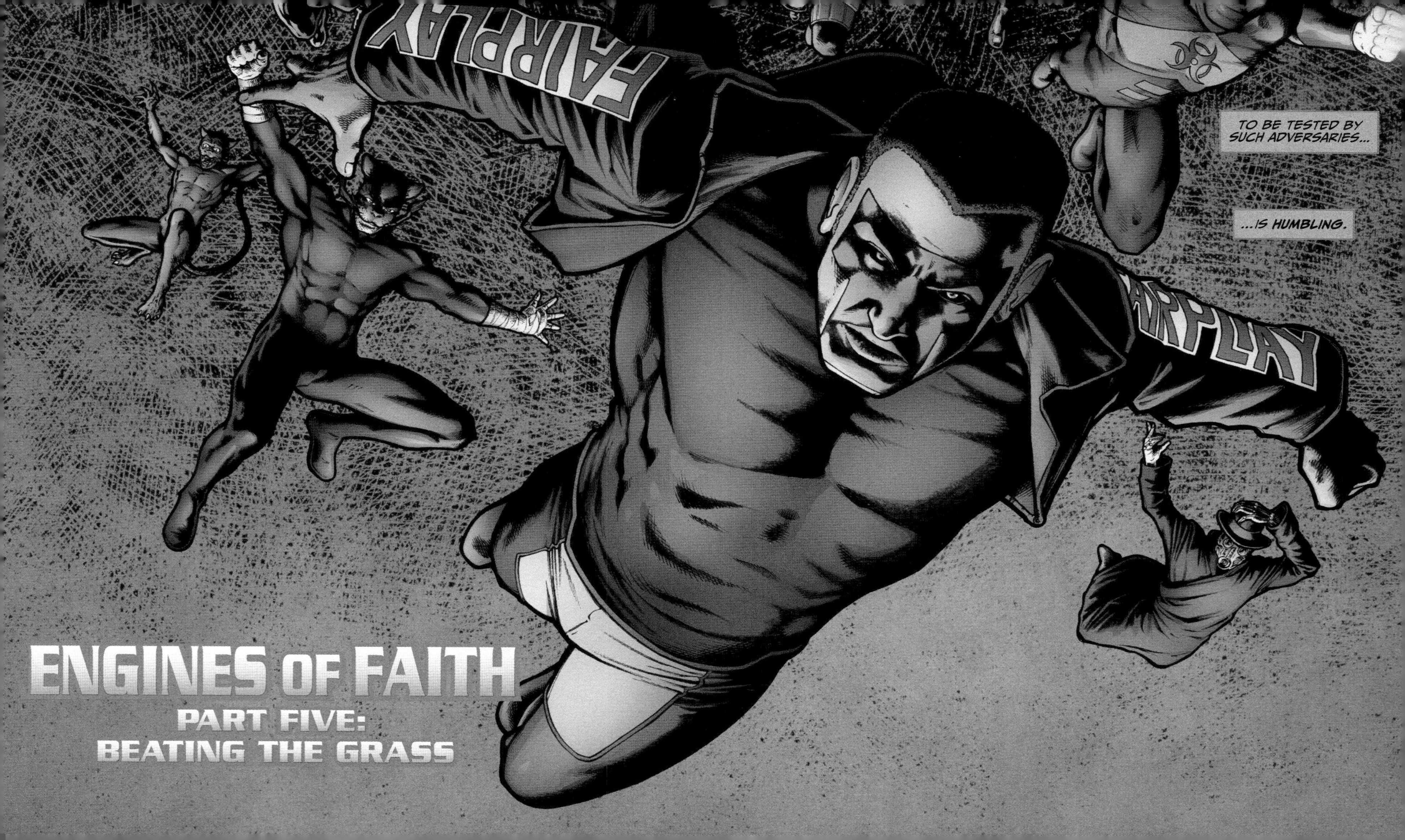
TO BE TESTED BY SUCH ADVERSARIES...
...IS HUMBLING.
FAIRPLAY
FAIRPLAY
ENGINES OF FAITH
PART FIVE:
BEATING THE GRASS

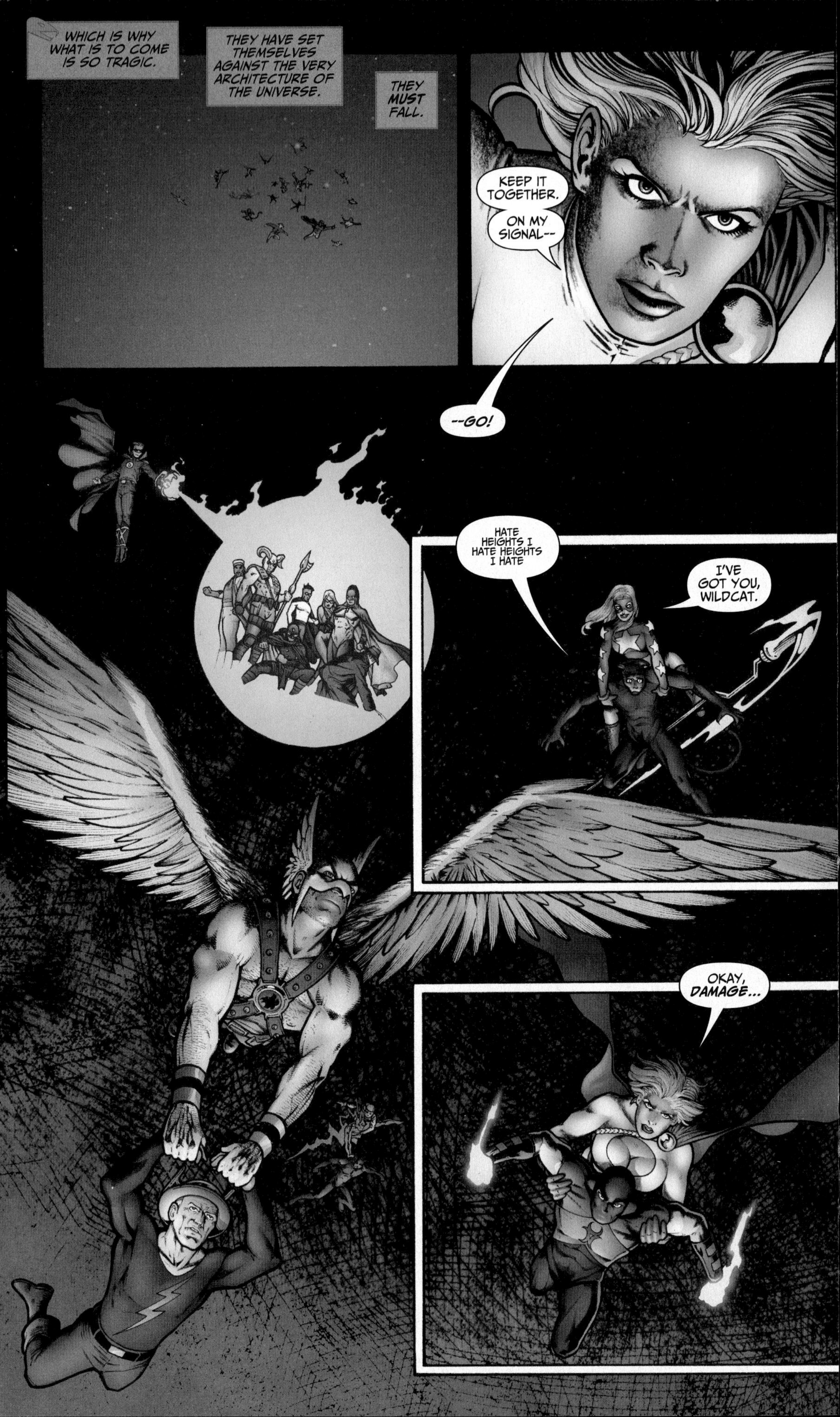
WHICH IS WHY WHAT IS TO COME IS SO TRAGIC.
THEY HAVE SET THEMSELVES AGAINST THE VERY ARCHITECTURE OF THE UNIVERSE.
THEY MUST FALL.
KEEP IT TOGETHER.
ON MY SIGNAL--
--GO!
HATE HEIGHTS I HATE HEIGHTS I HATE
I'VE GOT YOU, WILDCAT.
OKAY, DAMAGE...

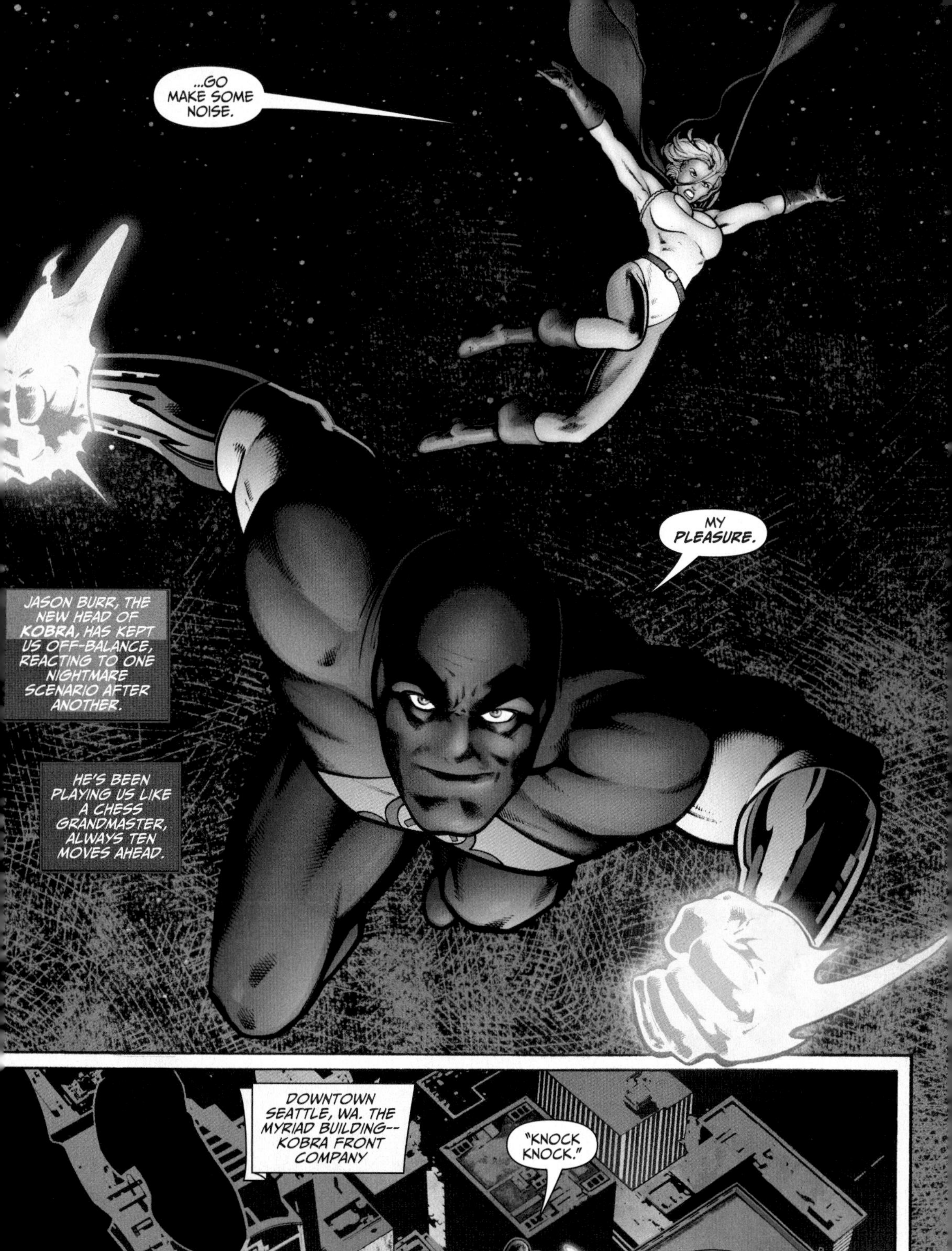
...GO MAKE SOME NOISE.
MY PLEASURE.
JASON BURR, THE NEW HEAD OF KOBRA, HAS KEPT US OFF-BALANCE, REACTING TO ONE NIGHTMARE SCENARIO AFTER ANOTHER.
HE'S BEEN PLAYING US LIKE A CHESS GRANDMASTER, ALWAYS TEN MOVES AHEAD.

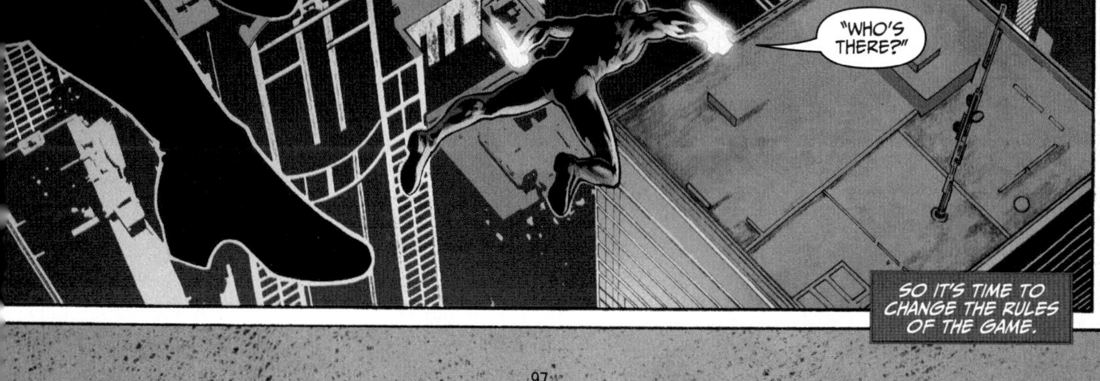
DOWNTOWN SEATTLE, WA. THE MYRIAD BUILDING-- KOBRA FRONT COMPANY
"KNOCK KNOCK."
"WHO'S THERE?"
SO IT'S TIME TO CHANGE THE RULES OF THE GAME.

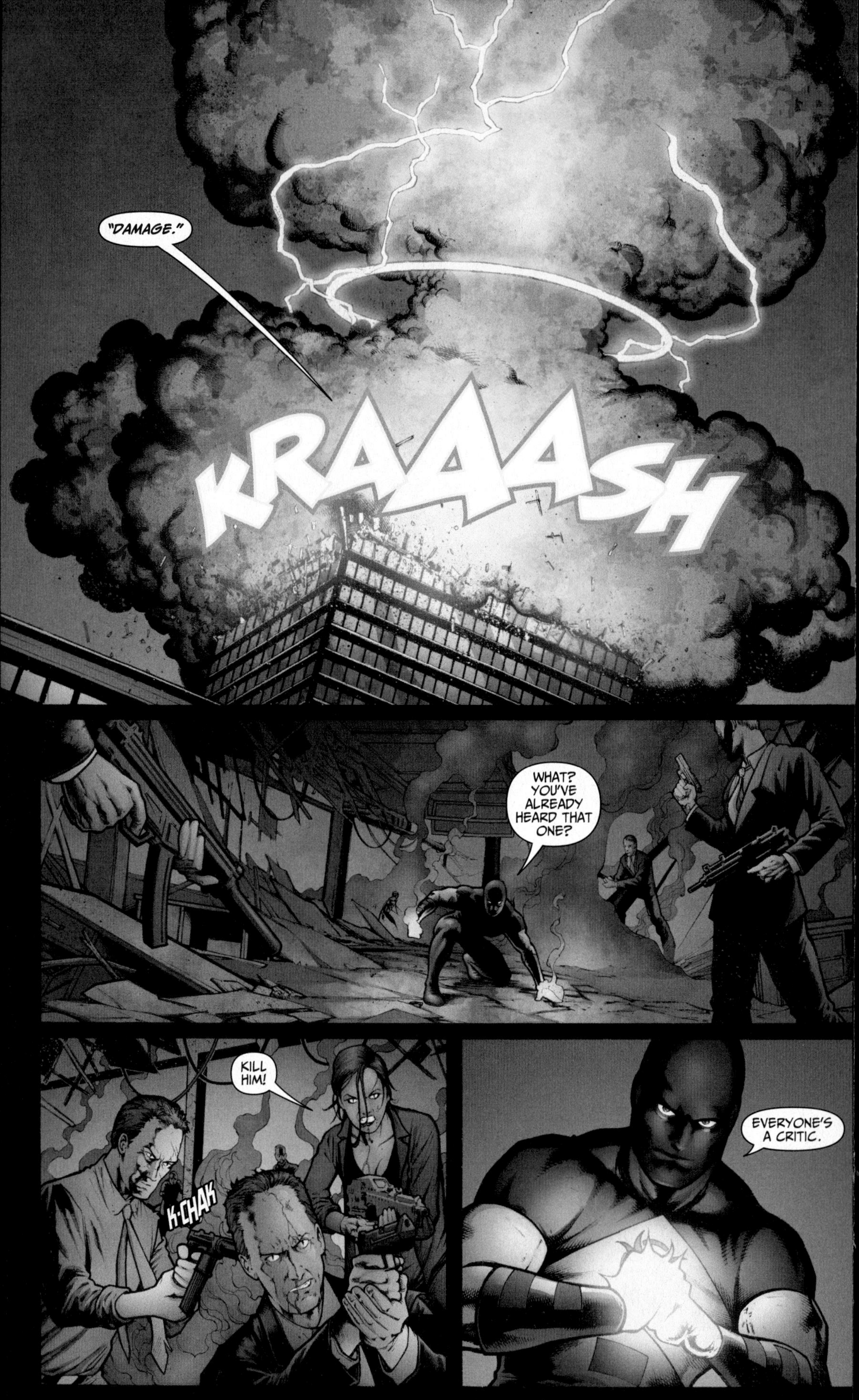
"DAMAGE."
KRAAASH
WHAT? YOU'VE ALREADY HEARD THAT ONE?
KILL HIM!
K-CHAK
EVERYONE'S A CRITIC.

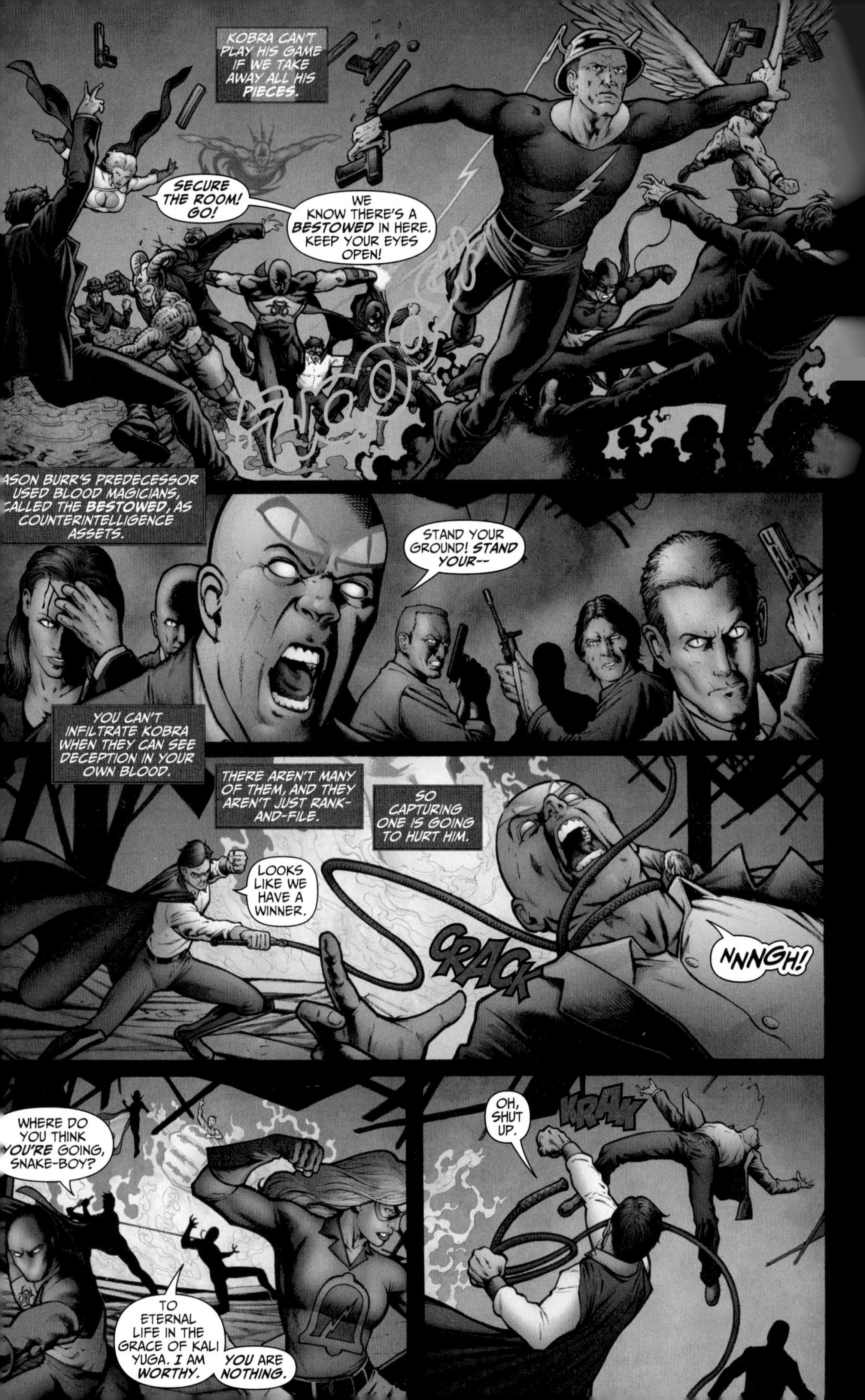

KOBRA CAN'T PLAY HIS GAME IF WE TAKE AWAY ALL HIS PIECES.
SECURE THE ROOM! GO!
WE KNOW THERE'S A BESTOWED IN HERE. KEEP YOUR EYES OPEN!
ASON BURR'S PREDECESSOR USED BLOOD MAGICIANS, CALLED THE BESTOWED, AS COUNTERINTELLIGENCE ASSETS.
STAND YOUR GROUND! STAND YOUR--
YOU CAN'T INFILTRATE KOBRA WHEN THEY CAN SEE DECEPTION IN YOUR OWN BLOOD.
THERE AREN'T MANY OF THEM, AND THEY AREN'T JUST RANK-AND-FILE.
SO CAPTURING ONE IS GOING TO HURT HIM.
LOOKS LIKE WE HAVE A WINNER.
CRACK
NNNGH!
WHERE DO YOU THINK YOU'RE GOING, SNAKE-BOY?
TO ETERNAL LIFE IN THE GRACE OF KALI YUGA. I AM WORTHY.
YOU ARE NOTHING.
OH, SHUT UP.
KRAK

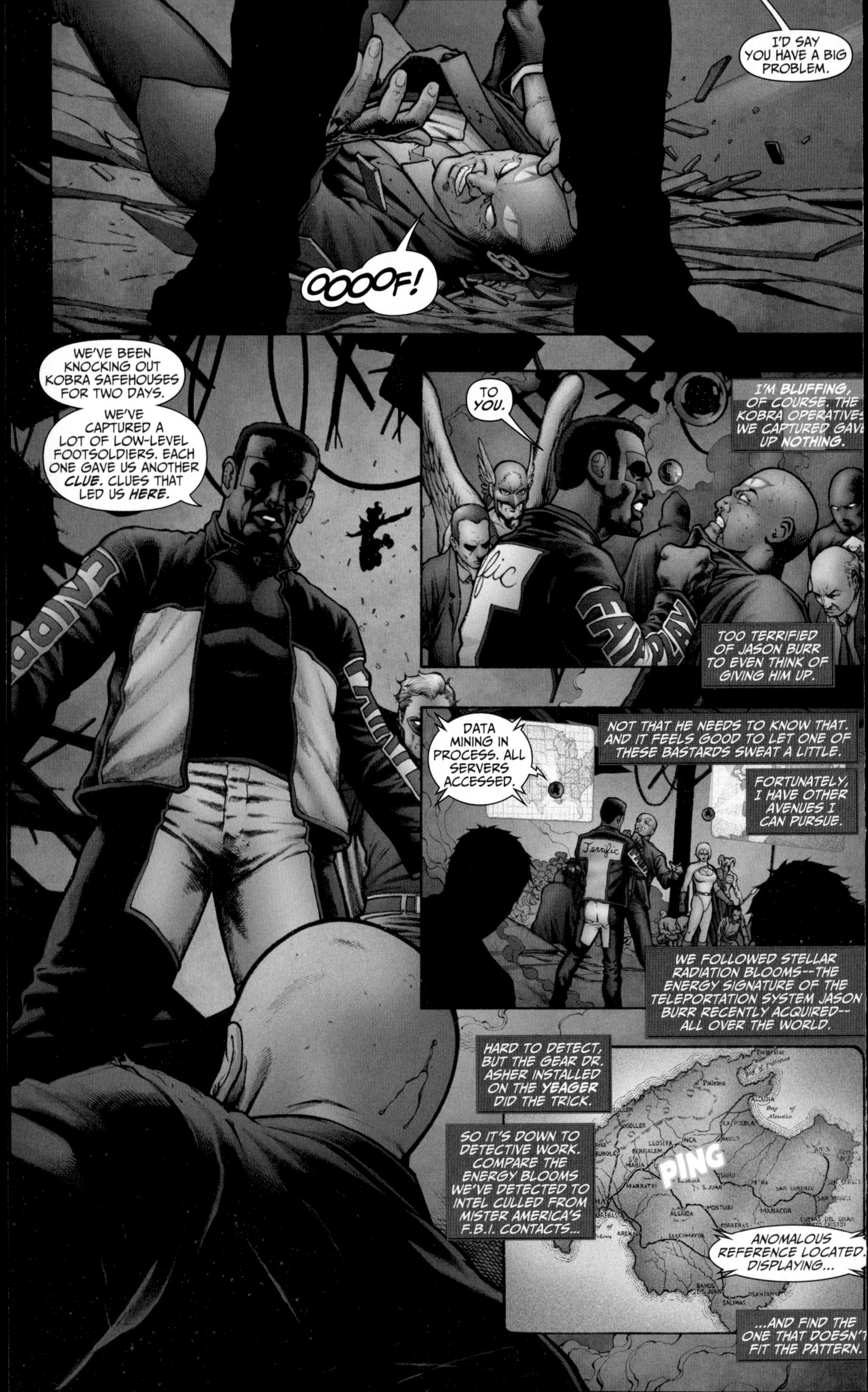
I'D SAY YOU HAVE A BIG PROBLEM.
OOOOF!
WE'VE BEEN KNOCKING OUT KOBRA SAFEHOUSES FOR TWO DAYS.
WE'VE CAPTURED A LOT OF LOW-LEVEL FOOTSOLDIERS. EACH ONE GAVE US ANOTHER CLUE. CLUES THAT LED US HERE.
TO YOU.
I'M BLUFFING, OF COURSE. THE KOBRA OPERATIVES WE CAPTURED GAVE UP NOTHING.
TOO TERRIFIED OF JASON BURR TO EVEN THINK OF GIVING HIM UP.
DATA MINING IN PROCESS. ALL SERVERS ACCESSED.
NOT THAT HE NEEDS TO KNOW THAT. AND IT FEELS GOOD TO LET ONE OF THESE BASTARDS SWEAT A LITTLE.
FORTUNATELY, I HAVE OTHER AVENUES I CAN PURSUE.
WE FOLLOWED STELLAR RADIATION BLOOMS--THE ENERGY SIGNATURE OF THE TELEPORTATION SYSTEM JASON BURR RECENTLY ACQUIRED--ALL OVER THE WORLD.
HARD TO DETECT, BUT THE GEAR DR. ASHER INSTALLED ON THE YEAGER DID THE TRICK.
SO IT'S DOWN TO DETECTIVE WORK. COMPARE THE ENERGY BLOOMS WE'VE DETECTED TO INTEL CULLED FROM MISTER AMERICA'S F.B.I. CONTACTS...
PING
ANOMALOUS REFERENCE LOCATED. DISPLAYING...
...AND FIND THE ONE THAT DOESN'T FIT THE PATTERN.

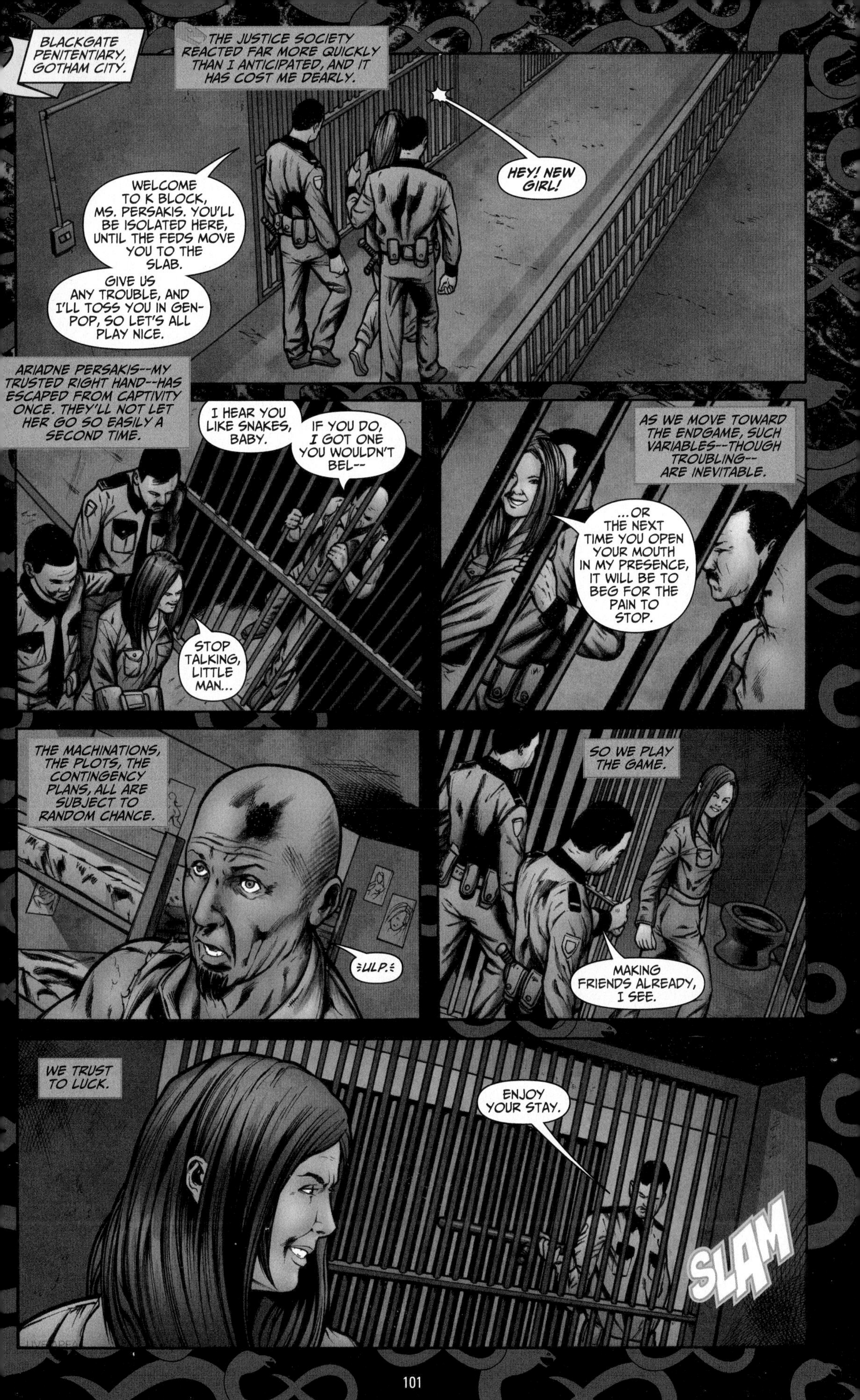
BLACKGATE PENITENTIARY, GOTHAM CITY.
THE JUSTICE SOCIETY REACTED FAR MORE QUICKLY THAN I ANTICIPATED, AND IT HAS COST ME DEARLY.
WELCOME TO K BLOCK, MS. PERSAKIS. YOU'LL BE ISOLATED HERE, UNTIL THE FEDS MOVE YOU TO THE SLAB.
GIVE US ANY TROUBLE, AND I'LL TOSS YOU IN GEN-POP, SO LET'S ALL PLAY NICE.
HEY! NEW GIRL!
ARIADNE PERSAKIS--MY TRUSTED RIGHT HAND--HAS ESCAPED FROM CAPTIVITY ONCE. THEY'LL NOT LET HER GO SO EASILY A SECOND TIME.
I HEAR YOU LIKE SNAKES, BABY.
IF YOU DO, I GOT ONE YOU WOULDN'T BEL--
STOP TALKING, LITTLE MAN...
AS WE MOVE TOWARD THE ENDGAME, SUCH VARIABLES--THOUGH TROUBLING--ARE INEVITABLE.
...OR THE NEXT TIME YOU OPEN YOUR MOUTH IN MY PRESENCE, IT WILL BE TO BEG FOR THE PAIN TO STOP.
THE MACHINATIONS, THE PLOTS, THE CONTINGENCY PLANS, ALL ARE SUBJECT TO RANDOM CHANCE.
ULP.
SO WE PLAY THE GAME.
MAKING FRIENDS ALREADY, I SEE.
WE TRUST TO LUCK.
ENJOY YOUR STAY.
SLAM

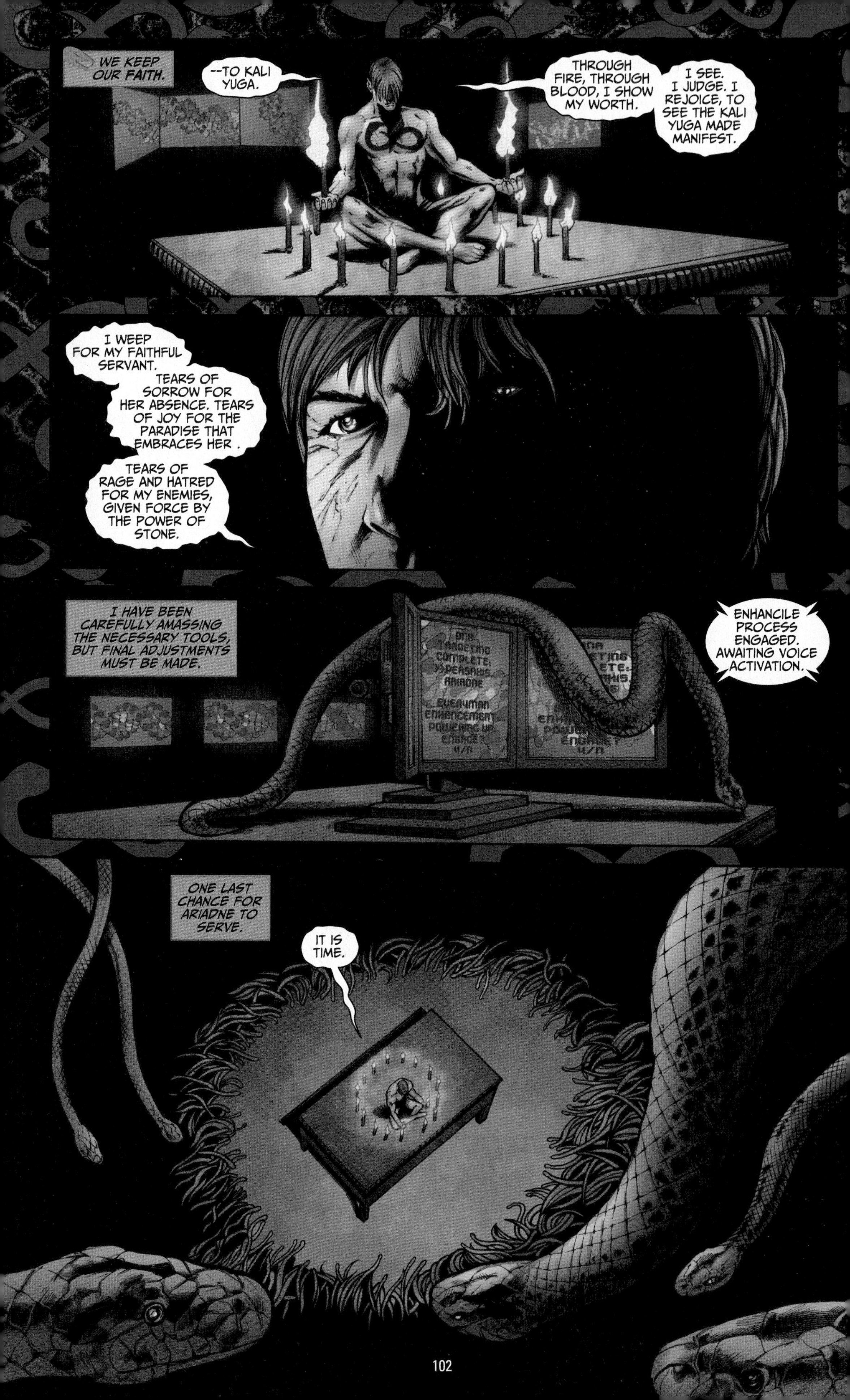
WE KEEP OUR FAITH.
--TO KALI YUGA.
THROUGH FIRE, THROUGH BLOOD, I SHOW MY WORTH.
I SEE. I JUDGE. I REJOICE, TO SEE THE KALI YUGA MADE MANIFEST.
I WEEP FOR MY FAITHFUL SERVANT.
TEARS OF SORROW FOR HER ABSENCE. TEARS OF JOY FOR THE PARADISE THAT EMBRACES HER .
TEARS OF RAGE AND HATRED FOR MY ENEMIES, GIVEN FORCE BY THE POWER OF STONE.
I HAVE BEEN CAREFULLY AMASSING THE NECESSARY TOOLS, BUT FINAL ADJUSTMENTS MUST BE MADE.
ENHANCILE PROCESS ENGAGED. AWAITING VOICE ACTIVATION.
ONE LAST CHANCE FOR ARIADNE TO SERVE.
IT IS TIME.

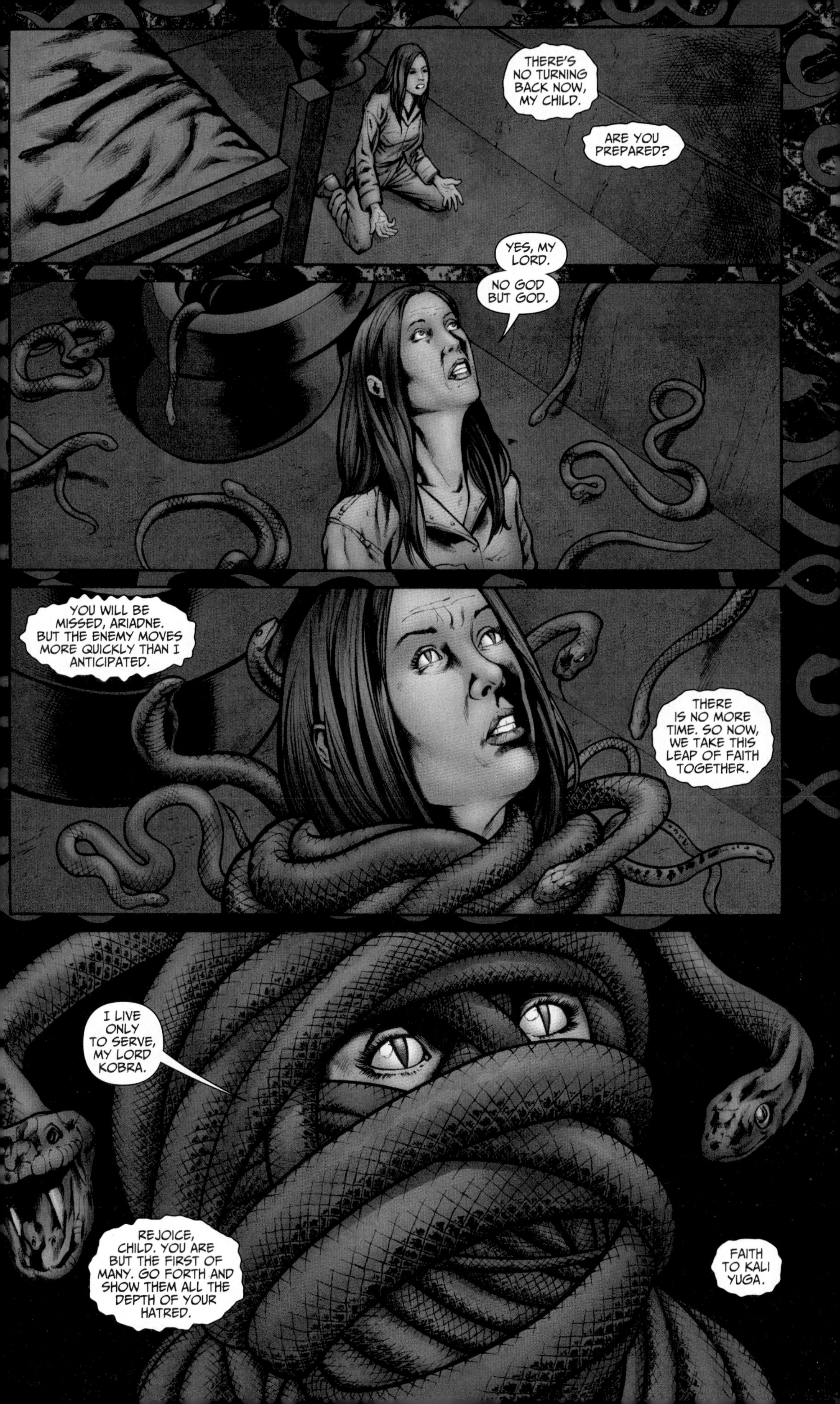
THERE'S NO TURNING BACK NOW, MY CHILD.
ARE YOU PREPARED?
YES, MY LORD.
NO GOD BUT GOD.
YOU WILL BE MISSED, ARIADNE. BUT THE ENEMY MOVES MORE QUICKLY THAN I ANTICIPATED.
THERE IS NO MORE TIME. SO NOW, WE TAKE THIS LEAP OF FAITH TOGETHER.
I LIVE ONLY TO SERVE, MY LORD KOBRA.
REJOICE, CHILD. YOU ARE BUT THE FIRST OF MANY. GO FORTH AND SHOW THEM ALL THE DEPTH OF YOUR HATRED.
FAITH TO KALI YUGA.

JESSICA MIDNIGHT IS THE ACTING BLACK QUEEN OF CHECKMATE WHILE SASHA BORDEAUX IS INACTIVE.

AND RIGHT NOW, SHE IS VERY ANGRY WITH ME.

--THE HELL ARE YOU *DOING*, MR. TERRIFIC?

IF YOU'RE RUNNING OPS AGAINST KOBRA, YO NEED TO NOTIFY M WE COULD HAVE RU SUPPORT, SENT IN FORENSICS--

CHECKMATE'S BEEN PENETRATED BY KOBRA. I COULDN'T TELL YOU.

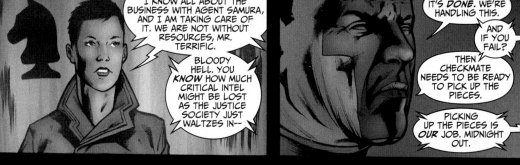

I KNOW ALL ABOUT THE BUSINESS WITH AGENT SAMURA, AND I AM TAKING CARE OF IT. WE ARE NOT WITHOUT RESOURCES, MR. TERRIFIC.

BLOODY HELL. YOU *KNOW* HOW MUCH CRITICAL INTEL MIGHT BE LOST AS THE JUSTICE SOCIETY JUST WALTZES IN--

IT'S *DONE*. WE'RE HANDLING THIS.

AND IF YOU FAIL?

THEN CHECKMATE NEEDS TO BE READY TO PICK UP THE PIECES.

PICKING UP THE PIECES IS *OUR* JOB. MIDNIGHT OUT.

...I *LIKE* HER.

YOU TWO COULD BE *RELATED*.

IN TWO DAYS, WE'VE LOCATED AND SMASHED A DOZEN KOBRA BASES. PRETTY GOOD START.

IT IS. BUT WE NEED TO KEEP MOVING. WE'RE CONTROLLING THE PACE NOW, AND WE NEED TO STAY IN CONTROL.

SO WE HIT THEM AGAIN. NOW.

GOOD. BECAUSE HITTING THEM IS *OUR* JOB.

AND FOR ONCE...

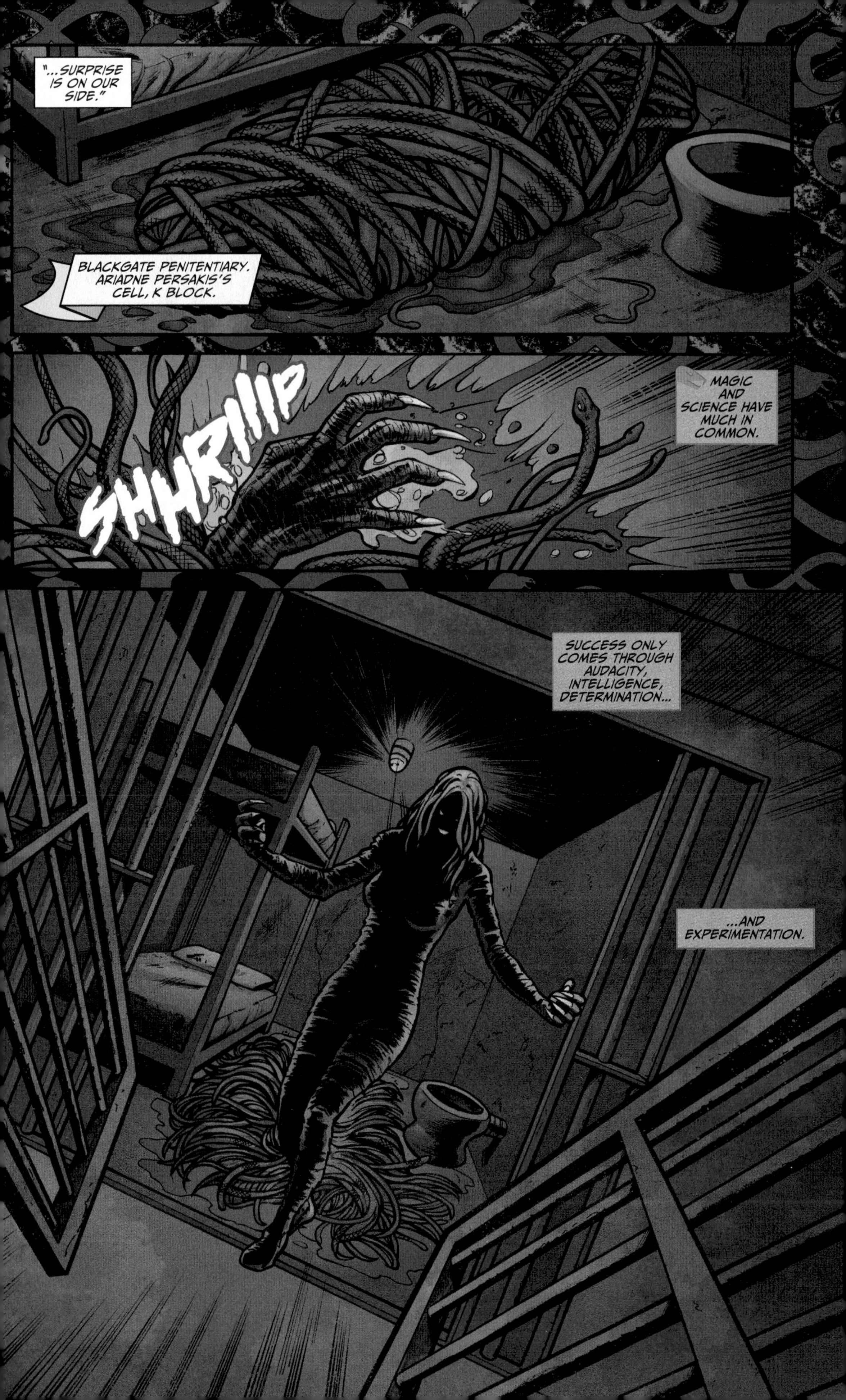
"...SURPRISE IS ON OUR SIDE."
BLACKGATE PENITENTIARY. ARIADNE PERSAKIS'S CELL, K BLOCK.
SHHRIIIP
MAGIC AND SCIENCE HAVE MUCH IN COMMON.
SUCCESS ONLY COMES THROUGH AUDACITY, INTELLIGENCE, DETERMINATION...
...AND EXPERIMENTATION.

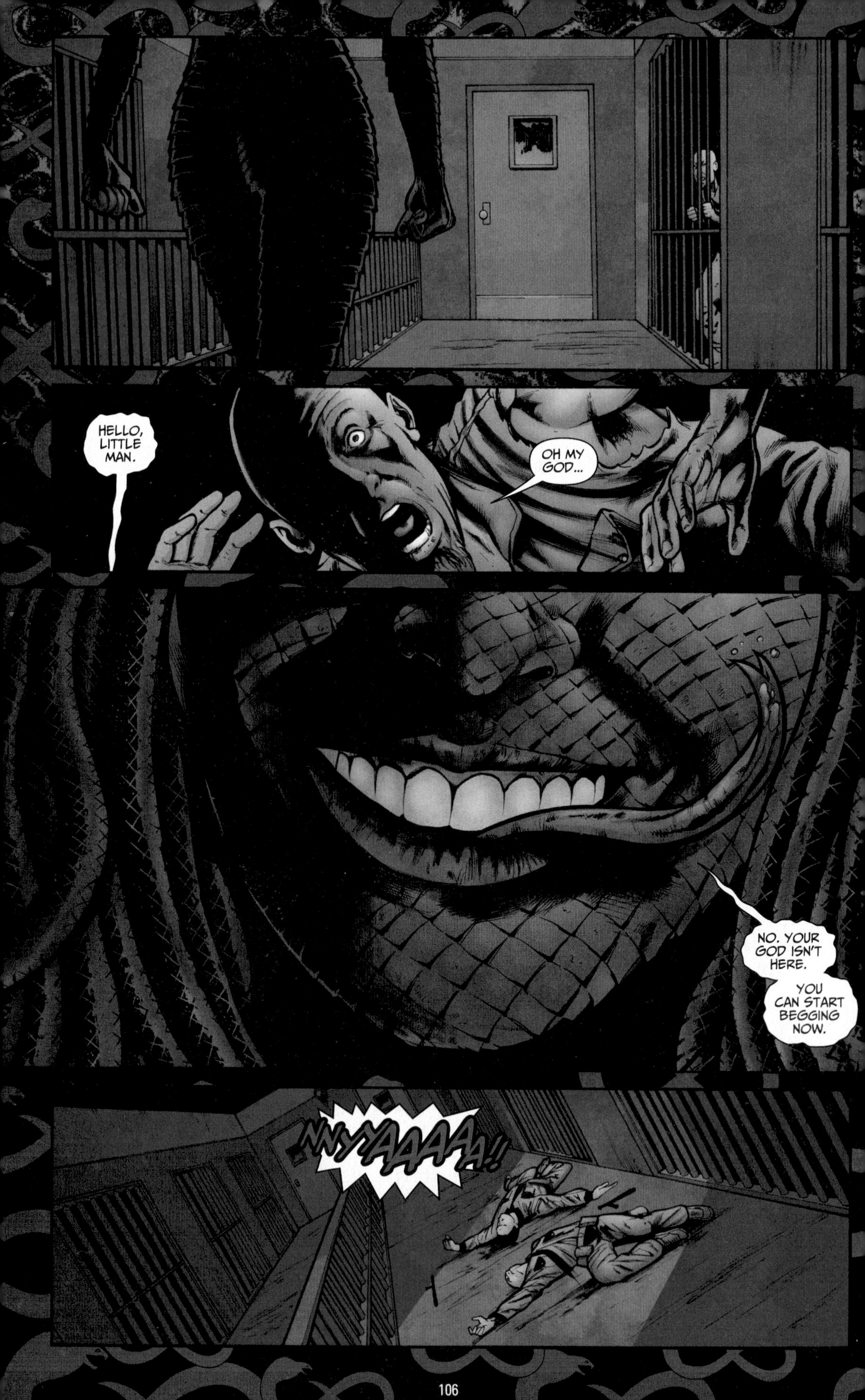
HELLO, LITTLE MAN.
OH MY GOD...
NO. YOUR GOD ISN'T HERE.
YOU CAN START BEGGING NOW.
NNYYAAAAA!!

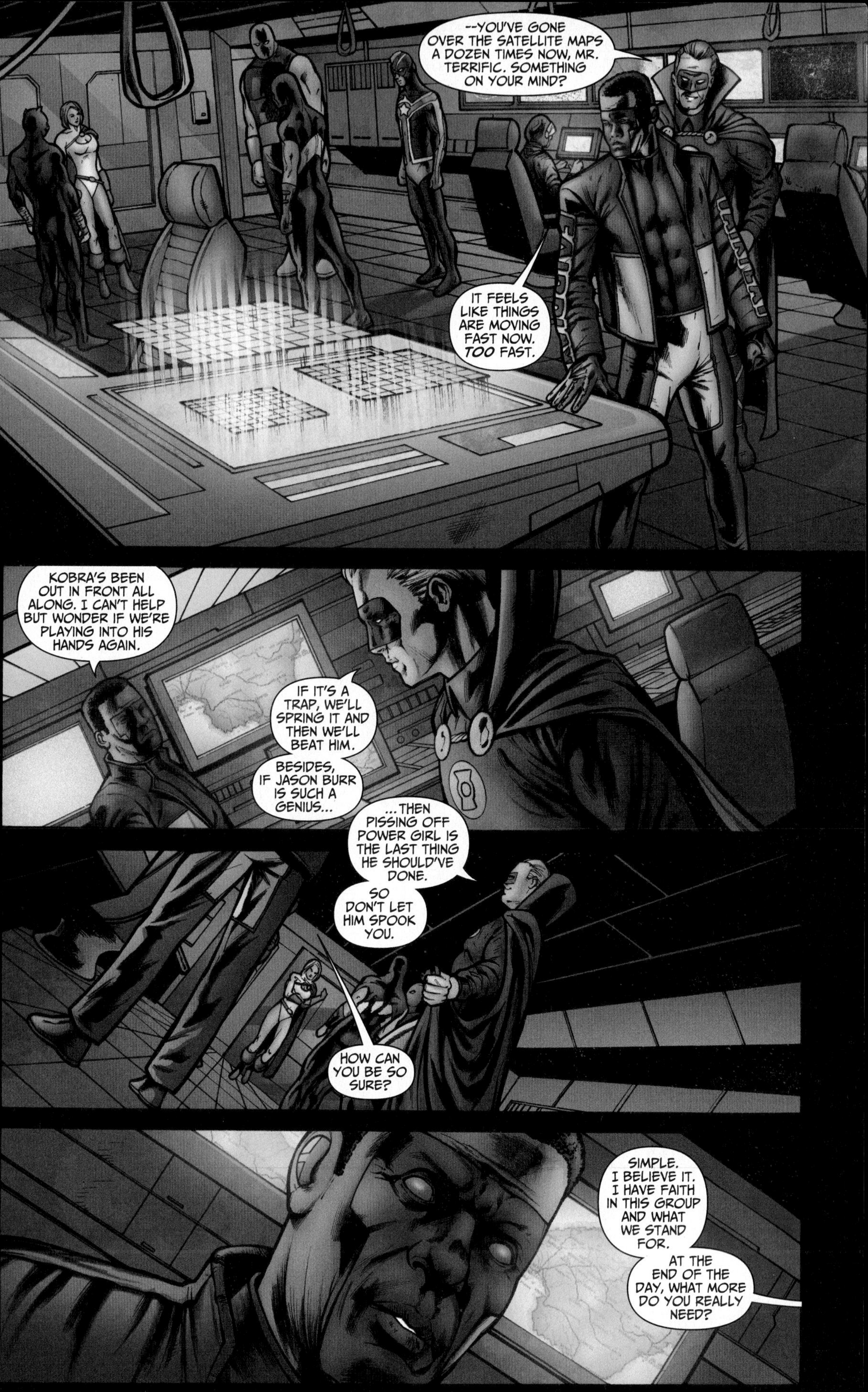
--YOU'VE GONE OVER THE SATELLITE MAPS A DOZEN TIMES NOW, MR. TERRIFIC. SOMETHING ON YOUR MIND?
IT FEELS LIKE THINGS ARE MOVING FAST NOW. *TOO* FAST.
KOBRA'S BEEN OUT IN FRONT ALL ALONG. I CAN'T HELP BUT WONDER IF WE'RE PLAYING INTO HIS HANDS AGAIN.
IF IT'S A TRAP, WE'LL SPRING IT AND THEN WE'LL BEAT HIM.
BESIDES, IF JASON BURR IS SUCH A GENIUS...
...THEN PISSING OFF POWER GIRL IS THE LAST THING HE SHOULD'VE DONE.
SO DON'T LET HIM SPOOK YOU.
HOW CAN YOU BE SO SURE?
SIMPLE. I BELIEVE IT. I HAVE FAITH IN THIS GROUP AND WHAT WE STAND FOR.
AT THE END OF THE DAY, WHAT MORE DO YOU REALLY NEED?

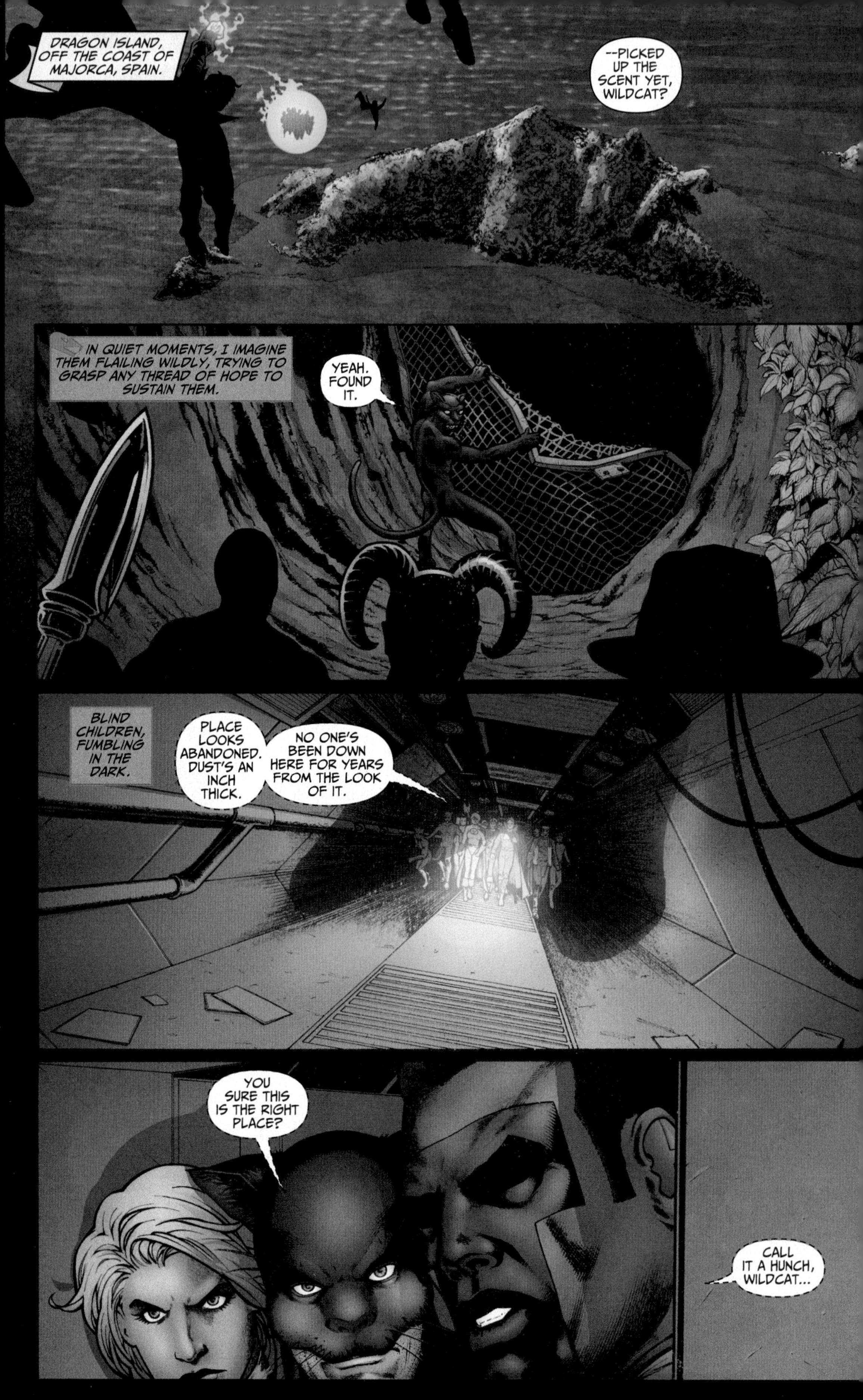

DRAGON ISLAND, OFF THE COAST OF MAJORCA, SPAIN.
--PICKED UP THE SCENT YET, WILDCAT?
IN QUIET MOMENTS, I IMAGINE THEM FLAILING WILDLY, TRYING TO GRASP ANY THREAD OF HOPE TO SUSTAIN THEM.
YEAH. FOUND IT.
BLIND CHILDREN, FUMBLING IN THE DARK.
PLACE LOOKS ABANDONED. DUST'S AN INCH THICK.
NO ONE'S BEEN DOWN HERE FOR YEARS FROM THE LOOK OF IT.
YOU SURE THIS IS THE RIGHT PLACE?
CALL IT A HUNCH, WILDCAT...

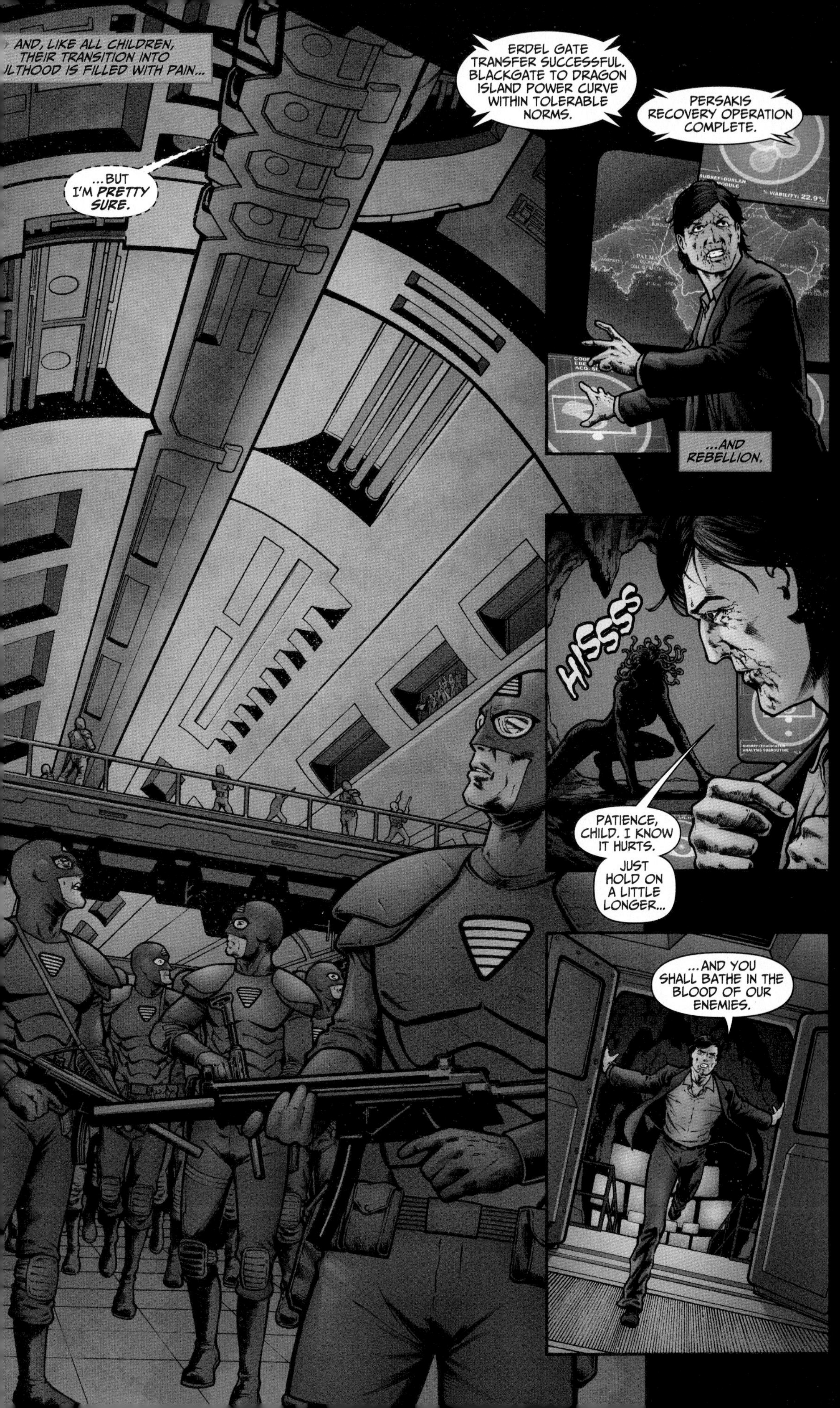
AND, LIKE ALL CHILDREN, THEIR TRANSITION INTO
ULTHOOD IS FILLED WITH PAIN...
...BUT I'M PRETTY SURE.
ERDEL GATE TRANSFER SUCCESSFUL. BLACKGATE TO DRAGON ISLAND POWER CURVE WITHIN TOLERABLE NORMS.
PERSAKIS RECOVERY OPERATION COMPLETE.
VIABILITY: 22.9%
...AND REBELLION.
HISSSS
PATIENCE, CHILD. I KNOW IT HURTS.
JUST HOLD ON A LITTLE LONGER...
...AND YOU SHALL BATHE IN THE BLOOD OF OUR ENEMIES.

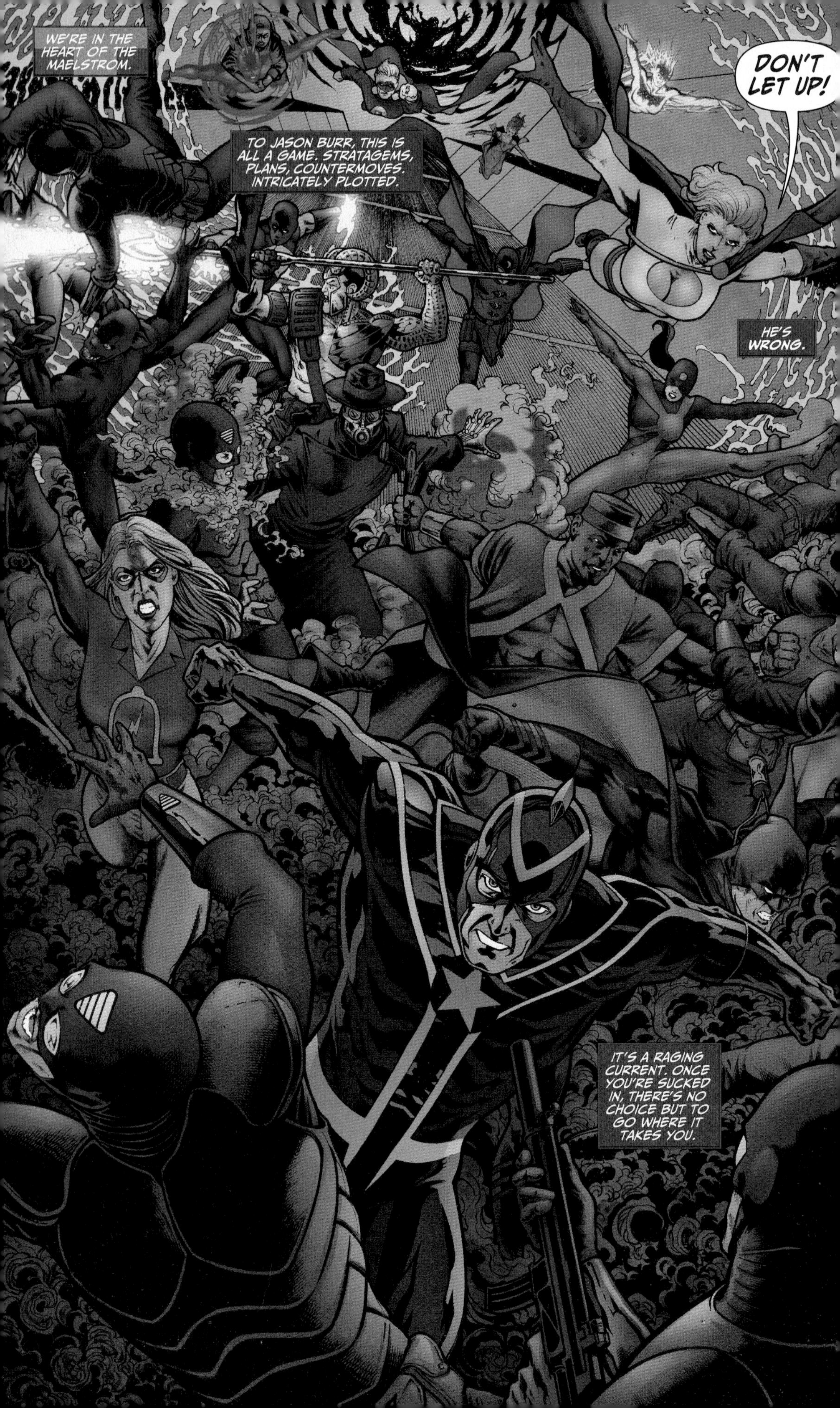
WE'RE IN THE HEART OF THE MAELSTROM.
DON'T LET UP!
TO JASON BURR, THIS IS ALL A GAME. STRATAGEMS, PLANS, COUNTERMOVES. INTRICATELY PLOTTED.
HE'S WRONG.
IT'S A RAGING CURRENT. ONCE YOU'RE SUCKED IN, THERE'S NO CHOICE BUT TO GO WHERE IT TAKES YOU.

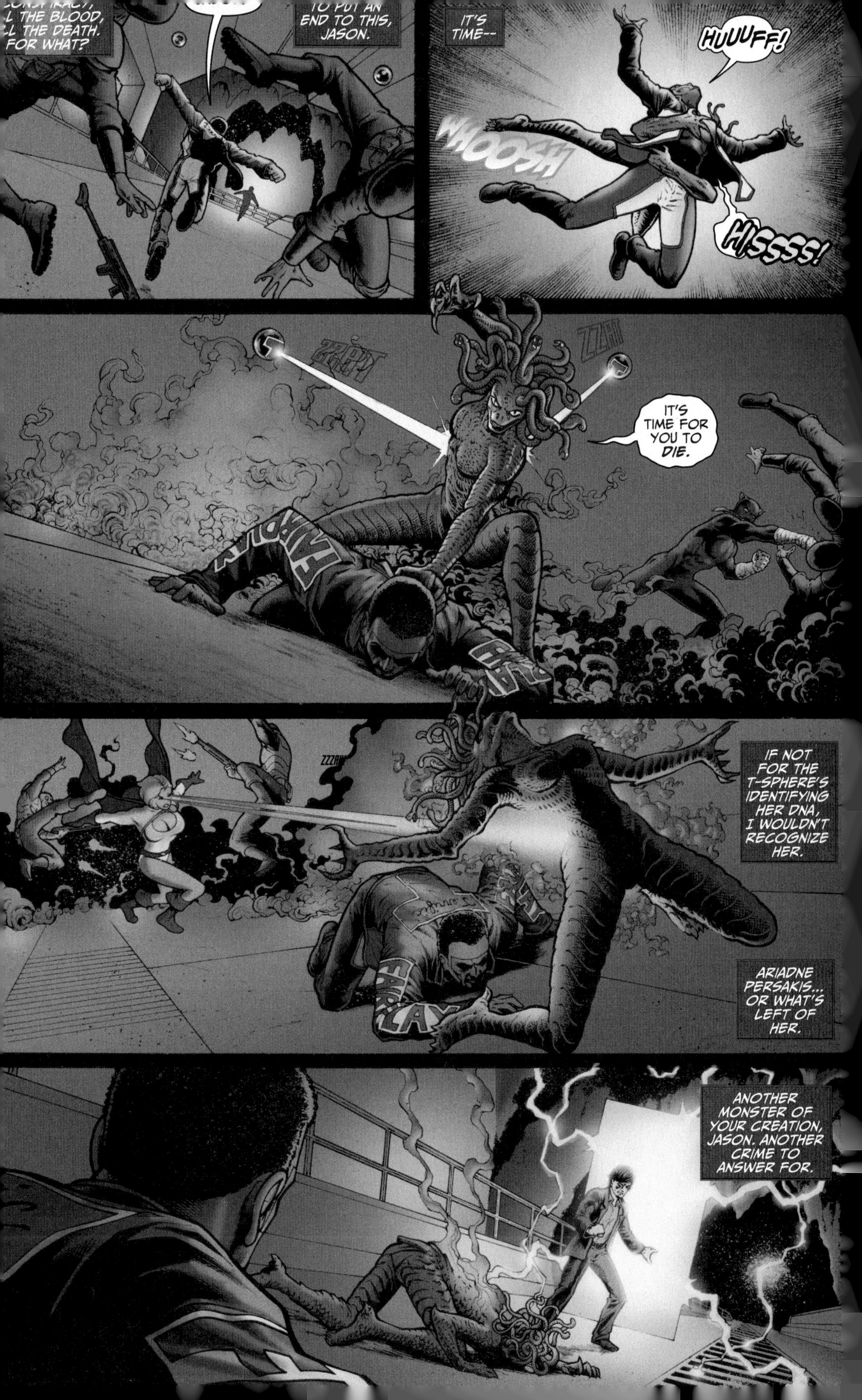
THE BLOOD,
THE DEATH.
FOR WHAT?
END TO THIS, JASON.
IT'S TIME--
HUUUFF!
WHOOSH
HISSSS!
IT'S TIME FOR YOU TO DIE.
IF NOT FOR THE T-SPHERE'S IDENTIFYING HER DNA, I WOULDN'T RECOGNIZE HER.
ARIADNE PERSAKIS... OR WHAT'S LEFT OF HER.
ANOTHER MONSTER OF YOUR CREATION, JASON. ANOTHER CRIME TO ANSWER FOR.

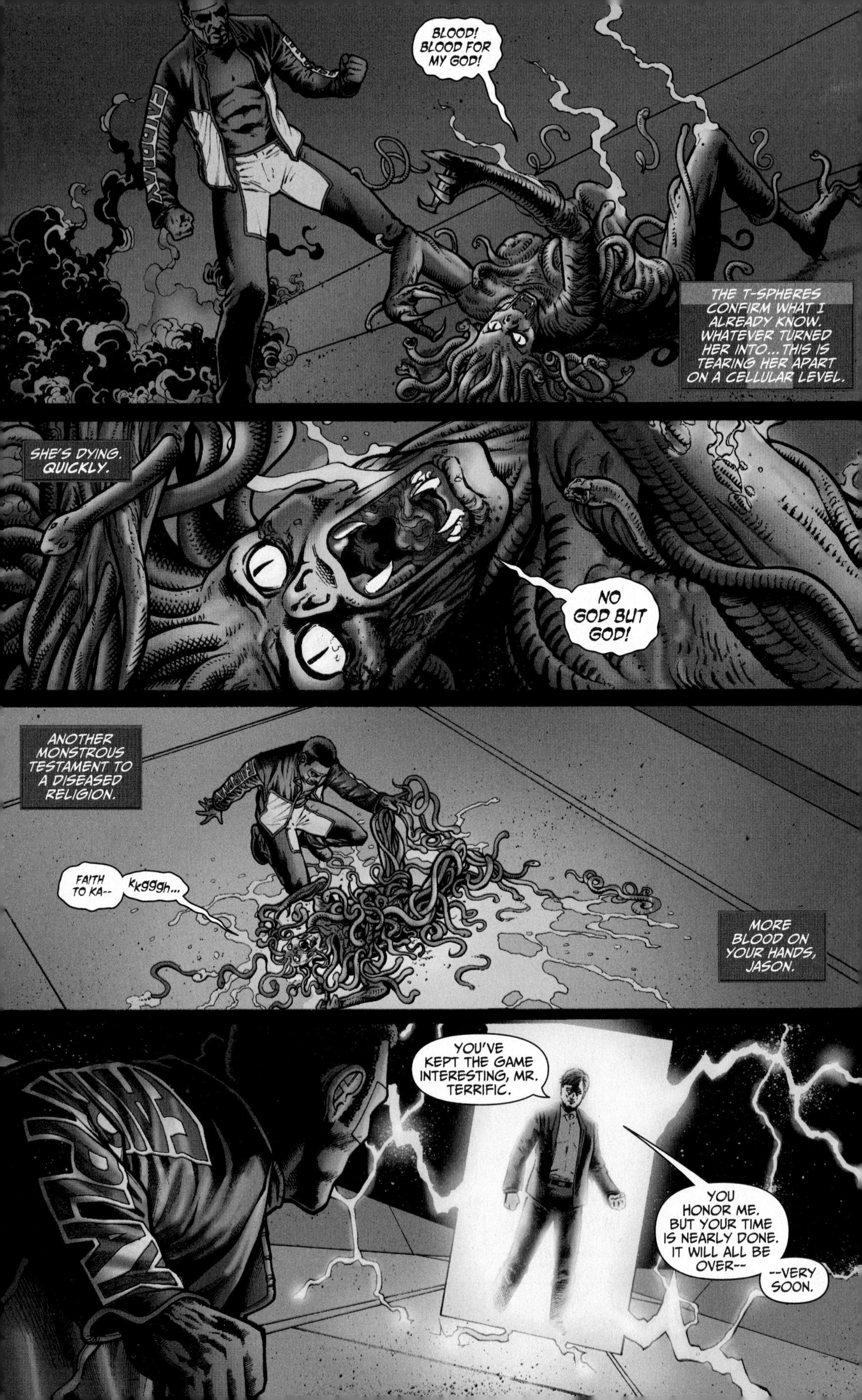
BLOOD! BLOOD FOR MY GOD!
THE T-SPHERES CONFIRM WHAT I ALREADY KNOW. WHATEVER TURNED HER INTO...THIS IS TEARING HER APART ON A CELLULAR LEVEL.
SHE'S DYING. QUICKLY.
NO GOD BUT GOD!
ANOTHER MONSTROUS TESTAMENT TO A DISEASED RELIGION.
FAITH TO KA--
kkgggh...
MORE BLOOD ON YOUR HANDS, JASON.
YOU'VE KEPT THE GAME INTERESTING, MR. TERRIFIC.
YOU HONOR ME. BUT YOUR TIME IS NEARLY DONE. IT WILL ALL BE OVER--
--VERY SOON.

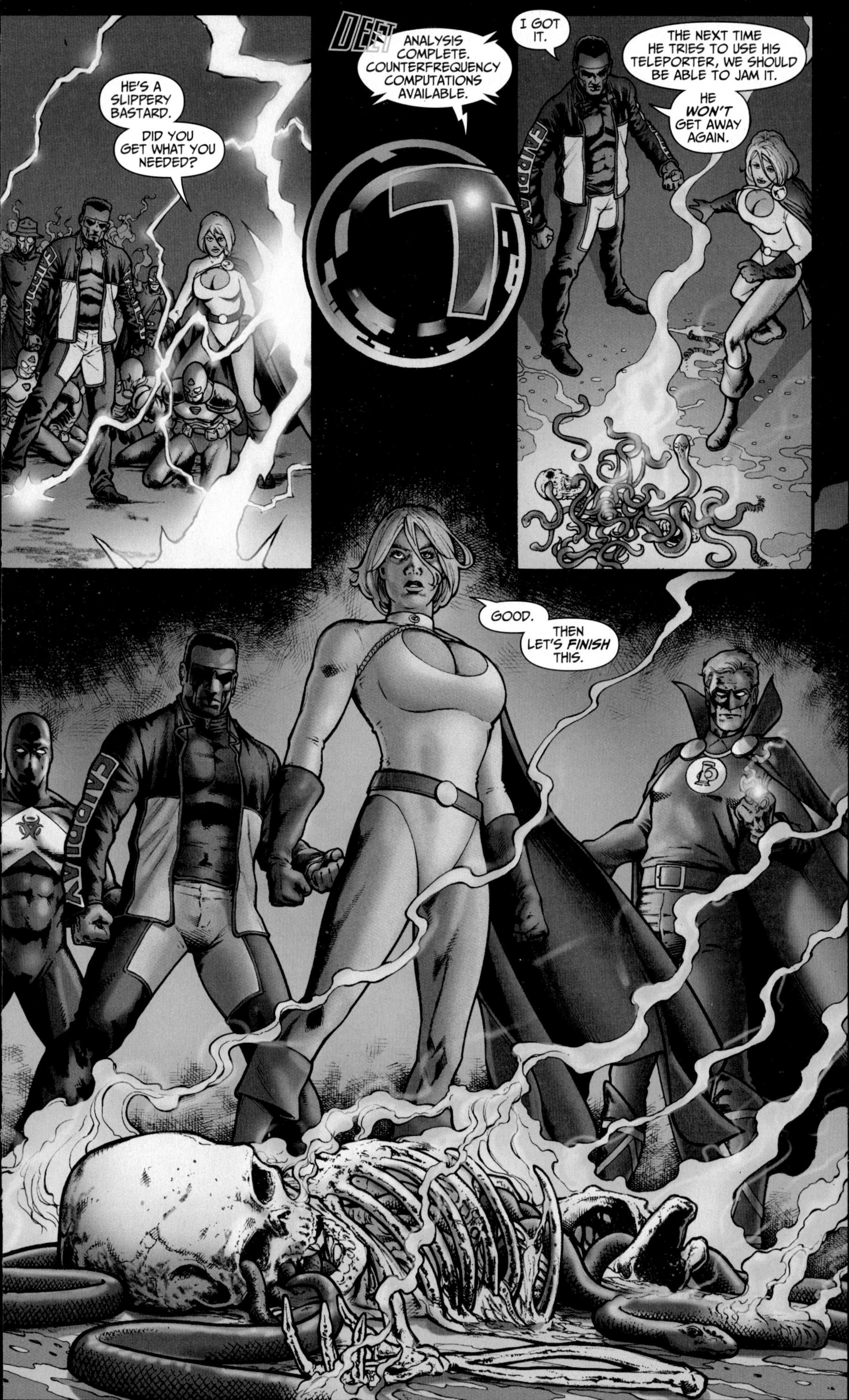
HE'S A SLIPPERY BASTARD.
DID YOU GET WHAT YOU NEEDED?
DEET
ANALYSIS COMPLETE. COUNTERFREQUENCY COMPUTATIONS AVAILABLE.
I GOT IT.
THE NEXT TIME HE TRIES TO USE HIS TELEPORTER, WE SHOULD BE ABLE TO JAM IT.
HE WON'T GET AWAY AGAIN.
GOOD.
THEN LET'S FINISH THIS.

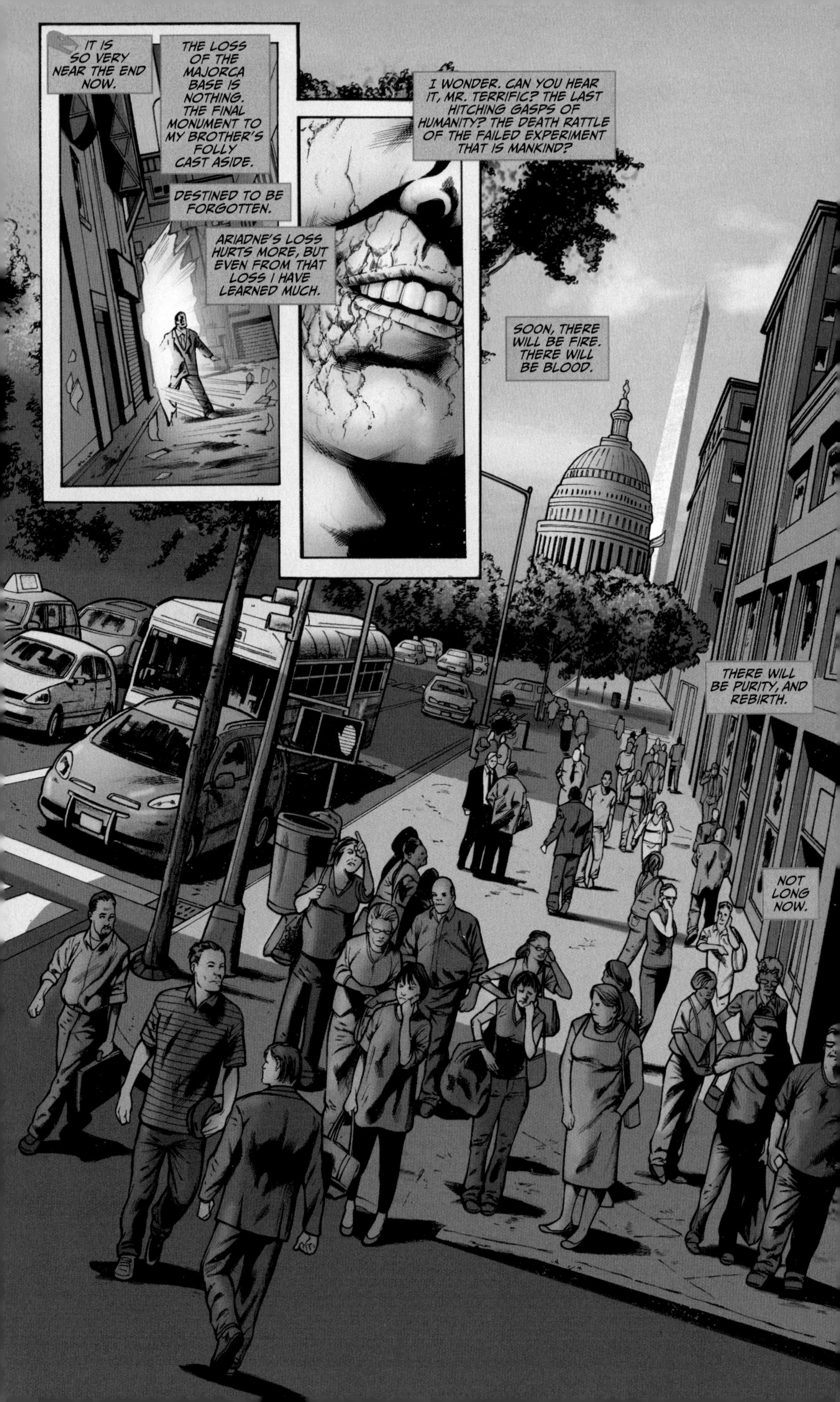
IT IS SO VERY NEAR THE END NOW.
THE LOSS OF THE MAJORCA BASE IS NOTHING. THE FINAL MONUMENT TO MY BROTHER'S FOLLY CAST ASIDE.
DESTINED TO BE FORGOTTEN.
ARIADNE'S LOSS HURTS MORE, BUT EVEN FROM THAT LOSS I HAVE LEARNED MUCH.
I WONDER. CAN YOU HEAR IT, MR. TERRIFIC? THE LAST HITCHING GASPS OF HUMANITY? THE DEATH RATTLE OF THE FAILED EXPERIMENT THAT IS MANKIND?
SOON, THERE WILL BE FIRE. THERE WILL BE BLOOD.
THERE WILL BE PURITY, AND REBIRTH.
NOT LONG NOW.

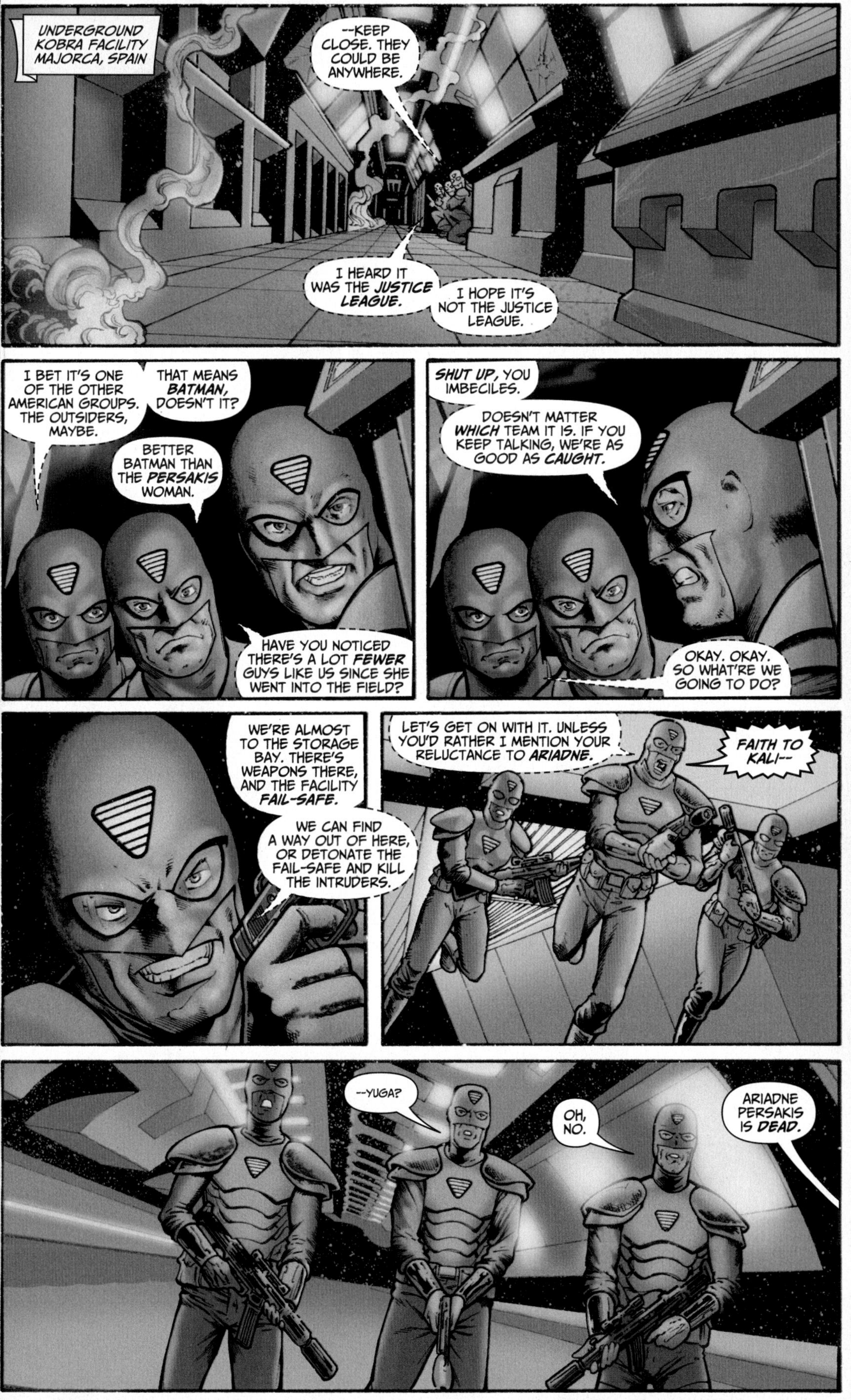

UNDERGROUND KOBRA FACILITY MAJORCA, SPAIN
--KEEP CLOSE. THEY COULD BE ANYWHERE.
I HEARD IT WAS THE JUSTICE LEAGUE.
I HOPE IT'S NOT THE JUSTICE LEAGUE.
I BET IT'S ONE OF THE OTHER AMERICAN GROUPS. THE OUTSIDERS, MAYBE.
THAT MEANS BATMAN, DOESN'T IT?
BETTER BATMAN THAN THE PERSAKIS WOMAN.
HAVE YOU NOTICED THERE'S A LOT FEWER GUYS LIKE US SINCE SHE WENT INTO THE FIELD?
SHUT UP, YOU IMBECILES.
DOESN'T MATTER WHICH TEAM IT IS. IF YOU KEEP TALKING, WE'RE AS GOOD AS CAUGHT.
OKAY. OKAY. SO WHAT'RE WE GOING TO DO?
WE'RE ALMOST TO THE STORAGE BAY. THERE'S WEAPONS THERE, AND THE FACILITY FAIL-SAFE.
WE CAN FIND A WAY OUT OF HERE, OR DETONATE THE FAIL-SAFE AND KILL THE INTRUDERS.
LET'S GET ON WITH IT. UNLESS YOU'D RATHER I MENTION YOUR RELUCTANCE TO ARIADNE.
FAITH TO KALI--
--YUGA?
OH, NO.
ARIADNE PERSAKIS IS DEAD.

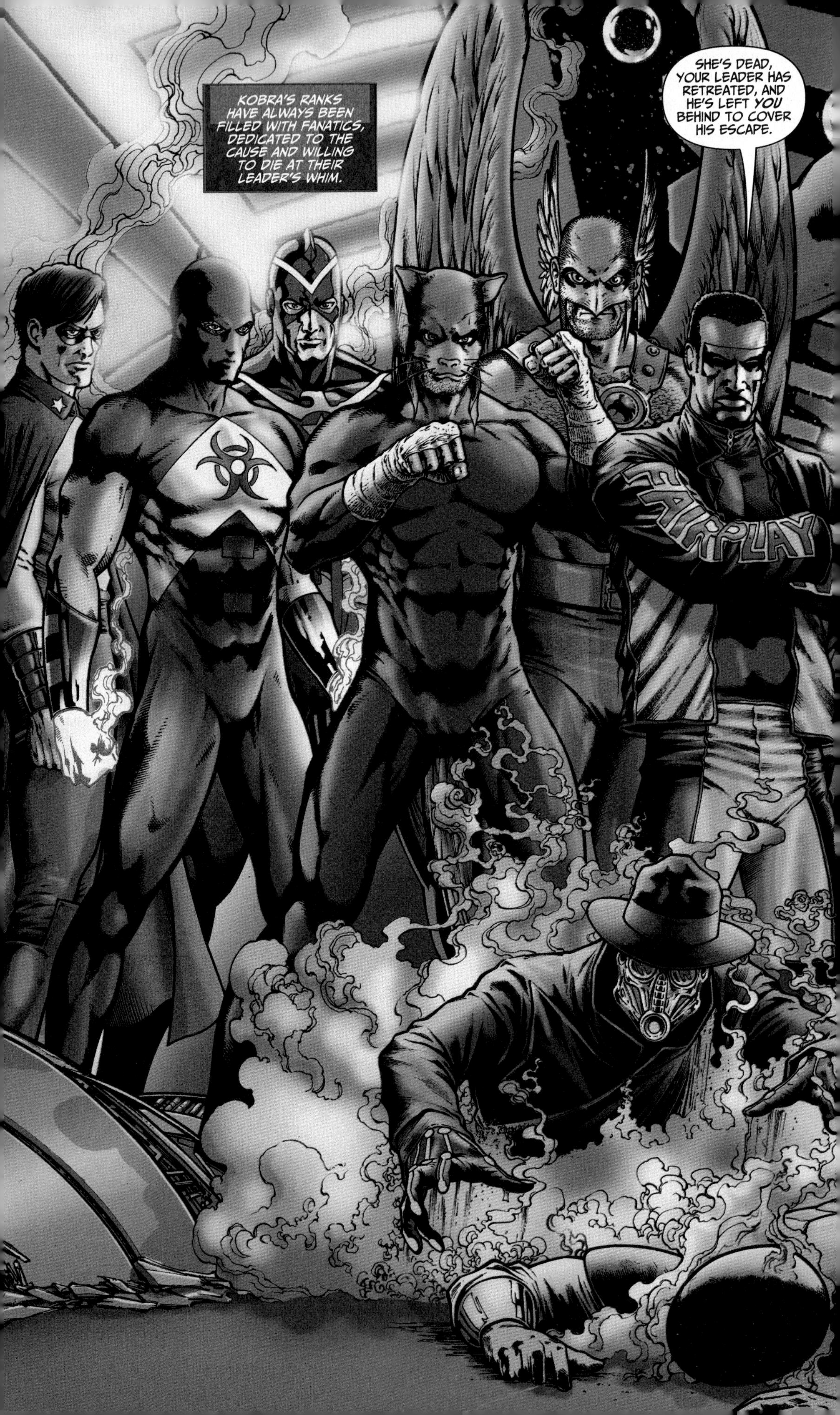
KOBRA'S RANKS HAVE ALWAYS BEEN FILLED WITH FANATICS, DEDICATED TO THE CAUSE AND WILLING TO DIE AT THEIR LEADER'S WHIM.
SHE'S DEAD, YOUR LEADER HAS RETREATED, AND HE'S LEFT *YOU* BEHIND TO COVER HIS ESCAPE.
FAIRPLAY

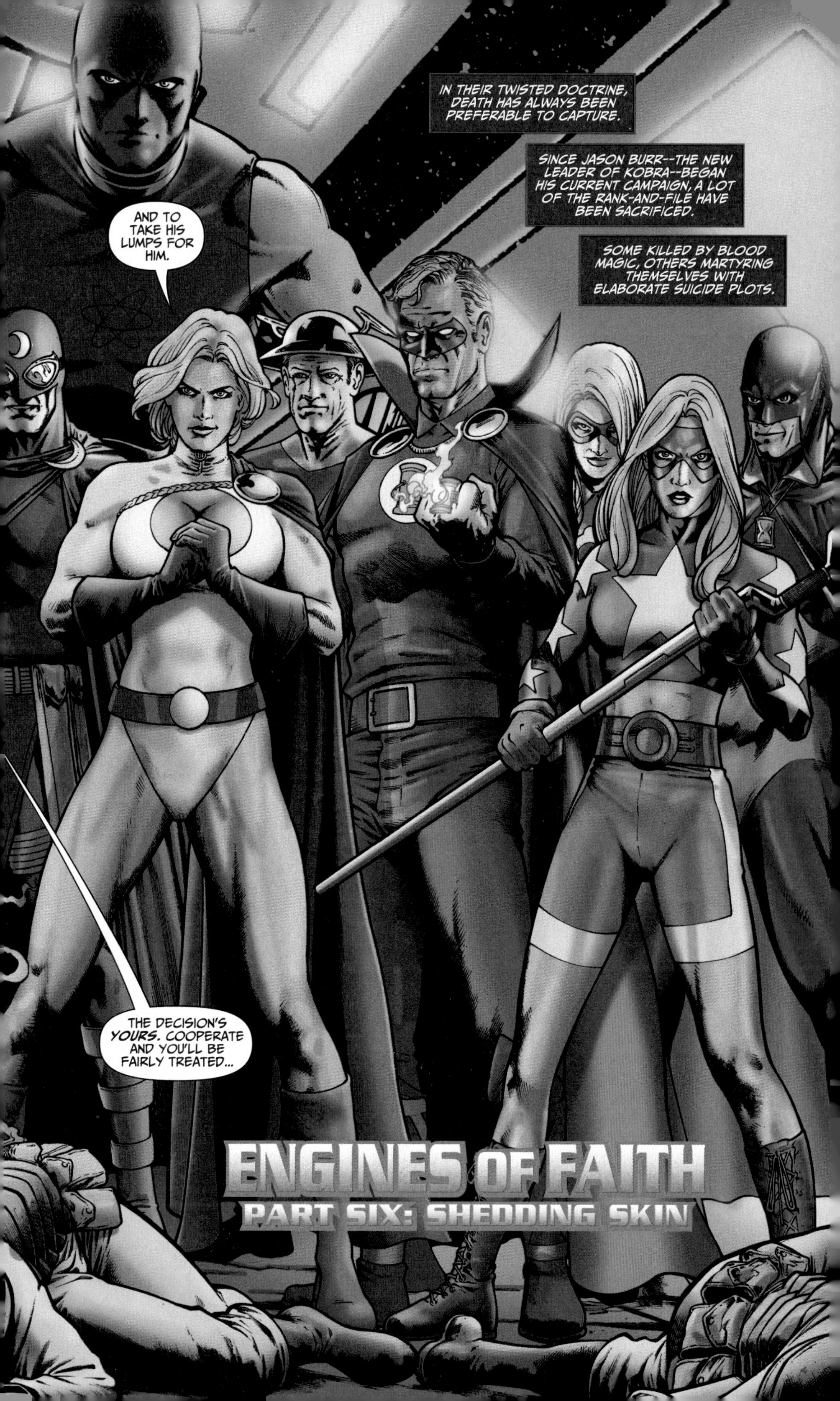

IN THEIR TWISTED DOCTRINE, DEATH HAS ALWAYS BEEN PREFERABLE TO CAPTURE.
SINCE JASON BURR--THE NEW LEADER OF KOBRA--BEGAN HIS CURRENT CAMPAIGN, A LOT OF THE RANK-AND-FILE HAVE BEEN SACRIFICED.
SOME KILLED BY BLOOD MAGIC, OTHERS MARTYRING THEMSELVES WITH ELABORATE SUICIDE PLOTS.
AND TO TAKE HIS LUMPS FOR HIM.
THE DECISION'S YOURS. COOPERATE AND YOU'LL BE FAIRLY TREATED...
ENGINES OF FAITH
PART SIX: SHEDDING SKIN

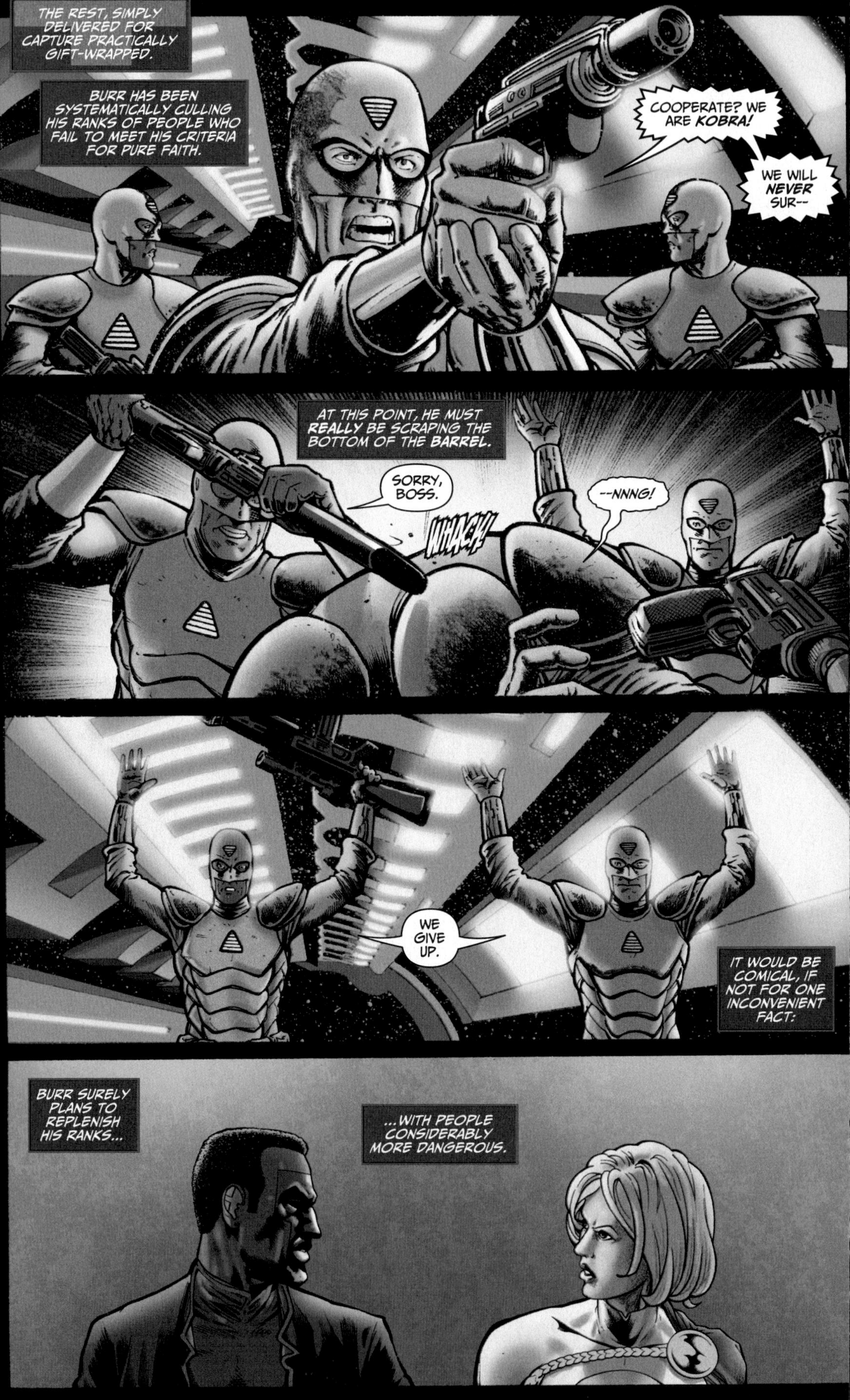
THE REST, SIMPLY DELIVERED FOR CAPTURE PRACTICALLY GIFT-WRAPPED.
BURR HAS BEEN SYSTEMATICALLY CULLING HIS RANKS OF PEOPLE WHO FAIL TO MEET HIS CRITERIA FOR PURE FAITH.
COOPERATE? WE ARE KOBRA!
WE WILL NEVER SUR--
AT THIS POINT, HE MUST REALLY BE SCRAPING THE BOTTOM OF THE BARREL.
SORRY, BOSS.
WHACK!
--NNNG!
WE GIVE UP.
IT WOULD BE COMICAL, IF NOT FOR ONE INCONVENIENT FACT:
BURR SURELY PLANS TO REPLENISH HIS RANKS...
...WITH PEOPLE CONSIDERABLY MORE DANGEROUS.

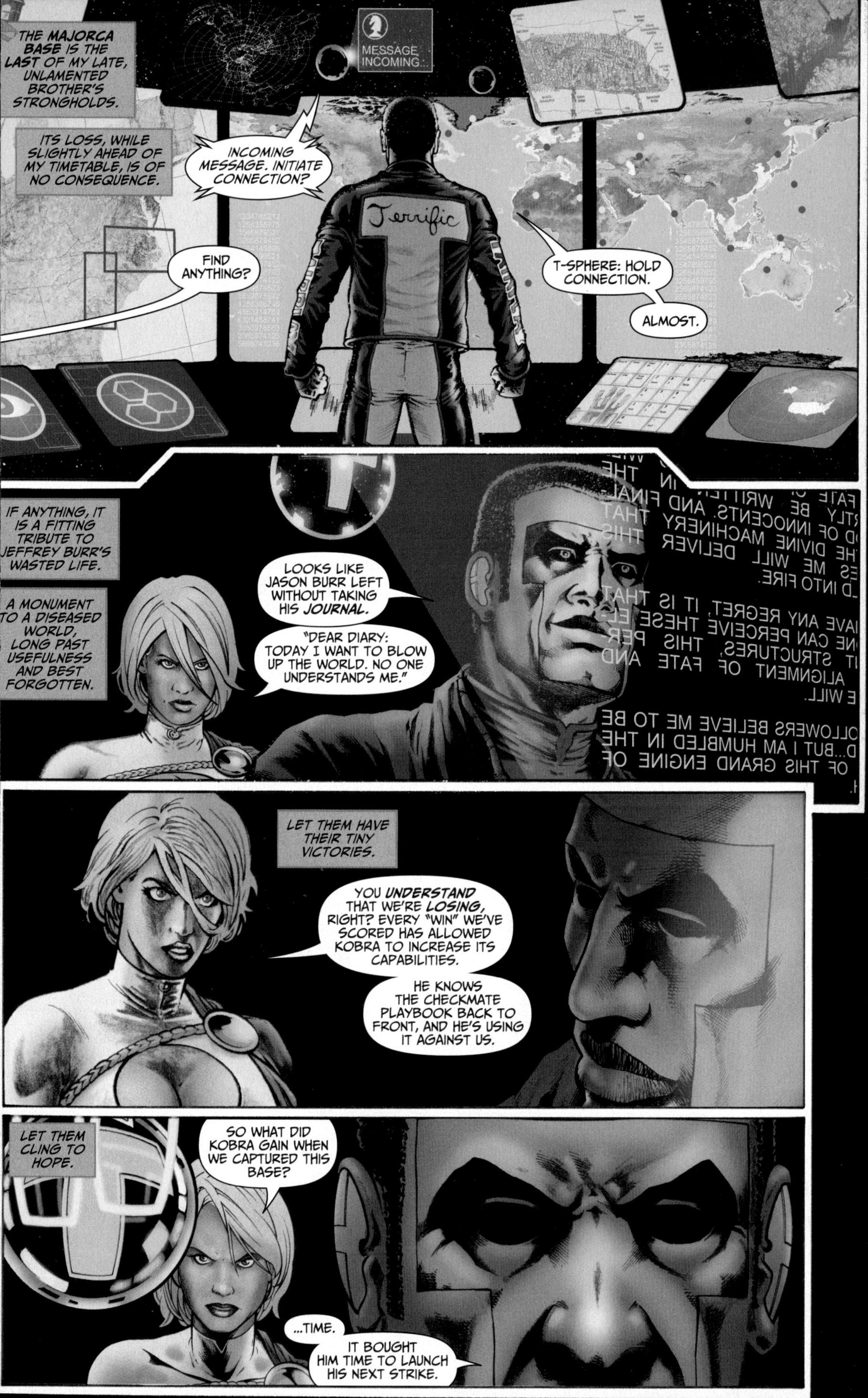
MESSAGE INCOMING...
THE MAJORCA BASE IS THE LAST OF MY LATE, UNLAMENTED BROTHER'S STRONGHOLDS.
ITS LOSS, WHILE SLIGHTLY AHEAD OF MY TIMETABLE, IS OF NO CONSEQUENCE.
INCOMING MESSAGE. INITIATE CONNECTION?
Terrific
FIND ANYTHING?
T-SPHERE: HOLD CONNECTION.
ALMOST.
IF ANYTHING, IT IS A FITTING TRIBUTE TO JEFFREY BURR'S WASTED LIFE.
A MONUMENT TO A DISEASED WORLD, LONG PAST USEFULNESS AND BEST FORGOTTEN.
LOOKS LIKE JASON BURR LEFT WITHOUT TAKING HIS JOURNAL.
"DEAR DIARY: TODAY I WANT TO BLOW UP THE WORLD. NO ONE UNDERSTANDS ME."
LET THEM HAVE THEIR TINY VICTORIES.
YOU UNDERSTAND THAT WE'RE LOSING, RIGHT? EVERY "WIN" WE'VE SCORED HAS ALLOWED KOBRA TO INCREASE ITS CAPABILITIES.
HE KNOWS THE CHECKMATE PLAYBOOK BACK TO FRONT, AND HE'S USING IT AGAINST US.
LET THEM CLING TO HOPE.
SO WHAT DID KOBRA GAIN WHEN WE CAPTURED THIS BASE?
...TIME.
IT BOUGHT HIM TIME TO LAUNCH HIS NEXT STRIKE.

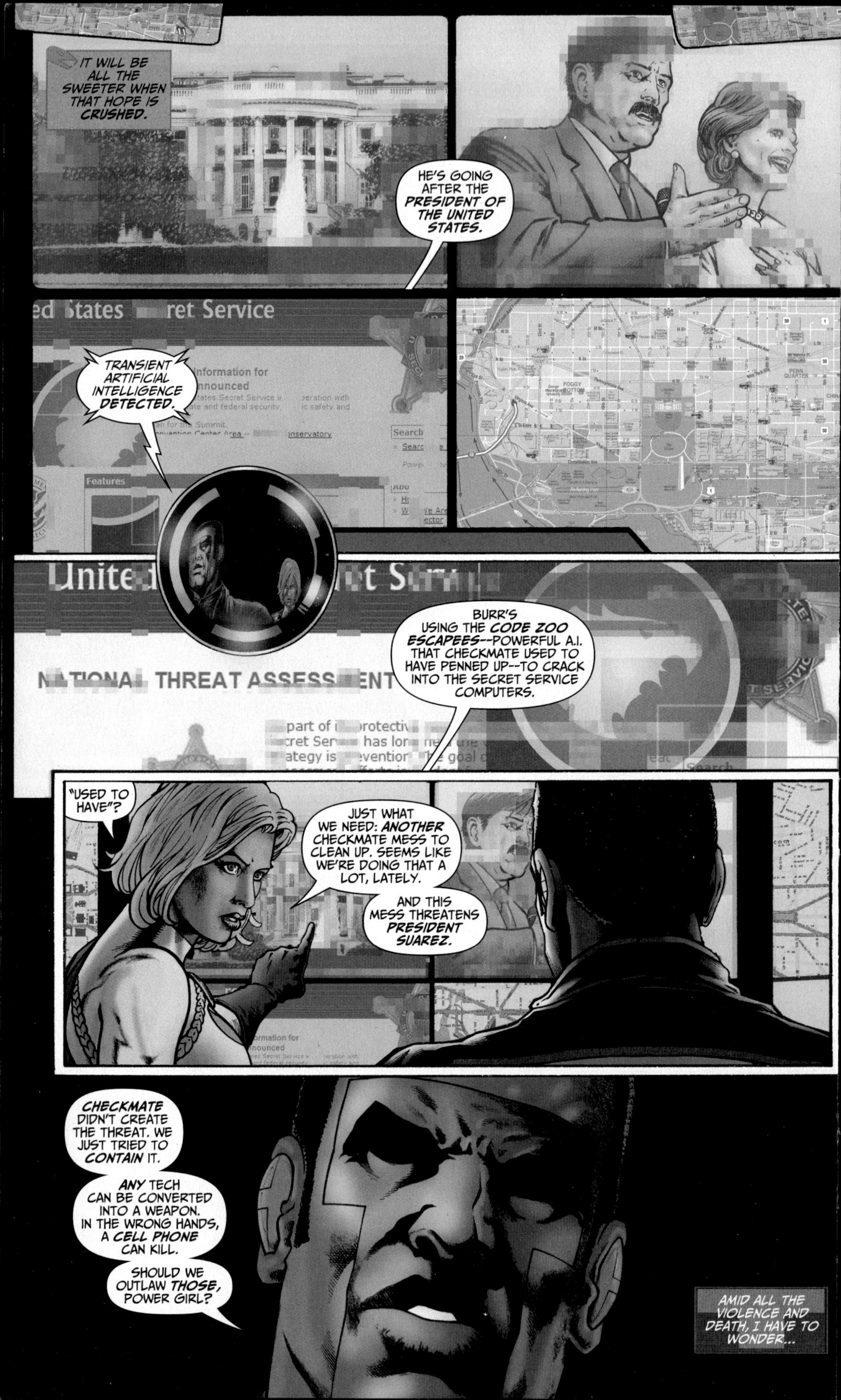
IT WILL BE ALL THE SWEETER WHEN THAT HOPE IS CRUSHED.
HE'S GOING AFTER THE PRESIDENT OF THE UNITED STATES.
TRANSIENT ARTIFICIAL INTELLIGENCE DETECTED.
BURR'S USING THE CODE ZOO ESCAPEES--POWERFUL A.I. THAT CHECKMATE USED TO HAVE PENNED UP--TO CRACK INTO THE SECRET SERVICE COMPUTERS.
"USED TO HAVE"?
JUST WHAT WE NEED: ANOTHER CHECKMATE MESS TO CLEAN UP. SEEMS LIKE WE'RE DOING THAT A LOT, LATELY.
AND THIS MESS THREATENS PRESIDENT SUAREZ.
CHECKMATE DIDN'T CREATE THE THREAT. WE JUST TRIED TO CONTAIN IT.
ANY TECH CAN BE CONVERTED INTO A WEAPON. IN THE WRONG HANDS, A CELL PHONE CAN KILL.
SHOULD WE OUTLAW THOSE, POWER GIRL?
AMID ALL THE VIOLENCE AND DEATH, I HAVE TO WONDER...

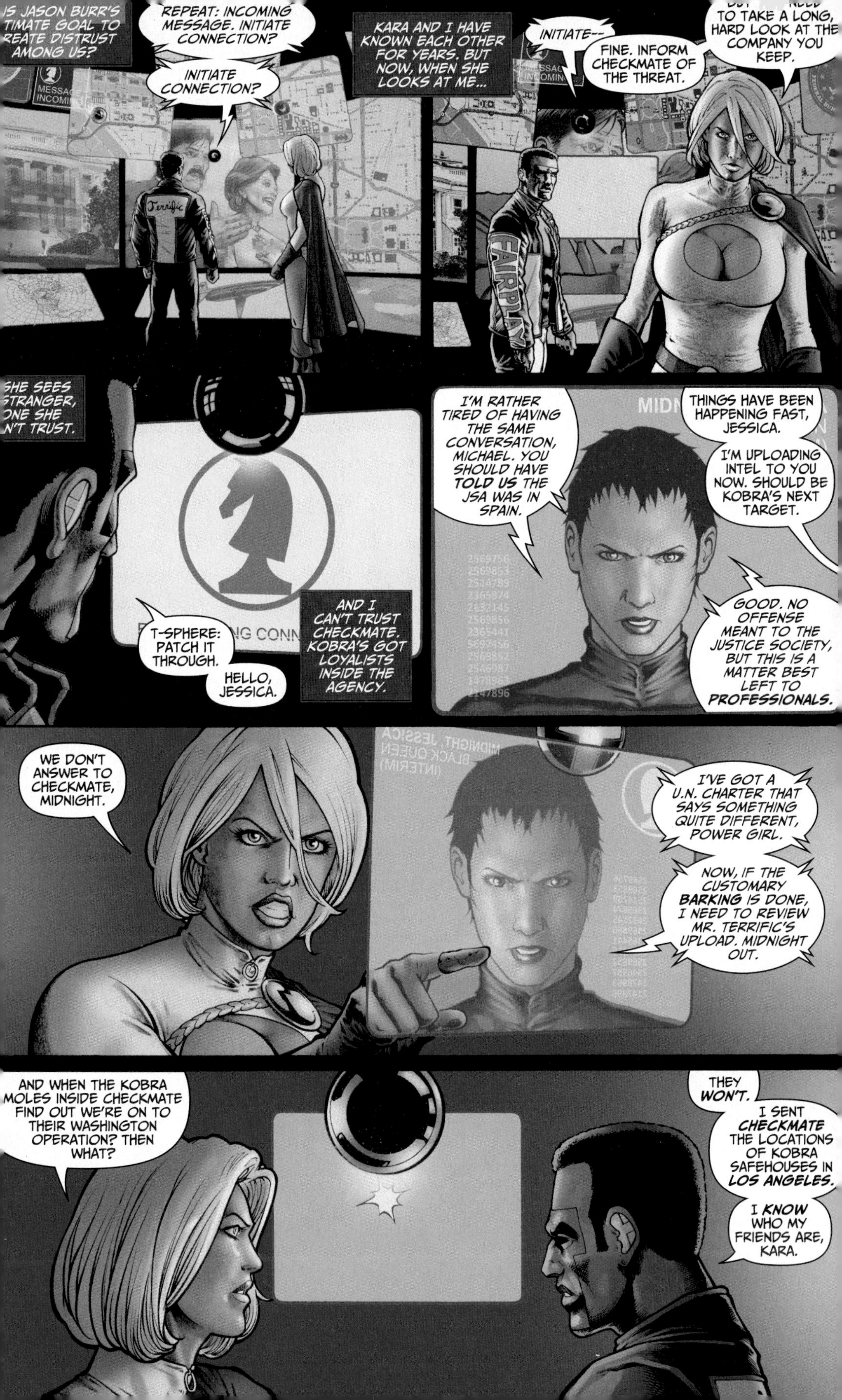
IS JASON BURR'S
TIMATE GOAL TO
REATE DISTRUST
AMONG US?
REPEAT: INCOMING MESSAGE. INITIATE CONNECTION?
INITIATE CONNECTION?
KARA AND I HAVE KNOWN EACH OTHER FOR YEARS. BUT NOW, WHEN SHE LOOKS AT ME...
INITIATE--
FINE. INFORM CHECKMATE OF THE THREAT.
TO TAKE A LONG, HARD LOOK AT THE COMPANY YOU KEEP.
HE SEES
TRANGER,
ONE SHE
N'T TRUST.
T-SPHERE: PATCH IT THROUGH.
HELLO, JESSICA.
AND I CAN'T TRUST CHECKMATE. KOBRA'S GOT LOYALISTS INSIDE THE AGENCY.
I'M RATHER TIRED OF HAVING THE SAME CONVERSATION, MICHAEL. YOU SHOULD HAVE TOLD US THE JSA WAS IN SPAIN.
THINGS HAVE BEEN HAPPENING FAST, JESSICA.
I'M UPLOADING INTEL TO YOU NOW. SHOULD BE KOBRA'S NEXT TARGET.
GOOD. NO OFFENSE MEANT TO THE JUSTICE SOCIETY, BUT THIS IS A MATTER BEST LEFT TO PROFESSIONALS.
WE DON'T ANSWER TO CHECKMATE, MIDNIGHT.
I'VE GOT A U.N. CHARTER THAT SAYS SOMETHING QUITE DIFFERENT, POWER GIRL.
NOW, IF THE CUSTOMARY BARKING IS DONE, I NEED TO REVIEW MR. TERRIFIC'S UPLOAD. MIDNIGHT OUT.
AND WHEN THE KOBRA MOLES INSIDE CHECKMATE FIND OUT WE'RE ON TO THEIR WASHINGTON OPERATION? THEN WHAT?
THEY WON'T.
I SENT CHECKMATE THE LOCATIONS OF KOBRA SAFEHOUSES IN LOS ANGELES.
I KNOW WHO MY FRIENDS ARE, KARA.

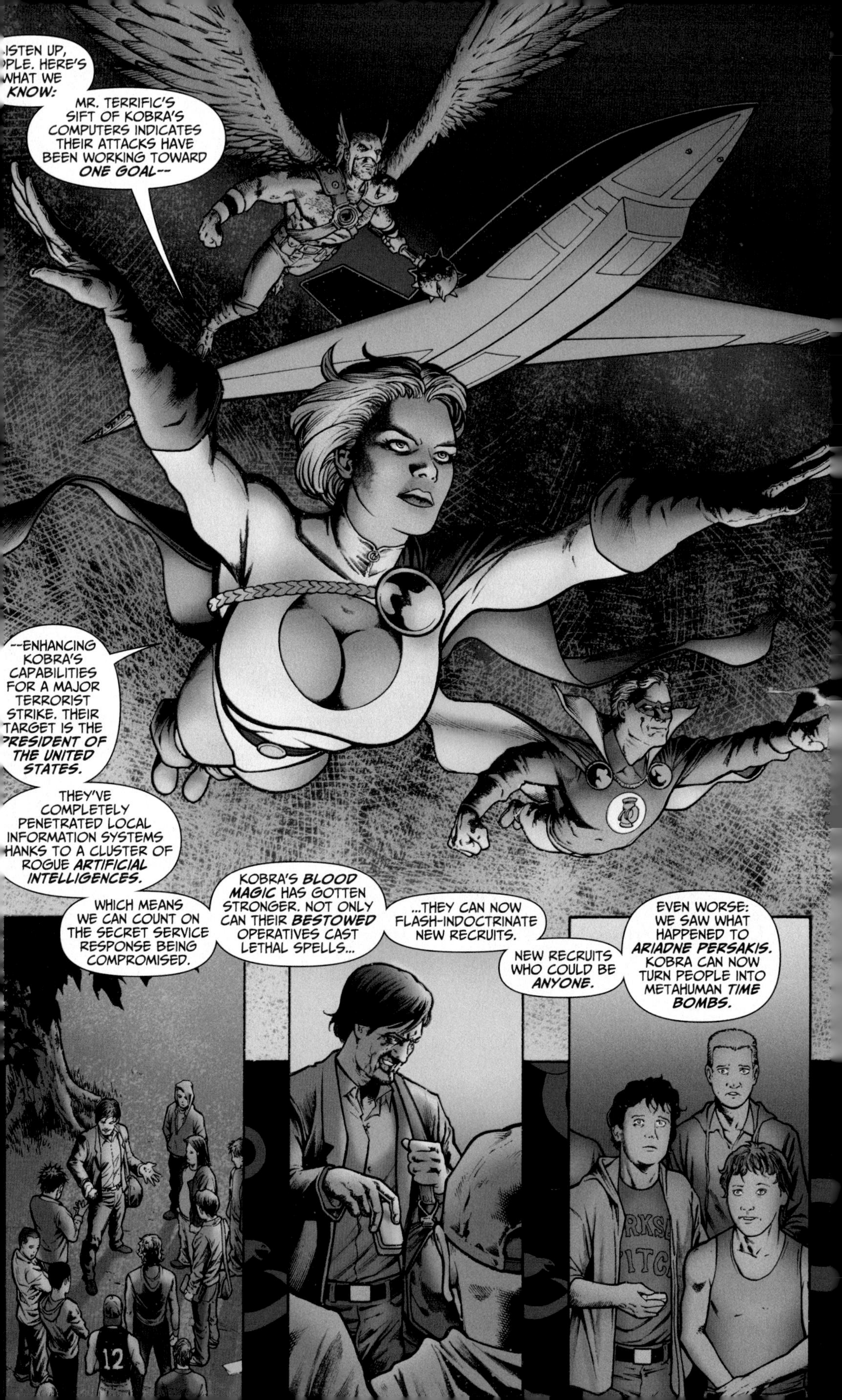

LISTEN UP, PEOPLE. HERE'S WHAT WE KNOW:
MR. TERRIFIC'S SIFT OF KOBRA'S COMPUTERS INDICATES THEIR ATTACKS HAVE BEEN WORKING TOWARD ONE GOAL--
--ENHANCING KOBRA'S CAPABILITIES FOR A MAJOR TERRORIST STRIKE. THEIR TARGET IS THE PRESIDENT OF THE UNITED STATES.
THEY'VE COMPLETELY PENETRATED LOCAL INFORMATION SYSTEMS THANKS TO A CLUSTER OF ROGUE ARTIFICIAL INTELLIGENCES.
WHICH MEANS WE CAN COUNT ON THE SECRET SERVICE RESPONSE BEING COMPROMISED.
KOBRA'S BLOOD MAGIC HAS GOTTEN STRONGER. NOT ONLY CAN THEIR BESTOWED OPERATIVES CAST LETHAL SPELLS...
...THEY CAN NOW FLASH-INDOCTRINATE NEW RECRUITS.
NEW RECRUITS WHO COULD BE ANYONE.
EVEN WORSE: WE SAW WHAT HAPPENED TO ARIADNE PERSAKIS. KOBRA CAN NOW TURN PEOPLE INTO METAHUMAN TIME BOMBS.

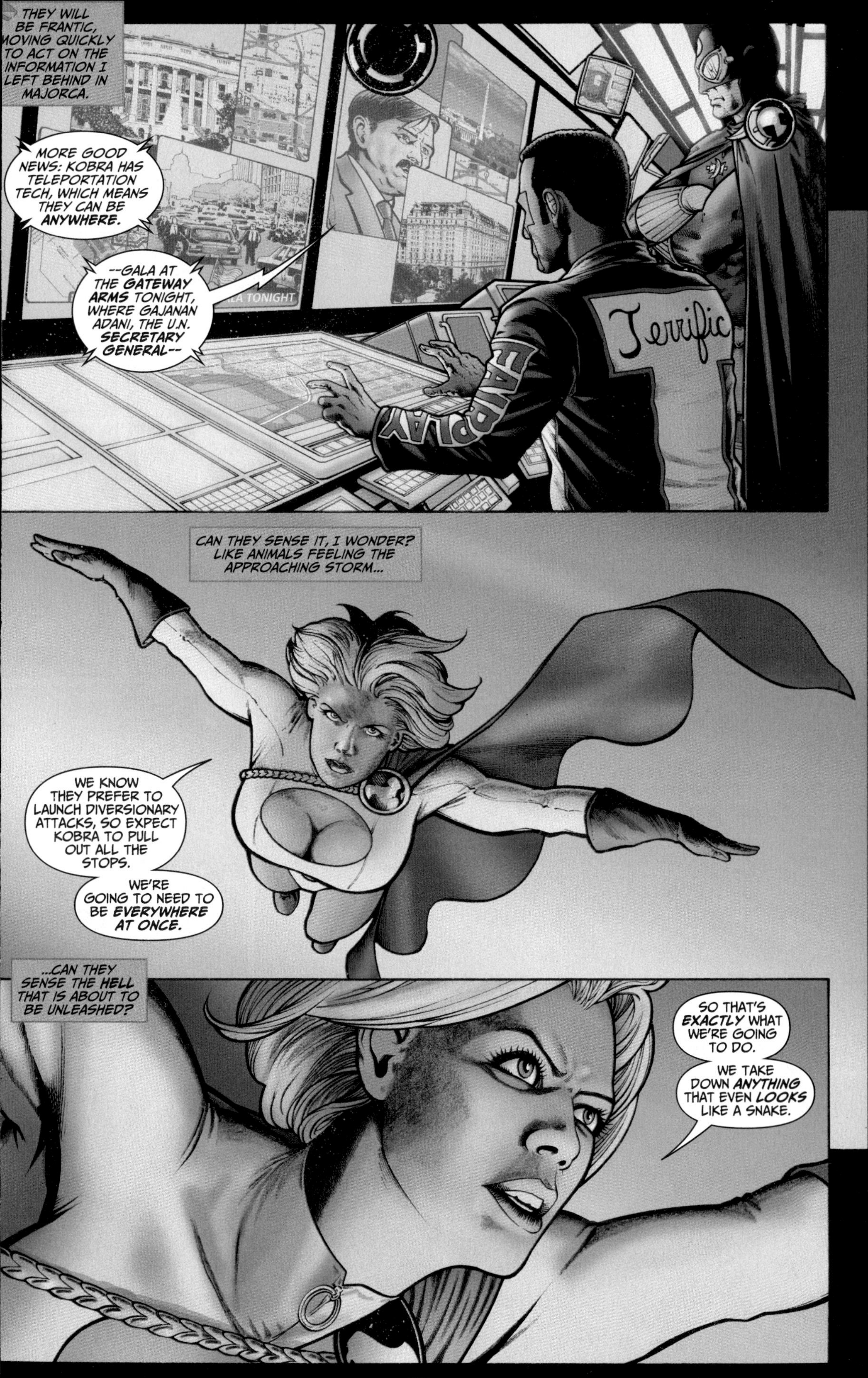
THEY WILL BE FRANTIC, MOVING QUICKLY TO ACT ON THE INFORMATION I LEFT BEHIND IN MAJORCA.
MORE GOOD NEWS: KOBRA HAS TELEPORTATION TECH, WHICH MEANS THEY CAN BE ANYWHERE.
--GALA AT THE GATEWAY ARMS TONIGHT, WHERE GAJANAN ADANI, THE U.N. SECRETARY GENERAL--
Terrific
FAIR PLAY
CAN THEY SENSE IT, I WONDER? LIKE ANIMALS FEELING THE APPROACHING STORM...
WE KNOW THEY PREFER TO LAUNCH DIVERSIONARY ATTACKS, SO EXPECT KOBRA TO PULL OUT ALL THE STOPS.
WE'RE GOING TO NEED TO BE EVERYWHERE AT ONCE.
...CAN THEY SENSE THE HELL THAT IS ABOUT TO BE UNLEASHED?
SO THAT'S EXACTLY WHAT WE'RE GOING TO DO.
WE TAKE DOWN ANYTHING THAT EVEN LOOKS LIKE A SNAKE.

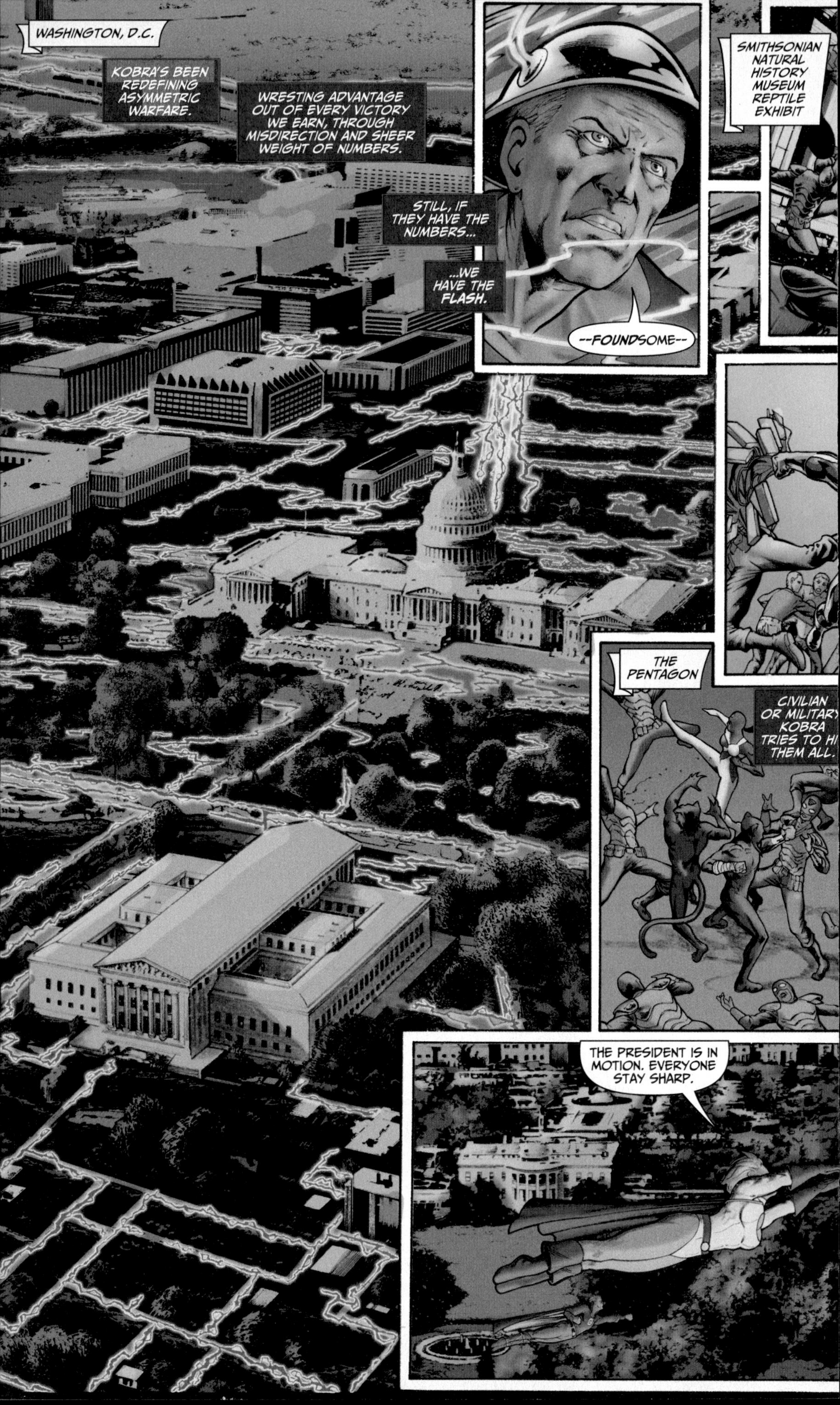
WASHINGTON, D.C.
KOBRA'S BEEN REDEFINING ASYMMETRIC WARFARE.
WRESTING ADVANTAGE OUT OF EVERY VICTORY WE EARN, THROUGH MISDIRECTION AND SHEER WEIGHT OF NUMBERS.
STILL, IF THEY HAVE THE NUMBERS...
...WE HAVE THE FLASH.
--FOUNDSOME--
SMITHSONIAN NATURAL HISTORY MUSEUM REPTILE EXHIBIT
THE PENTAGON
CIVILIAN OR MILITARY KOBRA TRIES TO HI THEM ALL.
THE PRESIDENT IS IN MOTION. EVERYONE STAY SHARP.

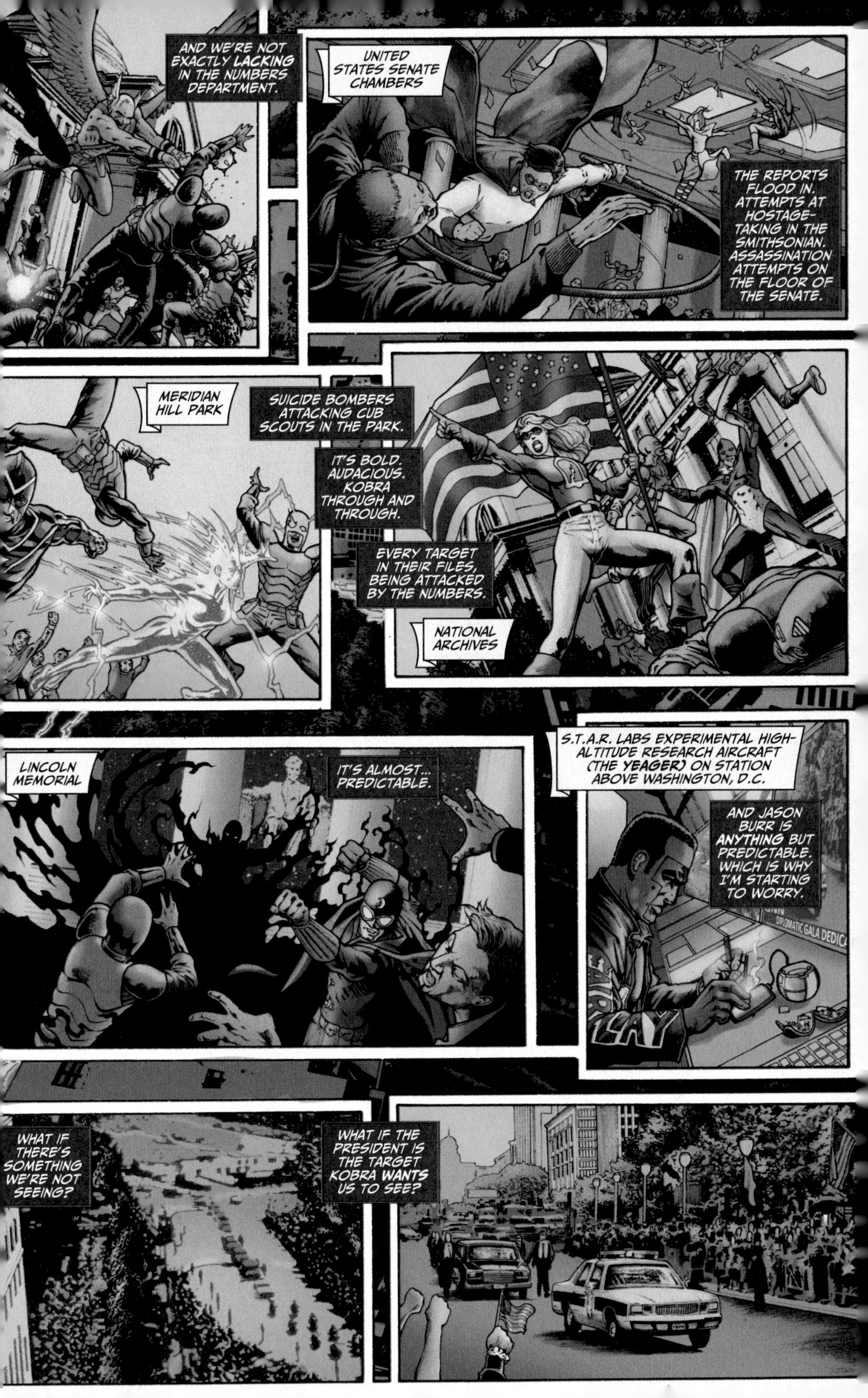
AND WE'RE NOT EXACTLY LACKING IN THE NUMBERS DEPARTMENT.
UNITED STATES SENATE CHAMBERS
THE REPORTS FLOOD IN. ATTEMPTS AT HOSTAGE-TAKING IN THE SMITHSONIAN. ASSASSINATION ATTEMPTS ON THE FLOOR OF THE SENATE.
MERIDIAN HILL PARK
SUICIDE BOMBERS ATTACKING CUB SCOUTS IN THE PARK.
IT'S BOLD. AUDACIOUS. KOBRA THROUGH AND THROUGH.
EVERY TARGET IN THEIR FILES, BEING ATTACKED BY THE NUMBERS.
NATIONAL ARCHIVES
LINCOLN MEMORIAL
IT'S ALMOST... PREDICTABLE.
S.T.A.R. LABS EXPERIMENTAL HIGH-ALTITUDE RESEARCH AIRCRAFT (THE YEAGER) ON STATION ABOVE WASHINGTON, D.C.
AND JASON BURR IS ANYTHING BUT PREDICTABLE. WHICH IS WHY I'M STARTING TO WORRY.
DIPLOMATIC GALA DEDICA
WHAT IF THERE'S SOMETHING WE'RE NOT SEEING?
WHAT IF THE PRESIDENT IS THE TARGET KOBRA WANTS US TO SEE?

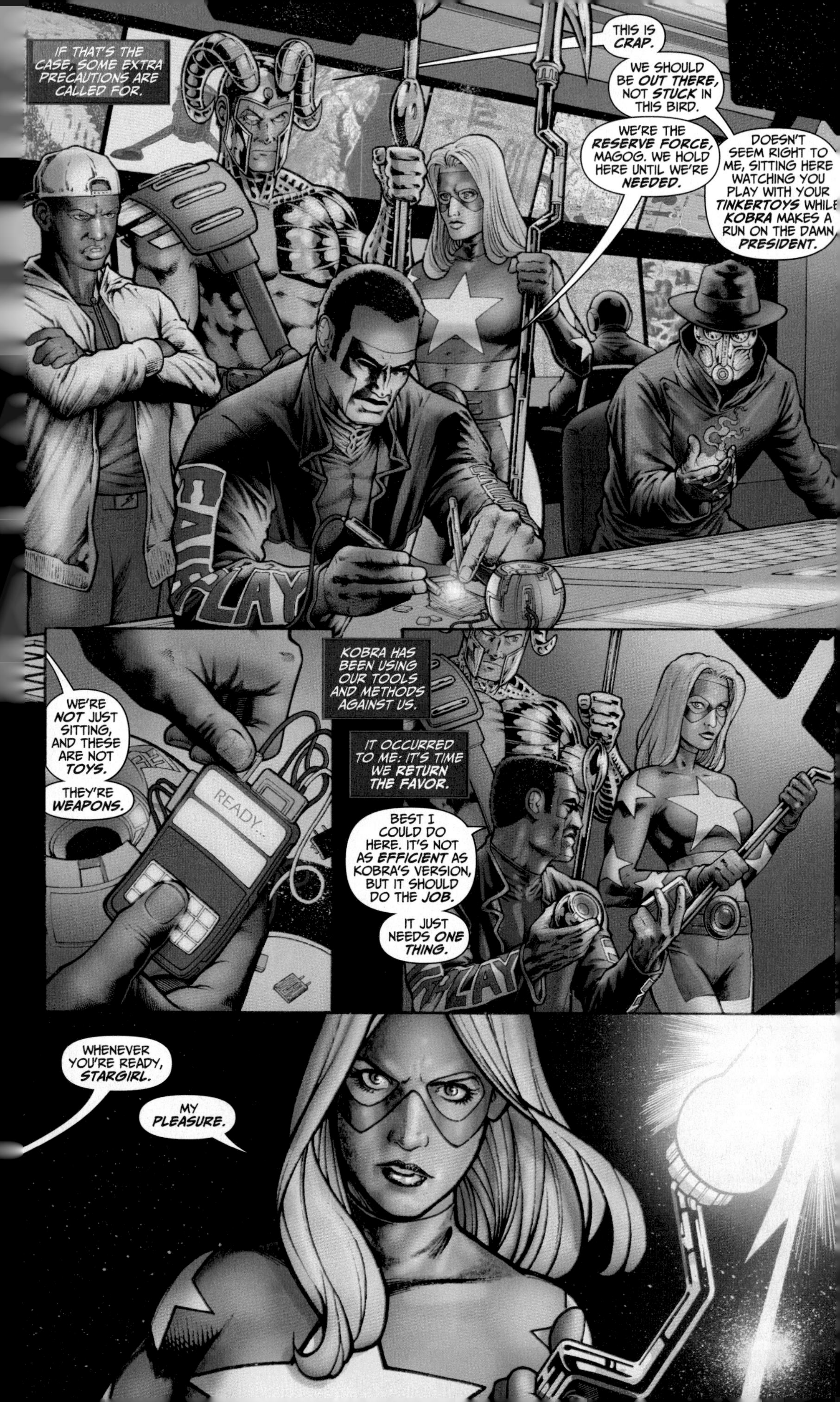

IF THAT'S THE CASE, SOME EXTRA PRECAUTIONS ARE CALLED FOR.
THIS IS CRAP.
WE SHOULD BE OUT THERE, NOT STUCK IN THIS BIRD.
WE'RE THE RESERVE FORCE, MAGOG. WE HOLD HERE UNTIL WE'RE NEEDED.
DOESN'T SEEM RIGHT TO ME, SITTING HERE WATCHING YOU PLAY WITH YOUR TINKERTOYS WHILE KOBRA MAKES A RUN ON THE DAMN PRESIDENT.
WE'RE NOT JUST SITTING, AND THESE ARE NOT TOYS.
THEY'RE WEAPONS.
READY...
KOBRA HAS BEEN USING OUR TOOLS AND METHODS AGAINST US.
IT OCCURRED TO ME: IT'S TIME WE RETURN THE FAVOR.
BEST I COULD DO HERE. IT'S NOT AS EFFICIENT AS KOBRA'S VERSION, BUT IT SHOULD DO THE JOB.
IT JUST NEEDS ONE THING.
WHENEVER YOU'RE READY, STARGIRL.
MY PLEASURE.

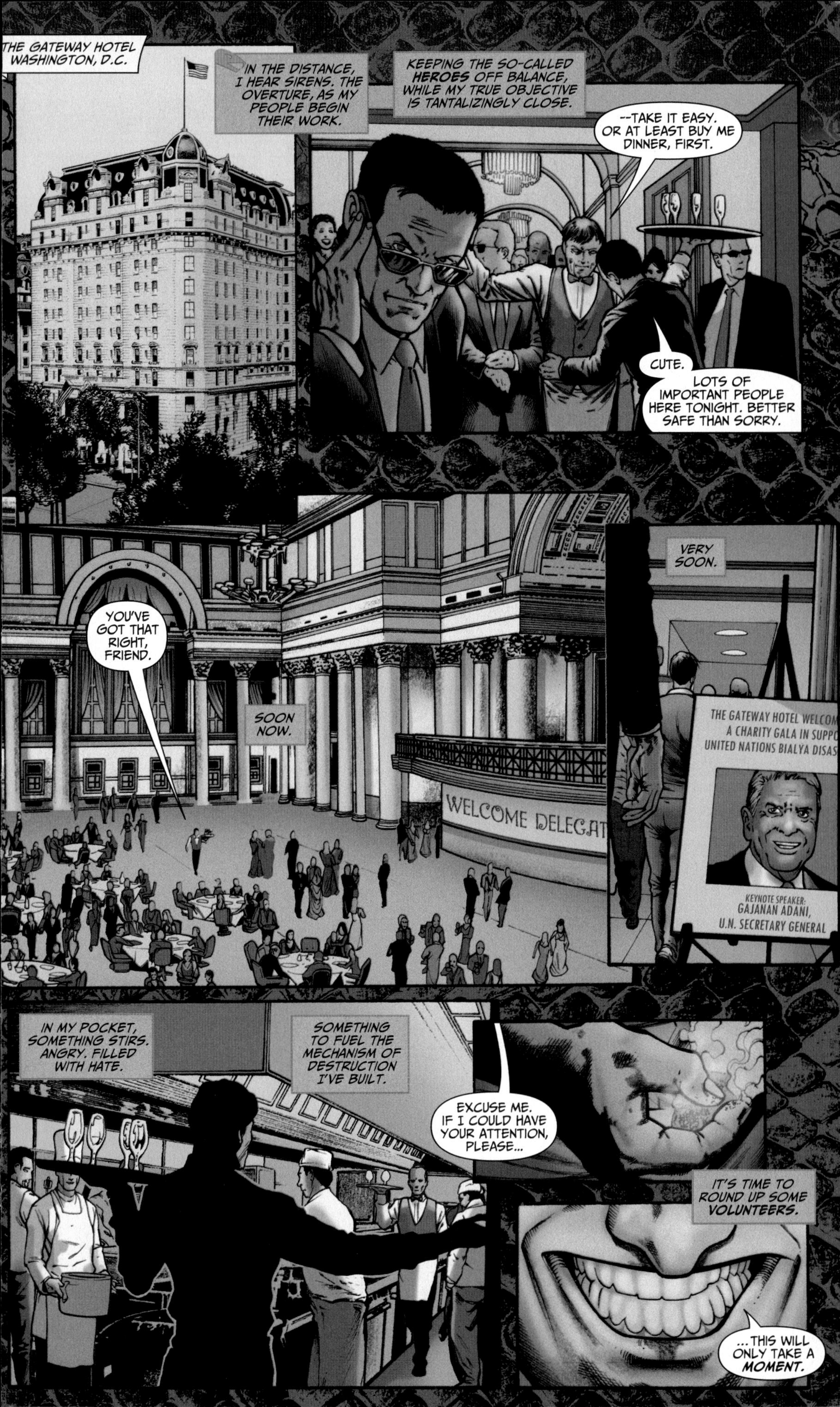
THE GATEWAY HOTEL WASHINGTON, D.C.
IN THE DISTANCE, I HEAR SIRENS. THE OVERTURE, AS MY PEOPLE BEGIN THEIR WORK.
KEEPING THE SO-CALLED HEROES OFF BALANCE, WHILE MY TRUE OBJECTIVE IS TANTALIZINGLY CLOSE.
--TAKE IT EASY. OR AT LEAST BUY ME DINNER, FIRST.
CUTE.
LOTS OF IMPORTANT PEOPLE HERE TONIGHT. BETTER SAFE THAN SORRY.
YOU'VE GOT THAT RIGHT, FRIEND.
SOON NOW.
WELCOME DELEGAT
VERY SOON.
THE GATEWAY HOTEL WELCOM
A CHARITY GALA IN SUPPO
UNITED NATIONS BIALYA DISAS
KEYNOTE SPEAKER:
GAJANAN ADANI,
U.N. SECRETARY GENERAL
IN MY POCKET, SOMETHING STIRS. ANGRY. FILLED WITH HATE.
SOMETHING TO FUEL THE MECHANISM OF DESTRUCTION I'VE BUILT.
EXCUSE ME. IF I COULD HAVE YOUR ATTENTION, PLEASE...
IT'S TIME TO ROUND UP SOME VOLUNTEERS.
...THIS WILL ONLY TAKE A MOMENT.

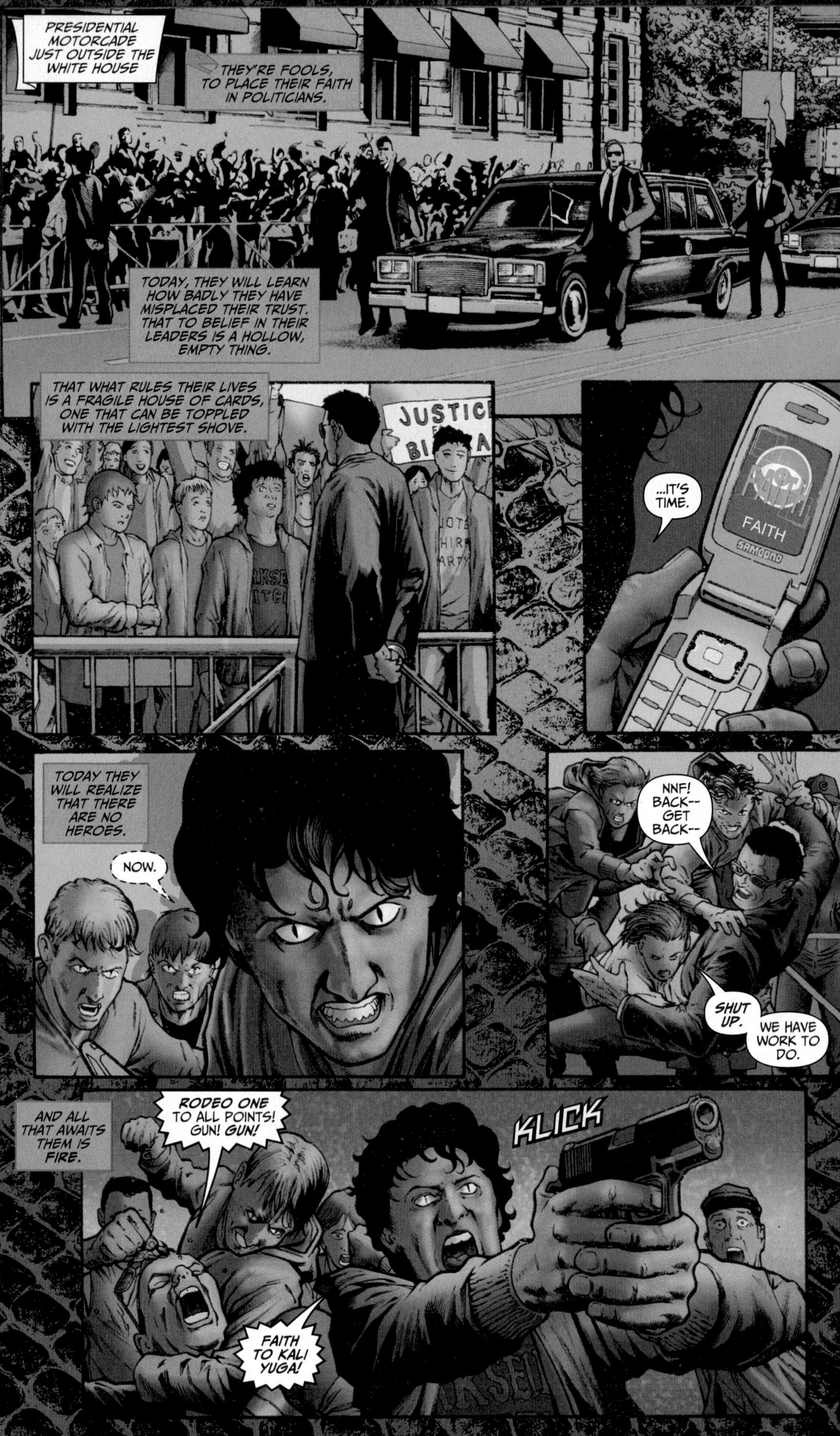
PRESIDENTIAL MOTORCADE JUST OUTSIDE THE WHITE HOUSE
THEY'RE FOOLS, TO PLACE THEIR FAITH IN POLITICIANS.
TODAY, THEY WILL LEARN HOW BADLY THEY HAVE MISPLACED THEIR TRUST. THAT TO BELIEF IN THEIR LEADERS IS A HOLLOW, EMPTY THING.
THAT WHAT RULES THEIR LIVES IS A FRAGILE HOUSE OF CARDS, ONE THAT CAN BE TOPPLED WITH THE LIGHTEST SHOVE.
JUSTICE
...IT'S TIME.
FAITH
TODAY THEY WILL REALIZE THAT THERE ARE NO HEROES.
NOW.
NNF! BACK-- GET BACK--
SHUT UP.
WE HAVE WORK TO DO.
AND ALL THAT AWAITS THEM IS FIRE.
RODEO ONE TO ALL POINTS! GUN! GUN!
KLICK
FAITH TO KALI YUGA!

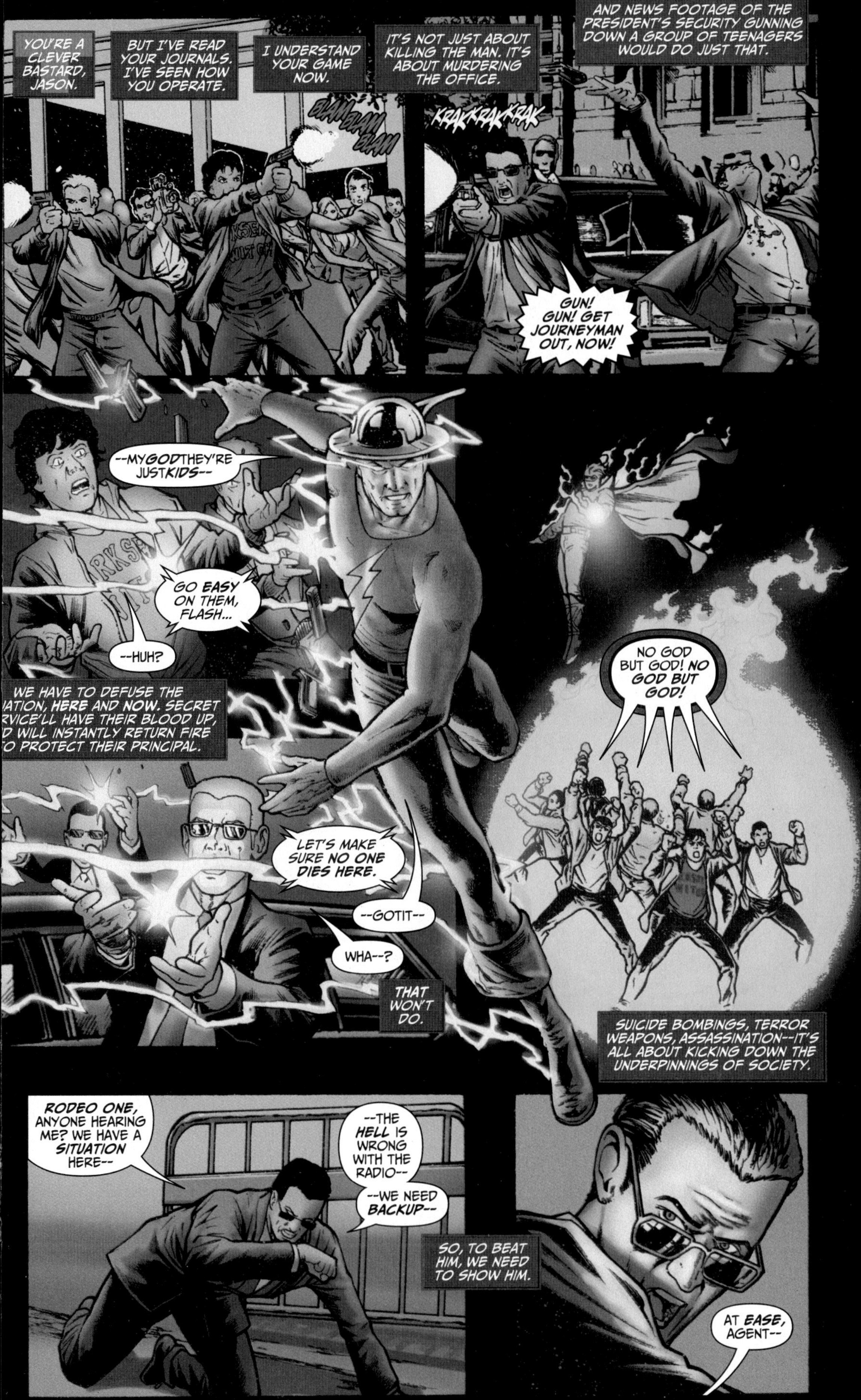

YOU'RE A CLEVER BASTARD, JASON.
BUT I'VE READ YOUR JOURNALS. I'VE SEEN HOW YOU OPERATE.
I UNDERSTAND YOUR GAME NOW.
BLAM BLAM BLAM
IT'S NOT JUST ABOUT KILLING THE MAN. IT'S ABOUT MURDERING THE OFFICE.
AND NEWS FOOTAGE OF THE PRESIDENT'S SECURITY GUNNING DOWN A GROUP OF TEENAGERS WOULD DO JUST THAT.
KRAKKRAKKRAK
GUN! GUN! GET JOURNEYMAN OUT, NOW!
--MYGODTHEY'RE JUSTKIDS--
GO EASY ON THEM, FLASH...
--HUH?
WE HAVE TO DEFUSE THE
IATION, HERE AND NOW. SECRET
RVICE'LL HAVE THEIR BLOOD UP,
D WILL INSTANTLY RETURN FIRE
TO PROTECT THEIR PRINCIPAL.
LET'S MAKE SURE NO ONE DIES HERE.
--GOTIT--
WHA--?
THAT WON'T DO.
NO GOD BUT GOD! NO GOD BUT GOD!
SUICIDE BOMBINGS, TERROR WEAPONS, ASSASSINATION--IT'S ALL ABOUT KICKING DOWN THE UNDERPINNINGS OF SOCIETY.
RODEO ONE, ANYONE HEARING ME? WE HAVE A SITUATION HERE--
--THE HELL IS WRONG WITH THE RADIO--
--WE NEED BACKUP--
SO, TO BEAT HIM, WE NEED TO SHOW HIM.
AT EASE, AGENT--

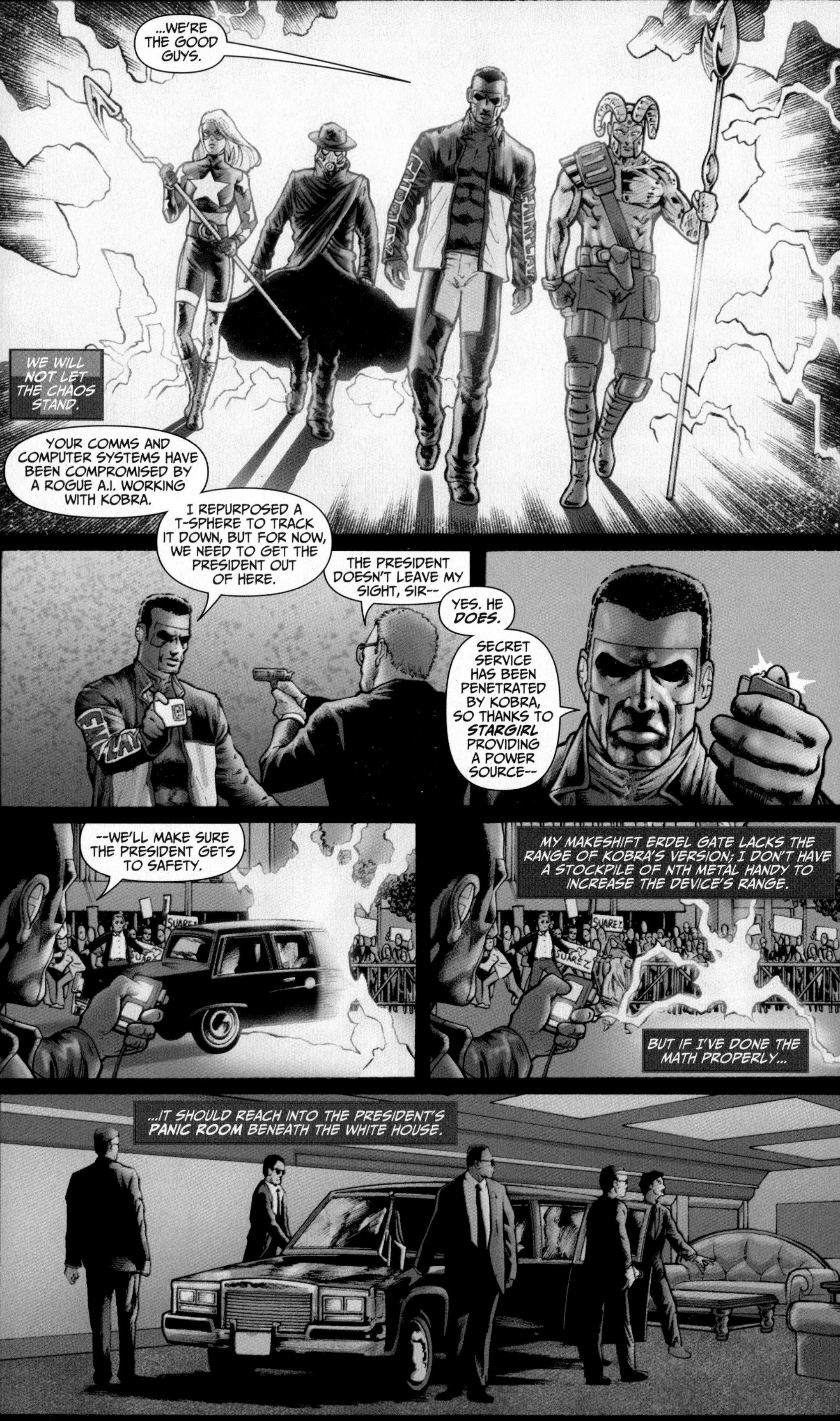

...WE'RE THE GOOD GUYS.
WE WILL NOT LET THE CHAOS STAND.
YOUR COMMS AND COMPUTER SYSTEMS HAVE BEEN COMPROMISED BY A ROGUE A.I. WORKING WITH KOBRA.
I REPURPOSED A T-SPHERE TO TRACK IT DOWN, BUT FOR NOW, WE NEED TO GET THE PRESIDENT OUT OF HERE.
THE PRESIDENT DOESN'T LEAVE MY SIGHT, SIR--
YES. HE DOES.
SECRET SERVICE HAS BEEN PENETRATED BY KOBRA, SO THANKS TO STARGIRL PROVIDING A POWER SOURCE--
--WE'LL MAKE SURE THE PRESIDENT GETS TO SAFETY.
SUAREZ
MY MAKESHIFT ERDEL GATE LACKS THE RANGE OF KOBRA'S VERSION; I DON'T HAVE A STOCKPILE OF NTH METAL HANDY TO INCREASE THE DEVICE'S RANGE.
SUAREZ
BUT IF I'VE DONE THE MATH PROPERLY...
...IT SHOULD REACH INTO THE PRESIDENT'S PANIC ROOM BENEATH THE WHITE HOUSE.

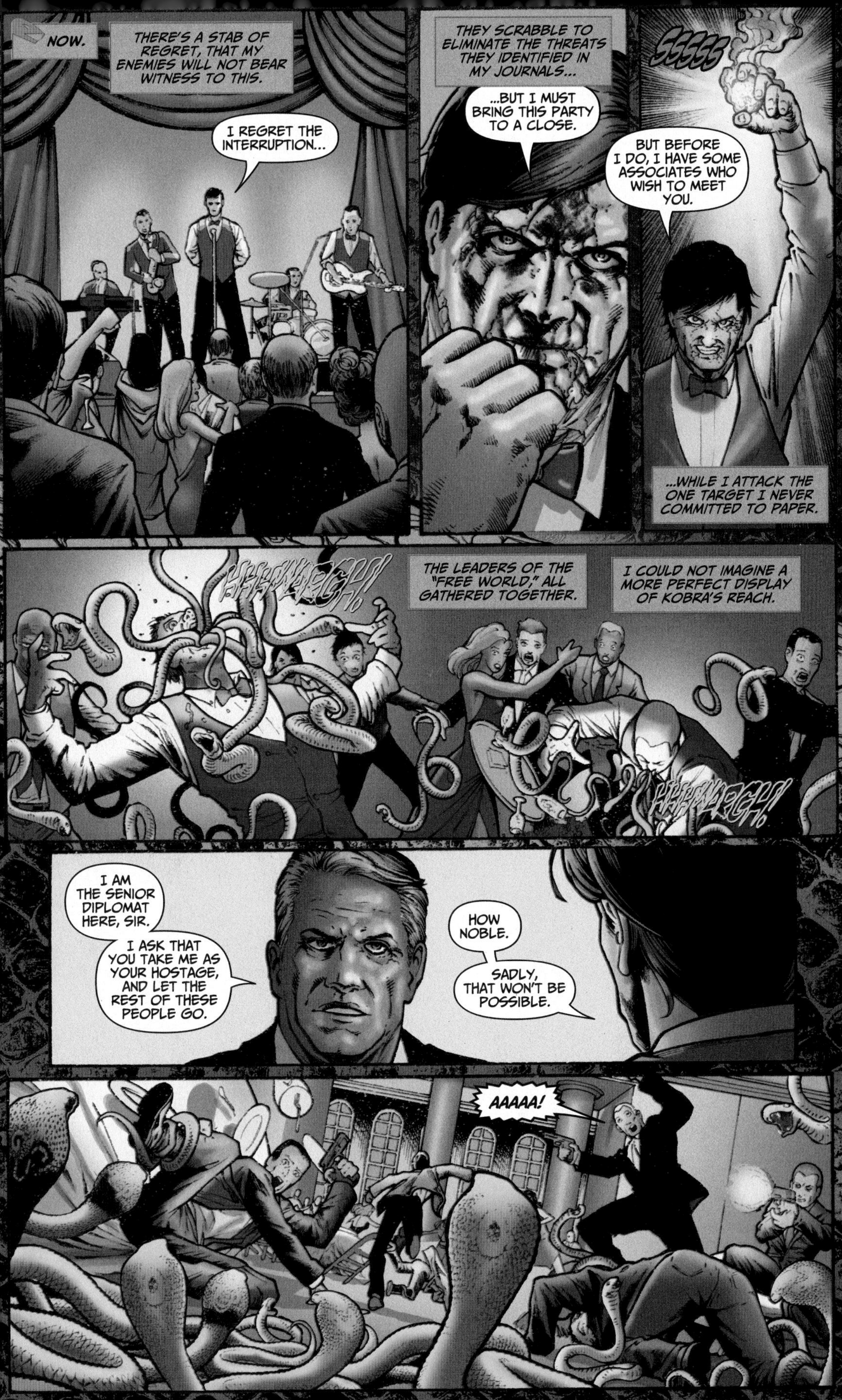
NOW.
THERE'S A STAB OF REGRET, THAT MY ENEMIES WILL NOT BEAR WITNESS TO THIS.
I REGRET THE INTERRUPTION...
THEY SCRABBLE TO ELIMINATE THE THREATS THEY IDENTIFIED IN MY JOURNALS...
...BUT I MUST BRING THIS PARTY TO A CLOSE.
SSSSS
BUT BEFORE I DO, I HAVE SOME ASSOCIATES WHO WISH TO MEET YOU.
...WHILE I ATTACK THE ONE TARGET I NEVER COMMITTED TO PAPER.
THE LEADERS OF THE "FREE WORLD," ALL GATHERED TOGETHER.
I COULD NOT IMAGINE A MORE PERFECT DISPLAY OF KOBRA'S REACH.
I AM THE SENIOR DIPLOMAT HERE, SIR.
I ASK THAT YOU TAKE ME AS YOUR HOSTAGE, AND LET THE REST OF THESE PEOPLE GO.
HOW NOBLE.
SADLY, THAT WON'T BE POSSIBLE.
AAAAA!

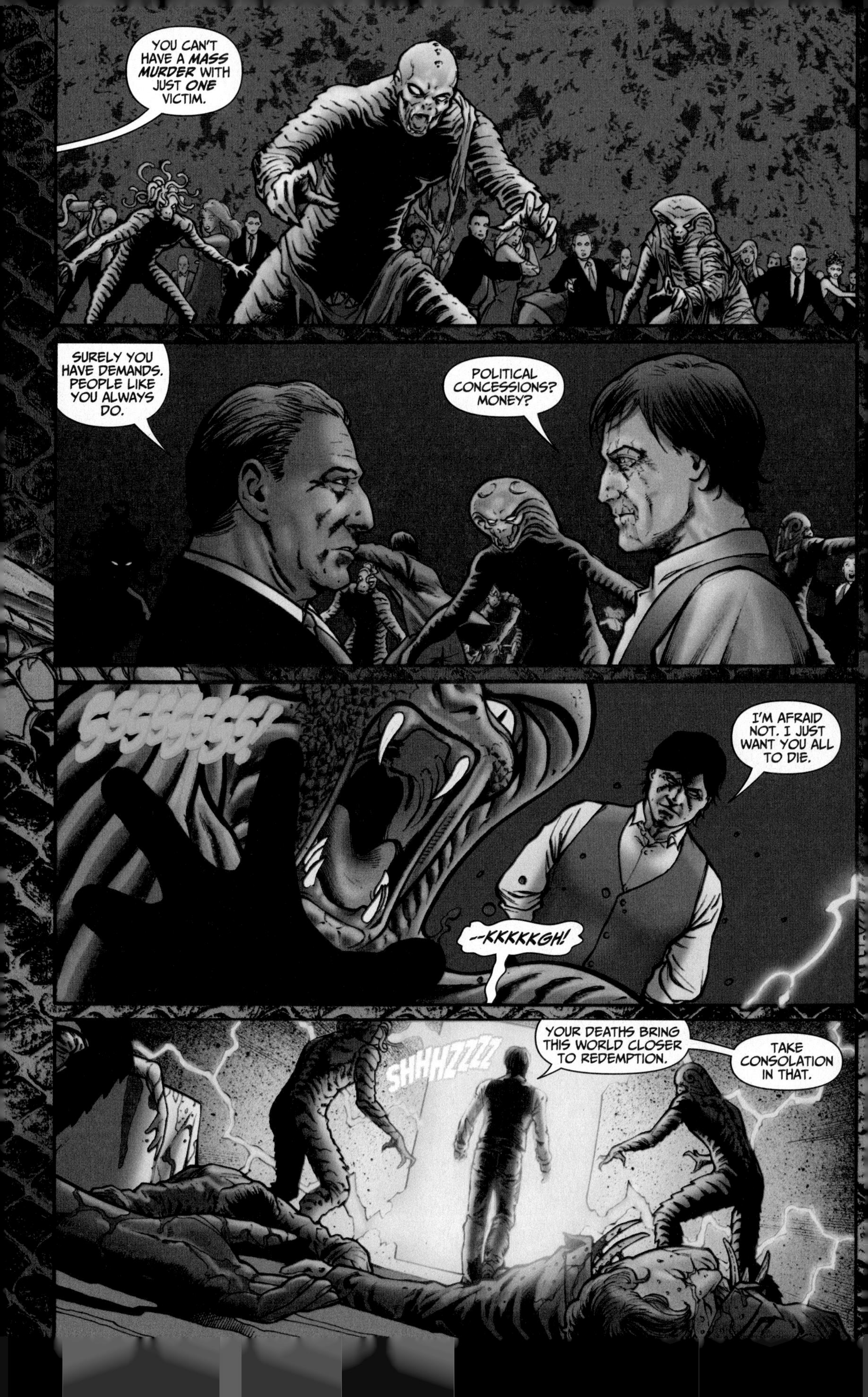
YOU CAN'T HAVE A MASS MURDER WITH JUST ONE VICTIM.
SURELY YOU HAVE DEMANDS. PEOPLE LIKE YOU ALWAYS DO.
POLITICAL CONCESSIONS? MONEY?
SSSSSSSS!
I'M AFRAID NOT. I JUST WANT YOU ALL TO DIE.
--KKKKKGH!
SHHHZZZZ
YOUR DEATHS BRING THIS WORLD CLOSER TO REDEMPTION.
TAKE CONSOLATION IN THAT.

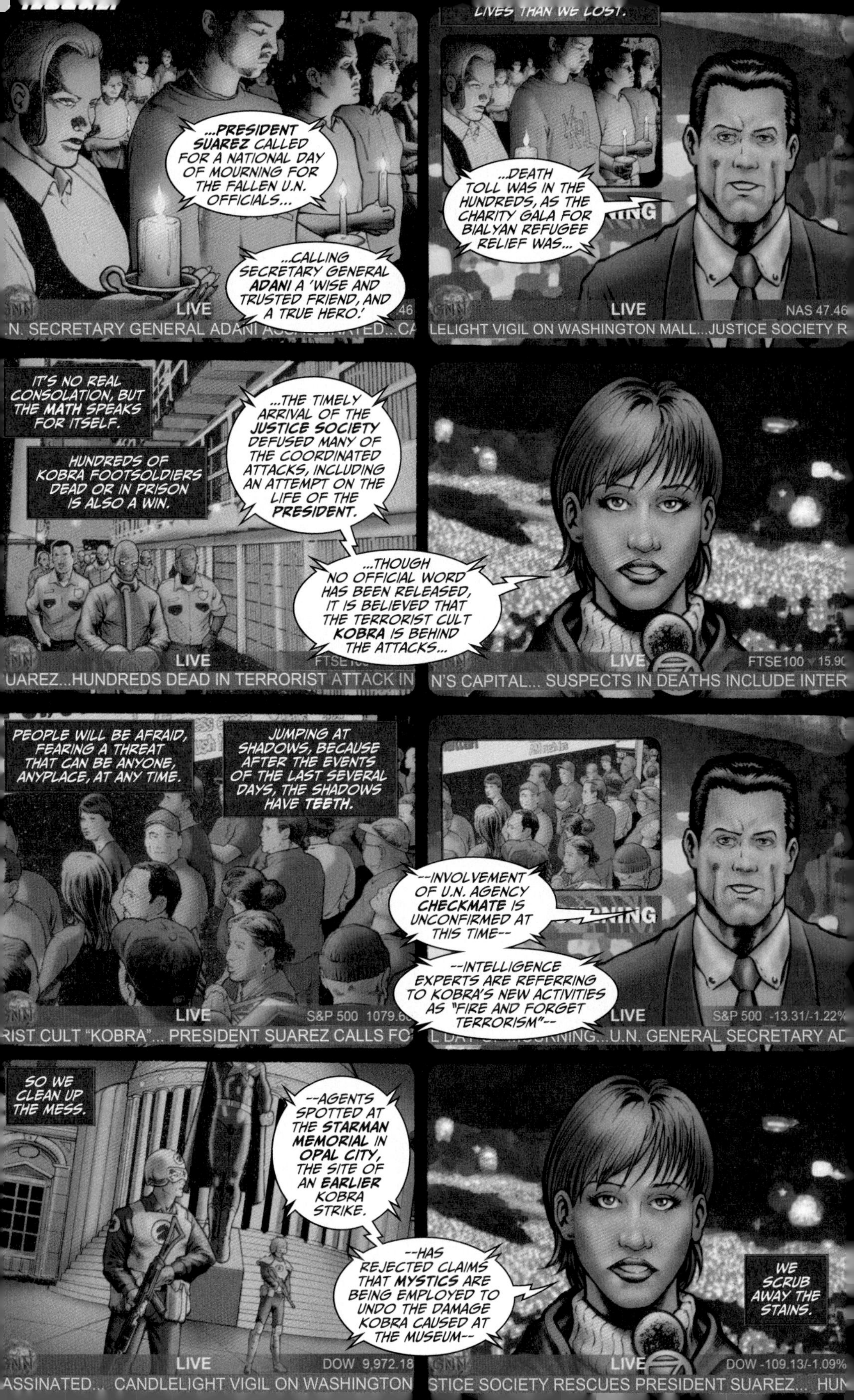
LIVES THAN WE LOST.
...PRESIDENT SUAREZ CALLED FOR A NATIONAL DAY OF MOURNING FOR THE FALLEN U.N. OFFICIALS...
...CALLING SECRETARY GENERAL ADANI A 'WISE AND TRUSTED FRIEND, AND A TRUE HERO.'
LIVE
.N. SECRETARY GENERAL ADANI ASSASSINATED...CA
...DEATH TOLL WAS IN THE HUNDREDS, AS THE CHARITY GALA FOR BIALYAN REFUGEE RELIEF WAS...
LIVE
NAS 47.46
LELIGHT VIGIL ON WASHINGTON MALL...JUSTICE SOCIETY R
IT'S NO REAL CONSOLATION, BUT THE MATH SPEAKS FOR ITSELF.
HUNDREDS OF KOBRA FOOTSOLDIERS DEAD OR IN PRISON IS ALSO A WIN.
...THE TIMELY ARRIVAL OF THE JUSTICE SOCIETY DEFUSED MANY OF THE COORDINATED ATTACKS, INCLUDING AN ATTEMPT ON THE LIFE OF THE PRESIDENT.
...THOUGH NO OFFICIAL WORD HAS BEEN RELEASED, IT IS BELIEVED THAT THE TERRORIST CULT KOBRA IS BEHIND THE ATTACKS...
LIVE
UAREZ...HUNDREDS DEAD IN TERRORIST ATTACK IN
LIVE
FTSE100 15.90
N'S CAPITAL... SUSPECTS IN DEATHS INCLUDE INTER
PEOPLE WILL BE AFRAID, FEARING A THREAT THAT CAN BE ANYONE, ANYPLACE, AT ANY TIME.
JUMPING AT SHADOWS, BECAUSE AFTER THE EVENTS OF THE LAST SEVERAL DAYS, THE SHADOWS HAVE TEETH.
LIVE
S&P 500 1079.6
RIST CULT "KOBRA"... PRESIDENT SUAREZ CALLS FO
--INVOLVEMENT OF U.N. AGENCY CHECKMATE IS UNCONFIRMED AT THIS TIME--
--INTELLIGENCE EXPERTS ARE REFERRING TO KOBRA'S NEW ACTIVITIES AS "FIRE AND FORGET TERRORISM"--
LIVE
S&P 500 -13.31/-1.22%
RNING...U.N. GENERAL SECRETARY AD
SO WE CLEAN UP THE MESS.
--AGENTS SPOTTED AT THE STARMAN MEMORIAL IN OPAL CITY, THE SITE OF AN EARLIER KOBRA STRIKE.
--HAS REJECTED CLAIMS THAT MYSTICS ARE BEING EMPLOYED TO UNDO THE DAMAGE KOBRA CAUSED AT THE MUSEUM--
LIVE
DOW 9,972.18
ASSINATED... CANDLELIGHT VIGIL ON WASHINGTON
WE SCRUB AWAY THE STAINS.
LIVE
DOW -109.13/-1.09%
STICE SOCIETY RESCUES PRESIDENT SUAREZ... HUN

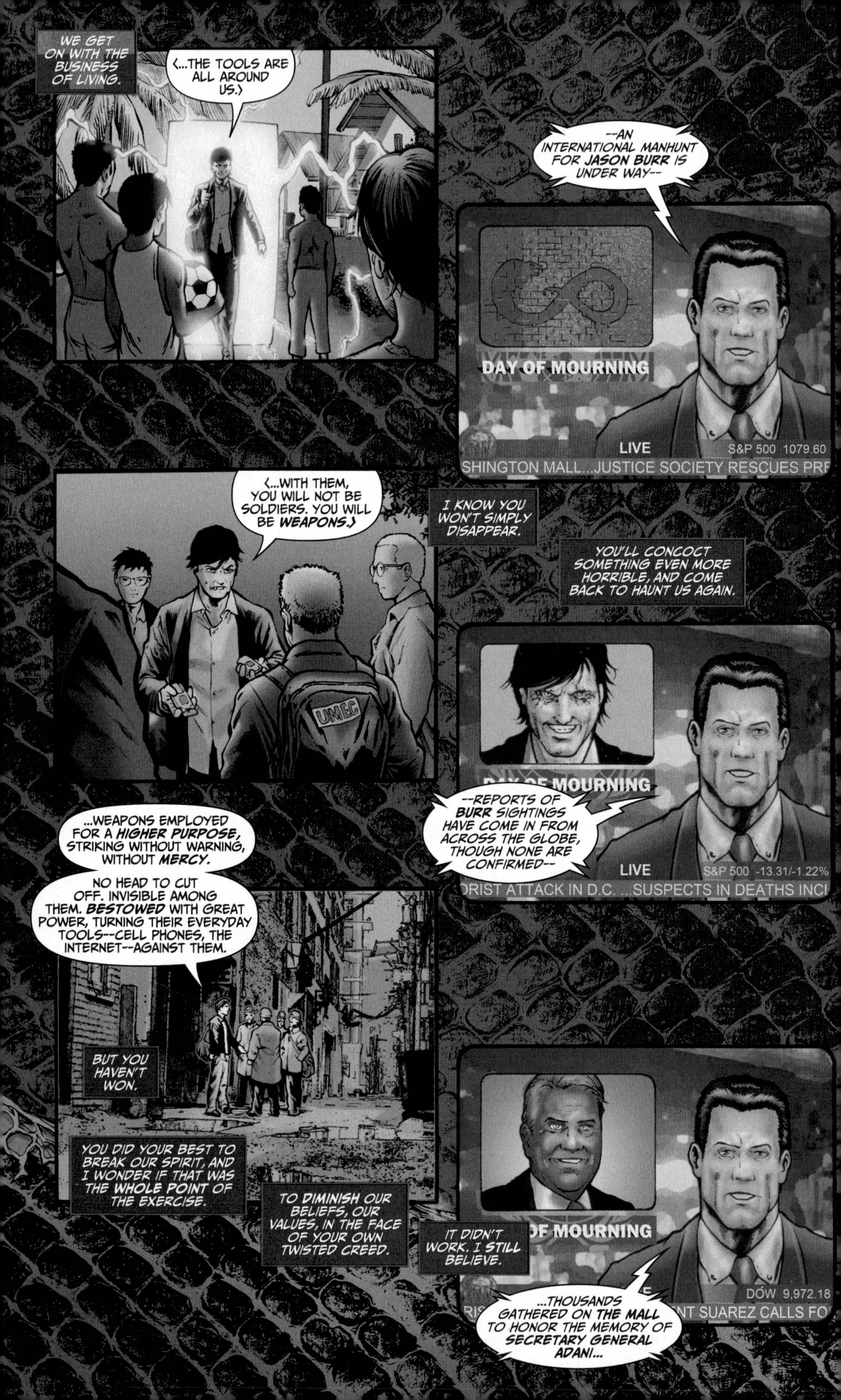
WE GET ON WITH THE BUSINESS OF LIVING.
<...THE TOOLS ARE ALL AROUND US.>
--AN INTERNATIONAL MANHUNT FOR JASON BURR IS UNDER WAY--
DAY OF MOURNING
LIVE
S&P 500 1079.60
SHINGTON MALL...JUSTICE SOCIETY RESCUES PR
<...WITH THEM, YOU WILL NOT BE SOLDIERS. YOU WILL BE WEAPONS.>
UMEC
I KNOW YOU WON'T SIMPLY DISAPPEAR.
YOU'LL CONCOCT SOMETHING EVEN MORE HORRIBLE, AND COME BACK TO HAUNT US AGAIN.
...WEAPONS EMPLOYED FOR A HIGHER PURPOSE, STRIKING WITHOUT WARNING, WITHOUT MERCY.
NO HEAD TO CUT OFF. INVISIBLE AMONG THEM. BESTOWED WITH GREAT POWER, TURNING THEIR EVERYDAY TOOLS--CELL PHONES, THE INTERNET--AGAINST THEM.
DAY OF MOURNING
--REPORTS OF BURR SIGHTINGS HAVE COME IN FROM ACROSS THE GLOBE, THOUGH NONE ARE CONFIRMED--
LIVE
S&P 500 -13.31/-1.22%
ORIST ATTACK IN D.C. ...SUSPECTS IN DEATHS INC
BUT YOU HAVEN'T WON.
YOU DID YOUR BEST TO BREAK OUR SPIRIT, AND I WONDER IF THAT WAS THE WHOLE POINT OF THE EXERCISE.
TO DIMINISH OUR BELIEFS, OUR VALUES, IN THE FACE OF YOUR OWN TWISTED CREED.
IT DIDN'T WORK. I STILL BELIEVE.
OF MOURNING
DOW 9,972.18
NT SUAREZ CALLS FO
...THOUSANDS GATHERED ON THE MALL TO HONOR THE MEMORY OF SECRETARY GENERAL ADANI...

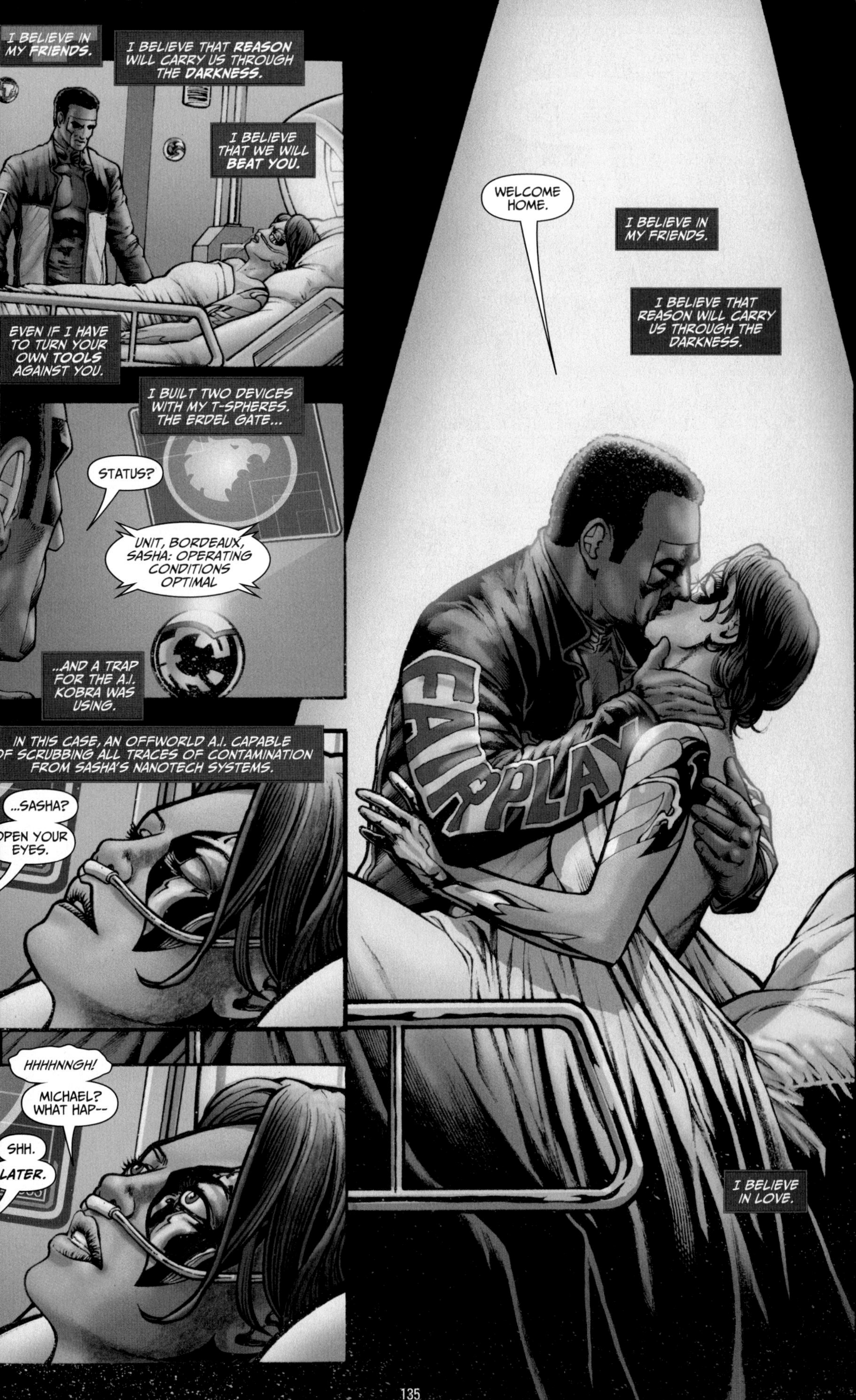

I BELIEVE IN MY FRIENDS.
I BELIEVE THAT REASON WILL CARRY US THROUGH THE DARKNESS.
I BELIEVE THAT WE WILL BEAT YOU.
EVEN IF I HAVE TO TURN YOUR OWN TOOLS AGAINST YOU.
I BUILT TWO DEVICES WITH MY T-SPHERES. THE ERDEL GATE...
STATUS?
UNIT, BORDEAUX, SASHA: OPERATING CONDITIONS OPTIMAL
..AND A TRAP FOR THE A.I. KOBRA WAS USING.
IN THIS CASE, AN OFFWORLD A.I. CAPABLE OF SCRUBBING ALL TRACES OF CONTAMINATION FROM SASHA'S NANOTECH SYSTEMS.
...SASHA?
OPEN YOUR EYES.
HHHHNNGH!
MICHAEL? WHAT HAP--
SHH.
LATER.
WELCOME HOME.
I BELIEVE IN MY FRIENDS.
I BELIEVE THAT REASON WILL CARRY US THROUGH THE DARKNESS.
FAIRPLAY
I BELIEVE IN LOVE.

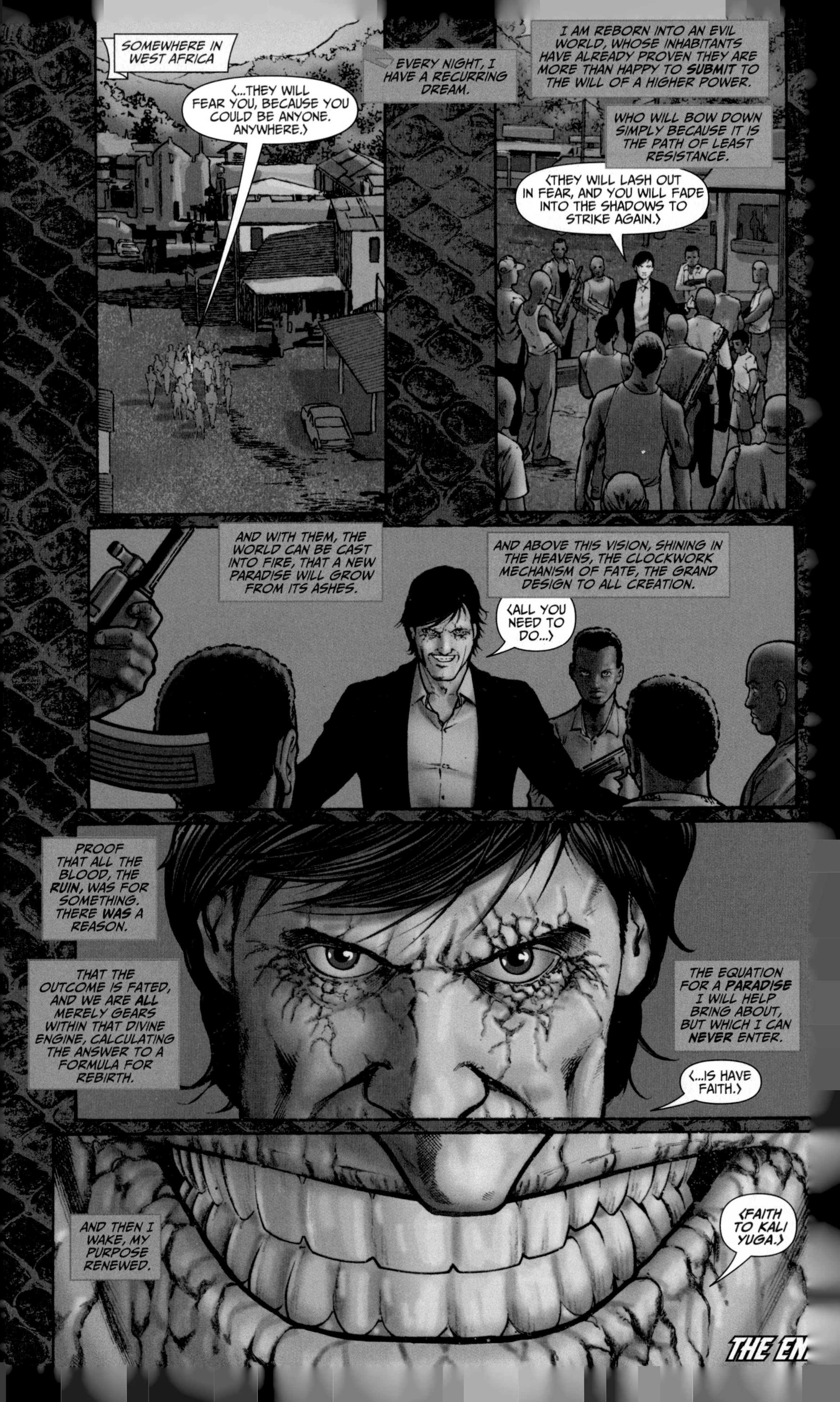
SOMEWHERE IN WEST AFRICA
EVERY NIGHT, I HAVE A RECURRING DREAM.
‹...THEY WILL FEAR YOU, BECAUSE YOU COULD BE ANYONE. ANYWHERE.›
I AM REBORN INTO AN EVIL WORLD, WHOSE INHABITANTS HAVE ALREADY PROVEN THEY ARE MORE THAN HAPPY TO SUBMIT TO THE WILL OF A HIGHER POWER.
WHO WILL BOW DOWN SIMPLY BECAUSE IT IS THE PATH OF LEAST RESISTANCE.
‹THEY WILL LASH OUT IN FEAR, AND YOU WILL FADE INTO THE SHADOWS TO STRIKE AGAIN.›
AND WITH THEM, THE WORLD CAN BE CAST INTO FIRE, THAT A NEW PARADISE WILL GROW FROM ITS ASHES.
AND ABOVE THIS VISION, SHINING IN THE HEAVENS, THE CLOCKWORK MECHANISM OF FATE, THE GRAND DESIGN TO ALL CREATION.
‹ALL YOU NEED TO DO...›
PROOF THAT ALL THE BLOOD, THE RUIN, WAS FOR SOMETHING. THERE WAS A REASON.
THAT THE OUTCOME IS FATED, AND WE ARE ALL MERELY GEARS WITHIN THAT DIVINE ENGINE, CALCULATING THE ANSWER TO A FORMULA FOR REBIRTH.
THE EQUATION FOR A PARADISE I WILL HELP BRING ABOUT, BUT WHICH I CAN NEVER ENTER.
‹...IS HAVE FAITH.›
AND THEN I WAKE, MY PURPOSE RENEWED.
‹FAITH TO KALI YUGA.›
THE EN

COVER
GALLERY

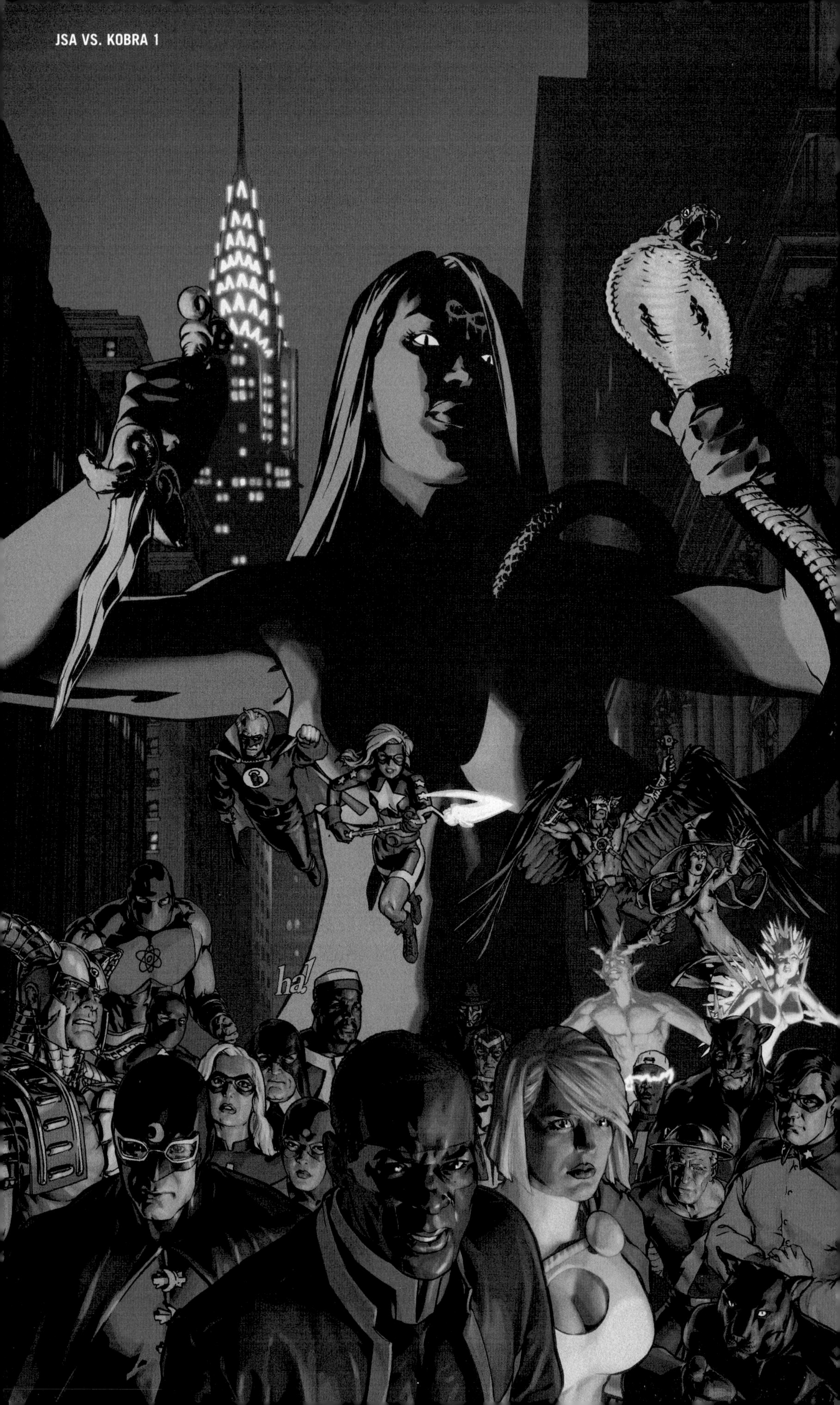
ha!

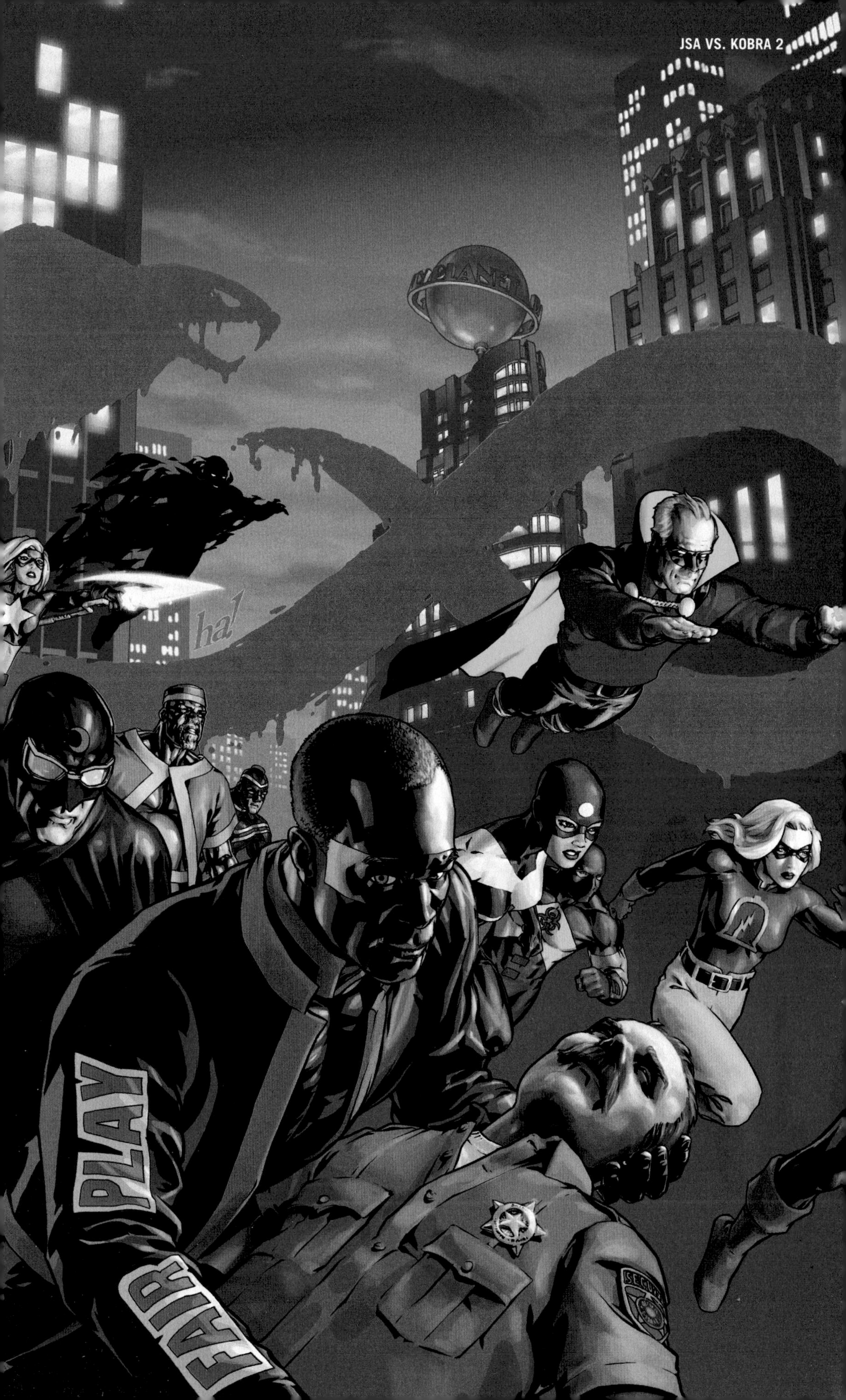
PLANET
ha!
PLAY
FAIR

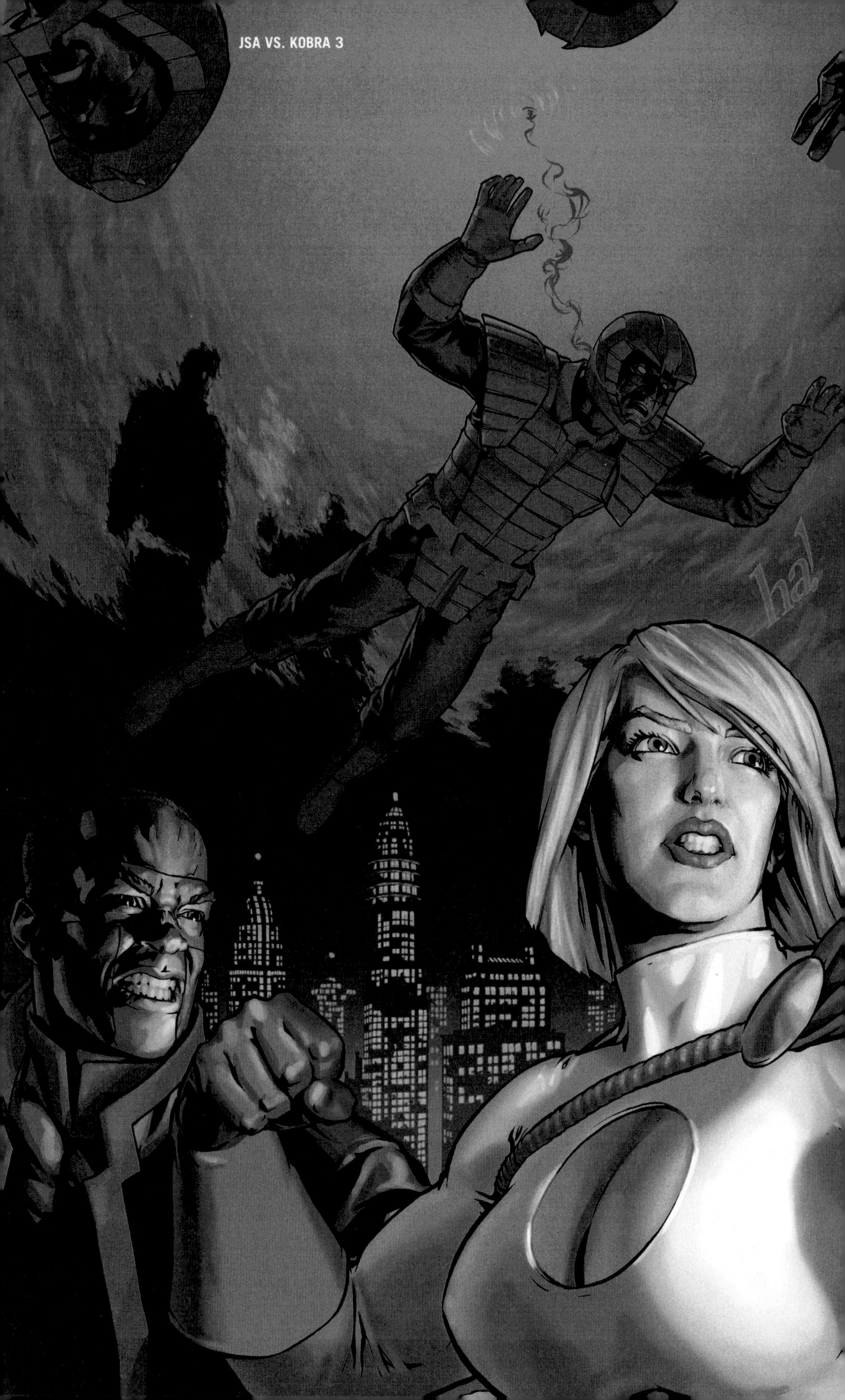
ha!

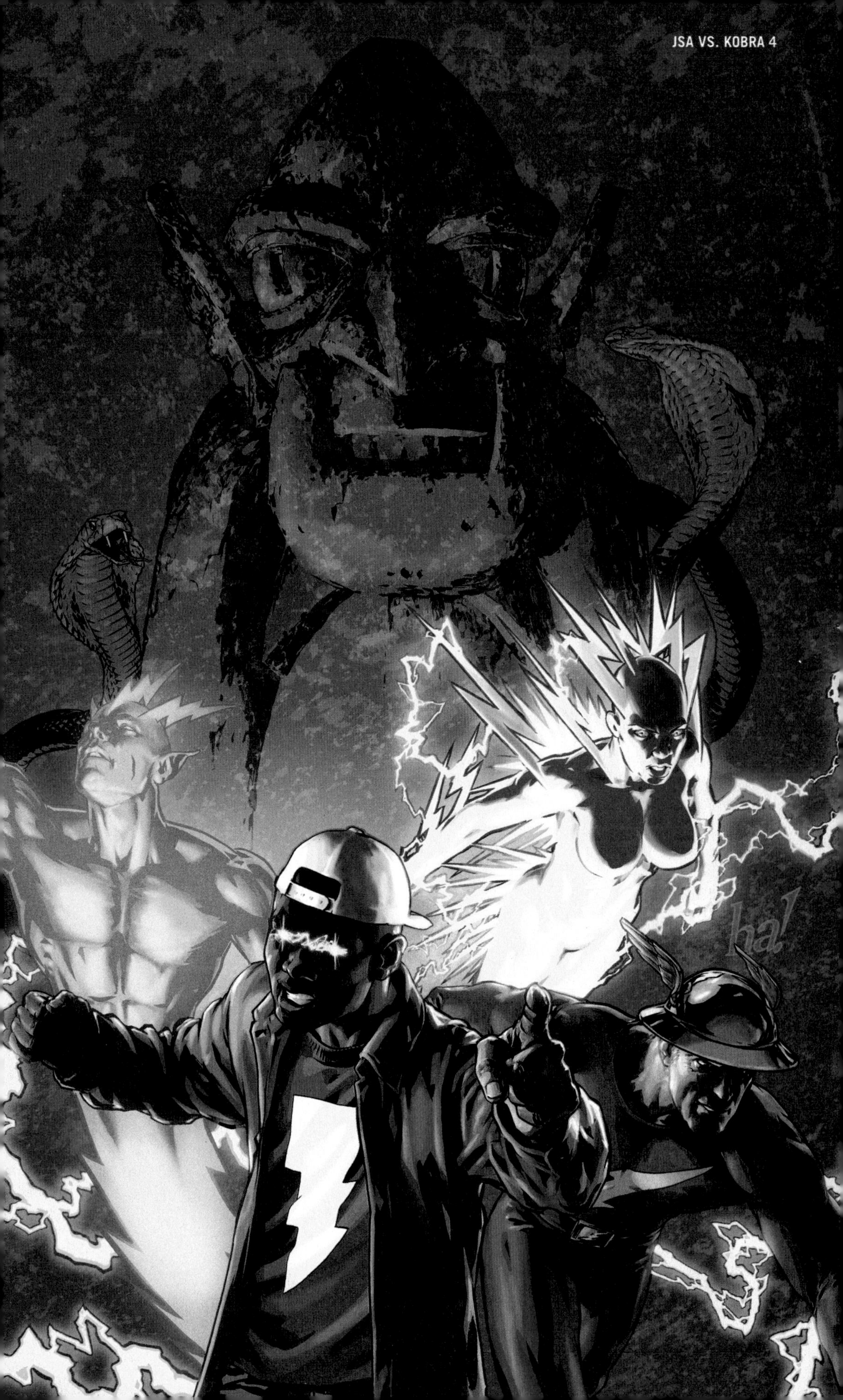
ha!

JSA VS. KOBRA 5

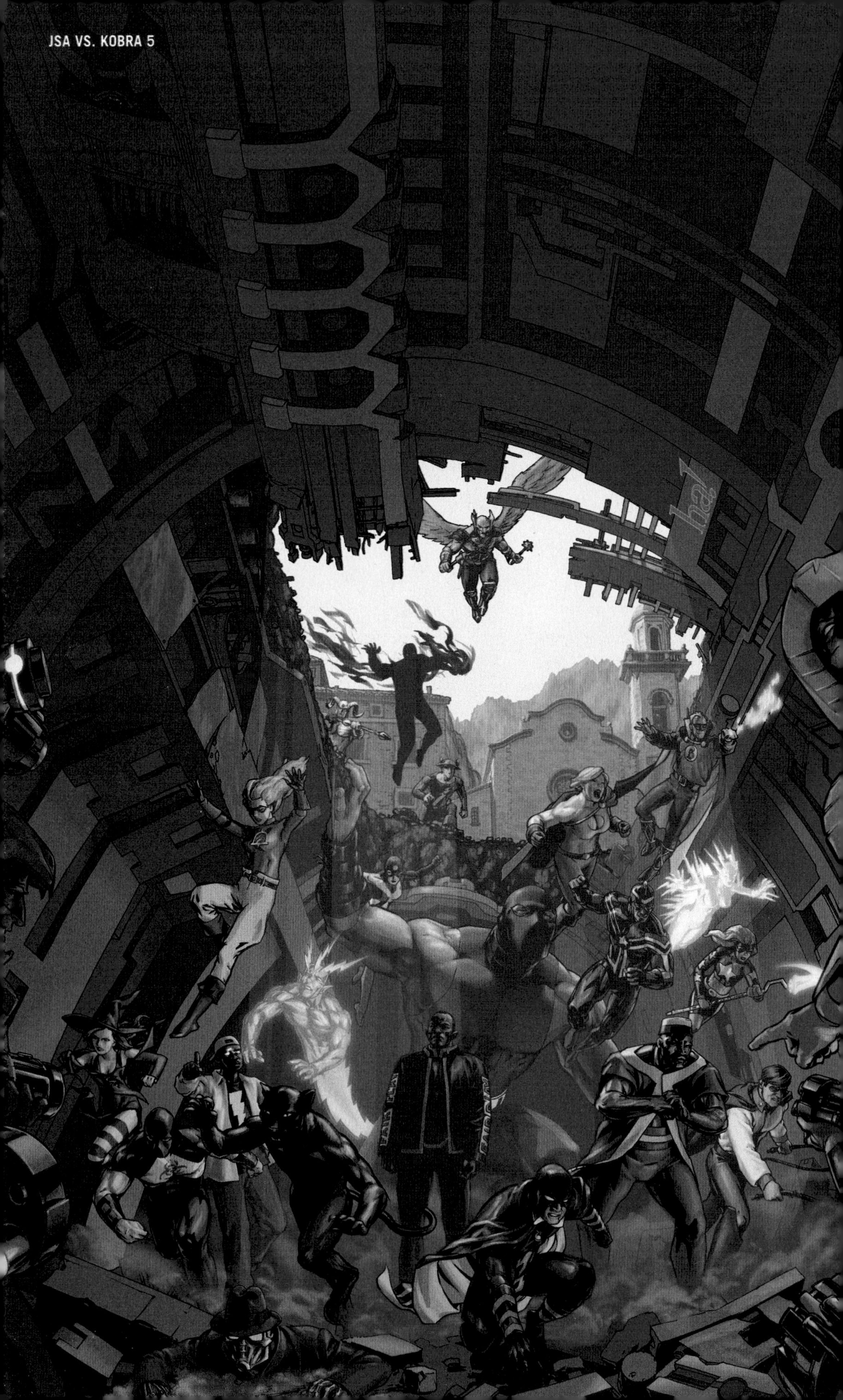

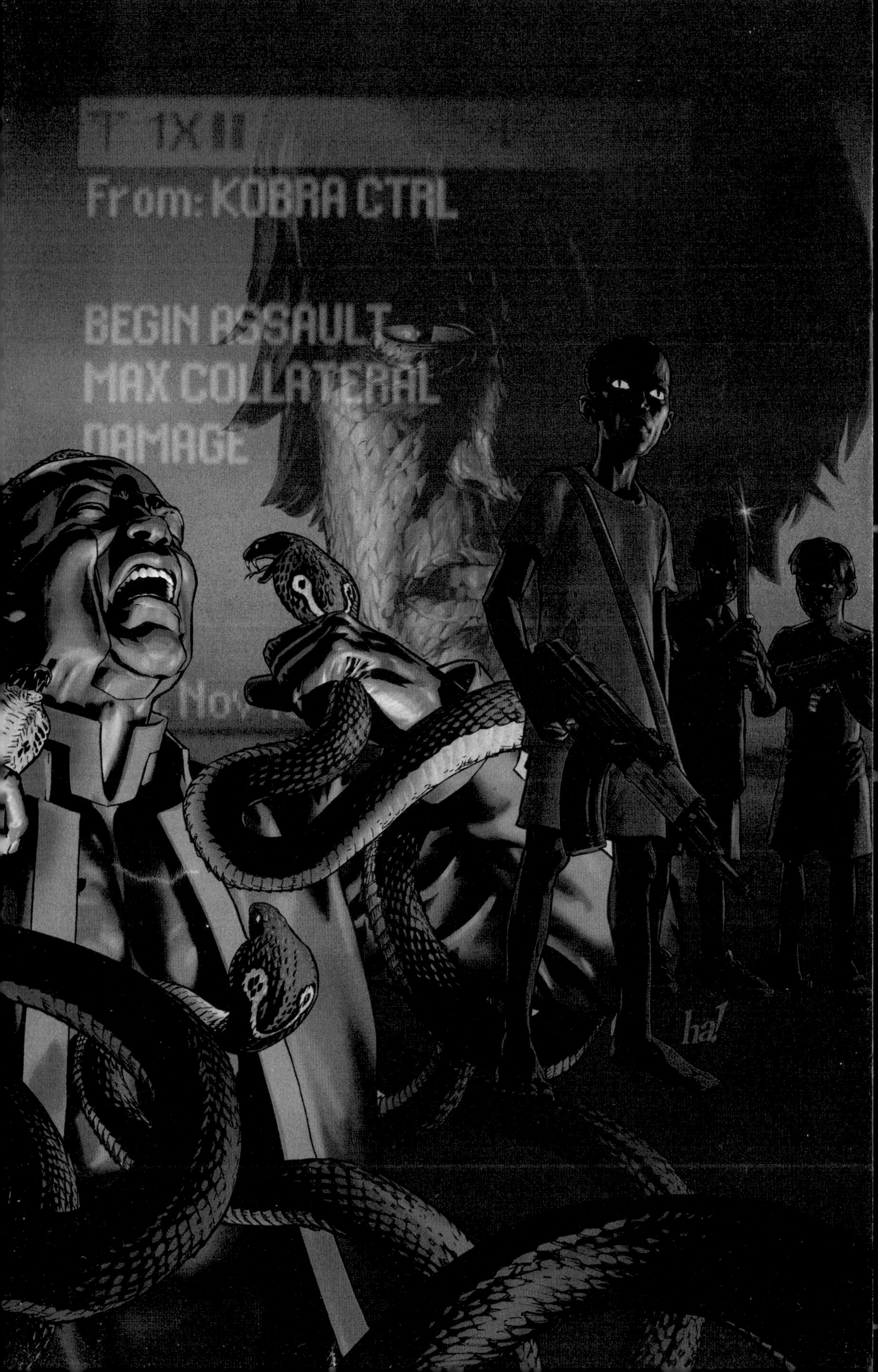
From: KOBRA CTRL
BEGIN ASSAULT
MAX COLLATERAL
DAMAGE
ha!

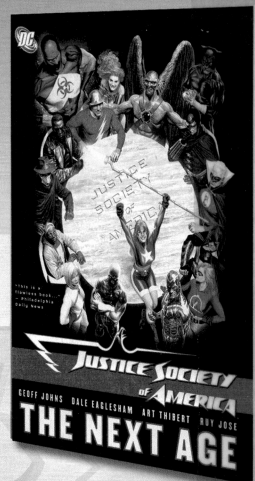